# THE FiLM FREAK CENTRAL 2007 ANNUAL

"Film reviews by people who actually love film? Thoughtful examinations of artistic issues instead of simplistic 'see it/don't see it' banality? Who are these guys, some kind of lefty, pinko oddballs out to force people to think for themselves? Oh, the horror!"

Keith Gordon
Director, *The Singing Detective*

"Walter Chaw's wit, wide range of cultural knowledge, and virtuosic command of film history make him one of the few essential critics writing about movies today."

Chris Terrio
Director, *Heights*

"FILM FREAK CENTRAL is my first and often last stop for honest, insightful, sharp film criticism in today's glutted world of screaming headlines, pandering superlatives, and dopey puns."

Rawson Marshall Thurber
Writer-Director, *Dodgeball: A True Underdog Story*

"Walter Chaw's reviews are lucid, rigorous, principled, and a pleasure to read, because whether they're highbrow or lowbrow, he wants movies to be exceptional."

Larry Fessenden
Writer-Director, *Wendigo*

"Had a bellyful of corporate-driven hacks touting the latest 'thrill ride of the summer'? Don't despair—Chaw and Chambers are here writing passionate, intelligent essays that are sometimes far more entertaining than the actual films they're reviewing."

Mark Hamill
Actor, *The Big Red One*, *Star Wars*

"Here they are, under one roof: hard-hitting, no-holds-barred, tell-all reviews. God bless Mr. Chaw for lurking in the shadows and pulling no punches."

Jim Wynorski
Director, *The Return of the Swamp Thing*

"Walter Chaw has film criticism's finest bullshit detector."

Vadim Perelman
Director, *The House of Sand and Fog*

PRINTED IN THE UNITED STATES OF AMERICA

Visit our website at www.filmfreakcentral.net

First edition published 2007 by Walter Chaw

Library of Congress Cataloging-in-Publication Data
Chambers, Bill.
    The film freak central 2007 annual / by Bill Chambers.
    p.cm.
    1.   Motion pictures. 1. Title.

*Cover design by Bill Chambers*

ISBN 978-0-6151-8377-0

# CONTENTS

*previously unpublished

# FOREWORD

**As Steve McQueen once famously** emoted (as blood flowed out of him during a botched rescue job at the end of *The Sand Pebbles*): "What the hell happened?"

At some point in my lifetime, film criticism gave over from the exotic tones of Canby, Kael, and CAHIERS DU CINEMA to the sad sounds of ONE GUY'S OPINION, THE MOVIE CHICKS, and PLANET SICK-BOY. What once seemed like a hallowed profession for wise, well-heeled journalists and intellectuals seems to have become a free-for-all for frustrated journal writers and loud-mouth kids who used to hang out at Denny's during the wee hours of the morning. Perhaps this burst of journalistic excess is the Information Highway equivalent of the French New Wave, but it feels a bit more like 'Daddy bought me a computer and now you're going to listen to me!' With the advent of the Internet came the inevitable crush of anybody being able to say anything—one giant step forward for 'freedom of speech,' one piercing blow for creativity and intelligence. People who once gathered at the railings of movie premieres to gawk at their favourite stars can now dictate studio policy from their bedrooms, merely by blathering on about their opinions in chat rooms or by sneaking into movie previews and being the first to spread pictures or breathless thoughts (with 'spoilers!') across the airwaves. Why get a star's autograph when you can now go online and mock their newest performance or hairstyle and make your friends 'LOL'?

It's a different critical world out there now, even from when my short career as a filmmaker began— it absolutely has become a world of fanboys and box-office results reported on the evening news. Movies are more about first weekends and DVD sales and less about artistry or great performances. Bloggers have something to say and if they say it loud enough people seem to listen. It's funny, what used to be hidden behind lock and key—remember the cute little gold bauble that adorned everyone's 'My Diary'?—has now become a free-for-all of 'Me, me, me!' Who knew how needy the general population was? Not me.

Mind you, I suppose this is the same as the increased accessibility that filmmakers have to production equipment these days. I wouldn't be here professionally if it hadn't become easier to get my hands on everything I needed to make a movie while living in a place like Fort Wayne, Indiana. People no longer have to go through the machinations of the studio system to make a picture and that's probably a good thing; many of my favourite films over the last forty years have been made by artists who broke free of tradition and hit the streets with a film or video camera and created something very close to art. And I suppose the fact that you or your brother wants to say something about a movie after you've seen it is OK by me, just don't expect me to take it very seriously. If I'm dumb enough to worry whether my film is "fresh" or "rotten" then it's my own damn fault, I suppose, and I'm getting what I deserve.

Even as a boy, I read film and theatre criticism and imagined a day when these witty and learned people might watch and write about something I had done. The fact that I now submit my work for approval from the likes of CREATIVE LOAFING and FILM SCHOOL REJECTS is simply the way of the world. Sad but true. As Brecht famously said about Hollywood, "Every morning, to earn my bread, I go to the market where lies are bought. Hopefully I take my place among the sellers." Who am I to talk?

So online critics, unite and blog your little hearts out about the next Marvel film or Comi-Con you attend in San Diego, but don't expect me to be moved or worried or excited about what you have to say. To be sure, this wide berth of new critics has spawned a few fine writers, but I suspect the overall effect has done nothing more than dull the senses of the average film artist or filmgoer. We now know that, yes, everybody has an opinion— this by no means suggests that they should all be voiced out loud or given any credence when they appear in print. Just because you can doesn't always mean you should.

I completely support the fact that anybody has a right to freely express the crap that they have to say about anything they see or experience or listen to. Knock yourselves out. After all, if one keeps it in perspective and remembers that criticism is a reactive medium and not an artistic one, you can stomach just about anything. And it's still thrilling to read the work of someone who really knows their stuff and writes with the savvy and freedom of an artist—it's just that that experience is more and more rare these days. It's a bit like the Woody Allen joke in *Annie Hall* about his teachers—I suspect that Mr. Allen might very well imagine that "film critic" ranks a notch below "gym teacher." Maybe two, in fact. After all, as George Steiner thoughtfully pointed out, "A critic casts a eunuch's shadow," and without the filmmakers who regularly put their work out there to be publicly poked and sniffed and praised and laughed at, critics probably wouldn't cast much of anything at all.

So Happy Birthday, FILM FREAK CENTRAL, and here's to your future! Now make me a believer.

**Neil LaBute**
Writer-director: *In the Company of Men,*
*Your Friends & Neighbors,*
*The Shape of Things*
November 30, 2007

# INTRODUCTION

**For whatever reason, writing this** introduction has been like that scene in *Pee-Wee's Big Adventure* where Pee-Wee's evacuating the blazing pet store and keeps putting off the snakes. For starters, it forces me to eat my words: elsewhere in these pages, in a passage reprinted from THE FILM FREAK CENTRAL BLOG, I "formally announce" that we will not be publishing an Annual in 2007. Just call me Nostradamus. I suppose I could've gone back and edited myself, but that seemed like the kind of George Lucas revisionism I regularly decry.

We changed our mind about the Annual in early October, which led to a scramble—credit where credit is due, mostly on Walter Chaw's part—to deliver a more complete snapshot of the movie year, as our online archive came up substantially short. What can I say? A certain melancholy hung over 2006 that led to a lot of inertia. I suppose it looks like we were "holding out" all this time simply to increase the purchase incentive of this book, but you can almost smell the ink drying on most of the 30 previously-unpublished reviews herein, a handful of which may still turn up online.

Inevitably, some titles continue to fall by the wayside—which is good news for the execrable *Clerks II*, but unfortunate for the ebullient *Dave Chappelle's Block Party*. At any rate, the self-imposed Christmas deadline forced us to make some real Sophie's choices. (*A Prairie Home Companion*, we hardly knew ya.) Included for the first time in earnest, though, are our reviews of the year's direct-to-DVD product, as the home market is gaining legitimacy in the eyes of movie buffs now that the studios have started using it as a dumping ground for red-headed stepchildren like *The Woods*.

Aside from middling sales of the previous two Annuals (for which I blame global warming), what initially put the kibosh on The Film Freak Central 2007 Annual is the fact that I've spent the better part of '07 with my right arm in a splint thanks to one seriously stubborn fracture—a fracture I incurred shortly after recovering from a hernia operation! So the prospect of assembling another Annual seemed daunting, if only physically. I frankly wasn't sure I had the stamina, especially with a site still to run.

But I am nothing if not the Jack Palance of editors, having put this baby together with one arm and a surplus of testosterone. Still, it wasn't macho pride that changed my mind, but rather the realization that we couldn't let FILM FREAK CENTRAL's tenth anniversary pass without fanfare: we needed to honour it in a material way—and in the process get some mileage out of that fancy "10" graphic watermarking the front-cover homage to Saul Bass.

My sincerest thanks to Neil LaBute, who graciously agreed to be this volume's special guest star even though Walter rakes his remake of *The Wicker Man* over the coals on page 239. (Of course, I have a sneaking suspicion that Mr. LaBute used this pulpit to take the mickey out of us.) Big props are also due Walter for bleeding himself dry to help make a page-count; Travis Hoover for doing a yeoman's job at the mothersite; Alex Jackson for, among other things, giving us permission to reprint his definitive *Snakes on a Plane* review; and our newest staff member Ian Pugh for his mad copywriting skillz.

I almost wish this wasn't the last one.

**Bill Chambers**
Toronto,
December 12, 2007

# PREFACE

**The year started on a** low.

It started, in fact, with the end of 2005, which was, for the first time since I started doing this as a job, also the first time I fell in line with the idea that the movies just weren't very good anymore. Still, there was stuff to celebrate in 2005: Terrence Malick's amazing *The New World*, Lodge Kerrigan's *Keane*, a pair of Herzog documentaries—not to mention Kore-eda's *Nobody Knows* and Ki-Duk's *3-Iron*, Cronenberg's remarkably sticky *A History of Violence*, *Rois et reine*, *King Kong*, Jet Li's eternally misunderstood *Unleashed*... And then it dawned on me that maybe 2005 only seemed down because the best films of the year were indicated by the extent to which they're crestfallen.

I think now that maybe I was just depressed, and that it's taken most of 2007 to get over it.

If we play with the idea that the movies of the post-9/11 period proceed, year by year, through different stages of mourning, I wonder if we can see 2002 as angry (*About Schmidt, Adaptation., Trouble Every Day*); 2003 as stunned (*Elephant, Spider, Kill Bill, Vol. 1, Hero*); 2004 as regret (*Spring, Summer, Fall, Winter... and Spring, Birth, Last Life in the Universe, Eternal Sunshine of the Spotless Mind*); 2005 as despair (*Last Days, Head-On, The New World, Caché*); and 2006? What to make of stuff like *Apocalypto* sitting in the same tub as *The Fountain, Talladega Nights*, and *A Scanner Darkly*? As *Vers la sud* and *Silent Hill* and *Children of Men*?

I have discovered in 2007 that I missed a lot of wonderful films in 2006—that I missed *Perfume* and *The Texas Chainsaw Massacre: The Beginning*, two great movies more alike than different. Both, for instance, feature identical birth scenes for their gifted protagonists, squirted out in an explosion of grue in abattoir settings by their monstrous mothers. Abandoned, tossed in the trash heap, picked up by well-meaning, psychotic guardians, and turned out to practise their God-given talents on an unsuspecting collection of sexy meat bags. 2006 is filthy with fairy tales: creation myths and monsters and child heroes (*Tideland, Pan's Labyrinth*, sure, but also *Superman Returns, House of Sand*, and so on)— even *The Descent* is about motherhood, isn't it? Birth fluids and pains and the UK ending includes a grail found. So is 2006 about regeneration? Partly (I don't want to go too far in that direction, because 2007 suggests a refutation of that), but moreover, I think 2006 is about fabling the apocalypse, recasting the end of civilization in terms of stories told by firelight.

2006 is about coming to terms.

The damnation of being imprisoned in yourself is that it's almost impossible to send up a periscope. I don't know if the process of pictures following 9/11 can be encapsulated so handily—an annual theme (I'm pretty sure that it can't, actually), in other words—but there's a moment every year that I put the book down, look off into the middle distance, and declare that I "get" it; and suddenly everything's slotted in obediently like sardines in the zeitgeist can. It's a quirk of the brain, this mania for gestalt, this desire for meaning and order—and this is how my version programs itself.

When they asked Pauline Kael why not write a memoir, Kael maintained that she already had. In the middle of the tenth anniversary of FILM FREAK CENTRAL, looking back at my six years with it, what I can say is "so there it is"—and thank God for Bill taking me in through this post-Wasteland period and providing me an outlet for my wandering. When I'm long gone, here's the hope: that my kids, and my kids' kids, will look at this site if it's archived somewhere in the ether, at these books if they're not dust—will drag a volume off the bookshelf in some pre-estate-sale rummaging and put an eyeball on it and marvel that no matter the cost, no matter the price to professional ambition, the people I pissed off, the friends I've lost, the bridges I've burned because I was too much of an asshole (too stupid, too egotistical, too afraid)—that despite all of that, I did my best to write true and to my bliss.

And that I was right.

**Walter Chaw**
Denver,
December 3, 2007

**PREVIOUSLY UNPUBLISHED**
**THE ABANDONED**
***½/****

*st.* Anastasia Hille, Karel Roden, Valentin Ganev, Paraskeva Djukelova
*sc.* Karim Hussain & Nacho Cerdà & Richard Stanley
*dir.* Nacho Cerdà

I've been waiting a long time for Nacho Cerdà's mainstream debut. I thought, in truth, that I'd wait in vain, given the nature of his legendary films. There would seem little to recommend in an exploitation picture about necrophilia (Cerdà's *Aftermath*), except that *Aftermath* is beautifully shot, existentially horrifying, and elegant, even, especially in comparison to its closest cinematic kin: Japan's brutish "Guinea Pig" series. His follow-up short, *Genesis*, is similarly lovely, a devastated telling of Pygmalion with a sculptor ossifying himself to give life to the graven image of his lost lover. It reminds in more ways than superficially of Clive Barker's "Human Remains" short story—another tale of a golem given terrible life at untenable expense. Teaming up with the often-brilliant pair of Karim Hussain and Richard Stanley to write *The Abandoned*, Cerdà firmly establishes himself as a director to be reckoned with, presenting a twist on the zombie genre that I've never seen before by allegorizing the hale bogeys as explicit reflections of the personal shadow rather than as shadows of collective despair. Not indicators of trends, in other words, but singular— individual—and inoculated against physical harm by their connection to their reluctant progenitors. *The Abandoned*, then, is a distillation of sorts of Cerdà's two short films: *Aftermath* for this picture's metaphorical auto-necrophilia; and *Genesis* for this picture's heroes' creation of personal projections, intimate golems of not only flesh and blood, but their flesh and blood, too. In a different but vital way, it could be said that *Abandoned* treats zombies—as all zombie pictures have before it, more or less—like a decidedly Christian pestilence.

Adopted Marie (Anastasia Hille: wonderful) returns to Russia to claim the ancestral home of her mysterious birth parents, finding out along the way that her mother was killed when Marie was an infant but mustered enough strength before dying to escape her murderer, her husband, with little Marie on the front seat. Hungry to know about her past with a zeal that Oedipus would have warned her about, she arrives at the farm (ringed with a river—and oh, Marie can't swim) to discover a long lost brother, Nicolai (Karel Roden), and a dead-eyed doppelgänger who trails after her as Marie drifts from room to haunted room. With flashbacks couched in the conceit that trauma has, *The Shining*-like, left its imprint in key locations around the farmhouse, *The Abandoned* distinguishes itself as a piece invested in discovering a meaningful, organic means to familiar ends. Consider, for instance, that the idea of imprinting here as a horror conceit mirrors Marie's curiosity about the portions of her persona that were shaped by her biology—not for nothing was Miike's "Masters of Horror" episode about abortion, torture, and true love called "Imprint". In relating its story of transgressing social norms in pursuit of biological imperatives, *The Abandoned* manages to make its external bogeys as integral as its thematic ones stay in the subtext. A scene in the partially-flooded and gradually narrowing cellar reveals the source of her and her brother's torment, doing so with a firm knowledge of what it means in these scenarios to descend into a flooded basement, raising the level of discourse and rendering the scene terrifying on progressively different levels for all the right reasons.

Lensed in an oppressive, beautiful style by ace cinematographer Xavi Giménez, *The Abandoned*'s look is fraught with the kind of terror spiced, pungently, ubiquitously, by the intrusion of the past. Its night scenes are almost tactile; Marie's arrival on the "island" and, much later, her "re-enactment" of the night of her mother's escape and her birth into the world, are painted in such velvet textures that the sensation is almost suffocating. I think that the intent of the whole of the film is to affect this near-literal internalization of Marie's journey to the self. Not as reductive as an invitation to personal introspection, the picture suggests a split in its characters between the divorced and the re-unified—taking in, along with all its other ambitions, the subject of cultural separation and the pull in adulthood to learn about what's been left behind in the unnatural separation of people from their homelands. Cerdà's fascinating mainly because he recognizes the usefulness of horror in better explicating archetypical concerns: not too fine a point to suggest that of all film's popular genres, horror in the line of potential sublimity may rank as highly as "poetry." *The Abandoned* is poetic in its upset: its gore is elegant and logical, and when it comes time for Marie to stand up against her other self, the progression of events is so unusual and lovely that I forgave the picture its too-conventional ending. A gem—and Cerdà is a star on the rise. (**Walter Chaw**)

## ACCEPTED
\*½/\*\*\*\*
st. Justin Long, Blake Lively, Anthony Heald, Lewis Black
sc. Adam Cooper & Bill Collage

and Mark Perez
*dir.* Steve Pink

Part of me is tempted to laud *Accepted* for daring to resurrect the late, lamented '80s campus comedy without satirizing it, but as the filmmakers haven't really modernized the genre in *any* respect, post or otherwise (not even its quaint aesthetic gets renovated to meet status quo techniques), the film is tediously anachronistic. A typecast Justin Long stars as Bartleby Gaines, a Max Fischer-esque over/underachiever who concocts a fake acceptance letter to a fake college after being rejected by every single school to which he applied. It's a stopgap solution to placate his increasingly disenchanted parents (Mark Derwin and Ann Cusack), but, of course, it will take a little elbow grease to sustain the ruse; before long Bartleby—tentatively linked to Melville's eponymous scrivener at best—and fellow pariahs Rory (*Strangers with Candy*'s Maria Thayer), Glen (Adam Herschman), Hands (Columbus Short), and Sherman (Jonah Hill) are slapping a fresh coat of paint on an abandoned psychiatric hospital and appointing Sherman's shoe-salesman uncle Ben (Lewis Black) the dean of their fictitious South Harmon Institute of Technology. I reckon the S.H.I.T. acronym would be a lot funnier had the characters never caught on, but the movie is nothing if not bet-hedging, going so far as to give our hero a blonde stick figure of a love interest (Blake Lively) rather than risk sexualizing the less broadly appealing Thayer. (One of *Accepted*'s obvious forebears, *Revenge of the Nerds*, shrewdly split the leading-man role in two, allowing for a tomboy complement to the cheerleader inamorata.) I reckon, too, that the picture would be funnier with an R rating on principle, and since the PG-13 generally means that the only booty flaunted is the money Bartleby makes in tuition fees when his sham starts reeling in co-eds from miles around, this alleged ode to hedonism is more accurately described as a celebration of capitalism. Told you the eighties were alive and well in *Accepted*. (**Bill Chambers**)

## ADAM & STEVE
\*/\*\*\*\*
*st.* Craig Chester, Malcolm Gets, Parker Posey, Chris Kattan
*w./d.* Craig Chester

Bill and I were on the phone one night, and we came up with a pleasant dream: what if a movie's stereotypical gay character—the one who gets all the bitchy repartee—actually wasn't funny? Be careful what you wish for: *Adam & Steve* is all stereotypes, all the time, and none of them are remotely funny. Only not by design, like in our fantasy—it's *meant* to be hilarious, meaning that you die of embarrassment on behalf of everyone involved. Although the film is supposed to be about a gay romance, its real theme is failure, and it's so terrified to seem like anything less than an outrageous good time that it tries too hard. (That the film's lone comedienne generally performs to crickets pretty much sums up the self-flagellant tone of the whole enterprise.) Hostile, ugly, and generally unpleasant to endure, it engenders fear intense enough to snuff out whatever lightness it might have had.

The film starts off badly with harsh, garish colours and the wit to match. It's 1987 at New York's Danceteria club, and goth Adam (writer-director Craig Chester) wanders in with fat friend Rhonda (Parker Posey) so that the former can gaze upon hot dancer Steve (Malcolm Gets); the evening ends with Adam hooked on coke as Steve takes a liquid dump in his apartment. Flash forward 17 years and Adam is a lonely ornithologist with self-deprecating tendencies and Steve is a psychiatrist with promiscuous ones. They meet again, fall in love, and have altercations with a jerk from

Jersey who throws bottles at them—but everything is fine until Steve realizes their old connection and stops the relationship out of shame. Not really the behaviour of someone in love, that, apparently, is how it is in gay Manhattan.

Like I say, the film frets and trembles over failure. The participants are to a one arrested adolescents: not in the sense that they're irresponsible but in the sense that they can never move on. Everybody's hung up on what happened in high school, with Rhonda still cracking fat jokes even though she's now noticeably slim and Steve's straight roommate Michael (Chris Kattan) still acting like the hilarious pothead well past the shtick's sell-by date. This would be a swell springboard to comedy had it been a satire, but *Adam & Steve* is a self-abusive jamboree that only evasively aims barbs at itself. Though the film dishes out happy endings and emotional progress as if in a charitable mood, the preceding cloud of gloom is impossible to dispel—and it makes for a highly uncomfortable, not-at-all-funny viewing.

Of course, the point of this wealth of self-deprecation is to reduce things to a manageable nothing, and in turn it reduces everyone in its path to a day-glo stereotype with a trait pinned to its outfit. Had a straight director run through the gay landscape with Chester's glib shorthand, he'd be quite justifiably attacked for his insensitivity—but since our auteur is looking for no emotional connection, the glosses on gym bunnies, promiscuity, and bashing are suitably numb. Or, rather, they would be were the issues they raise not so tender, if not serious: the running gag with the Jersey thug is more horrifying than it is amusing, all the more so for the casualness of its employment. Ranting aside, the more damaging part is to the core of seriousness that love is possible and the pain can be dispelled. While the movie rides to a happy conclusion, what precedes it calls its bluff—it's a film that can't commit and pushes you away when you try to engage it. *Adam & Steve* isn't so much about a romance with a shrink as it is a plea for a referral. (**Travis Mackenzie Hoover**)

## AKEELAH AND THE BEE
ZERO STARS/****
*st.* Laurence Fishburne, Angela Bassett, Keke Palmer, Curtis Armstrong
*w./d.* Doug Atchison

## THE OMEN
**½/****
*st.* Julia Stiles, Liev Schreiber, Mia Farrow, David Thewlis
*sc.* David Seltzer
*dir.* John Moore

## THE TEXAS CHAINSAW MASSACRE: THE BEGINNING
***½/****
*st.* Jordana Brewster, Taylor Handley, Diora Baird, R. Lee Ermey
*sc.* Sheldon Turner
*dir.* Jonathan Liebesman

Akeelah (Keke Palmer, in a fine debut) is a gifted speller trapped in a standard underdog sports-uplift intrigue, sage mentor strapped to her back (Laurence Fishburne, permanently slotted into the Morpheus role) and a deck of hard word flashcards stuffed in her hipsack. Doug Atchison's ghetto-baiting *Akeelah and the Bee* is deadening lockstep stuff that tries to capitalize on the brief renaissance of competitive spelling bees in a way so patronizing it's painful. In lieu of imagination and ambition, insert a training montage, a shop-worn backstory for the mentor that makes him as much in need of a surrogate daughter as our hero is in need of a surrogate father, and the standard plot arc wherein the ragtag downtrodden finds her voice in a society/class-uniting exhibition—the more grandiose the better. Because all

that garbage could be satisfied in about thirty minutes of screentime, the picture gives Akeelah a sickly romantic interest in cherub Javier (J.R. Villarreal) and an archenemy in dirty chink Dylan (Sean Michael). Dylan's father is the real miscreant, a 1940s era Yellow Peril caricature named Mr. Chiu (Ma Tzi) who's given to grave pronouncements about the silliness of black girls and the absolute imperial importance of son Dylan asserting his Asian-ness and kicking the nigger's ass at smart stuff. This does two things: it provides the film with drama it both sorely needs and doesn't need; and it reinforces every single stereotype held by middlebrow audiences. That *Akeelah and the Bee* also fails to surprise in its broad, blatant racism while trafficking in the surface-skipping, colour-blind masking of blacks is just symptomatic of more of that happy, well-meaning horseshit. Asians are a *favoured* minority, meaning we don't have to patronize them yet—just kick the hell out of their image in preparation for the next round in our Axis of Evil world tour. *Akeelah and the Bee*: breeding a generation of hateful little fuckers under the guise of promoting inner-city literacy.

A better film about a gifted youngster is John Moore's remake of Richard Donner's *The Omen*, which manages a couple of truly effective set design-driven set-pieces while fumbling the central relationships in their recasting. I love Liev Schreiber—seem to love him especially in remakes of hoary old genre faves—but he's too virile to embody the aging husband cuckolded (after a fashion—the word better fits what happens to the George Sanders character in Wolf Rilla's *Village of the Damned*) by his younger wife (Julia Stiles) and her mothering of an otherworldly spawn. Gregory Peck (then 60) of the original had about him a real desperation to prove his viability to much-younger wife Lee Remick (then 40)—to rescue her from the disappointment of a stillborn child and perhaps in the process make a statement about his own fitness. (For her part, there's a desire to reassure.) With the casting of Schreiber and Stiles (though separated by fourteen years, Schreiber's only 39), the focus shifts away from partner imbalance back to the basic procedural of "Who's Damien?", transferring the heartbeat of the New American Cinema of the '70s to the hopeless looking-backwards of the post-9/11 '00s. Where the 1976 picture fit nicely with contemporary *Rosemary's Baby* as generational terror allegories, this *Omen* shares a tub with the American *The Ring* in that each relocates the source of dread from a devil child to the inexplicable manipulation of photographs. Call it the corruption of technology as the last really scary thing left. (It's pithy that both pictures are remakes and by their very nature manipulations of old texts with new technologies.) Best is the casting of Mia Farrow as a mysterious, dog-loving nanny, resurrecting and repurposing her Rosemary performance for its instant recognition factor and lending it a disarming meekness foundering there under the surface of her obvious mania. By herself, Farrow in this film, in this way, works as all the post-modern deconstruction you need.

Which brings us to Jonathan Liebesman's oddly affecting *The Texas Chainsaw Massacre: The Beginning* (hereafter *The Beginning*), a prequel to Marcus Nispel's 2003 remake of (credited as co-producers) Tobe Hooper and Kim Henkel's grindhouse classic that strives ostensibly to give bogey Leatherface a name and a backstory. (It's "Tommy," and he's a freak other kids used to tease.) Stupid on paper, the film in execution is madly topical and involved in painting the victims as what's good and kind in this abattoir-world rather than, as in the other films, the bogeys. The message is no longer about the lengths to which family will go to stay together in swiftly-tilting circumstances, but rather of how experience is always inevitably mortal—and of how the

actions of our nation stain us by association as citizens. Brothers Dean (Taylor Handley) and Eric (Matt Bomer) are Vietnam-bound: Dean freshly drafted, Eric re-upping for a second tour to keep an eye on his peacenik sibling. They along with their girlfriends Chrissie (Jordana Brewster) and Bailey (Diora Baird) take an eleventh-hour trip to the Lone Star state to sow their oats before joining the fray. A familiar set-up, so it would seem, yet *The Beginning*'s sex is either in the rear-view or, it's suggested, made impossible by nerves over becoming cannon fodder for the American police action. The movie doesn't punish sexual activity—it reconfigures sexual activity (a bondage session between Dean and Bailey ends with her lament that "most guys are really into this") as a pursuit equivalent to indulging in the suffering of others. Find in that a pretty harsh equation of pandering with sending nubile youngsters to war. No accident that Tricky Dick is referenced herein, euphemism intact.

When Leatherface literally wears the face of one of his prettier victims, that sudden pang of pathos is about the desire indefatigable to assume the mantle of the privileged and recapture, in a literal way, the illusion of youth. It's a moment of true yearning, grisly though it may be, that occurs in the middle of what's been roundly dismissed as just another spam-in-a-cabin flick. *The Beginning* is sober filmmaking; when it's funny, it's funny on purpose, and an entire subplot concerning *Easy Rider*-inspired bikers (including one that apes Peter Fonda and suffers Fonda's character's same fate in that picture) is inspired. R. Lee Ermey returns as the subversion of authority (or as the essential hopelessness of investing any amount of trust in traditional institutions) to be used in the correct sentence in a scene where his drill sergeant persona is turned back on itself—then reasserted. The picture's scary, too, aided immeasurably by the assurance that no great harm will come to the bad guys (given that they're due for about thirty more kills before the events of the first film), making every faint hope subject to blue study. The implication is that there is no other fate for these young folks in this time than to die at the hands of brutal, power-hungry, cannibalistic cabals of old men and carnival freaks. The picture can be read as boot camp; at the end, individuality is ground into a bloody paste, making *The Beginning* a nigh-brilliant read of the entire genre as a lament for the faceless lost generations sent to die or get mutilated in Vietnam in the '70s and now, with the resurgence of the slasher form in mainstream cinema, Iraq. They're all young and beautiful— and they're all about to go screaming beneath the same ugly old machineries of pain. *The Beginning* is smart, well-shot, and disgusting, too. Not terrifying, but just nihilistic enough to reinforce our well-cultivated cynicism. (**WC**)

## ALL THE KING'S MEN
ZERO STARS/****
*st.* Sean Penn, Jude Law, Kate Winslet, James Gandolfini
*sc.* Steven Zaillian, based on the novel by Robert Penn Warren
*dir.* Steven Zaillian

SPOILER WARNING IN EFFECT. Ask most wags and they'll tell you that Sean Penn is the best actor of his generation; for a performance or two (consider that in *Dead Man Walking*, he goes the distance without the use of his hands), I'd be inclined to agree, but look at the way writer-director Steven Zaillian and, especially, composer James Horner, treat Penn in the long-delayed *All the King's Men*—and marvel at how little they think of their leading man. The second adaptation of Robert Penn Warren's 1946 Pulitzer Prize-winning novel about a populist-leaning stump-thumper modeled after Huey Long, the film garnered attention first for its sterling cast and

Tiffany pedigree, then for its sudden disappearance from last year's Oscar slate, only to appear now, without fanfare (save a gala screening at last week's TIFF), in the middle of what's traditionally a dumping ground for dead weight. And every time Penn delivers an allegedly rousing speech to a gaggle of hicks, proposing to nail the entrenched fat cats in the Big Easy's beleaguered senate to a rail, Horner's tiresome score endeavours to drown him out in a flood of sugared plastic emotion. Still, at least this sloppy brass orgy has a pulse, as opposed to Horner's "mournful theme," i.e. the one that accompanies the retarded voiceover narration of journalist Jack Burden (Jude Law), which sounds a lot like the piano exit music from the old "Incredible Hulk" TV show. If you believe your actors are capable of conveying emotion and nuance, you don't shoot them in sexy angles and luxury car commercial colour schemes while trying to drown them out in spasmodic torrents of empty, manipulative noise.

The story Willie Stark (Penn) going from a hick with no prospects to Governor of Louisiana is told through the soporific filter of Burden's association with the man as, initially, a bemused beat reporter and, finally, a leashed muckraker and media bulldog. His last task to dig up some dirt on Stark's enemy (and, as it happens, Burden's adoptive/maybe-real father), Judge Irwin (Anthony Hopkins), Burden all along is burdened (get it?)—and, by extension, so are we—by the spectre of one night spent with his long, lost love Anne (Kate Winslet). This matters because Stark is courting Anne's brother Andrew (Mark Ruffalo), hoping he'll lend his name to a new medical facility Stark is itching to build and, we presume, graft from— though the film's machinations are so Byzantine and confused that it's flat impossible to give much of a shit one way or another what happens to anyone in the picture. In a project that relies on the Greek-ness of Stark's rise from a grassroots-loving Mr. Smith to an entrenched politico lining his pockets and hiring gunmen as his drivers, it would have helped for Stark to appear to be genuine before gradually becoming corrupted by his hard-won power.

As it stands, there's not a moment that holds any bit of interest or taint of bigger truth, as *All the King's Men* trundles along its self-important, fatally-misguided way. It fails as political allegory, fails in truth in providing any kind of revelation. The performances run the gamut from Rhode Island Red (Penn) to Hopkins again trying to pass as a Yank and succeeding mostly in demonstrating that he's horribly limited and more than content to phone it in. It's unbelievably boring and ineffably alien, and when it comes time for Stark to meet his historically-mandated end, Zaillian, the screenwriter of *Schindler's List*, resorts to that film's black-and-white-into-red pretension. (Believe it or not, he even has the chutzpah left over to shove in a scene of blacks and hicks dropping flowers on Stark's memorial slab.) For how high it aspires, for how badly it wants to be taken as prestigious (badly enough to ask its trio of Brit A-listers to try on a Louisiana brogue with variously appalling results—none, however, as appalling as James Gandolfini's Tony Soprano-cum-Paul Prudhomme), *All the King's Men* is the frontrunner for, if nothing else, at least one end of year honour: so far, it's the worst movie I've seen all year. (**WC**)

A N I M A T E D
## THE ANT BULLY
*½/****
sc. John A. Davis, based on the book by John Nickle
dir. John A. Davis

If you read reviews with any degree of seriousness, you're probably not seeing that many animated kidpix anyway, and so remarking that *The Ant Bully* is

several cuts below the genre's low standards will fall on deaf ears. Still, I can't imagine an audience undemanding enough to not see through the film's cashing in on both the cachet of its source material (a storybook by John Nickle) and the CGI animation gold rush itself. The film is so unenthusiastic about doing its job that it's completely transparent, exposing its worship of the dollar at every turn of the screw. Even the creators of *Shrek* and their ilk seem to want to make the movie: there's no evidence of that with John A. Davis and his team of unmoved movers of pixels.

One more life lesson for the kiddies. Lucas Nickel (voice of Zach Tyler) is the stereotypical bullied little kid who takes out his frustrations on the front-yard ant colony. Little does he know that the ants have something in store for him: wizard ant Zoc (Nicolas Cage) has just perfected a potion that will shrink Lucas to ant-size. Strangely, once the deed is done, the ants don't simply rend him limb from limb—under the orders of the Queen (Meryl Streep), he will be taught the Way of the Ant under the tutelage of Hova (Julia Roberts). Everything goes great until, through the largesse of the most outrageous plot contrivances imaginable, an exterminator named Beals (Paul Giamatti) is contracted to snuff out the colony. It's up to the newly antefied Lucas to galvanize the insect community to stop the onslaught.

That Beals is hired through lies to and cajoling of an eight-year-old—the sole introduction to his character—tells you all you need to know about the sloppiness of the writing. The script is stripped down further than it has to be, with each character given one trait flogged mercilessly and each plot point lined up neatly to the narrative line. One expects at least a few digressions that develop incidental characters and offer wayward gags from the shoddiest examples of the genre, but the only eccentric thing about the whole enterprise is the idea of Nicolas Cage as a holier-than-thou ant wizard. Otherwise, we're handed the usual Sassy Black Voice Talent (Regina King as forager Neela) and the Not-Brave Brave Soldier (Bruce Campbell as scout Fugax) without any variations on already creaky themes.

By the time Beals has unleashed his fury on the insects, it's too late: *The Ant Bully* has failed to generate real interest in the colony that's in jeopardy. Bitter Zoc's tedious arguments with maternal Hova—who's spending far too much time with this human—become so rote that you half-wish the lot of them would be gassed into submission. That said, they're more tolerable than the horrific scenes featuring Lucas' grandmother (Lily Tomlin), she of the loose dentures and a flying-saucer fixation. (Her comedy is more burdensome than the narrative tension it's supposed to relieve.) Duty informs me to say that kids may not notice, but given the film's total failure at the box-office this summer, maybe the tots deserve more credit than they're usually offered. (**TMH**)

## APOCALYPTO (see: BLOOD DIAMOND)

## THE ARCHITECT
ZERO STARS/****
*st.* Anthony LaPaglia, Viola Davis, Isabella Rossellini, Hayden Panettiere
*w./d.* Matt Tauber

I am sick to death of pieces of shit like Matt Tauber's *The Architect*—sick of the White Guilt Trip, which here finds architect Leo (Anthony LaPaglia) the boogeyman behind all the cultural evils housed in the Cabrini-Green tenement he designed. When he protests to neo-Alfre Woodard Neely (Viola Davis) that he's just the mastermind behind the building's outline and thus unaccountable for the collapse of urban civilization housed

therein, the effect is one of outrage not at the arrogance of The Man, but at the cult of victimhood nursed by people like Tauber. By disempowering the film's blacks of even their own fall, Tauber performs an act of racism so odious that his next picture should be about these stock ghetto characters (the righteous mom, the good girl, the drug dealer, the dreamer) demanding an explanation as to why he's perpetuated these damning stereotypes in the guise of laying the paddle to hapless whitey. The picture meanwhile casts Isabella Rossellini as a variation on the same crazy suburban housewife Edie Falco played in *The Quiet* (and Juliette Binoche played in *Bee Season*—the better analogy for its complementary boy/girl child and rich/poor sub-dramas) and Hayden Panettiere as the teen-queen doing her best to get raped in the back of a semi-trailer, the better to allegorize her parents' disintegrating marriage and her brother's (Sebastian Sans) simultaneously-unfolding realization that he'd very much like to shag project-hustler-with-a-heart-of-gold Shawn (Paul James). Said events do not and do happen, respectively, with the gay union punished in typical gay-union fashion as Shawn swan-dives off Leo's precious edifice in an act of society-restoring self-loathing. Would that Shawn and Leo do the same as they gaze moonily into one another's eyes while the curtain falls on this umpteenth revival of contemptuous liberal cinema. My only question, doubly rhetorical because he might as well be if he isn't: is Tauber a Canadian filmmaker? (**WC**)

## ART SCHOOL CONFIDENTIAL
*½/****
*st.* Max Minghella, Sophia Myles, John Malkovich, Anjelica Huston
*sc.* Daniel Clowes
*dir.* Terry Zwigoff

SPOILER WARNING IN EFFECT. When Daniel Clowes and Terry Zwigoff sat down to adapt the former's

Ghost World for the screen, they divided up the task generationally, if you will, with the younger Clowes writing the Enid parts and Zwigoff writing the Seymour parts, which themselves have no correlative in the graphic novel. Clowes flew solo on the semi-autobiographical script for the pair's latest collaboration, *Art School Confidential*, and the main problem with it is that it's all Enid and no Seymour. In fact, the film is so relentlessly glib that the Enid doppelgänger who pops up now and again seems gratuitous—and moreover belabours a *Ghost World* comparison (much like the extended cameo from an unbilled Steve Buscemi) that only finds *Art School Confidential* wanting. The closest thing the movie has to a moral compass is Joel Moore's Bardo, one of those career students who becomes the Virgil to freshman Dante Jerome (Max Minghella). Adrift in a sea of *poseurs*, Jerome struggles in vain to win over his contemporaries, including comely life-drawing model Audrey (Sophia Myles). Meanwhile, a serial strangler trolling the campus for victims not only becomes Jerome's unwitting muse, but also provides one of his roommates, Vince (Ethan Suplee), with fodder for his thesis film.

Although the final scene of *Art School Confidential* apes that of Robert Bresson's *Pickpocket* as much as (if not more than, thanks to the tools of our hero's trade: his hands) *American Gigolo* does, all the secular misanthropy leading up to it is anything but Bressonian. As someone who took the odd art elective while enrolled in film school, I can vouch for the movie's credibility as satire—or, more precisely, burlesque: the classroom critiques are accurately depicted as a hazing ritual-cum-clusterfuck, while the artsy-fartsy types loitering in the background evince a documentary authenticity. Alas, these harmless jackasses—who don't interact so much as they mesh to form a wallpaper pattern—aren't

humanized beyond Bardo's pithy labels (i.e. "Nympho Slut," "Army Jacket," etc.), lest Clowes risk diluting the purity of his contempt for them. So much for success being the best revenge: Clowes obviously has an axe to grind (the excessive violence of the strangulation scenes (think Alfred Hitchcock's *Frenzy*) further demonstrates this), and as a result, *Art School Confidential* feels, to paraphrase filmmaker Thom Andersen, like a memoir written in crocodile tears.

There was a time, I think, when Clowes would've invested the grotesques on parade in *Art School Confidential* with at least two dimensions, even though the four-page story that inspired the film, written as a lark to fill the back pages of "Eightball", is no less snarky; perhaps he's finally succumbed to the cynicism that is the Achilles Heel of his prototypical antihero. Case in point, Audrey: in another issue of "Eightball", Clowes' celebrated, Crumb-esque alternative comic, a character wistfully recalls the physical defects (a scar here, a snaggletooth there) that epitomized the appeal of past lovers—a casual demolition of myths about male superficiality that *Art School Confidential* actively undermines by never challenging the empirically beautiful Myles' status as a grail object. Jerome even gets the girl, and everyone who doubted his supremacy winds up with egg on their face. However strong its undercurrent of self-loathing (the film student, Zwigoff's presumed avatar, is talentless; Bardo ultimately dismisses Jerome, Clowes' presumed avatar, as a "douchebag"), it's a movie that only a Rupert Pupkin could enjoy guilt-free. (**BC**)

## ASK THE DUST
*/****
st. Craig Chester, Malcolm Gets, Parker Posey, Chris Kattan
w./d. Craig Chester

As a male of the average chauvinist-pig variety, you find yourself inclined to give Robert Towne's *Ask the Dust* the benefit of the doubt because he's convinced Salma Hayek to strip naked a few times and roll around in the surf. And yet the realization dawns inescapable that no matter the acres of flesh, the film is every bit as horrible as that self-serious, neo-camp sexploitation classic *Original Sin* (another *noir* based on a lesser-known, period-dependent novel—that one by Cornell Woolrich, this one by John Fante), with only the gender/race roles reversed—that watching naked Angelina Jolie writhe around with Antonio Banderas can be every bit as disturbingly sexless as Hayek and Colin Farrell doing same. Promising to follow the James M. Cain pot-boiler formula with its dense voiceovers and *faux*-sordid, sepia-stained sexing, *Ask the Dust* is actually just inert, a painfully-overwritten, impossible-to-execute picture loaded down with self-conscious slatted shadows and mirrors (and all manner of *noir* affectations) that isn't only set in 1930s Los Angeles, but plays exactly as anachronistic and fusty as most films produced in the thirties, too. It's the kind of movie that makes much of a character's English-impaired malapropisms ("Not 'grew on me,' grew *in* me...like a baby," mewls Hayek's character in one of many excruciating proclamations); to its core, it's the kind of movie that sucks now and always has in exactly the same way.

The first problem is that it's not about anything. It's not about Los Angeles in the '30s because the suffering of the starving writer (Arturo Bandini (Farrell)), marooned in a *Barton Fink* hotel oubliette, is antiseptic. Starvation is something scored to a whimsical Spanish guitar and neatly solved by squandered drunken weirdo Hellfrick (Donald Sutherland) borrowing two bits at one point and returning fifteen cents in another, while Arturo's imminent eviction is mentioned in passing and then forgotten for a long stretch in-between. It's not about racism because although there's a lot of it going around in the picture (and in spite of much protestations as to its importance), it doesn't seem to colour the characters or their relationships in any meaningful way. It's not about writer's block because H.L. Mencken, in voiceover (provided by Richard Schickel, which is, indeed, your first warning), appears to buy Bandini's scribblings without much editorial insight. And it's not about love, because the actions and dialogue the erstwhile lovers share (an exchange about Camilla's (Hayek) shoes seals the deal: "Why, because they're too good for my legs?" "No, because your legs are too good for *them!*") are all alien and, almost without exception, unintentionally hilarious. It's so bad in a dedicated way that for much of its running time, *Ask the Dust* threatens to become an accidental satire of hardboiled L.A. *noir* epics with its gallery of grotesques anchored by a dickless, wholly unsympathetic ponce.

Farrell is, as usual, simultaneously fine and invisible (a quality that complements Malick's transcendentalism, if nothing else), and I've never thought much of Hayek as an actress save for that one bit with her toes in Robert Rodriguez's *From Dusk Till Dawn*, but whatever's wrong with the picture isn't the fault of its players. I will say that to its credit and for what it's worth, *Ask the Dust* is so certain about itself that it never ventures from its absurd approach into self-awareness, to say nothing of the kind of fully-justified self-loathing that might have salvaged Towne's already-foundering reputation. Set around the time of Towne's own seminal *Chinatown* script, it shares with it only that ironclad devotion to its style and sprung rhythms. In all other respects, it could be positioned as the exact contrary to it in terms of agility and gravity: the one the perfect modern screenplay, the other a weird riff on that screenplay with a chip on its shoulder and trying too damned hard—Herman vs. Joseph Mankiewicz, for instance, or the old Robert Towne versus the Tom Cruise-ified middlebrow edition. *Ask the Dust* is dreadful stuff, as stale, deluded, and sad as the cot in an old man's flophouse cubicle. (**WC**)

## AWESOME: I FUCKIN' SHOT THAT!

½* /****

*dir.* Nathanial Hörnblowér

Given that I was about halfway through a really nasty cold when I saw **The Beastie Boys**' *Awesome: I Fuckin' Shot That!*, I probably wasn't in the right frame of mind to judge its merits. With that disclaimer in place, this has to be the loudest movie I have ever seen. At the end of the ordeal, I felt as though band members Mike D, Adam Horowitz, and Adam Yauch had burrowed inside my brain and gone to work with an iron frying pan. I'll cop to preferring masochistic cinematic experiences in general and getting angry and frustrated by movies that want little more than to cheer me up— but from now on, I'm going to draw the line at **Beastie Boys** concert films. At their 2004 Madison Square Garden show, **The Beastie Boys** passed out cameras to fifty audience members with instructions to shoot anything that interested them; *Awesome: I Fuckin' Shot That!* was culled from their footage. It sounds like a pretty daffy idea, but the results are much better than you would expect—or, more accurately, they seem to reflect the vision of director Yauch (credited as Nathanial Hörnblowér). The visuals are every bit as aggressive as the music: they push you down, smash your skull against the pavement, and don't stop until they see the pink stuff. There are few moments where **The Beastie Boys** are not performing and there are few shots that don't underscore the music. It's cinematic, it's fast, and it leaves you bruised and wounded. Even outside of the headaches, based on what I've seen here I don't think I really care much for **The Beastie Boys**. Their pop-cultural references are broad and easy: *Scarface*, *Star Wars*, "Star Trek", Jackie Chan, high school proms, Nintendo, a viral video of boxing cats; they dedicate "Sabotage" to President Bush, and while the then-ten-year-old song does have a nice timeliness to it, it's still not particularly brilliant social commentary. I wish I could confirm this, but I think it was ex-**Devo** frontman Mark Mothersbaugh who said that punk rock could never take off in the States because the kids have too many toys to play with. Yeah. Hip-hop, the other half of **The Beastie Boys**' musical DNA, could never take off in the suburbs, either, for more or less the same reason. *Awesome: I Fuckin' Shot That!* is a film full of empty rage borne of a toy-drunk culture made by toy-drunk children. It's a portentous act of arrogance against good music, good filmmaking, and good taste. (**Alex Jackson**)

# B

## BABEL
*½/****

*st.* Brad Pitt, Cate Blanchett, Gael García Bernal, Kôji Yakusho
*sc.* Guillermo Arriaga
*dir.* Alejandro González Iñárritu

By this late date, the *Magnolia*-esque interconnected-lost-souls genre ought to have burned out. The films never meant anything, and when they did move us, it was in such an arbitrary, unfocused way that nothing intelligent could be gleaned from our self-interested pity. But here it is 2006 and I find myself reviewing *Babel*, which fills the tired bill to a chronologically-fractured T. I'd say that it isn't the worst of the genre, yet figuring out which one is suggests an academic exercise from which I'd rather be excused; suffice it to say that this globalized spin on the old saws is predictably pointless, with the added extra of none of its characters' actions resembling human behaviour even once. Instead of a powerful statement on the loneliness of individuals, we encounter a cavalier attitude towards the non-white and a prurient interest in the damaged sexuality of a teenage girl that destroys whatever patience we might have left.

The worst thing about *Babel* is that it gets your hopes up early on that it might actually have something to say. The film opens in Morocco with a rifle coming into the hands of a shepherd, who leaves his children in charge of both the rifle and his flock. The latter naturally get around to horseplay and fire a round at a tour bus. We're then whisked to America, where the apparent victim's illegal Mexican housekeeper is expected to take care of her kids — despite the tragedy's coinciding with her son's wedding. It

appears for a moment that the two disadvantaged parties are going to be used in some cultural-economic sense, with white victim Susan (Cate Blanchett) and her husband Richard (Brad Pitt) as the fulcrum of a race and class analysis. What do the inserts of teenage deaf-mute Cheiko (Rinko Kikuchi) have to do with anything? We're game for a few moments, hoping that the matter will clear itself up.

Alas, as we watch this girl struggle (unconvincingly) with her blocked sexuality and mother's suicide, it becomes increasingly clear that the burden of guilt will not rest on the shoulders of Richard and Susan, despite that they hired someone cheap and under the table; they will seem stoic as they wait in a village for help while the rest of the (white) tourists begin to selfishly fume. The shepherd and the maid (who's left with no choice but to take the children in her charge down to Mexico for the wedding) are the ones destined for punishment. And that girl — connected to the tragedy through the ministrations of her father, Yasujiro (Koji Yakusho) — shall tease her failed conquests by... flashing them. Yep, that'll show them.

It's obvious that director Alejandro González Iñárritu and screenwriter Guillermo Arriaga are flying by the seat of their pants. They sort of understand that the big game for the genre is to rope in various nationalities in the hopes of looking political, but they only show their inexplicable biases. They think that if they mix their own heritage (Mexico) with the dominant culture (America), throw in an in-the-news ethnicity (Arabs) and the hipster hotspot of the moment (Japan), they'll arrive at a Big Statement. Not quite. For starters, the Japanese segments belong on the cutting-room floor, as they have only the most tenuous relationship to the interwoven tragedies of the Morocco shooting and the concurrent disaster of dragging the children across the border. And the whiteys certainly beg for more kinks than the nice-guy ciphers on offer here.

Indeed, a controlled thesis isn't on the menu. Iñárritu and Arriaga are more interested in getting poor Cheiko's kit off in fits of sensationalism, or in mining the horrible consequences of going through customs with batshit Santiago (Gael García Bernal). It gooses you emotionally every few minutes so you don't notice that the disadvantaged are the ones who end up paying (even, bizarrely, the Mexicans—and it's not as though the filmmakers treat this as an ironic conundrum) while the distracting star-power of the white Americans prevails. This deserves to be treated as a sorrowful inequity, but in *Babel* there are no inequities, simply dumb luck and bad choices. Pitt and Blanchett shoulder their burden with cool grace and incredible cheekbones as a metaphorical Rome burns around them. Standard practice for the emotional pornographers masquerading as world-connecting artists, I fear. (**TMH**)

## DIRECT-TO-VIDEO ANIMATED
### BAMBI II
**\*\*/\*\*\*\***
*sc.* Alicia Kirk
*dir.* Brian Pimental

I'm It would be faintly disingenuous to cry bloody murder over a straight-to-video *Bambi* sequel: given Uncle Walt's own propensity for denaturing children's classics (and milking the new "classics" for cash), it's only fitting that the cream of his own canon would be whored out for what the market will bear. Still, *Bambi* is no ordinary Disney movie, but one whose awesome craft is matched only by its singular horror of the adult world. It's ludicrous, then, to pick up the story after the deer-kid has learned to talk and show him that being a grown-up isn't so bad. Not only does it generally

contradict the original, but it also blows off the primal fear and sadness that make *Bambi* as potent as it is.

Really, *Bambi II* isn't shoddy, and the writing's several cuts above the usual Disney-sequel (or "mid-quel") refuse. The animation is clean and smooth, the jokes aren't too stupid, and the moral isn't brutally hammered home. In fact, aside from a few thoroughly terrible non-diegetic songs, the whole thing is quite comfortable to watch. But let's face it: *Bambi* wasn't about comfort. Opening with Father Deer Prince (voice of Patrick Stewart, no less) seeking a replacement mother for his son, the new film sets us up for the lesson that Dad shouldn't be so unsparing a single parent, which is ridiculous, because *Bambi* says to stoically suck it up and get on with one's traumatized life. *Bambi II* essentially inverts the fear and loathing of its namesake in concluding that there's nothing a plucky young deer can't handle with the right encouragement—something the first film arrived at by equating "encouragement" with the violent death of your nurturing mother.

One could point to the mildly revisionist approach and argue that the new *Bambi* is trying to correct the old one's ideological crimes. The über-patriarchal tone of the original, with its manhood-is-resisting-all-pain message, has been replaced with lighter tones: there's a positive girl deer for gender balance, a bully-boy with budding antlers—who presumably grows up to be Bambi's nemesis from the original— as an example of bad sportsmanship, and a toning-down of the loner-male approach that has rightly disturbed the film's contemporary critics. But this isn't done out of genuine concern—it's done out of ass-covering cowardice. *Bambi II* so determined to whitewash its forebear's legacy that it says all the right things to create a nice, cozy atmosphere, when the recoverable genius of *Bambi* lies in not flinching while everything falls into chaos.

In its brilliant, twisted way, *Bambi*

offered strange comfort in the knowledge that we weren't the only ones to suffer the slings and arrows of a terrifying life—a comfort that no amount of warm-fuzzies can ever adequately approach. The irony of *Bambi II* is that Walt Disney's own efforts to erect safe havens in the form of theme parks and media empires have finally, triumphantly effaced his real achievement: the evoking of the fear that drives us into the arms of the loving parent. Now the snake has eaten its own tail to the point that it has winked out of existence, as not even the parent remains—just the pacifier meant to distract you from the wolf at the door. If you want comfort for your kids, this does the job, but if you want to perhaps give them a glimpse of the world to come, this won't do at all. As for the notion that family entertainment doesn't have to be innocuous mush, file your regrets at your local MPAA office. (**TMH**)

## BASIC INSTINCT 2
ZERO STARS/****
*st.* Sharon Stone, David Morrissey, Charlotte Rampling, David Thewlis
*sc.* Leora Barish & Henry Bean
*dir.* Michael Caton-Jones

Picture Chappaquiddick re-imagined as a Kylie Minogue video. Thus, auspiciously, begins Michael Caton-Jones' will-breaking *Basic Instinct 2*, a picture so magnificently awful that it demonstrates a special, indefinable kind of genius *en route* to being just another of the worst films in history. Schlock writer Catherine Tramell (Sharon Stone), who publishes under the *nom de plume* of "Woolf" (because she is one, get it?), is behind the wheel of a sporty little number as a drugged-up soccer hero fingers her snatch, climaxing at the moment she runs her racer through a glass crash barrier (?!) into an icy drink. (Perhaps the Thames—we're in Jolly Old England this time around.) Catherine then finds herself on the wrong side of the law

again, ordered to undergo sessions with brilliant British shrink Michael Glass (David Morrissey, who has Liam Neeson's face down pat) on behalf of Scotland Yard's finest, Washburn (David Thewlis). Washburn calls Tramell a "cunt" and a "bitch" and accuses Glass at one point of being beguiled by the "smell of her pussy," which is the sort of elderly banter the knitting cotillion might still find shocking—though it's light years more appalling than Tramell's pleased reference to Masters & Johnson and her constant litany of "cum" [sic] declarations. "He was alive, he was making me cum," she says, and, "I think of you when I cum," and so on and so forth, marking her vampy, thumb-on-the-turntable performance as the most hideous bit of creaky past-prime tarting-about since Mae West was dropping the same dusty come-ons in support hose and pancake makeup. All that's missing are references to Kinsey and "bloomers."

Because it's the type of film that doesn't know how to grow its own life, *Basic Instinct 2* dedicates much of its supporting cast to constantly affirming the brilliance and/or deviance of Tramell and Glass, when all evidence presented to our poor senses suggests exactly the opposite. Neither seems particularly bright or naughty, with Stone's baritone half-speed husking making her coquette turns as pathetic as her obnoxious minx. Morrissey, meanwhile, his face frozen in some nondescript neutral rictus, appears mainly stunned to be caught in something once subtitled "Risk Addiction." That's Glass' diagnosis of our lady Tramell (whose sole risky pastime after the opening stunt-driving is sucking on cigarettes lit by phallic British landmark lighters (like Big Ben, hardy har), causing both Freud and England to roll in their graves), and then the rest of *Basic Instinct 2* plays out like a porn film without any taboo sex, just risqué outfits and some sedate nudity packed around sordid sets and godawful screenwriting and direction. Consider the scene post-coitus where a towel-bedecked Glass trundles hilariously down a long flight of stairs while Caton-Jones decides, for maybe the first time in the movie, to simply let the scene play out. Or the line Tramell offers up to the gods of non-sequitur miscomprehension: "Even Oedipus didn't see his mother coming"—or is that "cumming"? Either way, it doesn't make any kind of sense in or out of context.

Nor does the squandering of Charlotte Rampling (understanding that to squander the pursed Rampling is really a difficult accomplishment) as Glass' puckered mentor, or poor Flora Montgomery as one of Glass' humiliating compensatory fucks, done doggie before she's interrupted by a cell phone call from Glass' abused ex (Indira Varma), upon whom hangs the picture's interminable, ridiculous denouement. The unfortunate shadow of the first film falls on this one, too, as every time Catherine perches herself on a chair/table/bench, we find ourselves staring at her crotch in anticipation of some acknowledgment of what is still Stone's only real claim to fame. Well, besides that she was married to a guy bitten on the toe by a frigging Komodo dragon.

To be fair, it's really the only thing of interest to do after a while. *Basic Instinct 2* is dreadful beyond description—you might be thinking that it's worth it in the same way that buying Farrah Fawcett's two late-'90s appearances in PLAYBOY (the first at Stone's current age of 48) was worth it, but you'd be wrong. You might also be thinking it's so bad that it's got to be funny, but you'd be wrong about that, too. *Basic Instinct 2* is the kind of horror that lingers on a shot of a magazine article long enough for you to read that every paragraph begins with the same sentence—and that sentence is "a perfectly good movie script could be made from..." Which is deceptive, too, because no one involved in any way, shape, or form with this misbegotten

death march would know a perfectly good movie script if it bit them on their perfectly toned, middle-aged buttock. (**WC**)

## BLACK CHRISTMAS
**\*/\*\*\*\***

*st.* Katie Cassidy, Michelle Trachtenberg, Mary Elizabeth Winstead, Andrea Martin
*sc.* Glen Morgan, based on the screenplay by Roy Moore
*dir.* Glen Morgan

The worst thing about Glen Morgan's *Black Christmas* is that there's too much of it. The original, by the tragically late Bob Clark, was a small masterpiece of economy, relying on little more than its one major set (a dormitory), an unseen killer, and some sorority sisters. But that was 1974, when nobody was paying any attention: by 2006, Hollywood had exchanged the cheap and the grungy for the overwritten and over-produced. The industry now demands rounded character arcs, and for this reason alone we're given a backstory for the film's slasher that nobody needed in addition to a padding-out of the action with forced cynicism and phoney characterizations. It's an overstuffed mess that fails miserably to evoke the fear and melancholy of a spectacularly defiled Christmas.

Genre fans the world over know the tale of a doomed sorority, invaded at Christmastime by a psycho-killer determined to pick off the residents one by one. Where Clark's film never made that much fuss over the murderer or his beginnings (beyond subtly dropping clues through the device of obscene phone calls that have become iconic in the annals of horror), *Black Christmas '06* is determined to matter more by providing a wholly unbelievable rationale for his actions—and somehow winds up being far more misogynist than the original. It appears that Billy Lenz (Robert Mann as an adult) was abused by his mother

(Karin Konival), bore witness to her murder of his father, and wound up fathering his own half-sister. Once again a harridan matriarch (shades of Hitchcock) is responsible for loosing a slasher upon the world, and this fact alone makes *Black Christmas '06* seem less fair than the free-floating angst of the earlier film.

Another problem with this origin story, incorporated into the picture as flashbacks, is that it repeatedly distracts from the main event: the Ten Little Indians-style dispatching of the sorority sisters that ought to be the movie's bread-and-butter. Worse, the sisters in question—caricatures like Lacey Chabert's daddy's-girl princess Dana and Michelle Trachtenberg's relatively normal cipher Melissa—aimlessly editorialize whenever possible about the Christmas season's superficiality, its pagan roots, and how much family get-togethers suck. Where the first film found its emotional center in the bitter disappointment of people dying during the holiday season, this one flails wildly without ever hitting a thesis and bogs things down with the un-scary and the not-resonant.

I suppose I wouldn't be complaining if anyone had actually pulled off said intrigues, but there's no design to the piece. *Black Christmas '74* was relentlessly paradigmatic in its delineation of murders, evasions, and distractions, whereas the remake is an amorphous mass that never quite gets at anything. Gorehounds might be pleased to note that this version (at least in this apparently unrated incarnation) is miles bloodier than its predecessor, but somehow it doesn't pack the same punch: Clark was acutely aware of the gravity of death and its attendant disappointments; Morgan and company are cartoonish to the last. It's no surprise that the film ends its onslaught at around the 75-minute mark only to restart for a lame second climax: with no sense of structure, *Black Christmas* is merely a series of failed bids for credibility. **(TMH)**

## THE BLACK DAHLIA (see: *HOLLYWOODLAND*)

## BLOOD DIAMOND
\*/\*\*\*\*
*st.* Leonardo DiCaprio, Jennifer Connelly, Djimon Hounsou, Michael Sheen
*sc.* Charles Leavitt
*dir.* Edward Zwick

## APOCALYPTO
\*\*\*/\*\*\*\*
*st.* Rudy Youngblood, Dalia Hernandez, Jonathan Brewer, Morris Birdyellowhead
*sc.* Mel Gibson & Farhad Safinia
*dir.* Mel Gibson

After sending Matthew Broderick to head a Negro battalion in the Civil War and Tom Cruise to witness—and survive—the end of Feudal Japan, director Edward Zwick dispatches Leonardo DiCaprio and Jennifer Connelly to Sierra Leone and its own diamond-fuelled Civil War to moralize endlessly from the superior ethical vantage afforded by time and privilege. (That they also lend a much-needed nougat centre to *Blood Diamond*'s thin chocolate coating goes without saying.) The Denzel Washington/Ken Watanabe token this time around is the oft-similarly-abused Djimon Hounsou: as the DC Comics-sounding Solomon Vandy, Hounsou seeks to trade a rare pink diamond for the life of his son, who's been molded by the evil Sierra Leonians into a soulless murdering/raping machine. Meanwhile, DiCaprio's South African fortune hunter Archer meets his match in humanitarian reporter Maddy (Connelly); it's the kind of dead weight from which flaccid romantic misadventures are made and reminds, if anything, of Joaquin Phoenix's cameo in *Hotel Rwanda* as a ventriloquist dummy for the filmmaker's belated activism. Maddy's an Aeolian Harp and Zwick is her hot air, and her scenes are the only ones in the film that don't resemble some ultra-violent, exotic serial interested in making a horror movie of the rest of the world and ennobled white knights in shining armour of the enlightened, Aryan Westerner. Archer's internal conflict in this context, then, isn't a nod to complexity (or a telegraph that *Blood Diamond* is *his* redemption story)—it's a statement that the worst of Us still has more power to change the darkest parts of the world than the best of Them. On second thought, take this film as sad proof of the point.

Women and children are butchered by kid-aged sociopaths, hands are lopped off, grand African vistas are fetishized, and big-budget chases give the picture the lustre of an old-fashioned Hollywood prestige piece—which, of course, *Blood Diamond* is, packed as it is to bloat with clichés and blacks as savage savages or the more palatable noble kind. It breaks its arm patting itself on the back, packing all the troubles of an exploited area into a series of facile, queasily pornographic images that exploit the area anew for its usefulness as a backdrop to two white people flirting together (see also: *The Interpreter*). Indeed, it seems there's no end to Sierra Leone's troubles. Like every Zwick film, *Blood Diamond* gathers a sort of grand epic momentum as it goes along, taking full advantage of its panoramic settings and demonstrating what feels like genuine glee in its bloodletting—and like every Zwick film, there comes a point when its "based on real events" vérité touches on a few troubling representational quagmires. Should the slaughter of countless crossfire innocents be quite this titillating? The trouble might be that there's nothing illicit about the pleasures of *Blood Diamond*—that whatever guilt that might possibly arise from the rock sitting on your wife's wedding ring is symbolically assuaged by the spiritual awakening of surrogate spoiler Archer (twice besmirched: once as a soldier of fortune, once as an Afrikaner); by the silent villain of people richer than you

(and maybe black, too, hence the invocation of "bling"); and by the familiar final-reel teat Zwick provides awards-season audiences.

No such chance to feel like they gave at the office awaits the unfortunates gathered for the genuinely-insane Mel Gibson's latest Guignol epic *Apocalypto*, a gore-steeped allegory of a theocracy ruled by arcane rituals, violence, and fear. Chases abound here as in *Blood Diamond*, the best of them involving a hungry jaguar that, to hear Gibson tell it, was the germ that sprouted into the film. The pictures also share the story of the noble savage overcoming impossible odds to reunite with his family: Jaguar Paw (Rudy Youngblood) is abducted from his subsequently raped-and-pillaged village by a master race of Mayans, managing to hide his kid and pregnant wife (Dalia Hernandez) before the atrocities unfold and embarking on an odyssey back to their side when he miraculously escapes sacrifice in the capital. Said odyssey (like the one in *Rescue Dawn*—the lesson of late is "Don't lose your shoes") involves Gibson's favourite mortifications of flaying and gaping side-wounds as great spurting geysers of blood drench the lush jungle setting in Gibson's martyr complex and rage. A cheese-fest epic full of breathtakingly stupid point-of-view shots, whip-pans, avalanches of human heads, and still-beating hearts shown to owners, Mola Ram-style, *Apocalypto* resembles a fever dream of Indian-fear not entirely unlike the legendary Italian exploitation flick *Cannibal Holocaust*. It's a strange brew that supports both the grindhouse charnel of *The Passion of the Christ* and the obscene naturalism of Werner Herzog, and I have to believe that it's only because of Gibson's persecutorial madness that *Apocalypto* coheres at all. Gibson might not be an admirable man, but he's turning into that rarity of a distinct filmmaker with the resources to do any damned thing he wants.

What most disappoints about *Apocalypto* is that it is, ironically, not particularly risible in any way. Its usefulness as allegory is blunted by its excess and insurmountable alienness (and, it goes without saying, its not being about Christ), while its decision to present itself entirely in a (modern) Indian dialect provides a further documentary remove. The very qualities—the detail and cultural subtleties—that drummed millions into genuflection for *The Passion of the Christ* feed into the familiarity afforded *Apocalypto* by its indulgence in colonial fear and loathing. No question that it means to be something more than a gruelling, kinetic chase through a train of thunderously-choreographed blockbuster moments, but because that's precisely what it is, the closest the film comes to delicacy is in its occasional inspiration of unintentional laughter.

Still, *Apocalypto* slots in solidly next to a spate of caveman action flicks from the last couple of years: stories about civilizations' end (and this film begins with Will Durant's famous post-mortem for the fall of the Roman Empire: "A great civilization is not conquered from without until it has destroyed itself from within") that have its survivors reconstructing the world along Old Testament guidewires. Just as Gibson's Christ is in steely ass-kicking mode when he rises from the dead in the closing moments of *The Passion of the Christ*, so, too, is *Apocalypto* constantly informed by the looming arrival of Spanish Conquistadors and the sanguine imposition of some more of that old-time religion. On second thought, I wonder if it's not a pretty useful allegory for the United States in the first part of the 21st century after all. (WC)

## BLOODRAYNE
ZERO STARS/****
*st*. Kristanna Loken, Michelle Rodriguez, Michael Madsen, Ben Kingsley
*sc*. Guinevere Turner
*dir*. Uwe Boll

It seems sort of pointless at this juncture to keep kicking at Uwe Boll—indeed, there's a minor backlash against all the lash, most of it dedicated to defending the Kraut Ed Wood along the lines of his latest, the excrescent *BloodRayne*, as being only as bad as ordinary bad films and not as bad as getting your eyelid caught on a nail. The secret to this bountiful wealth of backhanded praise, Boll has discovered, is found somewhere in the intersection of gratuitous gore and gratuitous nudity—both virtues forgiving a multitude of the director's other shortcomings (a tin ear, a blind eye, a plugger's grace, and so on), because it transforms his sword-and-sorcery saga into something that looks and sounds just like the crap most of us squandered our misspent youth surfing for on late night cable, tissue in one hand, lotion in the other. Without stretching too extravagantly, it's easy to see in that great sloppy act of pubescent self-abuse the very same method guiding Boll's hand at the camera through his ersatz trilogy of terrible. Fair to wonder a time or two over the course of the film if someone should invoke the Geneva Convention and get the fuck outta dodge. I guess there's a purpose to everything under the sun, and *BloodRayne*, based on a video game series of the same name, must be around to give hope to anyone with a camera in a country with a tax loophole that they, too, can make really bad movies with which to waste other peoples' lives.

BloodRayne (Kristanna Loken) is a half-vampire (like Blade without the funk) conceived of the union between her Victorian lady of a mother and arch-bloodsucker Ben Kingsley (cast as you would cast Keanu Reeves as a retarded surfer), going incognito here *sans* "Sir" so as not to sully his Oscar-winning reputation. Michael Madsen is here, too, and Michelle Rodriguez—

two names one hesitates to attach to a costume/period drama for the simple fact that they're horrible actors with no discernible range. (Rodriguez, especially, continues to patent her probably-lesbian, angry man-woman shtick, but to what end?) Ms. Rayne wishes to find her pa for a little 'splainin, figuring out somehow from someone that the best way to penetrate daddy dearest's demesne is to obtain a few artifacts in a *Conan the Destroyer/Red Sonya*/video game fashion. Why none of the evil henchmen think of opening a box said to contain one of the artifacts before bringing Blood before his majesty is a head-scratcher (just like why there's a training montage mid-film after our heroine has been kicking-ass for a full hour), if not as much as the fact of the picture's existence is. What I'm saying is you gotta pick your battles.

The gore is framed eternally center-stage, meaning that no matter what's happening, where it's happening, and at what point it's happening, Boll takes pains to shoot a carefully-structured, well (and differently) lit cutaway of the result. Cause for celebration in some circles, I'm sure, yet the gore is check-a-book-outta-the-library poor, and the leering quality of the cutaways renders them something of a mockery. You don't feel horror at the splatter, but rather a whole lotta disdain. (Check out Tom Savini's early work if you want to see how it's done on a low budget.) Ditto the nudity, most of it in a ridiculous establishing shot with vampire Meat Loaf surrounded by an arbitrarily-topless meat-puppet harem, while the money shot is reserved for Loken flashing half a tit during Brittany Murphy-sex, clinging to the side of someone like a chittering howler monkey as a jail cell door pounds out our pain in 4/4 time. The storytelling is patchy, the fight choreography is high-school drama club, and the dialogue and performances should win awards for consistency if nothing else.

I guess I ought to say that *BloodRayne* will be interesting to people who appreciate films that have no contact with film-craft—that are made by people who appear to have neither ever seen a film nor, more possibly, ever spared a moment contemplating what makes a film good or bad. There's a freedom about Boll's work that can, under the right circumstances, be seen as invigorating, a middle-finger to every asshole striving to create something of lasting value through hard work, respect for the medium, its history, the genre, and its audience, and the feeling of responsibility that if someone's trusting you with their money and time (producers, actors, and viewers alike), the least you can do is give something back that's more than this product of venal extrusion. Too conventional for dada, now, all Boll can claim is proof positive that you can get a subscription to HEAVY METAL magazine even in Germany. (**WC**)

## BOBBY
½*/****
*st.* Harry Belafonte, Joy Bryant, Nick Cannon, Emilio Estevez
*w./d.* Emilio Estevez

## FAST FOOD NATION
*/****
*st.* Patricia Arquette, Luis Guzman, Ethan Hawke, Ashley Johnson
*sc.* Eric Schlosser & Richard Linklater
*dir.* Richard Linklater

A completely pointless exercise in winsome, pathetic hand-wringing, the navel-gazing *Bobby* is just one of this year's inevitable examples of the power of nepotism in dictating who gets to continue churning out the worst films anyone's ever seen. Triple-threat Emilio Estevez (doing duties here as bad actor, bad director, and bad writer) continues his reign of terror unabated on the back of poor Bobby Kennedy, and those clips from RFK's speeches littering the picture are the only things remotely of interest. *Bobby* itself is a *Crash*-like roundelay of desperately manufactured bathos, covering the entire spectrum of miserable plotting and characterization from the old battleaxe (Sharon Stone) to the youngsters tripping on acid (to the tune of **Jefferson Airplane** and images of Vietnam carpet-bombing, natch) to the buttermilk-scrubbed ingénue (Lindsay Lohan) marrying her gay schoolmate (Elijah Wood—that casting admittedly the only hint that the schoolmate is gay) to save him from the draft to the non-drama of an Ambassador Hotel manager (William H. Macy) and his firing of a mildly-racist kitchen manager (Christian Slater). Is there any doubt that each and every one of these folks (and more: best to forget Martin Sheen and the still-execrable Helen Hunt pillow-talking until well-past the point of audience tolerance) will find themselves in the kitchen where/when Bobby meets his end? I imagine them as the cardboard cut-out "friends" Steve Martin's *Lonely Guy* uses to simulate a kickin' cocktail party, here repurposed to simulate "characters" in a movie that's supposed to mean something.

Just the idea of *Bobby* stinks of intense stupidity—of that taint of rich, intellectually infantile dolts dreaming up some sensitive, cardigan-wearing premise wherein a sainted icon's last day of life can be told through the eyes and mouths of "average" people. The great irony being that these champions of the average man represent said average man with such broad, clichéd, clumsy devices that they're every bit as condescending as the neo-conservative villains the picture wants so very much to vilify. When the conservative Right calls Hollywood a cesspool of shallow thinking left-wing wingnuts, *this* is what they're talking about. You can imagine Estevez and his aging yuppie fuckwit pals toking up and deciding that it'd be great to portray Bobby Kennedy's assassination through the eyes of lifeless workshop zombies representing the spectrum of some dimly-understood social strata affected by His martyrdom. Fresh-faced Latino everyman Freddy Rodriguez (cast as such here and in *Harsh Times*) provides the soul of the piece, buying a ticket to a Dodgers game for his father and himself in a holy rite that predicts his own martyrdom alongside the sainted Hyannis Portian—but *Bobby* reduces his sacrifice to the twin boons of passing his golden dockets to a sage, soothsaying chef (Laurence Fishburne, of course) and, later, his rosary to the fallen Catholic Himself. Latinos, as the film points out in a hilarious scene over mammy's berry cobbler, are the "new nigger," but closer to the truth that, between this and Richard Linklater's low-rent crotch punch *Fast Food Nation* (wherein Rodriguez, who was played by Michael Pena in *Crash*, is played by Wilmer Valderamma), Latinos (Mexicans) are the new Native Americans: noble savages entrusted with the full burden of conscience and outrage in these United States.

Other targets of *Fast Food Nation*, a fictionalized adaptation of Eric Schlosser's non-fiction exposé on the evil practices of the American retail infrastructure incorporated, include puppy mills, underage drinking, the very idea of Wal-Mart, minimum wage, economic caste systems, drugs, immigration, and, shoehorned in there somewhere, the cruel indignities of high-volume meat processing. Footage of the actual slaughter and butchering of doe-eyed cattle follows fast behind a sad analogy made between said cattle and all of docile America, suggesting that Linklater wants to parallel meat led to the slaughter with Americans led to mass-consumerism. As social satires go, it's somewhere in the neighbourhood of those late-night college bull sessions spent in a haze of marijuana and a hard-on for that girl who smells like rose oil and belongs to every activist organization on campus. (Who of course is going home with that callow asshole Emilio Estevez no matter how convincingly you pretend to give a shit about glaciers and owls.) By the end of its scattershot outrage, the only clear message is the condescending delivery of the factoid that cows die before they're turned into hamburgers. You're led to the uncomfortable, outrageous conclusion that the animals' deaths are more exploited (and rendered senseless) by *Fast Food Nation* itself than they are by the restaurants and meat packers the film does its best to condemn.

There are no strong statements in *Fast Food Nation*, just bumper stickers. It's a shame, because the subject of our literally and figuratively eating shit to maintain a certain lifestyle deserves to find articulation from mouthpieces more articulate than Linklater, Linklater favourite son Ethan Hawke, Bruce Willis, and Kris Kristofferson (performing the same function as Sam Elliot in the ultimately-as-useless but at least wry *Thank You For Smoking*), oozing onto the screen and slinking off to the beat of Linklater's patronizing compositions and interpolated cross-cutting of burger exec Don (Greg Kinnear) watching porn in his posh hotel room and a dozen Mexican nationals sharing a motor-inn bunk while waiting to perform their ten-dollar-an-hour dream jobs. Simply elaborating on the complexity of wicked fast food franchises offering naturalized Mexicans the chance to own a business and, perhaps, advance within the corporate structure while raping (again literally, with a plant super (Bobby Cannavale) putting the wood to his helpless charges) their own kind in the production-side would have instantly transformed *Fast Food Nation* into a thoughtful examination of the impossibility of our industrialized situation instead of an inchoate screed delivered by idiots to like-minded idiots.

What *Bobby* and *Fast Food Nation* share (besides the roundelay structure, the star-filled cast, the mindless liberal ranting made instantly quaint by our most recent Congressional elections—see also: *Crash*) is an intensely distasteful taint of superiority. That feeling that these people believe they're teaching anybody anything; that they're making an *important* film, nutritionally-rich with *messages* people like Roger Ebert will subsequently champion as such. It's not about art here, it's about instruction presumed to be long in coming—and while the far Right in this country believes (and not without profit) that its slavering base is comprised of backwards mental defectives, one of the charming attributes of the suffocatingly-correct far Left is that it didn't. No opportunity to explain itself is left trusted to audience intelligence; no awkward analogy left without instant clarification for those who might be having a little trouble understanding that the late '60s were a divided time (*just like today*, get it?) or that other people have to kill and prepare our meat because we'd rather pay them to do so than do it ourselves. Both roads lead to the conclusion inescapable that we as a culture are corrupt, bloated, materialistic, self-serving, and mean—points made with the reductivism and divisiveness these folks would quickly find in others and points made meaningless because they're illustrated with little intelligence and temperance. Not merely bad art, but bad politics, rhetoric, and thinking, too, *Bobby* and *Fast Food Nation* are born of the same punditry that most the United States has rejected: victims, both, of a rising tide towards the middle and an end, if one is hopeful, of the cheap hate-mongering and moron-baiting engaged in by either side of the culture war. (**WC**)

## BORAT: CULTURAL LEARNINGS OF AMERICA FOR MAKE BENEFIT GLORIOUS NATION OF KAZAKHSTAN
\*\*\*/\*\*\*\*

*dir.* Larry Charles

22

DOCUMENTARY
**THIS FILM IS NOT YET RATED**
*1/2/****
*dir.* Kirby Dick

British Comedian Sacha Baron Cohen, as his Kazakhstani journalist alter ego Borat, tells former Georgia senator Bob Barr that the cheese Barr's just eaten was made from his wife's breast milk, and he does it in such a way as to suggest the naïf savage stereotype's unaffected innocence as it preys on the secret bigot in us all. *Borat: Cultural Learnings of America for Make Benefit Glorious Nation of Kazakhstan* (hereafter *Borat*) lays on America's belief that the rest of the world is run and populated by ridiculous children alternately in need of careful guidance and firm scolding. The Borat character, then, is very much a creation of the shortsightedness of a condescending American intolerance, while his ability to infiltrate America's living rooms speaks to a complex national desire to fold the aliens it abhors to its breast in some sort of misplaced act of missionary grace. If we reduce the aim of evangelical Christianity down to the twin compulsions of damnation and salvation, what *Borat* really does is reveal the hypocrisy at the root of our professed acceptance and, more troublingly, highlight how divorced we are from the guiding principles of this sea to shining sea. In a film that does this much to expose the ugly undercurrent of homophobia, racism, and xenophobia in this country, it's no great surprise when New York subway riders threaten to kill Borat for kissing them on the lips in exuberantly misguided greeting—and the reactions of these Big Apple commuters strike me as refreshingly honest.

For the rest of what are most-often described as "cringe-inducing" moments, consider that although the targets in the picture are relatively soft (the kinds of provincial bumpkins *Borat* skewers are fairly common the world over, after all), the audience finds itself identifying with the dupes and the prudes, the rednecks and the retards. *Borat* is an astonishing meta-text because it has its cake and eats it, too: we laugh because we recognize that there's something horrific about a group of rodeo-goers agreeing *en masse* that Bush Jr. should drink the blood of every Iraqi man, woman, and child, as well as something impolite about pointing it out. The connection between the cultural mores of the millennial United States and those of Victorian England emerge in the margins of *Borat* when it's not busy shooting fish in a barrel. It seems that the only value left treasured in this country is civility, and once the lights come up on our beloved alien's Kool-Aid acid test, the odd realization dawns that we might be stuck in the quagmire in which we're stuck because the best intended were too deadened to affect any sort of meaningful change in time to matter. The assholes win since they're assholes and the rest of us are just cowed and appalled enough to turn away.

That willingness to ignore the rape and pillaging of our best intentions (and the best intentions of our founding fathers) tells us everything we need to know about the longevity and success of the MPAA's rating system, which takes identical works and weighs them according to the Goody Brown school of moral censorship. It's not that I think a ratings system is misguided in theory, it's that there's something essentially unAmerican about the way this system operates under a cloak of mystery and misdirection. The members aren't named (though *This Film is Not Yet Rated* unmasks them), the appeals process is secretive and presided over by a member of the clergy, and this collection of soccer moms and other sanctimonious prigs actually gather up the gumption to tell someone like Atom Egoyan how he should edit his films. Precedent isn't allowed as an argument and the reasons for a harsh rating can be as mysterious and capricious as "it just doesn't feel right"—while the old saw that you can show all the violence you want so long as you don't show a female orgasm is brought to the mat and wrestled with for a while. What bothers me about Kirby Dick's documentary *This Film is Not Yet Rated* is a bit with that asshole Michael Tucker, director of *Gunner Palace*, who rants that his film shouldn't have initially received an R rating: I found myself, unsurprisingly, disagreeing with everything he said. Ratings matter—but the process should be transparent. There shouldn't exist secret prisons and torture sanctioned by the American government and there shouldn't exist a board of hooded censors deciding which films get distribution and ad space and which get relegated to instant forgetfulness. It's not the fact of it that galls, in other words, it's the Gestapo tactics that offend. That being said, *This Film is Not Yet Rated* aims for obvious targets, provides a questionable service, and is ultimately a picture without either an audience or a point, as folks who care won't learn anything and folks who don't, can't. (WC)

## THE BREAK-UP
** /****

*st*. Vince Vaughn, Jennifer Aniston, Joey Lauren Adams, Ann-Margret
*sc*. Jeremy Garelick & Jay Lavender
*dir*. Peyton Reed

Vince Vaughn can never seem sincere, only dazed and slack, making his proto-slob Gary in Peyton Reed's infernal *The Break-Up* an odd object of desire for art gallery receptionist Brooke—or he would be if Brooke weren't played by vanilla pudding Jennifer Aniston. The problem with the picture is that it's *Who's Afraid of Virginia Woolf?* (or the more-often invoked *Scenes from a Marriage*)—with healthy doses of *Swingers* and *The 40 Year Old Virgin* to confuse the rancor—played by one-note actors who demonstrate not a soupçon of chemistry, thereby engendering zero rooting interest in their counterparts' reunion. (The fact that the two stars appear to have found love off camera regardless suggests the *Proof of Life* Effect for the anti-rom-com set.) You have to respect a picture that sports at least three or four scenes straight out of Hell and has the good sense at one point to mention it in so many words, like when Brooke comes home to find Gary engaged in some weird bacchanal, the two exchanging a long wordless look across the wasteland as the world comes to an end. But there's so little presence demonstrated by either of the principals that the movie finally feels disconnected and inconsequential.

It's something of a tradition in reviewing these films to point out the repugnantly fey gay comic relief (such as Brooke's brother Richard (John Michael Higgins) and co-worker Christopher (Justin Long)), and to speculate aloud how much better a picture it would have been were one of the sidekicks the main attraction, but no: although the gay comic relief is indeed repugnant and fey, none of *The Break-Up*'s characters are remotely interesting. It's a remarkable thing to discover about a film that boasts an ancillary cast of people like Ann Margret, Vincent D'Onofrio, Judy Davis, and Jason Bateman, each of whom is asked to play a minute or two of retrograde shtick before slinking off to wherever it is that bad workshop-plot shivs go to wither. (The central joke revolving around closeted Richard's flaming gayness appears to be that he's able to beat the shit out of Gary, which, in the broad scheme of things, is paternalistic bigotry rather than the other kind; in any case, Richard is summarily discarded once he's served his slapstick purpose.) This lack of character depth is germane to the conversation because it points to a holistic emptiness that robs *The Break-Up*'s darkest moments of insight and its lighter moments of revelation.

*The Break-Up* is anti-intellectual in a way that another film a little bit like it, Scorsese's *After Hours,* never was (an art gallery patron says he's loathe to pay money for something he could have painted himself—an odd point upon which to hang a barb when the truth is that most of the theoretical fans of this picture could also have directed it themselves), making a hero out of Gary before asking him to change to conform to some other idea of perfection. Brooke, on the other hand, is an arbitrarily mercurial doormat: in love with Gary only until the screenplay decides she's not and identified almost entirely by her haircut at the end—just as the actress who plays her has been for much of her career. Aniston's greatest skill is apparently being the *tabula rasa* upon which dim bulbs project their thoughts.

*The Break-Up*'s best moments are the aforementioned bacchanal, another in which Lupus (Cole Hauser), Gary's appropriately lupine brother, tries to pick up two women by describing a bizarre bondage/torture scenario, and a bit where best friend Johnny (Jon Favreau) can't be talked out of killing an innocent man out of macho kinship to Gary. The film is actually quite horrifying—it's not a comedy, really, not the least because it's not terribly funny. Still, what really bites is that the picture seems a missed opportunity. It isn't without insight, after all, into how men and women sometimes spawn something vile in the alchemy between them, but it reserves its ultimate horror for that moment where it wraps everything up with a wink and a shrug. *The Break-Up* is interesting solely because it's one of the starker examples of how neutered our culture has become. If only it had the courage to be as full of piss as it wants to be. (**WC**)

## BRICK
**\*\*½/\*\*\*\***
*st.* Joseph Gordon-Levitt, Lukas Haas, Nora Zehetner, Laura Dannon
*w./d.* Rian Johnson

*Brick* is a cult classic-in-the-making and one for which I harbour a goodly amount of affection. (I should say I admire its chutzpah, if not its ultimate success.) It's an experiment in screenwriting and matching shots, a gimmick stretched to feature-length by first-time hyphenate Rian Johnson that puts Raymond Chandler's hardboiled lexicon into the mouths of disconsolate teens seething at a high school somewhere in the twenty-first century. It would've been a fantastic *noir* except for that displacement, as its coolness decomposes every time the film contorts into an unnatural posture to honour its trick, nifty as it is. Consider *femme fatale* Laura (neo-Winnie Cooper Nora Zehetner): when she finally, inevitably, seduces our gumshoe Frye (the always-marvy Joseph Gordon-Levitt), for instance, it's hard to know whether they've slept together or just made out on someone's parents' bed. It matters. There's an inevitable infantilizing that goes hand in hand with the premise, which can be used to either its benefit (as when Kingpin's (Lukas Haas) mother fusses about like Scorsese's mom has a tendency to do in her son's pictures), or, as is more usual, its detriment (see: a ridiculously awkward meeting with the school's Vice Principal (Richard Roundtree)). As straight *noir, Brick* would be an easy project to get behind: it's post-modern and rejuvenating in the most respectful sense (more *Sin City* than *Dead Men Don't Wear Plaid*)—but to set it in a high school milieu, no matter the accomplishments of its cast (uniformly excellent), makes the whole production seem smug and, ultimately, just a little bit silly. A shame I didn't catch this about fifteen years ago. (**WC**)

## THE BRIDESMAID (La Demoiselle d'honneur)
*** / ****

*st.* Benoît Magimel, Laura Smet, Aurore Clément, Bernard Le Coq
*sc.* Pierre Leccia and Claude Chabrol, based on the novel by Ruth Rendell
*dir.* Claude Chabrol

Comparisons of *The Bridesmaid (La Demoiselle d'honneur)* to Hitchcock are almost inevitable, not only because such assessments are the lazy default position of critics when referencing suspense yarns, but also because *The Bridesmaid*'s director, Claude Chabrol, has carved out a career as the French heir apparent to the master's title. That said, the distinctions between the two filmmakers are probably more interesting than the similarities: Chabrol's overall style is considerably more relaxed than Hitchcock's, and his approach to character is finally less judgmental. Here, for instance, in lieu of assigning blame to the damaged *femme fatale* of the title, he notes the thrilling nature of her transgression and the unappetizing prospect of returning to normalcy after succumbing to her lethal charms. Chabrol has always put women in the driver's seat of perversity and sexual wilfulness—something Hitch never quite had either the guts or the sympathy to pull off.

We're confronted with this distinction in the film's earliest images. Handsome but schleppy Philippe Tardieu (Benoît Magimel of Haneke's *The Piano Teacher*) is aching to change the channel from a newscast reporting a bloody murder, but his sisters Sophie (Solène Bouton) and Patricia (Anna Mihalcea) mock him for his squeamishness and demand to keep watching. This establishes our man as a wannabe nice guy, one who's responsible in his salesman job and mindful of the feelings of his widowed mother, Christine (Aurore Clément). Enter Senta (Laura Smet), the titular bridesmaid who fills in at Sophie's wedding and sweeps Philippe off his feet. Unlike everything else in his well-ordered but boring life, she's unpredictable, impulsive, and passionate, though as time wears on, the lengths to which her amorality can go become a tad worrisome.

Everything's relative, of course—this is a movie where almost all of the male characters are shown to be weak or thoughtless. Senta is revealed to have a deadbeat dad, while Christine is granted a jerk boyfriend (Bernard Le Coq) who lies to her and makes off with a Tardieu family heirloom. Even Sophie's man Jacky (Eric Siegne) seems, like Philippe, a bit of a wus, setting the general assertiveness of the women in sharp relief. Senta proves to be a relative of the murderous duo of the late Chabrol masterpiece *La Cérémonie*: a societal outcast who can't help but gravitate towards the subversion of violence. We know she's crazy and violent, but given the male alternatives of dullness and contempt, what's a modern girl supposed to do?

Although it's based on a Ruth Rendell novel (as was *La Cérémonie*), *The Bridesmaid* doesn't take the outward form of a pulse-pounding thriller. It's almost thirty minutes in before Philippe and Senta meet; until then, the film prefers to record the rhythms of the Tardieu household as mother's disastrous relationship unfolds and Philippe burns with resentment to the point of swiping said heirloom (a bust of a woman named Flora) back from said jerk. He's clearly looking to break out of his routine, yet he doesn't exactly know it—and while we sense that something bad is going to happen, we're left to stew in the tension of unspoken desires and familial hostilities. Once the affair does commence, the imminent desperate acts are merely hinted at rather than telegraphed through streamlined narrative and jackhammer effects. Chabrol's Bazinian training serves him well: he establishes the rhythm of life as opposed to deploying shock tactics that tell us what to feel.

To be sure, *The Bridesmaid* is only good Chabrol; the crazy-woman-breaks-nebbish-out-of-rut story is a bit shop-worn regardless of the smart reading of the material. It's not the shattering tragedy of *La Cérémonie* or the cruelly sympathetic *Le Boucher*, and it merely hints at its thesis instead of putting it to the fore. Still, it's several cuts above the average thriller (French or American) and remains psychologically persuasive right up to the final close in on that antique bust. The film is a harmonious blend of pop constructs with a genuinely artistic sensibility—and vivid enough to suggest the growing unease of someone too locked into his mindset to identify what he really wants. It's worth less than a masterpiece, but several times more than the average. **(TMH)**

## DOCUMENTARY
### THE BRIDGE
\*/\*\*\*\*
*dir. Eric Steel*

The key moment in *The Bridge* comes during an interview with a photographer who happened to be on the Golden Gate Bridge just as a young woman was about to jump to her death. Not realizing that she was trying to commit suicide, he snapped a few pictures—and as soon as it sunk in, he immediately dragged her back to safety. We'd be happy to consider this man a hero and a saint were he not then ghoulish enough to not only steal a few photos of the girl's subsequent arrest, but also find it astounding that she decided to look back in his direction! It's this combination of sympathy and opportunism that defines Eric Steel's documentary, which, for all its motions towards "humanity," is grossly inappropriate in its violation of privacy and deeply morbid in its determination to collect footage of people's suicides, as if this will somehow give us deeper insight into the phenomenon. It doesn't and it

couldn't, but it sure is a great hook for someone looking to make a name in film.

As the title indicates, *The Bridge* is about the Golden Gate Bridge and its popularity as a final destination for the suicidal. Any analysis, however, is largely peripheral to the spectacle: there are melancholy images of people playing by the bridge, people walking on the bridge, people taking snapshots on the bridge, and—oh yes—people leaping off the bridge. Steel actually staked out the landmark with his camera and waited for random individuals to end their lives, without even so much as a "tasteful" amount of distance: he zoomed in as close as he could, following their bodies down until they hit the water. As accompanied by perspectives of goings-on on the bridge, it's all very sad and doomy. It's well-shot, cleanly edited, and rather accomplished for what it is—but what is that?

After completing the snuff portion of his film, Steel interviewed the families and friends of the deceased. Yet without any kind of framework for understanding these suicides, it registers as more rubbernecking. We're told that one jumper was a schizophrenic, one was the son of a depressive who always talked of death, one had lost his money and was feeling worthless... What, taken on their own, do these highly-abbreviated stories tell us? There's no thesis about the reasons for and patterns governing suicide, no discussion of the systems in place to deal with it, no sense of methodology in the distribution of information. Once Steel starts bringing in the bystanders, such as that photographer, or the family on vacation, you really wonder what he thinks he's playing at. Though he sort of captures the ripple effects of the deaths (that is, the guilt, anger, and confusion of the survivors left behind), it's entirely accidental—and so fleeting as to be almost imperceptible.

To be fair, many of the interviews are moving and will have anyone touched by the spectre of mental illness nodding in recognition. It's their use that rankles, their inclusion in an emotional gumbo that feels like crazy but comprehends nothing. Capping it off is Steel's fixation with the bridge itself: he's as fascinated by its suicidal magnetism as any of the jumpers drawn by its allure. When a final title crawl mentions that more people have killed themselves there than anywhere else in the world, does he believe he's helping? Or is he merely adding to the mystique that he pretends to be addressing? All kidding aside, this movie doesn't exactly make you think twice about killing yourself; its melancholy and confusion mirrors that of many of the people who jump. (**TMH**)

C

## CANDY (see: *NOTES ON A SCANDAL*)

A N I M A T E D
## CARS
*¹/₂/****
*sc.* John Lasseter & Philip Loren &
Kiel Murray
*dir.* John Lasseter

Soulless and anchorless, Pixar's *Cars* is the company's first all-around failure. It's got something to do with the lack of a human grounding: the only other time Pixar stumbled was with its similarly bleak *A Bug's Life* (that picture resorting, like *Cars*, to racial caricature as its primary tentpole), which is also the only other time the company has neglected to ground its story with homo sapien ballast. It's telling that a company pioneering machine-tooled animation so relies on that hint of humanity for its effectiveness; in its place, *Cars* resorts to cheap name-games (all the cities are car-parts except, dubiously, Los Angeles) as its primary gag and relies on a string of racing in-jokes (Darrell *Car*trip, get it? Yeah, me neither) to lubricate its worn-down gears. It's the product of the "Larry the Cable Guy" school of redneck effacement tacked onto a tired redemption romantic comedy, even more tired fish-out-of-water malarkey, and finally an inexplicable blanket criticism of all things urban. Sub-vaudeville gags with weak payoffs and rudderless execution are the things one would rightly expect from a DreamWorks flick—pity that their strain of high-concept lack of inspiration seems to respect no host.

Horror movies do a lot with city folk getting stranded in the boonies,

putting them at the mercy of mutant yokels bitter about their marginalization. Trace it back to *Psycho*, perhaps, and what happens to a nice momma's boy when the freeway bypasses his mom and pop. Thornier, the idea that a world existing entirely of cars (the cows are tractors) would inspire wonder and empathy in an audience of sentient beings is spectacularly misguided. But the real wonder of the bloated, meandering *Cars* is that in its tale of a self-obsessed jackass growing a heart way out there in the grassroots (but not without the help of a hot little Porsche, of course, thus fulfilling another DreamWorks/Disney dictum of the pretty mating only with the pretty), there's not one hint of the innovation and intelligence of Pixar's other films.

Lightning McQueen (voiced by Owen Wilson) is a hotshot NASCAR rookie, um, car, who hotdogs his way to a tie in an Aesop moment of hubris, necessitating a showdown with arch-nemesis Chick Hicks (Michael Keaton) and legend The King (Richard Petty). The opening race is beautifully rendered in a way that the processor of XBox 360 would have no trouble replicating, keynoted by a horrific crash made more horrific by the fact that these cars are living creatures. Pixar's corporate merging with Disney makes more sense now, recalling the way that salmon are treated in the Mouse House's otherwise completely-anthropomorphic *Brother Bear*: moments of callous stupidity, both, that speak to a wilful ignorance of how smart kids are.

McQueen, a self-obsessed speed-freak asshole a lot like namesake Steve McQueen (thus transforming the showdown with grizzled old Doc Hudson (Paul Newman) into a ghoulish '60s rematch between duelling idols McQueen and Newman), is stranded in a Podunk nowheresville that, we see in flashback, used to be a garish tourist trap before the department of transportation rendered it moot.

Inhabited by the bitter (Doc), the winsome (Sally (Bonnie Hunt)), and the inbred (Mater (Larry the Cable Guy)), the town of Radiator Springs is likewise home to Tony Shalhoub, reprising his accent from "Wings" and *Big Night* as a tire-store owner with a pet thing from *The Black Hole* (Guido Quaroni) who will have an inevitable date with glory once McQueen fulfills the suffocating strictures of the underdog sports uplift conceit that is *Cars'* skeletal substructure.

What the film resembles most, in fact, is a fattened-up version of *Duel*, complete with the same castration themes, urban/rural divide, anthropomorphized vehicles, and dusty races along back roads and dirt tracks—but it lacks those critical elements of real genius in its implementation and real purpose in its form. *Cars* is an edgeless, pointless love letter to racing freaks and car geeks, the greatest offense of which should be that it's so dumbed-down and wafer-thin that it says a lot about what its creators think of their target audience. Why should the stupidest, most facile, least-risky film Pixar's ever made be the one directed at NASCAR fans and other red-staters? Maybe it's not the olive branch from Tinsel Town we thought it was, after all. (**WC**)

## CASINO ROYALE
***/****

*st.* Daniel Craig, Eva Green, Mads Mikkelsen, Judi Dench
*sc.* Neal Purvis & Robert Wade and Paul Haggis, based on the novel by Ian Fleming
*dir.* Martin Campbell

A genuinely good updating of the James Bond mythos from plastic, moldering relic to bloody, sweaty sociopath drunk on his own virility and general misanthropy, Martin Campbell's *Casino Royale*—though the umpteenth chapter in a decades-old testosterone fever dream—is very much a part of this day and age. It's a film that makes sense of the franchise using a modern vernacular of vengeance, terrorism, Texas Hold 'Em, and paranoia. It's unnecessarily padded by at least fifteen minutes, but when it switches into gear it announces itself a worthy peer to the Jason Bourne films with action that's fantastically choreographed and alive with weight and violence. Most importantly, it finally has a protagonist who is, if not already, well on his way to becoming a serious psycho—postmodern man. What Daniel Craig brings to the role is a feral intelligence, this self-awareness that he's a bad person. Any good that he does is tainted by the knowledge that this Bond's only in it for the cheap thrills (drugs and murder, in particular) that lube his insect brain. *Casino Royale* summarizes the trend of detached, savage pictures from the last couple of years (*Miami Vice*, in particular, another bleak updating of a camp curio); when we talk about good action films now, we seem to be talking about the degree to which we have, as a culture, regressed to the Old Testament in matters of the heart and the hand. Call it "caveman vérité."

Bond has just been "00" certified, which, as you probably know, means that he has a "license to kill"—indiscriminately, it appears, as his superior M (Judi Dench) notes that he's already amassed a sizeable body count ten minutes into the picture. The brutal black-and-white prologue presages a nasty distillation of *On Her Majesty's Secret Service* into one difficult scene set in Venice that is the rare Bond set-piece to fully utilize the peculiarities of its locale. "The bitch is dead," says Craig at one point, and it lands like a hammer-blow in the middle of the urbane bullshit of the bulk of its twenty predecessors. Obvious in context, it's pretty easy to make the leap that *Casino Royale* is pissing on (the rest of) the franchise. Blood-weeping archvillain Le Chiffre (Mads Mikkelsen) observes that Bond has changed his shirt at one point; at another, someone has to defibrillate our previously-indestructible superhero. (His first words upon resurrection: "Are you okay?") All of it marks the picture as unusually smart about the shortcomings of its origins and dedicated to creating a work that will mean something to a contemporary audience. I imagine the ultimate effect of it to be that of a new *Star Wars* film directed by someone with a working frontal lobe—that is, the bar has actually been raised for maybe the first time in thirty years.

*Casino Royale* is fantasy in a world that's earned its darkness, a mature film that doesn't demand to be taken seriously but doesn't expect you to believe that the world is the same as it was when Sean Connery leered at Ursula Andress walking out of the surf like Venus on the half shell. In fact, when that scene is replicated in *Casino Royale*, it's Craig who's in the swimsuit, wearing a challenging look on his face that essentially invites the kind of torture he receives in the last half of the film, strapped to a chair with only his braggadocio and mental instability as armour. It's not about the misuse of women now, it's about being incapable of any kind of relationship that doesn't involve some degree of treachery and blood-letting. This Bond expresses an awareness that he's a murder or two away from losing his soul completely and then proceeds to kill an entire building of antagonists with his bare hands. It's nihilistic in the way that Scorsese's *The Departed* is nihilistic: both films are so hopeless that they destroy every signpost on their way back into the social breach that spit them out. It's the end product of our machineries of despair; that we see it as a renaissance speaks a little to the straits in which we find ourselves. (WC)

## PREVIOUSLY UNPUBLISHED
## CATCH A FIRE
**/****

*st.* Tim Robbins, Derek Luke, Bonnie

Henna, Mncedisi Shabangu
*sc.* Shawn Slovo
*dir.* Phillip Noyce

## PREVIOUSLY UNPUBLISHED
## TSOTSI
*/****

*st.* Presley Chweneyagae, Mothusi Magano, Kenneth Nkosi, Zenzo Ngqobe
*w./d.* Gavin Hood

South Africa is old news, man—didn't you hear? But that doesn't prevent two South African dramas from hitting the screens in 2006 (and what is it about 2006 that is so much like the end of the 1980s (the last time pictures about South Africa were dumped into the multiplex)?): Phillip Noyce's fact-based period piece (and half-assed allegory) *Catch a Fire* and Gavin Hood's half-assed allegory (and piece of shit) *Tsotsi*. Of the two, *Catch a Fire*, though obvious and unbearably proselytizing, is at least no worse than exactly what it is, i.e., a cross between Noyce's own comeback pictures *The Quiet American* and *Rabbit-Proof Fence*. (That is to say, an obvious serio-political, yes, *allegory* married to an uncontroversial, picaresque message flick.) *Tsotsi*, on the other hand, is a dimwitted redemption melodrama so flat in its execution and narrow in its scope that it could've been made anywhere, in any time, by almost anyone. Saying so shouldn't suggest that it's timeless, however, just that people are always producing crap like this when they want to make a name for themselves without offending anyone by being "relevant" or "edgy." *Tsotsi* is neither, of course, but the interesting question to ask is what in the zeitgeist has made it fashionable to cannibalize apartheid again for its rich thematic purposes? More, it's fair to wonder how Hood, in his film debut, has managed to base a picture in modern-day Cape Town that skirts the race issue altogether. The spectre of one of modernity's more shameful holdovers casts a pall over *Tsotsi*, naturally (the shadow of institutionalized bigotry is a long one), but the dedication with which Hood has endeavoured to tell a "universal" story that "could be set anywhere" has washed anything of real interest in the picture down to the lowest crime-story denominator. *Tsotsi* is an audition tape for Hollywood, and Hollywood responded by giving Hood the reins to the big-budget prestiger *Rendition*—which is just as dreadful as *Tsotsi*, but unlikely to win Hood another Oscar because without any blacks in it to feel superior to, it's just another gallon of hot air in a season filthy with the stuff.

*Catch a Fire* is the cliché-ized life story of ANC freedom fighter Patrick Chamusso (Derek Luke), who goes from family/company man to resolute anarchist/terrorist. After being frisked roadside and tortured for a crime he didn't commit, Patrick hulks out, joins the guerrillas, and tries to commit the crime he didn't commit. The bad guy is ogre Nic Vos (Tim Robbins), the mold-cast Afrikaner bogey played by Brendan Gleeson in *In My Country*, John Thaw in *Cry Freedom*, Jürgen Prochnow in *A Dry White Season*, Tim Roth in *A World Apart*, and so on, here representing all the corrupt, withered, neo-Third Reichisms of our hale Boer colonials. Funny how these biographies always tend towards the same Lifetime Channel narrative progressions, victims of the Hollywood-think that finds conventional drama in the unique lives of unique individuals and draws the string of the familiar from it long like a tapeworm from a bowel. By now, Noyce's eye for composition and way with pace serves mainly to render *Catch a Fire* a sugar pill of noble intentions and obvious political allegory culling from Bush Jr.'s campaign of torture and possibly race-/definitely religion-inspired crusades rationalized by defense-of-the-homeland justifications. Terrorism is identified as the last recourse of the righteous occupied and Chamusso as the true patriot for wanting the interlopers expelled from his homeland. Closing shots featuring the real Chamusso is more of the ol' *Rabbit-Proof Fence*, but Noyce makes the weird choice this time around to show Luke cavorting alongside his real-life model—a choice akin to having the corpse of Schindler doing a waltz with Liam Neeson to close out *Schindler's List*, or De Niro sparring with Jake LaMotta. It verges on smugly post-modern, but I think it was going for poignant somehow.

"Going for poignant somehow" is the best thing that could be said about *Tsotsi*, a contemporary flick about a hood ("Tsotsi" means thug, I guess) played one-note by Presley Chweneyagae, perfecting his smouldering stare and almost nothing else during the course of two hours of 'bad guy does the right thing when he becomes father to an orphan.' Sickening, saccharine, syrupy—all those things and more as Tsotsi carjacks a rich black woman, accidentally steals her baby boy in the process, and proceeds to make hash out of his life of crime. He learns of the world at the paralyzed hoofs of a paraplegic beggar, a single mom who becomes his charge's wet nurse, and, ironically, his gang-mate Butcher (Zenzo Ngqobe), the victim of Tsotsi's only actual murder. There's never any question whether Tsotsi is a nice guy, never any question that his path will inevitably lead to righteousness; *Tsotsi* is stunningly predictable, not for being a liberal love-in, but for being a *Three Godfathers*/*Three Men and a Baby*/*Tokyo Godfathers* manqué: sentimental, vaguely religious, and mostly a waste of time. There's one nice scene: Tsotsi goes back to the series of giant sewer pipes left in a field where he spent an emotional rainstorm as a child to find it overrun by a <u>Lord of the Flies</u> colony of feral youth. The rest of it—the ants crawling on the baby but not biting it, the decision to save lives instead of take them, the absolute terrifying zeal with which every moral crossroad is hammered into an unambiguous straight line—is for the birds. How you make a movie about South Africa that isn't about South Africa? The real question is why would anyone even fucking bother? (**WC**)

## CHARLOTTE'S WEB (see: *FLUSHED AWAY*)

## THE CHILD (L'Enfant)
**\*\*½/\*\*\*\***
*st.* Jérémie Renier, Déborah François, Jérémie Segard, Fabrizio Rongione
*w./d.* Jean-Pierre Dardenne & Luc Dardenne

## D O C U M E N T A R Y
## THE DEVIL AND DANIEL JOHNSTON
**\*\* /\*\*\*\***
*dir.* Jeff Feuerzeig

I believe the title is meant to indicate the arrested protagonist more than it is the baby he tries to sell on the black market, thus *The Child (L'Enfant)* — another of Belgian filmmakers Jean-Pierre and Luc Dardenne's mild, allegorical subversions of Robert Bresson and incrementally more violent subversions of the French New Wave — takes on *Pickpocket* via *Breathless*. In so doing, it conjures up this odd chimera of a stylistically backward-looking, formalist deconstruction, the first film of the Brothers (after *La Promesse, Rosetta,* and *The Son*) to feel this much like a knowing satire, to come so perilously close to being smug and post-modern that its style begins to become confused with its message. It could be a product of overfamiliarity with a fine and distinct sensibility (the last thing this kind of innovation can afford is to be outrun and second-guessed), or it could be that the Brothers are getting either bored of their shtick or fond of their reputation.

In any case, it's just a long way around to saying that *L'Enfant* is of course daring, technically impeccable, and aggressively humanist in its depiction of grimy mendacity, offering the faint possibility of grace to distract from the endless drudgery of the day-to-day. But it's a tougher sell this time for a number of reasons, not the least of which the interesting dilemma offered by a cad charismatic enough to give Milton's Old Scratch a run in the charm race. You do wonder if it's possible to cast Christian allegories with humanist cants any other way.

Bruno (Jérémie Renier) is a beautiful, towheaded Fagin, managing his street hoods in a leather jacket and Jean-Paul Belmondo's cap with the same casual equanimity with which he wrangles the sale of the infant son he's sired with girlfriend Sonia (Déborah François). He hasn't visited her in the hospital, but she still loves him in the way that coltish youngsters do in films like this, and they bicker and wrestle and fuck while the child is treated as an afterthought in the back of only our minds. (Sonia goes so far as to profess that her labour didn't hurt that much in just one example of the film's dearth of subtlety.) There's tension fabricated in the way the Dardennes put their camera off the shoulder of their actors — something mined with claustrophobic efficiency in the intensely graceful *The Son* that now plays a little like the indie equivalent of bullet-time for its self-consciousness. What still works is the defeat of the point-of-view shot: they show us the characters reacting to something they've seen for a beat or more before the subject of their gaze happens into frame. Though it's a device that forces a closer identification while simultaneously limiting audience omniscience to fairly interesting effect, none of it strikes me as the "documentary realism" that many have ascribed to the Dardennes as much as extraordinarily mannered and increasingly distracting, no matter its lingering power. The Dardennes seem to be moving toward making films that are intellectually interesting but tied to a moral/emotional rail.

As Bruno sells, then tries to

retrieve, the kid before the fuzz toss him in the slammer, the Dardennes furiously jam righteous poultry into their allegorical straw man at the expense of every other character in the thing with more complicated, more interesting, less predestined paths to redemption. (There's a reason <u>Oliver Twist</u> isn't about Fagin, after all.) *L'Enfant* proceeds along a straight line, lacking the revitalizing, cine-religious joy of *Breathless* and the revelatory repetition automation of Bresson, too, leaving the picture composed of half-measures, drab exteriors, and clay effigies. Bruno looks like a person, but he acts like an idea.

The same could be said of "outsider" musician Daniel Johnston, whose troubled life and mental illness were parlayed into cult fame after a piece on the Austin music scene ran on MTV in 1985 and catapulted him (after a fashion) to the underground limelight. Beloved by alterna-saints and legends like Kurt Cobain, **Sonic Youth**, and **Half Japanese**, he eventually landed himself a record deal with Atlantic that produced some lovely, even extraordinary, odes to sadness and loneliness. It's a sticky wicket, this Johnston thing for me, because my complete inability to separate Johnston's music from his chronic madness makes me wonder if I like his music because it's brilliant or because it's the product of a fascinatingly broken fountain.

In any case, it's too loaded a question for Jeff Feuerzeig's *The Devil and Daniel Johnston*, which does not, in itself, devalue the worth of the documentary, yet the lack of focus and the unabashed hagiographic intent does colour its ultimate value for me as anything but a shrine. Allying himself with the camera-philic Friedman clan of *Capturing the Friedmans* and *Tarnation*'s Jonathan Caouette, Feuerzeig compiles acres of interesting archival materials (old cassette recordings and home movies), including, in one fairly amazing scene, a document of Johnston's poor fundamentalist mother tearing him down—but even in that moment of near-revelation, the picture itself compares unfavourably with Terry Zwigoff's ambivalent, existentially traumatizing *Crumb*. There's a lot of blunt, distracting author intentionality in *The Devil and Daniel Johnston*, and like *L'Enfant*, that stamp of the creator draws a bold line from where the story's Faulknerian man-child begins and the salvation to which he's inevitably bound. It lacks insight in its 16mm point-of-view re-creations, doing its best to draw attention to itself, and though footage of late Johnston concerts reminded me poignantly of accounts that I've heard of Tiny Tim's last days on his "whiff of the pathetic" tour, still bitter about Miss Vicki and losing his falsetto, the picture is little more than a decently-compiled, fan-inspired research project as opposed to something organically resonant or artful. (**WC**)

## CHILDREN OF MEN
**** /****

*st.* Clive Owen, Julianne Moore, Chiwetel Ejiofor, Charlie Hunnam
*sc.* Alfonso Cuarón & Timothy J. Sexton and David Arata and Mark Fergus & Hawk Ostby, based on the novel by P.D. James
*dir.* Alfonso Cuarón

## LETTERS FROM IWO JIMA
***$^{1}/_{2}$/****

*st.* Ken Watanabe, Kazunari Ninomiya, Tsuyoshi Ihara, Ryo Kase
*sc.* Iris Yamashita, based on the book <u>Picture Letters from Commander in Chief</u> by Tadamichi Kuribayashi and Tsuyoko Yoshido
*dir.* Clint Eastwood

Stop on any single frame of Alfonso Cuarón's remarkable war idyll *Children of Men*—a film that's rarely in repose, sometimes seeming composed of one long, frantic shot—and I suspect the sharp-eyed, educated viewer would be able to cull a reference to modern art, most likely one about men reduced to their base animal nature. For me, the two visual landmarks come in the form of a cue to the cover design for **Pink Floyd**'s 1977 "Animals" when hero Theo (Clive Owen) goes to see his industrialist cousin Nigel (Danny Huston) for help and a re-creation of Richard Misrach's remarkable series of 1987 photographs documenting, among other things, a dead-animal pit in Nevada purportedly used to dispose of victims of a plutonium "hot spot." Both share a space with surrealism in the positioning of animals (artificial or deceased) in industrial spaces (London's Battersea Power Station is the iconic backdrop of the "Animals" cover) as mute commentary, perhaps, on man's destructive relationship with his environment—a read that jibes comfortably with the thrust of *Children of Men*, in which we're told that one day in the not-too-distant future, humans suddenly stop reproducing. (Fertile ground for science-fiction, this obsession with progeny (see: everything from <u>Frankenstein</u> to <u>I Am Legend</u>).) The picture opens with a Fleet Street terrorist bombing, a little like Terry Gilliam's dystopic *Brazil*—though rather than take the easier route of satirizing our current state of instability and free-floating paranoia, *Children of Men* makes a serious attempt to allegorize it.

It's home to the year's best action sequence in an extended, terrifying chase through the 2027 British countryside that establishes the stakes in this uncompromising enterprise as surprisingly high. And like most of 2006's best films, it expresses its violence as flat and unromantic, an ugly and insect pastime. As a reflection of our contemporary society, it's most effective in an Abu Ghraib/Guantanamo Bay sequence where refugees ("fugees," in the film's vernacular—essentially people without a British passport in a totalitarian future) hooded, tormented with dogs, are forced to stand, arms outstretched, in man-sized cages. Theo's father-figure Jasper (Michael Caine), a rural recluse who grows his own pot and tends to his catatonic wife, represents the failed idealism of the previous generation to express any real activism, tuning out a world made barren by its polarization and left to relive past glories in the hopes of one more chance to rebel. Religious fanaticism feeds intolerance, leading to a state of violent conformity and martial law as competing ideologies in the picture's present, serving to further obfuscate the ties that bind men to one idea of tolerance and understanding.

For all that, though, *Children of Men* isn't pessimistic. Theo, burnt-out and busy dying, discovers new purpose in the shepherding of Kee (Claire-Hope Ashitey), possibly the only pregnant woman on the planet, into the arms of a rumoured scientific resistance that has cast itself adrift in a boat to unearth the answers that will avert the slow death of humanity. When all human relationships fail, the film offers, it's that inability for humanity to quiet hope and forsake grace that'll save us. As in Mel Gibson's own apocalyptic vision of doom and the courage of the individual in the face of it, the picture climaxes with a birth (real or metaphorical, it hardly matters); a scene where the bloody storming of a tenement by Her Majesty's Finest is briefly suspended in mute, mutual genuflection before the sound of a baby's cries stands as very possibly the single most life-affirming moment in film this year. In the end, we're all of us here to defend our children. It's a simple message and simple messages are easy to forget. The miracle of Cuarón's films is that he presents the sanctity of our feelings for our children in ways as rugged, terrifying, and unsentimental as childhood. *Children of Men* is about a lot of things, including a sense of wonder in ourselves: how we're able to persevere in the face of our own mortality if we're just given (reminded of?) a cause worth fighting for.

Clint Eastwood's *Letters from Iwo Jima* unfolds during the last days of the futile stand of twenty-thousand Japanese soldiers on the black-sand shores of barren rock Iwo Jima, the conclusion to a conflict they started in China and Pearl Harbor with American steel. Commanding officer General Kuribayashi (Ken Watanabe), having received military training in the United States, tries in vain to rally his charges behind an idea of modern guerrilla warfare principles at almost complete odds with the Bushido code of valour and honour to which most of his underlings subscribe. Ultimately, it's his desire to offer a meaningful sacrifice for the children of his homeland (the kids of his home town sing a song of encouragement, broadcast to Kuribayashi in the final hours of the battle) as opposed to the meaningless sacrifice of caves full of auto-detonating footmen that is the picture's most complicated movement. It advocates honour in significant self-sacrifice, and it uses the example of a few of the enemy in our last popular war to illustrate it. Its obvious terrorist, fanatical stormtrooper Ito (Shido Nakamura), strings himself with landmines and vows to blow up an American tank by disguising himself as a corpse in a field of his fallen countrymen, yet in changing the perception of the Japanese soldiers entrenching themselves in an impossible situation, doesn't *Letters from Iwo Jima* posit the possibility that enemy combatants have intelligence, bravery, and integrity?

Treasonous in much of our current environment to even suggest such a thing, although the outrage over the indignity surrounding the recent execution of Saddam Hussein suggests a step towards recovery. Eastwood re-establishes his credibility with this, his own remarkable war idyll, finally finishing a thematic trilogy begun with *Unforgiven* and *A Perfect World* that deals with the idea that there is such a thing as an overriding morality guiding our lives. *Letters from Iwo Jima* is not so very different from Terrence Malick's *The Thin Red Line* in not only its single-voiced narration and disconnected narrative, but also its inspiring humanism, which essays the ugliness of either side of the conflict without damaging the idea that every combatant in every conflict in every period is as little and as much as a child of man. Through the simplicity of that message, Eastwood finds the freedom to explore the democratizing affect of war as it levels aristocrats with intellectuals, cowards with Olympians; the horror of modern warfare (eloquently in a moment with a dying horse, the last hurrah of the cavalry charge); and, as in *Unforgiven* and *A Perfect World*, the total incapacity of man to escape the brutal rites of passage that litter the way to self-awareness. Its moral relativism is liberating instead of restricting and, as is typical lately, saccharine—the triumph highlighted by a moment in which Olympian Nishi (Tsuyoshi Ihara) reads a dead American's letter from his mother and comes to a line ("Remember, always do what is right, because it is right") that lands as a potent condemnation of this country's foreign and domestic policy (since, ironically, somewhere around WWII) while also scoring a sour point as precisely the aegis behind which dangerous ideologues will veil their ignorance, intolerance, and bloodlust. *Letters from Iwo Jima* is about actions and consequences—that sense of wonder that we can embody the best versions of ourselves in the worst situations. That we can still do what's right when everything's wrong. (**WC**)

**CLICK**
ZERO STARS/\*\*\*\*
*st.* Adam Sandler, Kate Beckinsale, Christopher Walken, David Hasselhoff
*sc.* Steve Koren & Mark O'Keefe
*dir.* Frank Coraci

Adam Sandler would have you believe

that his latest film is about a man with a remote that controls the universe, but as the first fifteen minutes of *Click* manage to debase women, Arabs, and Southeast Asians in one fell swoop, you get the sinking feeling that the medium is not the message. In fact, the movie's high concept becomes a mere skeleton on which Sandler hangs his white male entitlement, which extends to reducing women to simple sex objects (good if you're Sandler's wife, bad if you're his daughter) and turning anyone outside the margins of the star's ex-frat-boy demographic into a victim of tyranny. That the plot engineers the *redemption* of this jackass is too much to bear—one whiff of his hostility and you'll want him thrown back into the pit.

I wish I had light, Anthony Lane witticisms with which to dismiss this movie: I could easily go to town on the narrative if the film's cruelty weren't so pervasive. Michael Newman (Sandler) is a harried architect who can't seem to find time for his family, meaning, of course, that he's going to be dealt a magical "Christmas Carol" comeuppance whereby he's shown the shambles his life is destined to become. Jacob Marley arrives in the covert form of inventor Morty (Christopher Walken), who has secret room in a Bed, Bath and Beyond where the existence-altering über-remote resides. Thus we're sent down the river on a familiar affirmative odyssey in which the remote starts fast-forwarding past small but significant moments, forcing him to face that family is more important than blah, blah, blah.

Only problem is, the world that surrounds Michael exists to facilitate the power of his angry male corpus. Dealt with dismissively even when she's right, wife Donna (Kate Beckinsale) is a hottie most often seen wearing short-short pyjamas and tight spaghetti-strap tops. That Donna never ages beyond a few streaks of grey in her hair is pretty much all you need to know about the film's opinion of women—until you get a taste of

Michael's horror at his daughter's development, that is. Samantha Newman (Katie Cassidy) is perhaps the most demeaned character of the year, a pair of breasts for the protag to worry about (and for the rest of the production to ogle) and then shunt aside for the more pressing issue of favourite son Ben (Jake Hoffmann).

What of the rest of the populace? Simple: you are the target and Sandler is the shooter. If you're Japanese, you're uptight and obnoxious; if you're Arab, you're uptight, obnoxious, and have a funny name; if you're not a hot secretary, you're uptight and actually a man—in fact, if you're anyone outside of Michael's race, gender, or geographical orientation you're an annoyance to be treated with contempt. It's not exactly bigotry that's the problem, it's hostility: you're left with the impression that Sandler and company are letting off steam with these cheap shots. That they subsequently pull a 180 and try to be "redemptive" is no excuse—my skin was crawling throughout the running time as the hero acted like a bully towards every unfortunate passerby.

No, Anthony Lane is not with me today. *Click* deserves a response as heavy-handed as its seething macho aggression, a firm "no" to its *laissez-faire* acceptance of the most appalling behaviour and its ill-tasting chaser of Hollywood uplift. It's the worst movie since *Madea's Family Reunion*, with the pair making an apt double bill: both are lazily directed, both are profoundly unfunny, and both traffic in repugnant ideology while pretending to have solid priorities. It manages to elicit nostalgia for the firm moral centres of Brett Ratner and Michael Bay; I never thought I'd live to see the day. (**TMH**)

## CONVERSATIONS WITH OTHER WOMEN
**\*\*¹/₂/\*\*\*\***

st. Aaron Eckhart, Helena Bonham Carter, Nora Zehetner, Eric Eidem
sc. Gabrielle Zevin

*dir.* Hans Canosa

There's no real arguing with *Conversations with Other Women*—you either buy into its common program of relationship angst and mid-life crisis or you don't. Although director Hans Canosa tries to juice things up with a split-screen technique that's less unctuous than the description might suggest, it's still the same Woody Allen-ish trip through romantic failure via witty banter. There's an extent to which this can be entirely watchable, and at no point does the film grind to a halt and become a chore to sit through. Its concept is a tad far-fetched, however, and the insights gleaned from the chance encounter of two people at a wedding reception are nothing you can't find in the pages of any major glossy mag.

Aaron Eckhart and Helena Bonham Carter play those two nameless people, both in their late-thirties and facing the void. The former approaches the latter at a wedding reception and strikes up a conversation. He's flirtatious; she's standoffish. He's divorced but dating a 23-year-old; she's divorced and remarried to a doctor. He's the brother of the bride; she's the last-minute replacement for a fallen bridesmaid. And so the man tries to put the moves on the woman and she puts up defenses—though he somehow manages to talk his way into her room despite her apparent ability to see right through him. The split-screen effect that separates them in the frame also reveals their past history together—a past of which the woman doesn't appear entirely cognizant.

A big problem with this set-up is that one has to swallow the idea that two people who had a long-term relationship would be at some point unrecognizable to one another—or, at least, that one would fail to be recognized by the other. Wisely, the script by Gabrielle Zevin makes this flaw a part of its ultimate design, and it sketches the psychology of the pair with a fair amount of accuracy. (Zevin is aided by Canosa's bisected frame and its ability to partition not just space but time as well.) For their parts, Eckhart and Carter commit totally to the script, their performances seamless and entirely credible. The only thing left is to give us a compelling reason to care—and as well-executed as the film is, it's not entirely successful in delivering those particular goods.

One registers the approaching-mid-life dissatisfaction of these characters without actually feeling it. The leads' problems are more badges of honour than points of inquiry—they're sources of "conflict" and "drama" as opposed to actual interrogations into the feelings of a certain age bracket. One watches willingly but uninvolved; we nod at the allusions to emotion without being genuinely absorbed or enlightened. Mostly, *Conversations with Other Women* is cant about midlife crises split into both genders, and while that may provide some comfort, it doesn't really draw any straight conclusions. There's no massive and gaping flaw in the design of the movie, it's just that it builds on well-trod ground and never reaches very high. (TMH)

## THE COVENANT (see: *THE PROTECTOR*)

## CRANK
**\*\*<sup>1</sup>/<sub>2</sub>/\*\*\*\***
*st.* Jason Statham, Amy Smart, Jose Pablo Cantillo, Dwight Yoakam
*w./d.* Neveldine/Taylor

Consider the moment where French-fu schlockmeister Jason Statham marches through downtown traffic clad in a hospital smock, black socks, and boots while sporting a giant erection and ask yourself what more you could want from a dumb action movie called *Crank*. Seriously. A crotch-first fusion of Rudolph Maté's *D.O.A.* and "Grand Theft Auto", it defines that genre of video game-inspired non-sequitur mayhem indicated by epileptic edits, CGI-aided wire-fu, and John Woo gunplay by offering a high concept (hero is dying of a rare Chinese toxin that can be held in abeyance only with a steady infusion of adrenaline) as its narrative/excuse to exist. Chev (Statham) is a sociopathic hitman, injected with the abovementioned toxin and shot like a rocket across the mean streets in search of his murderer. Short time (and as it happens, *Crank* is a lot like Dabney Coleman's surprisingly funny *Short Time*, too) inspiring sentimentality in the ol' so-and-so, Chev finds time in his mad dash to pick up dim-bulb girlfriend Eve (an unbelievably hot Amy Smart), who's of course amenable to a couple of public displays of affection. One, in the middle of Chinatown, betrays a little intelligence in the objectification of a school bus full of Asian schoolgirls; the other—in which Eve gives Chev a hummer while he's in full flight from carloads of gun-bearing baddies—fulfills the holy trinity of puerile wish-fulfillment: bullets, crashes, and blow-jobs.

*Crank* fulfills a lot of puerile wish-fulfillment, truth be told, by dispensing with the pleasantries of plot and character development in favour of strippers, girls in bikinis, dumb nymphet girlfriends, gay sidekicks who get killed via erotic asphyxiation, motorcycles, helicopters, guns, and the Chinese mafia. Anyone without the good fortune to be a white male is, in fact, offered the full weight of objective tribal disapproval, mistrust, and sadism. Hateful and misanthropic, it's the caveman aesthetic unadorned and a pretty fair representation of an awesome video game chock-a-block with collateral damage opportunities and a scene where the hero is defibrillated at his own behest. It's an amplification of Luc Besson-pushed pieces like *The Transporter* (which themselves owed their existence to Hong Kong's action carnival of the 1980s), riding a wave of trendy Eastern *wuxia pian* conventions in a fascinating case of East-West cultural diffusion. Fair to note that Woo, Ringo Lam, et al were influenced by Sam Peckinpah (and John Ford by way of Akira Kurosawa by way of Sergio Leone), but the immediate lineage seems clear as a bell: *Crank* is like a product translated from Chinese to French to English for American consumption. The end product of all that distillation is the super-concentrated silt at the bottom of a chemistry experiment that has no possible purpose to it but to deliver whatever limited jolt of which it's capable. It's simultaneously the defense and the weakness of the piece, this ability to do what it does without a hint of pretension, but because it's so much of a type, it's doomed to be confused with just about every other film that's identical to it—down to Statham, down to the restlessness, down to the juiced-up impotent rage. (**WC**)

## CURIOUS GEORGE (see: *NIGHT AT THE MUSEUM*)

## CURSE OF THE GOLDEN FLOWER
**\*\*½/\*\*\*\***
*st.* Chow Yun Fat, Gong Li, Jay Chou, Liu Ye
*sc.* Zhang Yimou, Wu Nan, Bian Zhihong
*dir.* Zhang Yimou

I recently had the opportunity to see for the first time the cut of Zhang Yimou's virtuoso *Hero* prepared for Yankee viewers, complete with the subtitles and framing cards slapped on by American distributors. Before now, the only contact I'd had with the film was through a region-free DVD from Hong Kong that preceded the U.S. theatrical release by a couple of years. (After buying the rights to it, Miramax, you'll recall, decided to sit on it until such time as its unleashing wouldn't somehow interfere with timeless masterpieces of misguided schlock like

*Cold Mountain.*) Anyway, I was appalled. The extent to which *Hero* has been dumbed-down—the insertion of "our country" for a term that means, in Mandarin, "beneath the sky" drums up this weird nationalistic gumbo at the end where, before, it was sober and idealistic—manages to paint Zhang as the worst kind of toad. There's an animated map at the beginning now, I guess to show the great unwashed American moron that there is land outside the range of purple mountains majesty, while much mystical bullshit about "over two thousand years ago" mainly obscures the fact that *Hero* takes place well over two thousand years ago. I feel a lot of anger towards what's been done to one of the best films ever to come out of the Mainland to make it more suited for white consumption, both because of the sacrilege and because whoever's responsible has a lot of answering to do for how far they've undersold the intelligence of Western audiences. I finally understand why a lot of people in the United States didn't think much of *Hero*: the version I saw was a Zhang Yimou picture, whereas the version most in this country saw was a Miramax picture.

I mention this only because my "first" screening of *Hero* roughly coincides with the DVD release of the conclusion to the loose trilogy that it began, *Curse of the Golden Flower*. If *Hero* is about nationalism and the very Asian resolve to equate history with mythology and *House of Flying Daggers* is a return to Zhang's claustrophobic gender/sex satires, then *Curse of the Golden Flower* marries Zhang's withering political allegories *Ju Dou* and *Red Sorghum* to the poetics of the fall essayed in the underestimated *Shanghai Triad*—the last time before now, as it happens, that Zhang paired with his muse, Gong Li. That it doesn't work very well is almost beside the point for auteurists following this *wuxia pian* cycle, and indeed there's profit in reading these pictures as a roadmap for Zhang back to the

smaller, oft-banned pictures that made his name as the most instantly—and easily—championed of the Fifth Generation Chinese directors. There's only so long that someone like Zhang can spend in the wilderness of big-budget spectaculars before his instincts begin to reassert themselves, not just in little pictures like *Riding Alone for Thousands of Miles* but in the middle of all that gloriously empty bombast as well. By far the worst of the three films, *Curse of the Golden Flower* might nevertheless be the most beautiful (testifying to an inverse proportional scale that holds true more often than not), its long halls shot in stained-glass primaries and its fields of gold almost orgiastic in their unapologetic excess. There's not a shot here that isn't fevered—and, perhaps predictably, it's overwhelming; then deadening; then common.

Wash away the lurid colour and what remains is a Greek drama involving incest, fratricide, courtly intrigue, poisoned tinctures, bastard heirs, and bloody reprisals. The Tudors had nothing on this Tang Dynasty, presided over by Emperor Ping (Chow Yun Fat, still struggling with his Mandarin), the wife (Gong) he's slowly poisoning with a brain-devouring fungus, his feuding sons Jai (Jay Chou), Wan (Liu Ye), and Yu (Qin Junjie), and hordes of retainers, physicians, courtesans, and so on. Seems someone's accidentally sleeping with their half-sister, someone else is purposefully sleeping with her stepson, and still someone else has a secret about the Emperor that will permanently unhinge the youngest son, who appears to be something of a brat besides. Lots of screaming and bodice-ripping is interspersed with a few grand fight sequences that, by this point in the genre's development cross-culture, are almost boring for their familiarity. I'll maintain that the West has yet to learn how to film a swordfight with the grace and kineticism of this Yuen Woo-ping-inspired fight choreography (though

Yuen's absence from this film is nonetheless noticeable—it's like someone choreographing Fosse who is not Fosse), but without much at stake in *Curse of the Golden Flower*, it all starts to veer into the silly.

What holds firm is the idea that this government is corrupted by dirty tricks and ugly secrets—that Gong's Empress might represent the will of a people oppressed and slowly poisoned by a mind-destroying brew; the film is incredibly bracing in its open sedition. I'm a little bit surprised that the Chinese didn't ban it: earlier in his career, Zhang's portrayal of the ruling class as a fat, petulant infant earned him the door. (I do wonder if Zhang didn't parlay his new status as the architect of the Beijing Games' opening ceremonies into a blind eye.) More, the final battle where a revolutionary army assembled behind the idealistic Crown Prince Wan is mowed down in a courtyard decorated for a looming festival—the blood of the aftermath quickly washed away like a magic trick, sweeping a pile of corpses under the carpet—marks *Curse of the Golden Flower* as possibly the first mainstream Chinese representation of the massacre at Tiannamen Square. That few if any stateside reviews of the picture have mentioned this adds fat to the fire that this desperate sacrifice of the young and idealistic was, indeed, utterly futile, swept under history's carpet like the film's most disturbing sequence depicting mass, machine-efficient forgetfulness. The picture's epilogue, almost Orestiean in its dinner-table bloodlust, underscores the idea that the fire of change has been extinguished and the ashes scattered, the naming of the Empress "Phoenix" something more bitter than hopeful. The sacrifice of the nameless, off-caste hero in *Hero* for the sake of a culturally unified China finds itself at a dead end in *Curse of the Golden Flower*. (**WC**)

# THE DA VINCI CODE

ZERO STARS/****
*st.* Tom Hanks, Audrey Tautou, Ian McKellen, Jean Reno
*sc.* Akiva Goldsman, based on the novel by Dan Brown
*dir.* Ron Howard

The greatest threat that Dan Brown's novel, and now Ron Howard's film of the same, poses to spirituality is the same threat that any bad art presents the human soul. *The Da Vinci Code* is a retarded attempt to summarize painstaking scholarship and liturgy into broadly digestible gruel. In the eyes of many, it's what the Christian Bible is to centuries of pagan mythology and millennia of cultural anthropology: the greatest stories ever told, retold in a form that illiterates and the gullible can appreciate. It's nothing more and nothing less than The Celestine Prophecy (itself adapted for the silver screen this *annus mirabilus*) for fallen Catholics and armchair intellectuals: books so poorly-written, so bereft of poetry and grace, that they cannot offend (or repel) the unschooled and the indiscriminate with their oblique-ness, each *about* poetry and grace so brusquely raped and "decoded" that the "conspiracy"—the great mystery of great art—is laid bare as bad thriller material. It's skipping forward to read the last page of the book—and the wrong book at that. Is it really ironic that Ron Howard, who has never directed a graceful scene, has never had a film with a hint of a whiff or subtext (his version of "genius at work" is a holodeck (see: *A Beautiful Mind* and now *The Da Vinci Code*)) is the chosen one for the adaptation (along with partner in extreme, middlebrow-pleasing mendacity Akiva Goldsman)

of an obscenely popular book (60-million copies sold and counting) that makes anyone with a half a brain crazy with grief for the plight of the sublime in our culture?

This may be a sign of the apocalypse, though not in the way the zealots on either side would have you believe. The danger of both the book and the movie is that they have people believing they've read literature or seen a film of substance when this just isn't the case. It's no great secret that our culture has become "dumbed down" (I'm not surprised that many wear this as a badge of brute honour)—but the real cultural fallout is not how stupid and venal our most popular cultural artifacts are (they always were, after all), it's in our collective willingness to buy what we're sold, wholesale. And that infects more than the cineplex: "intelligence" is a maligned ideal and ironic in most public usage—using the correct words and referencing anything from before the last five years is pretentious. When we want philosophy we go to sub-Carlos Castanedas like Dan Brown. When we want uplift we go to sub-Stanley Kramers like Paul Haggis and Ron Howard. When we want moral leadership, we look to calcified, devalued, debunked pundits like the Vatican, George W. Bush, and Oprah.

Start in *The Da Vinci Code* with the mythical discipline of "symbology": a malapropism invented by idiots so as not to confuse their flock with real words like "semiotics" or "epistemology." It's like calling psychiatry "talk-about-it-ology." (Defenders of the text beware, because the thing you defend purports to be in love with the importance of language.) Our good Harvard professor Langdon (Tom Hanks, acting throughout like he's trying to pass a stone) is a professor of "Symbology," you see, and he opens *The Da Vinci Code* giving a Power Point lecture in Paris about how first "symbology" is the study of symbols (duh), and then—those who don't read (or drive, or walk around their town), prepare to be startled—how symbols are a form of language.

The rest of the film follows this pattern: a term or person or thing is introduced and someone will explain it and then someone will use it in a sentence. Sir Isaac Newton was a scientist who "discovered" gravity; Sir Isaac Newton angered the Church. When Langdon hijacks a Blackberry to access Google, he narrates himself typing in key words as well as his ostensible reasons for using those key words before someone else explains to him why his fuzzy search keeps bringing up some guy named "Alexander Pope." Langdon isn't talking to himself for his own benefit: Langdon's dialogue is Howard/Goldsman's message to us that they think we're incredibly, unbelievably dense and desperately in need of a hand to hold through every tiny step of this undercooked thriller (trust no one, indeed) and the specious scholarship holding it all together by the skin of its controversy. Langdon, as it happens, also looks like an idiot because he has to not alienate moviegoers, thus it's lucky that everyone else in the film acts like an idiot, too. (What these mutual declarations of ignorance really do is drag the proceedings out to a deadening 149 minutes.) It says volumes to me that Catholic church sees something as inept as *The Da Vinci Code* as a threat: talk about knowing your audience.

The source postures itself as a reaction to the violent paternalism of the traditional church, and yet its main female character, Sophie (Audrey Tautou—and of course her character's name is "Sophie" and of course she's played by Audrey Tautou), a noted cryptographer, is completely helpless throughout to solve any puzzles and made not once, but twice, the squealing prize at the end of a hostage-takers knife/gun. She and Langdon go gallivanting around Europe, acquiring sage Sir Leigh Teabing (Ian McKellen—of course and of course)

along the way. A grail scholar, Teabing—who, with his two canes and feral, mad scientist energy, reminds me a lot of the middle stage of Brundlefly—is searching for the secret of the Holy Grail, which, *The Da Vinci Code* implies, is just like the Jewel in *The Jewel of the Nile*. (Sad to note that the two films are not dissimilar.) If you have a working pre-frontal, you can puzzle out the thriller elements of this piece of shit within ten minutes. If your internal narrative bogs down, there's always the sudden appearance of a murderous albino monk/hitman (Paul Bettany) to defibrillate the wheezing ol' geezer. Or, better yet, how about another inutile expository flashback to hold the place of actual character development, lest Howard, heaven forfend, invoke his arch nemesis "nuance"?

Whenever Langdon is confronted with a puzzle, he provides the only tension ("It's meaningless...unless!"), and the solution is either invariably broad and breathtakingly obvious (Encyclopedia Brown could have solved this puzzle in two pages) or forever occluded and dismissed with a pursed lip and a terse nod. Hanks seems lost with this material; no question Howard is. He shoots a street poster of "Les Miserables: The Opera" and then posits French gendarme Jean Reno as the film's ideological Valjean. It's juvenile and it's desperate, but most of all, it demonstrates that *The Grinch, EdTV, The Missing, Cinderella Man, Far and Away, A Beautiful Mind, Backdraft*, and so on and so forth, in all their ignorance, misogyny, and slick facility, were no accident. Find in *The Da Vinci Code* the perfect storm of every personal, creative weakness that Howard, Goldsman, and Brown have managed to slide by the world, brought to the proscenium in stark, ugly light. That loud gasp is the exhalation of millions of fans of the book, blaming the film for popping their balloon when the truth of it is that it was never full of anything but torpid hot air in the first place. The picture's not without value, then, if it can make a joke of the book—the fear, though, is that it makes a martyr of it. (**WC**)

## THE DEATH OF MR. LAZARESCU
## (Moartea domnului Lazarescu)
\*\*\*\*/\*\*\*\*

*st.* Luminita Gheorghiu, Ion Fiscuteanu, Gabriel Spahiu, Doru Ana
*sc.* Cristi Puiu & Razvan Radulescu
*dir.* Cristi Puiu

## OLD JOY
\*\*\*/\*\*\*\*

*st.* Daniel London, Will Oldham, Tanya Smith, Robin Rosenberg
*sc.* Jonathan Raymond & Kelly Reichardt
*dir.* Kelly Reichardt

My only real problem with Cristi Puiu's remarkable *The Death of Mr. Lazarescu* is that it sees itself as Divine Comedy rather than as The Trial: a cautionary tale instead of the absurdist fable that it can only be read as, and a series of circles leading, through diminishment, towards the salvation of future episodes rather than a singular journey from impossible situation to inevitable extermination. There's too much hope in Puiu's nihilistic film about the detachment and ironic misanthropy of those entrusted with the care of others (even if that hope comes in the form of just one sympathetic paramedic and then the doctor who finally agrees to operate on our hero)—too many successes, however hollow, for a film about bureaucracy's devilishly-unsolvable knot. Despite its length, it reminds a good bit of Ezra Pound's tone poem "In a Station of the Metro" (in its entirety: "The apparition of these faces in a crowd;/Petals on a wet, black bough.")—its title, in other words, deeply complicit in the mood and an understanding of the metaphor of the piece. Can it be that at the end of this endurance test and probe of personal morality that all the film really had to say is that you die by yourself? That said, it's hard to find too strenuous an argument with Puiu's almost miraculously "naturalistic" picture, and harder still to fault it overmuch for its portrait of a pilgrim subjected to the horrors of an institutionalized inhumanity that we hope to only have the misfortune of suffering once and then only at the end of our lives.

Dante Lazarescu (Ion Fiscuteanu), better dubbed "Franz," has endured a four-day headache that he has tried to self-medicate with various over-the-counter medications and liquor. He calls an ambulance, asks his neighbours for help, pukes on himself (twice), and suffers the first of about 152 minutes' worth of jibes and questions about whether he's really sick or just on an extended bender. The picture is a landmark achievement of quiet observation and seamless editing that makes it look and feel like one long, uninterrupted take in the last night (we presume from the title) on Earth for an old guy, estranged from family, lacking in friends, in bed with the bottle, and at the mercy of caregivers too beaten by the absurdity of their profession in this place and time to allow themselves to care. Ancillary conversations, we discover, are soon the only connections we're allowed in the picture as Lazarescu, already a cipher, becomes an incoherent catalyzing agent to the last stages of his journey. He's not the star, he's the centre, and in a visceral way the film is a first-person POV piece where we find ourselves sutured, eyeball-to-brainstem, to the mute patient as he's driven around Bucharest by long-suffering paramedic Mioara (Luminita Gheorghiu), trying to plow through the System's red-tape to get an ailing, miserable, stinking old bastard a shot at a couple more years of abused life. A moral litmus at the least for its audience of white, educated, liberal filmgoers who would give a three-hour Romanian picture about a dying hermit with social behaviour disorders a look, it's a rallying point for the privileged—an argument, pro or con, for or against socialized health care; for quantifying the relative value of a human life; for the definition of heroism in confused situations; and on and on into cocktail staff-party legend. By making the starting point of the conversation a blank, we're invited to be the fill-in-the—and it's not a big surprise that those fast-clamouring to the post of righteous martyr are the ones least likely to endure a similar trial.

Still and all, *The Death of Mr. Lazarescu*, perhaps because of its opacity, has a lingering, nigh-unforgettable aftertaste to it that approaches the best, in theory, of *avant-garde* cinema. It's the film Andy Warhol or Frederick Wiseman would have made had they the wit and self-deprecation to do so, an exercise in *vérité* that simplifies its politics and reduces its emotionalism to strike at the heart of the auto-ennobled arthouse audience and its attendant, unimaginative critical tides. The film is great, but not because of its existential stickiness (the title tells you to gird for it, for God's sake). It's great because there's actually a chance here to successfully argue the opposite, unenlightened viewpoint: that the tragic bus accident that's clogging Bucharest's late-night emergency response arteries is, in fact, the greater good—that doctors overworked and underappreciated already should be forgiven for not wanting to operate on a wino of no visible means who would be taking away from children immediately and others trickily, but obviously, more deserving into the future. It's possible to see Mr. Lazarescu as a guy who doesn't deserve that liver as much as the eight-year-old transplant recipient, who doesn't need to be exhausting that brain surgeon as much as that six-year-old accident victim. The picture is brilliant because it allows us to be honest about the value of life: not those boring maudits about how you die alone and your life is worthless and you're a piece of meat to medical professionals, but that life is a dirty, ugly thing, valuable only to its owner and even then not a right but a commodity to be guarded jealously. We appreciate altruism—some appreciate the opportunity to applaud it even more, to be sure. But *The Death of Mr. Lazarescu* is a Rorschach to ferret out the assholes who have to make life and death choices that, by their nature, doom some to neglect, in addition to the assholes who like to make Mr. Lazarescu the focal point of their outrage at a system they perceive to be without mercy. A funny stance to be taken by the party so in love with the idea of "nuance."

Kelly Reichart's *Old Joy* is more like a David Gordon Green film than *The Death of Mr. Lazarescu*'s oft-commented upon passing glance at the Dardenne Brothers' oeuvre (though, honestly, how the Belgian filmmakers' extreme artifice compares to Puiu's almost total lack of the same can be considered comparable is beyond me), an American picture about silences broken by awkward spurts of dialogue in a natural, green setting. Old pals Mark (Daniel London) and Kurt (Will Oldham) get together for a spur-of-the-moment overnight camping trip into the Oregon Cascades in search of some hot springs. Armed with pot, beer, and the weight of decades of friendship about to suffer the crucible of Mark and wife Tanya's entry into parenthood, the two get lost, camp in a clearing festooned with litter, talk quietly about nothing at all, and part after one clarifying moment of nostalgia in the suspended middle of nowhere. It's not as subtle as it'd like us to believe—there are lines as fraught as any in Wes Anderson's purposefully self-conscious talkers ("Boy, you sure do hold on to things!" says outcast Kurt about Mark's pack-ratting...or is it?)—but in a film as free of dialogue as this one, everything they *do* say becomes food for coffeehouse mastication. *Old Joy* is neither literal nor symbolic, neither allegorical nor naturalistic—it's a two-man reading exercise staged in a small theatre. The fact that it works as well as it does is testament to the native talent of all involved, if no great monument to their sense of their own ideological ostentation. This notion of escape into an illusory prelapsarian state is one that will be examined to more profit by many of the amazing mainstream films of 2007; call it one of those Old Testament "pre-echoes" of the coming of a lord in that it's almost more interesting in the rear-view than it should have been at the time. Objectively, for what it is, there's a tenderness there and, intriguingly, something to say about growing up, growing apart, and the wisdom to let it happen without fireworks and gunplay. Nice to report that *Old Joy* is, if not much else, grown up about it. (**WC**)

## DECK THE HALLS (see: *FLUSHED AWAY*)

## DÉJÀ VU
**\*\*½/\*\*\*\***
*st.* Denzel Washington, Val Kilmer, Paula Patton, Jim Caviezel
*sc.* Bill Marsilii & Terry Rossio
*dir.* Tony Scott

Who woulda thunk that crap-meister Tony Scott could be so in tune with the spirit of the times? Scott follows up *Man on Fire*—a vile piece of revenge-on-foreign-soil wish-fulfillment schlock—and *Domino* (another slice of the vigilante kind) with *Déjà Vu*, a time-travel fantasy complete with a horrifying act of domestic terrorism that noble ATF agent Carlin (Denzel Washington) is offered the chance, through the providence of limited time travel, to prevent. It's one of those questions, right? Would you smother infant Hitler in his cradle to prevent

the tears that will follow—and, if you did, would it change the course of history or just substitute that Adolf for another? Alas, Scott ultimately degrades this fun cocktail party conundrum into an action-movie finale involving heartbreakingly beautiful love interest Claire (Paula Patton), clean-Marine grassroots sicko Carroll (Jim Caviezel, doing *High Crimes* all over again), and a ferryboat full of people crossing over from Katrina-ravaged New Orleans. Working in the picture's favour is that it's thick with national calamity, making one wonder if Scott would even get a movie made anymore were he not so quick to jab a needle into the collective jugular. The pall of our recent history hangs over the proceedings like a borrowed mourning veil, but Scott muse Washington is so good—and the film's premise so loopy—that *en route* to touching the steadily more tiresome post-9/11 bases of illegal/omniscient surveillance and sour regret, *Déjà Vu* actually breathes a little. It's the best Tony Scott film since the underestimated, unofficial *The Conversation* sequel *Enemy of the State*, which ran over on the same technophobic ground. Call it another science-fiction romance to join this season's already-bursting slate of *Children of Men*, *Stranger Than Fiction*, and *The Fountain*.

It's not really spoiling things for anyone who's seen a Tony Scott film to reveal that *Déjà Vu* opens with a horrific explosion. Agent Carlin's quest for the culprit leads to the monitor-strewn lair of Dr. Denny (Adam Goldberg) and FBI spook Pryzwarra (Val Kilmer), where what's initially explained as a complex satellite surveillance system is in reality a limited, joystick-controllable wormhole that allows our crimefighters to peek through one moving window, four-and-a-half days into the past. Carlin becomes obsessed with the possibility that he could change history in a meaningful enough way to, if not prevent the destruction of the loaded ferry, at least save the life of the young woman connected incidentally to the event with whom he's developed an odd fascination. The early scenes of Carlin "stalking" Claire through her apartment, four days before the tragedy that will end her life, take on qualities of, of all things, Michael Powell's *Peeping Tom*: it's the sickest kind of *Memento mori*, something not unlike a snuff film starring yourself; and for a while, *Déjà Vu* almost serves as an indictment of our role as voyeurs in a darkened room. It identifies, in the process, our playing at detective as our alter ego (Carlin in this case) goes through the paces on our behalf. Too much to say that the film is a think-piece, but as the machine's abilities and limitations are explored, it's an altogether different kind of movie than you'd expect.

What's most unusual is that *Déjà Vu* is self-consciously a picture with a quasi-religious, moral centre in taking pains to address possible objections to its premise. When the machine causes a power surge, for instance, it shows doctors in the middle of a surgery calmly waiting for their backup generators to kick in—and after hero Carlin causes a ghastly car crash on the interstate, we have a moment where he calls the paramedics on behalf of his victims. It's the antidote to Tony Scott movies, in other words—the anti-*Bruce Almighty*, in which an act of romantic whimsy (much like Carlin's dedication to saving his *Laura*-like lady-fair) causes without comment or immediate consequence to the protagonists a devastating tsunami half a world away. Whatever you think of the picture, when it talks about destiny and a benevolent god's intervention in the lives of men, it avoids hypocrisy by controlling and acknowledging, in its own omnisciently-manipulated terrarium, the cost of its violence. At its heart, though, it's still just a macho fantasy of redemption and re-fighting, Rambo-like, battles we've already lost while rekindling romances with high school sweethearts who've long moved

on. Its last reel, especially, jettisons smarts with extreme prejudice in favour of more chases, explosions, damsels in distress, and gruesome executions of deserving targets. Better than it should be, *Déjà Vu* is finally swallowed by its creator's desire to slake the bloodlust of an audience already beaten by the images on the daily news. How much better a film this would be in less pandering hands. (**WC**)

## THE DEPARTED
***/****

*st.* Leonardo DiCaprio, Matt Damon, Jack Nicholson, Mark Wahlberg
*sc.* William Monahan
*dir.* Martin Scorsese

Martin Scorsese's *The Departed* is his funniest—and most nihilistic—film since *After Hours*, which remains for me the most *enjoyable* of his pictures, not the least for its travelogue of the Wasteland, complete with a gallery of freaks and grotesque statuary. It's a bleak, Kirkegaardian thing more oppressive as fraught cityscape than Travis Bickle's New York, seeing as how there's no filter of the unreasonable to buffer against the assertion that scum does, indeed, need to be washed off those mean streets. That city finds a doppelgänger in the blasted, depressed Boston of *The Departed*, whose set-pieces unfurl inside dives, abandoned warehouses, and condemned buildings, and in which we find the only relationship worth saving is between a brilliantly profane Massachusetts State Trooper Sergeant, Dignam (Mark Wahlberg), and his captain in the Special Investigations Unit, Queenan (Martin Sheen). The brutality with which that relationship is preserved, in fact, ultimately delineates this as a rare comedy (in the traditional sense) among Scorsese's long legacy of American tragedies, albeit one that's laced with poison and the unmistakable taint of a post-millennial/post-apocalyptic stench.

*The Departed* joins the ranks of other post-lapsarian dirges like *Sin City*, "Deadwood", and Michael Mann's *Miami Vice*, where men rebuild a fallen society from ashes and chaos according to bestial, masculine guidelines. Even the title, *The Departed*, refers to the soft euphemism for a corpse in Catholic burial liturgy. If Scorsese is a Joyce of our visual history, this is his <u>The Dead</u>. It feels like a letter from someone who's given up passing among the living. Good boy Sullivan (Matt Damon) and bad boy Costigan (Leonardo DiCaprio) each attend the police academy, but the good family Sullivan's from is The Family run by mad Frank (Jack Nicholson) and the bad lineage from which Costigan hails is a long dead and not-long-lamented airport janitor. So Sullivan is a mole in the police for Frank, while Costigan is a mole for the cops in Frank's camp. They both love the same police counsellor, Madolyn (Vera Farmiga, in a star-making turn), and they're both suspiciously perfect for their respective rackets. There're father/son issues, of course, and issues of aspiration, and because Scorsese is our country's most conspicuous Catholic, there are a great deal of guilty mother issues, culminating in a moment where a framed portrait of the Virgin Mary is used as a weapon.

But there's none of the doomed Romanticism of the bulk of Scorsese's other films—that feeling of lost brotherhood or a romance worth dying for. And without that weight of jeopardy, the belief that there's a reason to persevere, *The Departed* is extraordinarily cynical. It name-checks the Patriot Act in Captain Ellerby's (Alec Baldwin) glee at being able to set up surveillance without the sticky impediment of the Constitution; and it sets up a love triangle that will serve as the catalyst for the hilarious parade of head-shots that constitutes its last half hour (and is predicted by an early moment in the Academy during a

ballistics lecture). But what to make of the 149 minutes preceding that last, lingering shot of a rat sitting on a balcony? Is it the punchline to the oft-repeated warning that "this city is full of rats"?

Faith and trust is all a bad fucking joke, Scorsese suggests with *The Departed*. When Frank says that in the past, if he smelled an informant among his crew he'd kill the lot of them and let God sort it out, Scorsese pays it off in his Guignol finale. When Costigan complains that he's become the instrument of a mass murderer, well, sure enough, that mass murderer is Scorsese. The film is a grinning death's head—Joe Pesci's clown elevated to Jack Nicholson making a rat's face and bathed in a red filter before inviting his Nubian girlfriend to roll on a bed of cocaine until she's numb. Even with the soundtrack (silky smooth at the opening, with Frank's rise scored to **The Rolling Stones**' "Gimme Shelter" in the Scorsese style), Scorsese has by the tail of the second hour already begun to fuck with the rhythm, cutting his montages with harsh jumps and starts and then tossing in a grungier version of **Pink Floyd**'s "Comfortably Numb" as his final word on the state of this insular world. Adapted from Hong Kong's *Infernal Affairs* trilogy by William Monahan (the screenplay is a delight—the real star of the film), *The Departed* is another product of a closed society hopelessly wriggling beneath the fist of a repressive regime. "You learn a lot by the way things eat," says toys in the attic Frank, "you should eat something." Find in that a filmmaker arriving at the end of some kind of rope and producing a difficult meal that goes down in a rush of extraordinarily tasty technical proficiency while leaving a genuinely vile aftertaste. It's not about emptiness, it's an example of it. It seems reductive to say it, but *The Departed* is the film Scorsese should have made in 2006. (**WC**)

## THE DESCENT

\*\*\*/\*\*\*\*

*st.* Shauna Macdonald, Natalie Mendoza, Alex Reid, Saskia Mulder

*w./d.* Neil Marshall

Beginning in the same way as countless other genre pictures (the city folks go to a cabin and have boring, perfunctory, character-defining chatter), Neil Marshall's often-terrifying, often-brilliant *The Descent* subsequently manages to describe for long stretches a complicated, Jungian labyrinth of regret and shadow-projections and doubling through dank explorations of a vaginal, womb-like metaphor for the subconscious. There's a moment where our avatar, Sarah (Shauna Macdonald), emerges from a gore bath and stands reborn into the very avenging feminist totem of Carrie post-prom: it's just one of three "births" Sarah endures (four if you count a dream sequence in a hospital early on), the last of which stands in tribute to the final sting of *Carrie*. It's possible, in fact, to split the film into quarters according to its recurrent motifs of gestation-into-discharge following penetration.

Described in the United States (and anticipated for almost a year; the film is already long on DVD in the UK with its original ending intact) as the distaff version of last year's underestimated *The Cave*, *The Descent* is a tougher, more thematically rich horror film loaded with panic-attacks that sound like Lamaze breathing, lines like "down the pipe," and a way of photographing water seeping off subterranean walls that casts everything in intensely biological terms. Mention it once and leave it be: there's something rich to the way that Marshall has his bitch goddesses marshal fire and do violence to eyes—and for all the exposition, there's a wealth of understatement in the use of both a child's birthday cake and a dominant motif in recent "feminine avenger" cinema (*Kill Bill, Sympathy for Lady Vengeance*), that of the loss of a child and its rippling, toweringly symbolic toll on the rest of civilization. *Our* civilization.

Sarah is widowed and left grieving for her daughter in the opening minutes of the film. When we rejoin her in twelve months' time in remote Appalachia (the travel brochure for which should read "What's an Appalachian outing without a gruesome compound fracture?"), we find Sarah in the company of five spelunking women—including former best-mate Juno (Natalie Jackson Mendoza), whose namesake (a jealous, omniscient, omnipotent goddess) is our first clue—invested in Sarah "having a good time" following her stay in bereavement hell. The trek into the wilderness to highlight their isolation, the discovery of the animal carcass to bring home the idea that these people of modernity are about to be reintroduced to their mortal animalism...every time-honoured and weather-beaten convention is paid proper obeisance by genre-loving Marshall, who has, in fact, name-checked *Deliverance*, *Alien*, and *The Shining* as prime inspirations/sources for this film, which is honest of him and mostly accurate. I'd replace *The Shining* with Nicholas Roeg's *Don't Look Now*, however, in that there's a suggestion throughout that the ghost of Sarah's child is trying to warn her. Once in the cave systems, *The Descent* becomes genuinely claustrophobic and harrowing, with the setting providing the bulk of discomfort long before the monsters of the Id hop up out of the bubbling deep.

*The Descent*'s gore is a marvel of weight and consequence. A gash on a hand is made to look like a bleeding vagina while a broken bone is handled with all the care of a tetherball on an aggressive playground. When these characters scale rock, it's accompanied by groans and cries of exertion—none of the weightless acrobatics of Sylvester Stallone or Tom Cruise (or even the Piper Perabo character from

*The Cave*). There's a physical toll to their actions, and that sense of material karma seeps into the film's foreboding of spiritual karma. Every action in the set-up has a reaction in the cave; Marshall handles the sacrifice/redemption cycle of his characters with true grit and a genuine lack of apology.

Eat or be eaten, the quick and the dead, even the cultural relativity of Levi-Strauss' The Raw and the Cooked are embedded in *The Descent*'s complex order—there are whole semesters to be mined from not only the film's gender philosophies but also the filmmaker's reconstitution of male archetypes around female icons. (Consider that the savagery Sarah exhibits near the end of the film—especially towards her ostensible partners—would be something unthinkable for a male hero wanting to retain his "heroism.") Not hurting things, certainly, is that while the picture's humming for almost the whole of its last half, it's one of the scariest, most purposefully lawless horror movies in an age that celebrates slick exploitation garbage like *Hostel* for breaking new ground. Indeed, *The Descent* breaks old, no, *ancient* ground and does so with conviction and serious chops (note how in one scene after Juno pulls herself out of a lake, the camera begins, subtly, to stalk her). Segueing from his satirical/hysterical werewolf flick *Dog Soldiers*, Marshall's on something of a roll. (**WC**)

## THE DEVIL AND DANIEL JOHNSTON
## (see: *THE CHILD*)

## THE DEVIL WEARS PRADA
*¹/₂*/****
*st.* Meryl Streep, Anne Hathaway, Stanley Tucci, Simon Baker
*sc.* Aline Brosh McKenna, based on the novel by Lauren Weisberger
*dir.* David Frankel

"Sex and the City" fashion porn married to *The Princess Diaries* 'tween ugly-duckling uplift, David Frankel's facile sitcom *The Devil Wears Prada* allows Meryl Streep free reign to craft the titular, nattily-attired hellspawn. Her presence here gives the film the kind of starfuck quotient tied to Jack Nicholson genre vehicles once upon a time; without much effort, one can imagine a carnival barker pulling the wide-eyed bumpkins into the freak tent with the promise of blue-chip capering. Alas, Streep disappoints by turning in a human performance as an Anna Wintour manqué, drifting about as "Miranda Priestly" in Cruella DeVil mane and couture, operating a publishing empire (fictional RUNWAY MAGAZINE substituting for VOGUE, though Madonna's "Vogue" features prominently in the soundtrack for the terminally dim) with a soft voice and a sibilant brittleness.

The film's biggest error in judgment might be that instead of providing an outsider's view of what is, to many, a mysterious world full of arcane concepts and values, *The Devil Wears Prada* mires its narrative in sophomoric romantic melodrama (will Andy break up with her doe-eyed, blue-collar boyfriend (Adrian Grenier), or will she end up with dashing freelance journalist Christian (Simon Baker)?) and a slippery morality that proudly proclaims its superiority to something that is, as Miranda has eloquently articulated, inextricably woven into our consciousness. It's a problem when your best actors (Streep and Stanley Tucci) argue so well on the side of the enemy while the hero (Hathaway) is so pure that there's never much of a question as to her alleged corruption. She's not staring into an abyss, she's fucking up a great job opportunity in a fascinating field. She's less the noble victim than the naïf making a bad mistake following her sous chef beau to Beantown.

Two scenes suggest the film that could have been. The first finds dowdy new assistant Andy (Anne Hathaway) giggling at the silliness of high fashion only to get a brilliant rundown on the evolution of her bag-lady cerulean sweater, the second features Streep, *sans* makeup, revealing what it's like to be a woman in a tank full of men. The rest of it is the typical I-don't-even-recognize-you-anymore bullshit so threadbare and hand-me-down that the fashion mavens of the film would be the first to deride it. It's the performances that save the film to the extent that it can be saved, really, and Hathaway is fast becoming the girl with whom I most want to associate the word "breathless." She's all eyes and awkward and already too charming to play these Sandra Bullock frumps. Stanley Tucci continues his career-long homage to Peter Sellers as a long-suffering fashion consultant at the magazine who longs for a room of his own; Emily Blunt provides a broken climber decked out in red-rimmed eyes and a runny nose; and of course there's Streep's dynamic understatement.

Without them, *The Devil Wears Prada* is just a feature-length version of the opening credits of "The Mary Tyler Moore Show", with Meryl Streep as Lou Grant and a big ol' rapturous toss of the hat the solution to those prickly body-image conundrums that surface when Miranda calls size-6 beauty Andy "fat"—and Andy obligingly shrinks down to a size 4. It'd raise more eyebrows if it wasn't exactly the kind of retarded girl-movie message sold every three months to those most vulnerable to it. We've finally come full-circle from the outrage of Naomi Wolf's The Beauty Myth to the casual acceptance that beautiful girls are stupid and frumpy girls are smart. Surrender as progress: God bless America. (**WC**)

# DON'T COME KNOCKING
** /****

*st.* Sam Shepard, Jessica Lange, Tim Roth, Gabriel Mann
*sc.* Sam Shepard, based on his play

*dir.* Wim Wenders

Howard Spence (Sam Shepard) is a has-been western star knocked down a few pegs by alcohol, drugs, and groupies—and so like any good anti-hero, he takes off in the middle of shooting a film, on horseback, to reunite with his long-estranged mother (Eva Marie Saint) before heading off to Butte, Montana in search of a long-lost bastard son (Gabriel Mann). He has a few conversations with the barmaid (Jessica Lange) he knocked up once upon a time, while a sullen girl (Sarah Polley) carrying a blue urn stalks him around town, offering the occasional cryptic message before retreating again into the wallpaper. But what glorious wallpaper it is, with Wim Wenders and his cinematographer Franz Lustig finding in Butte a myth of the American West frozen in bright, primary, Edward Hopper amber. Twin painters of isolation and suspension, Wenders and Hopper—since long about *The American Friend*—have been on a mission to redraw the psychic divorce of one American from another in minor chords and long, drawn-out tremolos. *Don't Come Knocking*, though, is only minor Wenders, and I do wonder if giving over too much faith in the flagging abilities of Shepard to write a script worth shooting has cost him his pitch this time around.

At his best, Wenders is besotted by a collective framework of invisible tenterhooks that bind one person to another—more as ideas than as meat—across great, empty divides. It's what made the German New Wave director such a perfect match for the vastness of the deserts of the United States and that favoured genre son: the road movie. Even there, in the middle of nothing, he increases our sense of isolation by shooting from places at some remove, depositing his protagonists at a lonesome altitude from which to look down upon, and up, and across. In his underestimated, prescient *The End of Violence*, the

Gabriel Byrne character sits in the Griffith's Park Observatory, high above Los Angeles, watching an array of video monitors upon which he witnesses a violent abduction—an image of an ambivalent angel carried over from Wenders' *Wings of Desire*, as well as something he'll carry forward to all the rooftop vistas of *Million Dollar Hotel* and now into *Don't Come Knocking*, in which he reunites with playwright Sam Shepard for the first time since *Paris, Texas* to create a remake, of sorts, of that classic, only without the urgency or sense of freshness. Blame Shepard's self-conscious, mortally stage-bound script (or maybe it's the lack of a musical muse this time around), because when Wenders spins his camera around Shepard in a 24-hour pan (an audacious, show-stopping bit of flashy auteur existentialism), *Don't Come Knocking* finds that invisible framework and plucks it like a guitar string. For a few moments, the world revolves around Howard Spence (Shepard) and we get a good, long look at how it's all come apart for him.

Too much of the film is given over to the unchallenging, to the easy gag and the predictable development; it's a far cry from the anti-narrative *noir* of Wenders' Patricia Highsmith adaptation. You can almost feel Wenders relaxing, trusting Shepard to do the narrative lifting, but all that's squeezed from that turnip is desperation of the unbecoming kind: a legend of a certain flavour trying hard to recapture a little of that old black magic with broad strokes and braggadocio. Ironically more than literally, *Don't Come Knocking* is a better diorama of the old hero turned anachronism and object of sympathy. For Wenders' part, the picture is breathtakingly beautiful and, visually, ineffably sad. Howard's mother's glass vantage high on a Nevada bluff recalls the director's fascination with metaphysical crow's nests and introspective spyglasses even as Shepard's idea of comic *noir* inversion

in a slicked-down insurance investigator (Tim Roth) threatens to bring the whole house down. It's a film at eternal tension between Wenders' transcendentalism and Shepard's Ozymandian pretense—one in the air and the other buried in the sand. "Look on my works, ye Mighty, and despair!" says Shelley's poem, and then: "Round the decay/Of that colossal wreck, boundless and bare/The lone and level sands stretch far away." Like Wenders building on Shepard. All the non-visual Romanticism of the piece is still better expressed in fourteen lines from two hundred years ago. (**WC**)

## DOWN IN THE VALLEY
*/****
*st.* Edward Norton, Evan Rachel Wood, David Morse, Rory Culkin
*w./d.* David Jacobson

Almost worth it for a scene on the set of a western where our deranged fabulist hero Harlan (Edward Norton) finally finds a home, David Jacobson's *Down in the Valley* is otherwise so much pretentious hoohah waving its indie banner like a parasol. Rather than serve to illustrate a point about form and function à la Gus Van Sant's shot-for-shot remake of *Psycho*, what Jacobson's film does is strain its affection for (affectation of?) *Taxi Driver*, to the point of re-enacting the sacred "You talkin' to me?" sequence—to the point of actually perverting Scorsese's satire into your typical avenging-father/straying-daughter intrigue. It's possible of course to boil Travis Bickle's odyssey down to that, but to call *Down in the Valley* "reductive" is too kind: this is *Taxi Driver* recast as a protect-your-children-from-bad-dates picture, one that turns its back on the dreamlife of a crocodile in favour of the restoration of familial strata. It fails the courage test—going so far as to subtly pose an anti-Second Amendment suggestion—after failing, more damnably, to rationalize its pilfering of perhaps the definitive yawp in modern American cinema. Shake *Down in the Valley* hard enough and out falls another produced-by vanity piece for Norton to exercise his blank (as in Miyazaki-forest-sprite blank), squinty-eyed Method for the approval of his rapidly-shrinking circle of admirers. As far as the Norton mystique goes, Ryan Gosling is cheaper and prettier.

Harlan believes he's a cowpoke from some Anthony Mann *noir* (a chase in the dark and fog underscores the connection), and when he meets teenaged Tobe (Evan Rachel Wood) at a gas station and she invites him to spend a day at the beach with her and her pubescent buddies, well, who wouldn't? Nah—truth is, most people Harlan's age would resist, meaning that for the first little while *Down in the Valley* is twisted in just the right *Badlands* way. Hopes that its start has set the stage for the lawless doom of Terrence Malick's lapsarian road trip are quickly extinguished, though—how much better would the picture be were Harlan, like Malick's Kit, denied a backstory and dropped, inexplicably, into the middle of a young girl's sexual dawn? When *Down in the Valley* loses its nerve (as it does often and dedicatedly), it decides that it's no longer enough to have had Harlan simply materialize—it has to offer a past spent in a loony bin, complete with a frustrated Loomis hunting him down, vengeful father (David Morse) at his side. The daddy is twice-enraged, as a matter of fact: not only is his daughter under Harlan's sway, but Harlan's Old West phantasmagoria seduced his young son (Rory Culkin) as well. Thus is the father figure supplanted as both object of desire and role model. Morse gives the role an exceptional amount of depth and complexity; if the film has an anti-hero, equal parts noble and ignoble, it's him.

All of this skirts the issue of how much *Down in the Valley* is a distended, infected boil in desperate need of a good lancing. It's full of itself, and its shambling corpulence as an entertainment speaks to Norton's bad habit of reading his own press. It's self-important, announcing itself as a Statement Movie even as it busily makes no discernible statement about anything in particular save that Norton thinks of himself as Robert De Niro and Paul Schrader rolled into one noisome package. In fairness, all that might really be missing is anything tangible to rebel against beyond the idea of making a picture with a budget—ironic because Norton's best films are products of the studio system (neither *Fight Club* nor *25th Hour* are exactly zero-budget indies) and because the Norton-produced *The Illusionist* is much more condescending while being several shades less daring than Christopher Nolan's big-budget duelling magician piece *The Prestige*. If subject matter and premise become indistinct in the grey area between mainstream and indie, then the only distinction left is lack of experience, funding, and established talent. (What's more, it's easy to forget that everybody's favourite maverick flick *Taxi Driver* appeared magically under the Columbia banner courtesy the producers of *The Sting*.) Watching *Down in the Valley* is a lot like having a conversation with one of those wieners who believes that the only valuable cinema is the kind that surfaces for a week at the last surviving arthouse in their Podunk burg—using obscurity as the sole criteria for success in a way as hollow and gutless as the opposition that consults box-office returns as the provenance of quality. (**WC**)

## DRAWING RESTRAINT 9
**\*\*1/2/\*\*\*\***

*st.* Matthew Barney, Björk, Shigeru Akahori, Koji Maki
*w./d.* Matthew Barney

Where Matthew Barney's *Drawing Restraint 9* falls short of his brilliant, seminal *Cremaster* series is in its decision to focus on the exploitation of natural resources from whaling through to oil—as filtered through the prism of Japanese industry (using Shinto as the primary test)—rather than on, as in *Cremaster*, the process and scope of myth-making from the Celts to the Masons to Gary Gilmore. The focus is too discrete for the far-reaching archetypes Barney's disquieting, biomechanical surrealism suggests (he's somewhere at the fulcrum between Salvador Dali and David Cronenberg)—the attempt to articulate the perversity of man's exploitation of their natural resources seems a little like what it is: an artist too good and too provocative to waste his time on something that sells so trite. There's a problem as well with how quickly Barney drops his breathtaking mass processional scenes, telescoping his continuing extrapolation of religiosity and ritual (Barney is to post-modernism what Manet was to realism) down to the pinpoint of a disturbing conjugal circle-mutilation between him and Björk in a half-flooded stateroom on what appears to be a cyborg whaler, the Nisshin Maru, berthed and born in Hiroshima and afloat, now, in Nagasaki Bay. Clinched in an intimate embrace, the couple feed each other sashimi from flesh carved and torn from one another's legs—paring away their humanity as the crew of the fourth-generation whaling vessel ("Four means death in Japanese," their host offers) carve a giant mold of whale fat into cubes on the deck of the ship.

Preceding this is a tea ritual consisting of a bile-green liquid infused with ambergris and served in shells that mirror Barney and Björk Shinto marriage gowns, which are adorned with the carapaces of sea creatures. Find logic here in Barney's choice of the Japanese culture as the looking glass through which he filters his thoughts on the madness of man's ideological divorce (and inseparability) from his truer nature. It's a refashioning of a culture that has taken the elevation of ceremony to something like fervour, while the spectre of nuclear holocaust hangs over their mass veneration of equal, disparate draughts of big-eyed cute and nihilistic horror. (Powder-pop vs. bukkake.) Stripped of their formalism, the film's pearl divers, the whaler's preparation of their haul, and the marriage ceremony's flensing ritual birthing thrashing, aquatic creatures reveal, in the twitches and convulsions, our lizard brains freed of the lie of civilization.

It's not too great a stretch to see that the effect of *Drawing Restraint 9* could have been an Ozu film or a Wallace Stevens poem—and its appearance in a United States post-9/11 (our own little version of Armageddon from above) feels less like an accident than like a cry of recognition. Rocks bleed petroleum jelly (not a bad analog for geological amniotic fluid) while a giant cylinder of volcanic issue, this film's lunar monolith, subs in the picture's visual vernacular for the limited resource plundered in Man's heedless forward ambition. The film's liquid baseline stands in contrast to *Cremaster*'s priapismic constructions—but that confrontation between the mercurial with the eternal, the eternally-mutable force with the immutable effigy, doesn't quite yield the kind of introspective, existential epiphany of which Barney's art is capable. What remains, once unmoored from the illusion of circumstance, is a visually-arresting, sometimes impossible-to-watch art installation about how man falls away from his self only to return to the dank fold of the collective through ritual, religion, and the ineffable tides of art that bind. It's a lovely thought, but it's not a surprising one; going out on that proverbial limb, it all might be much ado about nothing. (**WC**)

## DREAMGIRLS
** /****
*st.* Jamie Foxx, Beyoncé Knowles, Eddie Murphy, Danny Glover

*sc.* Bill Condon, based on the play by Tom Eyen
*dir.* Bill Condon

Hailed as one of the more innovatively-staged musicals in the modern pantheon of such entertainments, *Dreamgirls*, transferred to the big screen, is nothing special in the way of something trying way too hard to dazzle. It's the plain girl swathed in a gallon of makeup: there's so much misdirection that you actually try harder to dig up a foundation that can't bear the scrutiny. Said base for *Dreamgirls* is of course one of the most successful Broadway musicals (6 Tonys, 1,522 performances) from an era that counts "Les Miz", Andrew Lloyd Weber's dreadful operettas, and, what, "A Chorus Line"(?), among its chief rivals. You want to attribute its Broadway success to its spinning stage, choreographed and motorized $3.2M tower set, and coy deconstruction of bitch-goddess Diana Ross and her **Supremes**, but it's hard not to wonder if it merely benefits from the relative quality of its competition. Then again, its success is likely the by-product of a fairly consistent mass appetite for cookie-cutter musical biopics, which have been self-satirized to near-total inconsequence first by VH1's "Behind the Music" series, then to quickly-diminishing returns at the multiplex by *Ray* and *Walk the Line*.

*Dreamgirls*, at least, already hedged its bets on Broadway by allowing hero-diva Effie a happy ending when her real-life template, Florence Ballard, died penniless, drunk, and alone at the age of 32. It seems a miscalculation in the sense that were Effie to die in this film version of some Victorian wasting disease, it would have all but guaranteed an awards night coronation for "American Idol" also-ran Jennifer Hudson. Instead, *Dreamgirls* positions itself somewhere between critical-adoration and geek-love, owing its life to the cooling legacy of Rob Marshall's *Chicago*

(without acknowledging the summit littered with the high-profile corpses of *The Producers* and *Rent*) and wary to toe the line in a way that even fondly-remembered family fare like Fred Zinnemann's *Oklahoma!* never did.

Diana Ross, called Deena (Beyoncé Knowles) in this incarnation, falls in love with Berry Gordy Jr. (or "Curtis" (Jamie Foxx)) before or after Curtis installs her as the lead singer of an up-and-coming Motown trio. This miffs Etta James-ian belter Effie (Hudson), who, having previously been the one splitting time between Curtis' bed and lead on stage, excuses herself from the "Dreams" girl megagroup on the eve of its becoming the biggest musical attraction in the country. Rags-to-riches to disappointments and divorce are graphed along a Darwin chart of bad wigs as *Dreamgirls* also spares a moment or two for the sad saga of Jimmy "Thunder" Early (Eddie Murphy), a composite of several soul singers that reduces suspiciously to the reanimated corpse of Murphy's SNL "James Brown Celebrity Hot Tub" goof. His whole performance is ridiculous, with the pathos of his "black" singing going out of vogue in the white-appealing Motown not only covered more effectively by Effie's third-act rise from the ashes, but also made hollow by Murphy's star-persona and stale, past-date perspiration. (You inevitably catch yourself anticipating a cameo from Joe Piscopo's Frank Sinatra.) It's a comeback in the sense that anything Murphy is in now that doesn't involve a lot of children and fart gags is an improvement, but I was mostly left with nostalgia over how innovative a performer he actually used to be.

*Dreamgirls* suffers, too, from a form of schizophrenia in trying to balance the character flaws and career ambitions of Deena, Curtis, and Effie. Deena's the idealist who wants to be an artist, although hers is strictly a cross-racial appeal comprised of equal parts "unthreatening" and bland; pragmatic Curtis, as the one character in the piece who understands how this world works (greasing palms in payola scams and removing the "too black" Effie as the Dreams' face), is tunnel-visioned when it comes to nurturing human connections; and Effie is the ego-deficient blusterer whose lack of substance is interesting to discover as a flaw in an abrasive, gaudy person and not so much in an abrasive, gaudy film. If *Dreamgirls* were more aligned with Jimmy Early's unruly, chaotic dedication to himself and his unpopular vision—even though it may have consigned *Dreamgirls* and its dreams of mainstream acceptance to the same ghetto as the super-charged, admirably-uncompromised *Idlewild*—there might be something more to celebrate here than Hudson's full guns a-blazing screaming. Not surprisingly, as the only star of the film not already a star, she stands out in a story about non-stars who don't know they're going to be famous and, worse, are saddled with the responsibility of being influential. She's the only one who isn't recognizable as a single name, without that gleam in her eye that says she knows more than she should, and whose ego isn't already tied to the immense emptiness of celebrity.

The whole of *Dreamgirls* is a product of lowered expectations and hopeful qualifications. The songs for the most part aren't that catchy (*but they're pretty good for that period of musical theatre*), the book is corny and canned (*but not compared to...*), and the performances are sweaty but remote (*but Beyoncé, Eddie, and Hudson do unexpected work*). Out of time, irrelevant, and orphaned without the intimacy of the stage (an avalanche of hype notwithstanding), *Dreamgirls* is just another overlong and expensive end-of-year mediocrity that may benefit from that overcompensating paternal propensity to over-tip the help. The picture has already picked out a dress and composed an acceptance speech, I think, because it's already proved itself acceptable to folks capable of paying for tickets on the Great White Way (generally, peers of the folks with an Academy membership) and will be the kind of minority picture that, like *The Pursuit of Happyness*, reassures the ruling class that minorities succeed only when they make money for or entertain us. (Preferably both.) This year's *Brokeback Mountain* in a lot of ways, *Dreamgirls* is the movie over which it's impolite not to fawn. (**WC**)

E

## EIGHT BELOW

½*/****

*st.* Paul Walker, Bruce Greenwood,
Moon Bloodgood, Jason Biggs
*sc.* David DeGilio
*dir.* Frank Marshall

There are situations and statements, questions and propositions, that are so stupid by their nature that they actually approach Zen. And then there's Frank Marshall's arctic dogs-and-dude melodrama *Eight Below*, which plays for all the world like not only the world's most unwelcome sequel (to *Snow Dogs*), but also a companion piece to *March of the Penguins*. It is, in simplest terms, a pandering blight—a straight line (nay, flatline) from unsurprising set-up to unsurprising resolution, every bit the equivalent of a line of footprints in the snow between two known points. Opening with one of film history's most wooden leading men, Paul Walker, and "nice Jewish boy" comic relief Jason Biggs sitting in a hundred-degree steam room before running out into a 30-below autumn day in Antarctica, *Eight Below* immediately teaches us that human beings heated to a toasty 110 degrees do not steam when exposed to sub-zero temperatures and, more, that if you should ever visit the South Pole, your breath will never, ever show. It's full of fun facts like that, but it saves its most fascinating revelations for the intricacies of canine interactions, including their complex gift-giving behaviours, advanced speech, abstract philosophical concepts, and eerie ability to go for at least fifteen days at a time without food or water. It even wrests an explanation from the universal loam as to what Walker was put on this earth for: to be upstaged by eight dogs, someone named Moon Bloodgood, Jason Biggs, and miles of white. It goes without saying that those scenes Walker plays against Bruce Greenwood have the queasy, guilty fascination of a baby seal getting mauled by a polar bear.

Walker's dog-sled master Gerry is enlisted to take hotshot scientist Dr. McClaren (Greenwood) to some mountain in the pristine wasteland in search of some meteorite that just happens to be lying on top of the snow directly in their path. McClaren is the stupidest scientist in the world, needing to be rescued constantly from his mortal errors in judgment, and when a storm rolls in, forcing the evacuation of the little outfit *sans* pooches, it's McClaren who's given the lion's share of responsibility for the dog-like Gerry's never-in-doubt reunion with his people-like charges. Trumpeting that it's based on a true story, *Eight Below* is actually based on a Japanese film called *Nankyoku Monogatari* that was sort of suggested by a true story in which only two of eight abandoned dogs survived a few months in the wild. In Disney's hands, that death count is turned upside-down. I can't help but think that it would've felt cozier if its set-up weren't identical to that of John Carpenter's *The Thing*, but alas, I can't find much pleasure in a postcard and a dog calendar deadened by periodic episodes involving Walker doing his best to approximate a heartbeat.

But *Eight Below* knows which side its bread is buttered on and so it shows a dog playing poker, dogs kissing, dogs mourning, dogs telling other dogs to sit while organizing a hunting party, dogs fighting a CGI leopard seal ("More. Leopard. Than. Seal. I. Say," offers Gerry), dogs barking at the Northern Lights, and, most importantly, dogs not killing and eating their human counterparts after months of isolation and starvation. I did like the scene where Gerry's perfunctory love-interest Kate (Bloodgood) says that she's dating an engineer and Gerry asks, "A. Train. Engineer?" in a way that confirms Walker didn't understand the line as a joke, but didn't care for the scene where Gerry consults a wise old Native American for spiritual wisdom. Nor, in truth, did I appreciate Mark Isham's invasive James Horner score, his "Micky Mouse'ing" of every dog scene with whimsical musical emoticons that confirm the idea that the picture believes—correctly, granted—that its audience is comprised of ignorant sheep desperate for herding.

The standard hate mail in response to my reviews of films that suck in this way is that I must not understand what it's like to be a parent in search of movies to watch with their children, and what can I say? I'd rather sit in the park with my toddler than thrust her before a black hole like *Eight Below*. It's how Hollywood trains children to accept certain modes of storytelling and to accept being condescended to with a cheerful lack of discrimination. Call it a gateway drug for the drippy dope dealt by peddlers like Garry Marshall and Shawn Levy and Michael Bay: you can try to nip it in the bud, or you can tacitly agree to keep breeding adults as suggestible and pliant as two-year-olds. I mean, there comes a point where we must recognize that this insatiable desire to accept any old feel-good garbage without question has become more than just a problem at the Cineplex. **(WC)**

## ERAGON

ZERO STARS/****
*st.* Edward Speleers, Jeremy Irons, Sienna Guillory, John Malkovich
*sc.* Peter Buchman and Lawrence Konner & Mark Rosenthal, based on the novel by Christopher Paolini
*dir.* Stefen Fangmeier

Fears that veteran F/X man Stefen Fangmeier's directorial debut *Eragon*, a feature-length adaptation of a fifteen-year-old trying on Anne McCaffrey's jodhpurs, would be the sequel to *Dragonheart* nobody wanted prove unwarranted, as *Eragon* is actually the sequel to *BloodRayne* that nobody wanted. It's ugly as sin, with the much-vaunted dragon at its centre (voiced by Rachel Weisz), designed by skilled craftspeople from both Peter Jackson's WETA workshop and Industrial Light and Magic, looking fatally inorganic to its environment. Not helping matters, the titular rider (Edward Speleers) resembles a younger, equally rubbery David Lee Roth and sports the acting chops of the same. Eragon is the towheaded farmboy who heeds a call to glory to save Sienna Guillory's beautiful Princess Arya ("Help me Eragon, you're my only hope") while gaining a mysterious old hermit mentor (Jeremy Irons—the poor sod should've learned his lesson with *Dungeons & Dragons*) who dies during a daring raid on the Death Star—er, on the castle keep of Darth Vader, er, King Galbatorix (John Malkovich). Alas, this Luke Skywalker also has an Uncle Owen (Uncle Garrow (Alun Armstrong)), and his Darth Vader has a henchman (Robert Carlyle) who at one point kills an underling general and declares the second-in-command "promoted." *Eragon* is a rip-off and a bad one, a carbon copy made on one of those old mimeograph machines: washed out, juvenile (even weighed against the not-exactly-mature example of *Star Wars*), and nigh unbearable for anyone so much as cursorily familiar with genre fare.

The sets are amateurish and the performances all the more so. Although it's tempting to be glib and say that Malkovich is the only person alive capable of delivering a line like "My missing stone causes me pain. Do not prolong my suffering," the truth is that no one can deliver that line; every syllable of dialogue in this misbegotten disaster is unspeakable. Luckily, what's expected of the cast is not acting, but reacting—mainly to a dragon phantom that spends most of its time looking wise—and wondering whether *Eragon* is more like *Dungeons & Dragons* or some gay kid playing with a He-Man action figure. The battles are stultifying at best, retarded at worst, and examples in any case of the poor stuntwork and non-choreography that typifies Uwe Boll's aggressive failures. With *Star Wars* the best picture that *Eragon* could hope to be compared to, also note glimpses of the male-bonding phallus-fight flirtation of Peter Hyams' crazy-bad *The Musketeer* (another film in which a lofty talent roster (Stephen Rea, Tim Roth) plays second fiddle to a chunk of wax in tights) and the inevitable comparisons to Jackson's Tolkein adaptations.

There's no sense of grand epic scope or ambition in *Eragon*, though—the whole thing feels like a children's pageant you endure in a neighbour's backyard one afternoon. Having never read the books (it's a trilogy, I guess, and the end of this one sets the stage for the inevitable sequel), I don't know if they're also as crappy, but far from inspiring me to pick them up, the picture has inspired me to stare at a blank wall for a few hours in the hope that Djimon Hounsou in extensions and an oddly-fey breast plate will fade from memory. Stupid, sexy Hounsou. *Eragon* is godawful by every measure, if not really dispiriting in the way that a lot of cash-grabs are: you don't get a sense they were trying to make a bad movie inasmuch as this was absolutely the best they could do. (It's an object of pity more than one of derision.) It's possible that children familiar with the book will be happy to fill in the narrative gaps and vacuous characterizations, but it's hard for me to believe there's another audience for the picture. While the presence of Carlyle, Malkovich, and Irons would at least seem to point to some camp pleasure in the margins, take this as fair warning that there's nothing remotely pleasurable about any single moment of *Eragon*. Better to rent the theatrical cut of *Star Wars* while you still can and call it a day. (**WC**)

PREVIOUSLY UNPUBLISHED
ANIMATED
**EVERYONE'S HERO**
½*/****
sc. Robert Kurtz and Jeff Hand
dir. Christopher Reeve, Dan St. Pierre

An appalling melancholy casts a long shadow over *Everyone's Hero*, which possesses possibly the worst idea for a movie ever carried through to fruition, shepherded there by sainted martyrs Christopher and Dana Reeve. (I'm not certain how much impact our Man of Steel ultimately had on the outcome, though, as he died more than two years before the release of the picture.) This is the story of a little boy, Yankee Irving (Jake T. Austin), who's just dreadful at baseball and therefore destined to be a great baseball player. I realize that Michael Jordan was cut from his high-school basketball team and Einstein failed high-school physics, but all this self-esteem, 'sky's the limit' bullshit spoon-fed to the children of our beloved country has resulted in confident-to-the-point-of-arrogant kiddos who regularly rank last in the world in standardized tests—but first in "can do" attitude. The reason Brad Bird's *Ratatouille* and *The Incredibles* are so spectacular is because they posit that someone gifted can come from any background, not that anyone can be anything they want. Yankee is befriended by a talking baseball (voiced by Rob Reiner) and, eventually, by Babe Ruth's talking bat (Whoopi Goldberg); and after traveling cross-country to reunite The Babe's wood with The Babe himself in the final game of the World Series, Yankee gets the chance to bat in the Big Show.

It seems unsporting to pick at *Everyone's Hero* for not making any sense, but it doesn't make any sense and, a bigger problem, it doesn't appear to respect any internal logic, either. Yankee is accused of stealing Babe's bat, thereby costing his dad (Mandy Patinkin) his job as Yankee Stadium janitor and compelling Yankee to chase down the real culprit, Cubs pitcher Lefty Maginnis (William H. Macy). Why is there a talking baseball to aid Yankee in his search? It feels like what it is: an attempt to apply the *Toy Story* model to sports dreams—but a child's evergreen belief that their toys come to life when they're not looking (or that their bikes can fly, or that they're secretly superheroes/wizards) is a far cry from carrying on a conversation with a fucking baseball. That's pathetic. It's a poverty joke like the Irish kid whose parents give him a potato painted like a turtle for a pet. Making the ball a kvetching nebbish is even more indecipherable, particularly in a picture that has a sequence on a Negro League team bus where it's clear that the inspiration isn't Satchel Page, but the Harlem Globetrotters. The film is, in other words, as retarded about race as it is about children's fantasies. If your child is talking to his football, it's time to splurge and buy him a dog.

Once every attempt to rationalize it is abandoned, what remains are flat slapstick sequences and interludes with evil Cubs manager Napoleon Cross (Robin Williams) improvising desperately like a comic out of season for at least two decades now. I'm going to throw this out there, that the only way Robin Williams could resuscitate any kind of credibility now is if Quentin Tarantino were to cast him as a villain. Williams ia only ever good under a tight, tight rein (consequently, he was only ever good in his ten minutes in Kenneth Branagh's *Dead Again*), and Tarantino might be the one director left who can keep a firm hand at the bridle and still allow him the freak-energy that makes him interesting instead of zombefied. Anymore, Williams' name on a marquee is a warning instead of an invitation, and his participation in an animated film is the direst warning of all. The flick looks good, but as technology gets cheaper and easier to use, what does that matter, either? *Everyone's Hero* is directionless and lacking utterly in inspiration—it's senseless and lifeless and the extent to which the doomed Reeves' involvement has been touted in its publicity reeks with sour exploitation. It's a dispiriting slog the only function for which is to displace *The Sandlot* as the worst kiddie baseball flick ever made. (**WC**)

# F

## FACTOTUM (see: HOLLYWOODLAND)

## FAILURE TO LAUNCH

ZERO STARS/****
st. Matthew McConaughey, Sarah Jessica Parker, Zooey Deschanel, Justin Bartha
sc. Tom J. Astle & Matt Ember
dir. Tom Dey

Starring professional unctuous petroleum spill Matthew McConaughey as Tripp, a carefree stallion still making a stable of his parent's house, Tom Dey's excruciating *Failure to Launch* is two things and both of them suck: a romantic comedy and a boorish fraternity slapstick, mashed together like a jumped track mashes together train cars. When Tripp is ready to break up with a girl too interested in something resembling an adult relationship, the modus is to screw her at his place and hope that his folks walk in on them. So what do his adoring parents (Kathy Bates and Terry Bradshaw: she's not naked this time, he is—let's call it a draw) do but hire an unctuous tan line named Paula (Sarah Jessica Parker) to pretend to be his girlfriend? Yes, they get their boy a whore, who, in a particularly uncomfortable scene in a particularly uncomfortable film, mumbles her way around an excuse as to why she's fucked her client to keep him from breaking up with her. Now that's professionalism for you. (At least in *The Wedding Date*, the jane had the decency to pay for her own escort.) If you don't think it's loathsome when the Bradshaw character, ogling Paula, says, "I'm payin' fer it, I'll stare if I want to," then have I got a movie for you.

All this is so very "Sex and the City", thus, to appease the young male demographic for whom "Sex and the City" is like a barium enema (let's face it, it's no holiday for any demographic), Dey and company insert a series of slapstick vignettes involving Tripp being attacked by a chipmunk, a dolphin, and a lizard, thereby rendering the picture thoroughly unwatchable for everyone. There's unresolved tension over which one is the more irredeemable miscreant in this mess, and there's a strange revelation that Tripp (who has never moved out of the house, we're told) is actually not a parasitic, arrested loser sucking like a barnacle to the ample undercarriage of his clueless kinfolk, but actually a soulful huckster still mourning the death of a sainted girlfriend. This allows for the introduction of a precocious "nephew" character to dispense cherubic wisdom like a play-doh factory while unsuccessfully ghosting Tripp every bit of the soulfulness his character does not otherwise earn. Of course this "nephew" is black.

Other sidekicks for Tripp include a pair of affable, invisible, wallpaper ne'er-do-wells; for Paula, we have deadpan nihilist Kit (Zooey Deschanel, doing this role now around the clock), who will, of course, fall for one of Tripp's buddies after he gives the kiss of life to a mockingbird. The description would fit a work of surrealism, and that's because there's so little energy in the production, so much desperation in its obvious recorded-in-a-coffee-can overdubbing, late rewrites, and other sundry post-production panic button quick-fixes, that its seams show in every old-person sexuality joke and impossible to reconcile paint ball sequence. There's a bizarre attempt to make sense of the two halves late in the game, something to do with why otherwise tame wildlife (like Parker) would suddenly attack toothy Tripp, but all this succeeds in doing is to introduce another exhibit into the mounting evidence that *Failure to Launch* is a badly-calibrated geek button for an audience of sexualized children. If you listen closely, you can almost hear the colossal failure crank grinding—and the great tragedy of it is that this film has its audience, didn't cost much to produce, and will justify its own existence financially, guaranteeing iterations of exactly the same kind of feckless malfunction again and again. You can glimpse eternity in this thing (or at least a hint of your own mortality), and if it's not the worst movie I've ever seen it's only because intimate knowledge of its endless ancestors and inevitable offspring resists the sweet refuge of hyperbole. (**WC**)

**FALL TO GRACE (see: QUINCEAÑERA)**

**FAMILY**
½*/****
*st.* Renee Humphrey, Boyd Kestner, Tanner Richie, Joseph Russo II
*sc.* Hudson Shock
*dir.* J.M. Logan

Long-time FX man J.M. Logan makes his directorial debut with the sometimes-handsome but more-often tedious *Family*, which is not, as the title might lead one to assume, a gay flick or another telling of Charlie Manson's summer of love. Instead, find in it a retread of *Freeway* by way of *The Hitcher* by way of *Kalifornia* by way of *Breakdown* and *Children of the Corn IV* and every other mother-loving *noir*/Americana/road-trip flick you can name. Mistaking cheap Final Cut Pro editing somersaults for character-development and scares, the picture finally washes out as a poorly-written, poorly- paced and performed "psychological thriller." The bad guy delivers endless spit-soaked monologues, the anti-heroine spends most of her time emoting dully against her dull co-stars, and an early scene where someone has to ad-lib a conversation into a pay phone actually makes one long for the relative buff of Bob Newhart's antiquated telephone shtick. It's the lack of professionalism that rankles, really—that undeniable feeling that you're wasting your time here on someone's pet project, and that the most *Family* will ever claim is that it was directed by the self-described "visual effects producer" for *The Passion of the Christ*.

None of Logan's mastery within his field is on display here, though. A decidedly more mundane story of escaped-con Jean (Renée Humphrey) hitching a ride with ex-cop Eldon (Boyd Kestner, not bad with little to work with) and his young son Cole (Tanner Richie), *Family* is your standard cross-country journey of self-discovery. Secrets? Sure. Surprises? Almost none. But there *is* an interminable amount of deadening dialogue shot back and forth across the front seat of a car as classical music blares in almost complete misunderstanding of how score is used in a motion picture. Character development is necessarily minimal, given that skeletons in closets are used exclusively as the plot points in what passes for plot in *Family*, but nothing (such as tension, for instance, or compelling set-pieces, or an interesting premise) rushes in to fill the void. What's left is a foregone conclusion rambled towards with a surfeit of energy and an excess of blah. More's the pity, as a few moments (including a tense visit to a roadside grocery and a shower gone wrong) hold the potential for shock—or, at least, for exploitation. But alas, *Family*'s as stingy with the cheap thrills as it is with the sophisticated ones; no amount of stutter-cuts and bursts of exposition replayed like a skipped record can substitute for actual involvement in the tale.

Lacking much of anything else to talk about, champions and critics of *Family* alike inevitably fall back on a discussion of its use of a 24p digital camera (with a sepia filter firmly in place throughout) and of how it looks relative to other HiDef productions. What I'll say is that Michael Mann is probably the only person right now who understands how to properly use this technology as a celluloid substitute—and what he understands best is that digital photography is cold, not warm. I should add that *Family* is very much a film about process: about a freshman screenwriter trotting out his page-bound kinder a good half-dozen rewrites shy of presentable; and about a freshman director able to afford expensive toys, offering a film that is mostly just a demonstration of how high-end equipment allows you to achieve a David Fincher aesthetic without the accompanying cargo of dread and subtext. It's a commercial for technique—desktop editing suites and mounting pictures on a comparative shoestring that have the very shellac cast of thrillers of some substance. All *Family* really manages, then, is to underscore the impenetrable truism that, with time and resources, you can carve a duck out of clay, but it takes something ineffable to make it quack. (**WC**)

## FAST FOOD NATION (see: *BOBBY*)

## D O C U M E N T A R Y
### FAVELA RISING
\*\*\* /\*\*\*\*
*dirs.* Jeff Zimbalist, Matt Mochary

A beautifully-shot, surprisingly optimistic documentary about favela ("slum") problem in Rio de Janeiro (brought to popular Western attention with a sick, slick sort of glee in *City of God*), Zimbalist and Mochary's *Favela Rising* follows Anderson Sa—founder of percussionist group **AfroReggae**—in his attempts to offer the minors in the favelas an alternative to becoming drug traffickers, outlaws, and/or statistics. Between bloody crime

scenes, harrowing accounts of police corruption and brutality, and a chilling interview with a little boy who expresses an ardent desire to grow up to become a murderer earning $650/week (that's roughly $637/week more than the average "honest" salary), the picture inserts shots of Sa's band performing to packed crowds and gaining apprentices at the rate of one for every three to wind up in the cartels. Nearly four thousand of the city's children were murdered during state of perpetual drug war between 1997 and 2001—and against that impossible tide, we find Sa and his band, the product of what they call "The Shiva Effect": hope reborn from chaos and destruction. If the musical sequences run long and if it all ultimately has something of a deadening effect, the aftertaste at the least is as sweet as faith in the enduring power of art. (**WC**)

## FEAST
\*\* /\*\*\*\*
*st.* Balthazar Getty, Henry Rollins, Navi Rawat, Clu Gulager
*sc.* Patrick Melton & Marcus Dunstan
*dir.* John Gulager

## D I R E C T - T O - V I D E O
### THE WOODS
\*\*\*½/\*\*\*\*
*st.* Agnes Bruckner, Patricia Clarkson, Rachel Nichols, Bruce Campbell
*sc.* David Ross
*dir.* Lucky McKee

I'm surprised that more great films aren't shuttled to the direct-to-video twilight zone, seeing as how mainstream taste-makers, particularly in regards to genre pictures, seem primarily invested in churning out the same pre-masticated gruel. At the very least, prefab garbage like *School for Scoundrels* might as well have been dumped on the home market without a ripple in the fabric of daily life.

(Something like Liliana Cavani's *Ripley's Game*, on the other hand, deserved a theatrical release: disguised as a dtv unload, it's the best thriller in years.) Between their low budgets, how they perform without bankable leads, and how they pretty much guarantee a healthy return on their investments, it's almost inexplicable that horror movies get exiled to Blockbuster as often as they do. You can learn a lot about a people from the mythologies they construct to frighten and warn, although because horror films are bankable product (and always were), they fall prey to the same venal, filthy lucre-inspired pitfalls of formula drudgery. Still, I like to refer to them as the "indicator species" of our cultural swamp in that they're not only ugly, dirty, bottom-feeding, what have you, but also the first species of entertainment to reflect the elements polluting the spirit of this exact moment in our social history. If you can find the pulse of it, a horror movie will tell you a lot about that quickening in your own chest when you watch the evening news.

That intense contemporary meta-currency might be the most interesting thing about John Gulager's serviceable *Feast*, the harvest of the third and final season of "Project Greenlight", Live Planet's reality show in which a series of stupid decisions pairs a few mismatched aspirants in the marathon of producing a feature-length motion picture. Too intimate a knowledge of the struggles in making *Feast* colour it with endless distractions: is heroine Tuffy (Krista Allen), for instance, wearing the bra that shows her nipples from scene-to-scene? And why did I have no idea that its star, Henry Rollins, was even in the thing despite having watched every episode? Gulager on the program comes off as something of a nebbish initially, blossoming into a minor hero standing up for his vision against the monolithic Weinsteins—and the first thing that comes clear in the picture is that, just visually, it looks remarkably good. It lost me early, though, with a series of character-introduction title cards that, besides being over-written, felt a little desperate to be too cool for itself, actually functioning a time or two as silent-movie exposition or, worse, commentary from the god of snark. The way that films like *Feast* work is that, tongue in cheek or not, they present themselves as deadly serious. Once you wink, you look embarrassed and, moreover, insecure and ashamed.

Tuffy is a single mom, truck-stop waitress, and sometime-whore who, along with the usual suspects, finds herself barricaded in a remote honkytonk while toothy beasties do their best to break in. It's only a matter of time, of course, until she's called into action in the Ripley mold. Spam-in-a-cabin in every gory aspect of the sub-genre, the film works when it works because its cast is committed and, in the case of Rollins, not to mention (John's dad) Clu Gulager as a grizzled barkeep with a pump-action hog-leg in his drink, inspired. Stealing the show is Jenny Wade as "piece of ass" Honey Pie, the victim of the Guignol equivalent of a money shot and possessor of the moment that is the best, most canny and hilarious commentary on the genre in a film that, most of the time, tries too hard. As for the goods, the action sequences, alas, are so confused and hyperactive that it's impossible to commit to the mayhem—more's the pity, as once the ill-defined monsters are brought at last into focus, they prove themselves well-conceived and fearsome. The consequences, especially, of the creature's attacks (including a particularly funny fate for actor Jason Mewes, playing himself) are ugly enough, and the feeling pervasive is that if *Feast* had only trusted the meat of the text to provide the extratextual exegesis on its own, we might have really had something here.

As it is, the picture is smarter than you expect—funnier and nastier, too; a minor diversion, if also a minor disappointment. In terms of the

Weinsteins' release philosophy, however, favouring the bigger-budgeted stinker *Pulse* over *Feast* (the former getting a splashy theatrical release, the latter relegated to a couple of midnight screenings before its prompt banishment to DVD), the film suddenly attains cult cachet: proof again that little engines that could don't make it over that pass in the dream factory. Should *Feast* gain an audience on video, credit its treatment and, by direct comparison, its relative worthiness. Maybe the Weinsteins know what they're doing, after all.

It's hard to say the same about the braintrust at Sony that would drop Lucky McKee's exceptional *The Woods* (produced under UA stewardship and left to founder, much as *Feast* was born to Miramax and retained by the Weinstein Group) without so much as a midnight peek. Just the sound design and visuals would merit this film a screening or two (no direct-to-video picture since *Ripley's Game* has so deserved the big screen), but the picture, McKee's follow-up to the well-regarded *May*, is genuinely frightening, sharp as a tack, and impeccably executed. The very fairytale for a young girl's sexual awakening that its title suggests, *The Woods* centres around troubled Heather (Agnes Bruckner, exceptional), exiled to exclusive boarding school Falburn Academy after she sets fire to a tree in her front yard. Her long-suffering parents (Bruce and Emma Campbell, apparently no relation) entrust her to the icy ministrations of headmistress Ms. Traverse (Patricia Clarkson) and her staff of twitchy, patrician harridans. Shades of *Suspiria*, to be sure (and late-night flights through haunted woods dominate the middle portion), but shades, too, of *Heathers* in bullying blonde Samantha (Rachel Nichols), before the picture brushes up against the similar pubescent humiliations and vengeance-taking of *Carrie*.

A splash of blood on a wrinkled parchment initiates the proceedings: a metaphor for menstruation, of course, or the loss of virginity, and only the first of several startlingly evocative images McKee tosses onto the screen. Though strange happenings and missing students are the bedrock for this strain of genre edifice, the ivy through the cracks of *The Woods* incorporates a couple of creepy/loaded Leslie Gore tunes that Heather and sadsack pal Marcy (budding star Lauren Birkell) listen to in private rapture—and the most lascivious use of tree roots since *The Evil Dead*. Of course the milk is poisoned, of course the hand that silences is split like a ripe fruit, and of course the voices in Heather's head suggest an initiation into the mysteries of the feminine. Yet *The Woods* isn't bereft of originality as much as it is rich with archetype. It's a repository of genre intelligence and a repackaging of superstitions surrounding the practice and abuse of witchcraft, transforming the fires that are its bookend into an echo of the historical remedy—in addition to the suggestion of cleansing and rebirth that said remedy purported to deliver. Consider its Oedipal coda, with Heather's father the would-be rescuer of this maiden-fair following the dispatching of her mother via the tentacled limb of a rogue tree: it's something as breathless and charged in its own way as Bruce Campbell's return to the axe-wielding avatar that remains his most enduring creation. (**WC**)

**FETCHING CODY**
ZERO STARS/****
*st.* Jay Baruchel, Sarah Lind, Jim Byrnes, Robert Kaiser
*w./d.* David Ray

Canada is a nation of amateurs. Some terrible national weakness has taught us to be sheepishly inexact, as if trying to tell a story or form a coherent argument were about showing up and meekly filling in time as opposed to a complex array of intellectual and aesthetic decisions. We'll do the job, but we won't do it precisely—and frequently, the results are empty shells like *Fetching Cody*. I wouldn't be nearly so angry about its failure if I didn't know that there were more like it— long, unbroken streams of arrested preadolescents looking to get points for being "serious" and "meaningful"— coming down the pipeline. Critics are probably the largest segment of the population who'll see them, which probably accounts for why we're terse in our dismissals: we know we'll wind up talking to no one but ourselves.

Despite taking place in Vancouver's downtown east side (an area that claims the highest HIV transmission rates due to shooting-up in North America), the film gives us a peppy opening with two lovey-dovey kids chasing a balloon on a bicycle. There is some extremely clunky exposition letting us know that Art (Jay Baruchel) and Cody (Sarah Lind) are street kids and drug users, but it doesn't really sink in: Art's Catholic School hoodie makes him look resoundingly middle-class, while Cody resembles an angry runaway straight out of a music video. There's a transvestite hooker named Sabrina (Robert Kaiser) and a smaller runaway child, but they seem airlifted in—at no point does verisimilitude kick in to persuade us of anything we're seeing. Nothing has been referenced back to its original model; it's a bunch of people shooting blindly in the dark.

Eventually, Cody has the bad form to OD, meaning Art gets left in the lurch. Luckily, his homeless buddy Harvey (Jim Byrnes) has found a discarded recliner that doubles as a time machine. Yes, you read that right: *Fetching Cody* is parasitic on *The Butterfly Effect* and allows Art to travel back in time to try and un-fuck-up his paramour's life. Only it makes the crucial error of playing the temporal hijinks for laughs, with Art trying to rescue the pubescent Cody from menstrual embarrassment, watching

her suicidal gay brother Holden (Lucas Blaney) blow the top of his head off, and abruptly ending Cody's relationship with a lunkhead boyfriend through the strategic (re)placement of Christmas gifts. Thus the film wants us to take it seriously yet sabotages any hope of that happening—leaving us confused, annoyed, even seriously embarrassed.

The DVD release of *Fetching Cody* features rationales from writer-director David Ray to the effect that he a) did all manner of research on street kids; b) wanted to introduce a "dark," "Grimm fairytale" element to the proceedings; and c) felt that some "humour" should be introduced. Unfortunately, a) plays like a point-form printout, not a well-sketched milieu; b) winds up making the proceedings seem glib; and c) is so weak and unfunny as to be cringe-inducing. More to the point, these elements are thought of *in isolation from each other*. That is, street kids, dark fairytales, and humour are individual concepts stitched together instead of synthesized—an intelligent blending of forms (see: Robert Coover) is missing. The film feels like it's ticking off requirements on a list, and it does so out of half-understood duty rather than self-initiated interest.

In a world with Gus Van Sant and Lodge Kerrigan and the Dardenne brothers, the destitute and marginal need not suffer such indignities. Unfortunately, none of those luminaries lives in Canada. For here, you can get away with the most facile of political tracts and be showered with grant money—and while I'm not against public funding *per se*, I am against the childish criteria by which both standard art films and Stursberg-era pop films have been judged. Money isn't the only thing that's required: we also need something that can inculcate the massive undertaking that is an aesthetic process. Otherwise, we will continue to allow our timid filmmakers to wreak havoc on unsuspecting "social issues," or hide behind their good intentions instead of firmly and fully stating a case. It's time for our filmmakers to start elaborating and stop name-checking, before more *Fetching Codys* blight our cinemas for their obligatory one-week runs. **(TMH)**

## FINAL DESTINATION 3
*** /****
*st.* Mary Elizabeth Winstead, Ryan Merriman, Kris Lemche, Crystal Lowe
*sc.* Glen Morgan & James Wong
*dir.* James Wong

Jettisoning any attempt to perpetuate the ponderous lore of the first two films, *Final Destination 3* docks at the arrivals gate with a full payload of wry sadism and satirical high school archetypes and nothing but grim exploitation nihilism on its mind. It's the perfect post-9/11 horror film in its way, and sure enough, 9/11 is invoked in an extraordinarily inappropriate photo of the WTC with the shadow of an airplane crossing its middle, which our dour, spoil-sport heroine presents in support of her thesis that photos taken of our soon-to-be-victims might provide clues as to their imminent demise. For the indoctrinated, the machinations of the picture are familiar: a small group of would-be teens avoids a Byzantine—and disgusting—fate, only to be hunted down by "death" (as a concept) and dismembered like flesh puppets ground in the gears of Rube Goldbergian contraptions. (Rube Goldberg with the unsavoury predilections of the Marquis de Sade, that is.) The calamity this time around is a hilariously sprung roller coaster, and the dour, virginal OCD headcase who has the premonition and survives is Wendy (Mary Elizabeth Winstead), doing her level best to warn her fellow survivors but succeeding mainly in being our front-row surrogate witness to the most gleeful assemblage of remorseless bloodletting since, well, *Final Destination 2.*

There's a strong feeling this time around that creators James Wong and Glen Morgan have tapped into a dank universal thrum, locating the cloud of doom that currently hangs over the United States by throwing a cast of teensploitation types under the proverbial bus. They undermine the expected by refusing to offer a surcease from their characters' sorrows: replacing the slasher resolution of the "good girl" winning out and restoring society is the idea of a terrorist alert level set constantly at red. Something terrible, God knows what it is, is going to happen—it's going to get you and your loved ones right where you live, work, and play. ("Fuck you, Ben Franklin" is the film's funniest, and oddest, complaint.) And no matter what you do or how smart you are, you'll never see it coming, and there's no one, ultimately, to ever hold accountable for the mayhem. Take away the authority figures (unreliable in any case (parents and police are complete non-entities here)) and let a pathological be worrier the hero before making every single thing she's concerned about a vile, messy, completely unavoidable reality and you have all the ingredients of the pernicious id roiling in the secret think-pan of most thoughtful Americans.

Start with the hilariously vacuous valley girls Ashley (Chelan Simmons) and Ashlynn (Crystal Lowe), punctuating their invitation to sour Wendy to go tanning with them with "That was *so* totally nice of us!" and meeting their mutual demise in a Kentucky-fried kind of way, though not before taking off their tops. The only two functions of pretty, stupid girls in films like *Final Destination 3* is for them to first get naked and then to die, and director Wong obliges, yet what separates this picture from other slashers with less on the mind is that the torture of its characters is so non-sexual and protracted that between peals of laughter, you may experience a moment of surprised existential doubt about your participation in their sexual objectification and, crucially, in the funhouse objectification of their deaths. It seems a punishment of their vanity, a read that holds water particularly in that another death—of star football player Lewis (Texas Battle)—comes at the end of a commensurate display of frightening machismo. But *Final Destination 3* seems mainly interesting in taking every single character type introduced as timeless in *The Breakfast Club* and deconstructing them narratively before literally. There is no tactic that works in the film: the nerds, the jocks, the yearbook club, the Heathers, and the Goths are equally impotent in avoiding a grisly fate. If there's a thread that unites the picture's mouse trap vignettes, it's the oft-repeated debate between the value of knowledge versus the bliss of ignorance—and if you're tired of talking about how so many of our films now are about home invasion and vengeance and hopelessness and terror, maybe it's a good time to talk about how this film and others like it (*Saw II*, for instance, or *Open Water*) are about how terrible is knowledge when it brings no profit to the wise. Or, more to the point, how useless is outrage when the train jumps the tracks. (**WC**)

# FIREWALL
*\*1/2/\*\*\*\**
*st.* Harrison Ford, Paul Bettany, Virginia Madsen, Mary Lynn Rajskub
*sc.* Joe Forte
*dir.* Richard Loncraine

Because 63-year-old Harrison Ford is pushing mandatory retirement age in most industries, his new movie *Firewall* is aimed squarely at an older, more affluent, less savvy demographic. Casting the aging demigod as a greying bank executive extorted by the usual band of eurotrash techno-terrorists holding his perfect family hostage, it's a fable of paranoia that

finds evil in not only the modern cell phone bogey, but other mysterious beasts like iPods, phone cameras, GPS devices, fax machines, and online banking, too. Its never-explained title, in fact, refers to a technology that protects against malignant computer codes floating around the World Wide Web—but rather than try to define this for an audience that's ideally long-resistant to such cogent explanations, it makes the "firewall" a literal thing by devolving into another homeland security allegory, with the craggy paterfamilias meting out sweet vengeance against a gaggle of interlopers. Better to have called it "Antivirus"—but Michael Bay's probably reserved that title for his kick-ass foreign terrorist/avian flu metaphor.

Ford stars as one of his "Jacks" (not "Ryan," his Tom Clancy hero, nor "Trainer", his *Working Girl* persona, but rather a chimera of the two), Jack Stanfield, father of two (Carly Schroeder and Jimmy Bennett, the latter the same forlorn-looking kid terrorized to similar effect in *Hostage* and *The Amityville Horror*), husband of requisite clutcher/screamer Beth (Virginia Madsen). Jack is VP of Security at a mid-sized bank about to be taken over by a larger financial institution. He has a partner (Robert Forster), but that character is so mangled and misused as to function handily as an emergency brake, yanked whenever the movie threatens to develop some cheerful momentum. Mary Lynn Rajskub portrays the assistant to another Jack (after "Bauer" of Fox's "24"), Janet this time, and so when mousy Janet lends this Jack her laptop, there's a tiny, microscopic flash of po-mo hipness in an arthritic script by Joe Forte that otherwise plays like the stuffiest episode of "Frasier". Predictably (and much like the opening of *The Clearing*), Jack's idyllic life is one day interrupted by a band of high-tech bank robbers led by puffy Bill Cox (Paul Bettany), who spews the usual threats and ultimatums in the usual oily, continental fashion, moving one to fantasize about how slightly more interesting the film would've been had Ford played the bad guy, forced to retire without health care or a pension (like, say, dozens of veteran United Airlines pilots) and pushed to serious violent crimes against some young punk with a tech degree.

Alas, *Firewall* goes along its linear path with nary a thought of deviating from its ultimate destination: a mano-a-mano between the old grey lion and the young cub in a battle of wile and scrap. The rest is a strung-together series of none-too-disguised excuses for Jack to throw down in an insurance-company audition to get Ford covered for one more round as Indiana Jones. The potentially interesting bits (such as the suggestion that Jack is in a technological fishbowl at the mercy of his tormentors, or the Alan Arkin and Robert Forster cameos) are dropped as soon as humanly possible in a terminal case of missed opportunity. What's left is pretty frugal, indeed: a loosely-sketched, moronic master plot complete with a final slow-motion shot so saccharine and hilarious that it looks to be on loan from Ford's sometime-collaborator and child prince of the stupid ending Steven Spielberg. *Firewall* joins Ford's earring and Calista Flockhart as things he should've outgrown by now—and if you so desired, you could identify the movements of the picture as a retrogression from *Air Force One* to *The Fugitive* to *Patriot Games*. Call it a sad case of arrested development, though of course it's sacrilege to entertain such thoughts about Han Solo. That guy is *awesome*. (**WC**)

## PREVIOUSLY UNPUBLISHED
## ANIMATED
## FLUSHED AWAY
**\*\*$^1/_2$/\*\*\*\***

*sc.* Dick Clement & Ian La Frenais and Chris Lloyd & Joe Keenan and Will Davies
*dirs.* David Bowers, Sam Fell

## PREVIOUSLY UNPUBLISHED
## DECK THE HALLS
ZERO STARS/**\*\*\*\***
*st.* Danny DeVito, Matthew Broderick, Kristin Davis, Kristin Chenoweth
*sc.* Matt Corman & Chris Ord and Don Rhymer
*dir.* John Whitesell

## PREVIOUSLY UNPUBLISHED
## CHARLOTTE'S WEB
**\*\* /\*\*\*\***

*st.* Julia Roberts, Dakota Fanning, Steve Buscemi, John Cleese
*sc.* Susannah Grant and Karey Kirkpatrick, based on the novel by E.B. White
*dir.* Gary Winick

Unabashedly, irreverently British, Aardman's *Flushed Away*—something of a chimera between digital animation and the traditional stop-motion which stood as the limey company's stock and trade—casts its French characters as literal frogs; its Yanks as loud-mouthed tourists chronically underfoot; and its Brits as buck-toothed, terminally-polite blokes accidentally thrust into bursts of derring-do. Dry as a soda cracker and packed to the rafters with taking the piss out of other movies, the film is marked with Aardman's wit, even if there's something undeniably lost in the translation when human hands aren't literally involved in the physical manipulation of actual models. What's gained, however, is scope and elasticity in the sets and action sequences, the best of which include a sewer-bound miniature London filthy with rats and their slug chorus; a chase using the company's stock foodie obsession (some of the baddies ride cake mixers subbing for jet skis) complete with a slow-mo Christopher Cross romantic interlude; and a finale involving what looks like the lost director's cut epilogue of *The Abyss*. The downfall of the agility is a surplus of high-speed crotch gags and what can seem at times like a visual cacophony.

Roddy (voiced by Hugh Jackman) lives a life of lonesome luxury in a gilded cage in Kensington, calling dolls his friends in a quick homage to the *Toy Story* franchise before finding his life in turmoil when he's maliciously flushed down a toilet. Once in the underneath, he's thrust into a *Romancing the Stone* quest for a red ruby on the arm of steamboat captain Rita (Kate Winslet), in full flight from tragic archvillain The Toad (Ian McKellen) and his henchman Le Frog (Jean Reno). In a creative film's most brilliant sequence, The Toad delivers a monologue through a video cell phone strapped to the front of a frog mime. It's sort of impossible to describe. Even a cheap joke at the expense of the French's propensity to surrender lands with a well-timed, and well-appreciated, sense of good-natured ribbing. The problem with the thing is that all it really seems to be is a collection of gags adding up to nothing much. Its pace headlong and its craft suddenly pedestrian when robbed of Aardman's gentle humanity and painstaking labors, *Flushed Away* is just another movie in great need of something more substantive than pop-culture riffs, post-modern auto-criticism, and the diminished returns of doo-wop slugs. Not a disaster by any stretch, it's consigned to the fate of being the least of a storied studio's productions: fun but, save a couple of ingenious moments, instantly and uncharacteristically forgettable.

Would that *Deck the Halls* were so easy to forget. The latest offering from Shawn Levy-ite John Whitesell as well as the latest attempt to cash in on the holiday family market with a piece of knocked-off, half-assed, embarrassing, profit-driven hackery, this one stars Matthew Broderick and Danny DeVito as feuding neighbors: the one a button-up suburban climber, the other a *nouveau riche* huckster intent, along with his bimbo wife and daughters, on creating a holiday light display obscene enough to be visible from outer space. After the bulk of it is blown on ugly behavior and badly-timed slapstick, no points for guessing that it's all going to end with a horse-gagging portion of forced sentimentality. This is the kind of movie Steve Martin used to star in with John Candy, or Chevy Chase with anybody: the uptight one needing to loosen up and the free-spirit, lower-classed stooge who does the reaming. It's the kind of film that mines for humor in a policeman's secret occupation dressing up in women's underthings, revealing a degree of ugly intolerance that's the anchor for most films like this: conformity is king; what's become of Christmas bridges all spans. (What's become of DeVito (essentially resurrecting his character from Barry Levinson's *Tin Men*) is similarly upsetting, though not as much as what's happened to Broderick.) It's like a porno flick: all elaborately-staged simulations bathed at the end with sticky money shots—only worse because *Deck the Halls* pretends to be a warm paeon to togetherness and family instead of just a way to get your money by giving you something to jerk off to.

If Christmas isn't sacrosanct in a country founded by pilgrims and overtaken now by various Puritan whack-jobs, what chance does E.B. White's <u>Charlotte's Web</u> have? Certainly not Charles Nichols and Iwao Takamoto's well-remembered 1973 animated version (which actually hasn't aged all that great, what with Paul Lynde's Templeton and Charles Nelson Reilly, for fuck's sake, turning good swatches of it into instant camp); and certainly not a certain reverence for one of the most unabashedly-disturbing pieces of children's literature of all time. Steve Buscemi replaces Lynde as the erstwhile rat's vocal avatar in Gary Winick's *Charlotte's Web*, a *Babe*-ified live-action version awash with CGI-enhanced and animatronic animals, none less artificial than boggle-eyed Dakota Fanning as soulful farmgirl Fern.

Screenwriter Susannah Grant (she of *faux*-minist uplift sagas *28 Days*, *In Her Shoes*, *Erin Brockovich*, *Catch and Release*, and so on) writing the adaptation has a certain infernal logic to it, bringing to the project a sense of being pleased with itself that makes the whole thing as inexorable as a coronation march. The better question is whether an adaptation of the book should have been attempted even if the intention of the thing wasn't to bloat it to feature-length with a pair of jive-talking, stoner crows (Thomas Haden Church, André Benjamin), fart jokes, and pratfalls. There's a real dignity to White's novel: its take on inevitability; its calm acknowledgement of doom; its sober celebration of love; and, above everything, the power of words. The book is so much about language that it's a highly questionable endeavor to translate it into a visual medium — almost like a movie version of <u>To the Lighthouse</u>, or anything by Gertrude Stein. It's a project doomed to failure the moment someone like Grant, fond of crass over-statement and wholesale emotional pandering, is tabbed to pen it.

Fern (Fanning) saves runt Wilbur (voiced by Dominic Scott Kay) from her daddy's axe and raises it to the eve of his Christmas martyrdom when kindly barn spider Charlotte (voiced by Julia Roberts) decides to make Wilbur her project. She starts weaving laudatory words into her web above the barn doors through which Wilbur is framed, thus demonstrating in a weird, wonderful sort of way how rural people are heavily influenced by the things they read. Can *Charlotte's Web* be interpreted as a Christian allegory about the original function of the Bible as an instrument wielded by the literate to "harvest" the illiterate? I guess, but as the picture spends the bulk of its running time with "awww" shots of the pig and innumerable animal pun jokes belched out by everyone from John Cleese (as a sheep) to Kathy Bates (as a cow) to, gulp, Oprah (as a goose), it's fast

indistinguishable from any other relatively innocuous children's flick about making your children callow and mostly harmless. Strange how the best parts of the film are its title sequences, which subtly animate Garth Williams' classic illustrations (they remind of the opening sequence to 1977's *The Many Adventures of Winnie the Pooh*) — the closing one to a saccharine Sarah McLachlan tune that nonetheless captures the spooky inevitability of the source material. Bookending an adaptation of a *literary* children's book that just doesn't hear the music, the only bits that haunt and inspire are, pithily, the bits high on restraint and completely *sans* dialogue. The best way to adapt a book like this is to make it as much a creature of whatever new medium as it is of words in its book form. What remains of Winick's try is a *Charlotte's Web* that, no matter the technological miracles employed in its creation, only comes to life when it has the courage to be dignified. (**WC**)

## DOCUMENTARY

# 49 UP
****/****
*dir.* Michael Apted

A riddle wrapped in an already impossibly complex enigma, the seventh instalment of "The Up Series" examines not only the interconnective tissue that guides our lives, but also what it means, exactly, to know oneself as one ages. At 49, the Uppers have more or less settled into a permanent lifestyle, and they're torn between looking back at five-decade lochs of life and trying to determine what's left. They grew up during a time of immense social upheaval and eventually followed the natural order to become the Establishment themselves. A direct companion piece and counterpoint to *28 Up* (the peak vs. the descent?), *49 Up* finds the subjects once again understanding just how much control they have over this series, their actions to that end now encompassing a desire to keep prying eyes away from their business. Several loudly refuse to allow Apted to film their spouses because it intrudes on their intimate lives; John, meanwhile, returns to the fold after his second fourteen-year hiatus, perhaps only because the recent reality-TV boom has finally offered him a pulpit from which to smirkingly criticize the project. But while this is yet another indication of how much this man hates Apted and his documentaries, it also manages to establish "The Up Series"—and, by extension, the generation John represents—as a trendsetter gradually being replaced by hipper successors. Once again, the Uppers feel annoyed and violated by the camera, but those feelings don't lie with the intrusion itself so much as the fear that they will be anchored to the series' perceived obsolescence—just another reminder (along with receding hairlines, dulling reflexes, and grandchildren) of rapidly-advancing age as they approach the half-century threshold. Notice that the Uppers most open and willing to participate are those who are imbued with "new" presences in their personal lives: Bruce, who now has two children; Nick, remarried; and Tony, who recently acquired his long-desired holiday home in Spain and had a stage production written about his life.

That mutual fear has formed an empathetic bond among the participants. We've only seen them all together twice on film (once at 7, once at 21), and there's little indication that they've socialized with one another much beyond those instances—even Bruce and Neil, such good friends at 42 (derelict Neil lived in Bruce's home for several months and later read at his wedding), have drifted apart. And yet they refer to themselves in relation to each other more often than they have at any other point in the series, usually as "us"—a united front against Apted. Prompted by a question of whether she worries that her son takes after her,

Jackie pulls the filmmaker into an argument, and eventually concludes: "You will edit this as you see fit. I have no control over that. You definitely come across as [saying] this is your idea of what you want to do, and how you see us, and that's how you portray us... This one may be, may be, the first one that's about us, rather than your perception of us." Jackie is responding to Apted's typically sneering attitude towards his trio of East End girls ("I like it when you shout at me" is the last straw), and her statement reflects knowledge that the director's patronization tempts her fellow subjects to fight back.

Interviews and commentary tracks have shown Apted to be by and large a kind, humble fellow—and Jackie finally suspects that his haughtier moments are a put-on, specifically designed to cut through the bullshit and force his subjects to uncover their "true" selves, observer effect be damned. If true, though the gambit worked spectacularly for the filmmaker in 28 Up, Jackie's opened up a whole new line of discussion, that being a question of the "truth" that such manipulation can offer. (Apted continues his train of reverse-psychology here to try to convince unwilling participants: Suzy's segment, the shortest of the bunch, ends with her promise that she will "bow out" of the series, then an abrupt cut to black; and Charles, who apparently attempted to file suit when Apted refused to remove his image from this film, is only given a curt narration that denies us the usual explanation of where he's been since 21.) With that out in the open, the Uppers are once again thrown into a role of indignation, and in finding another way to question Apted's ethics, they've peeled back another layer of reality to reveal yet another aspect of life—the endless cycles of self-awareness. Where it will all lead, of course, will have to wait for 2012 and 56 Up. (**Ian Pugh**)

## THE FOUNTAIN
****/****

*st.* Hugh Jackman, Rachel Weisz,
Ellen Burstyn, Mark Margolis
*w./d.* Darren Aronofsky

As deeply emotional and damnably frustrating as any work of pure individual vision must be, Darren Aronofsky's long-gestating *The Fountain* is officially devastating from about thirty-minutes in and buoyed by its singular vision for the remainder. A film that defines the fatigued term "ambitious," it's the story of Man's need to transcend the physical, to defeat mortality, to address the divine that takes the form of what the director has called "science-fiction for the new millennium." Is it arrogant to seek to redefine an entire genre? No doubt— but it's that exact genus of hubris under the microscope in *The Fountain*, with its three interwoven storylines concerning the courage to explore new worlds armed and shielded only (and enough) by dogged, ragged faith, and so Aronofsky's arrogance becomes, only as it should be, the connective fibre that binds his film together. *The Fountain* is philosophy, posing questions about the nature of art, of communication, of the truly *big* questions of existence. And because it's good philosophy, it doesn't seek to answer the mysteries of our intellectual life, but rather offers as the only humanist answer another mystery: love. It's oblique to the point of opaque for long stretches of its "future" passage (involving the voyage to a nebula wrapped around a dying star in what appears to be a bubble housing a hilltop and a tree) and verges on the brink of camp in "past" segments set during the Age of Discovery and the Spanish Inquisition, yet it finds its core—its thematic and emotional anchor—in the "present" with a research scientist's race against his wife's voracious cancer.

The heroes of all three timelines are explorers played by Hugh Jackman, while Rachel Weisz embodies his inamoratas—and throughout, there's a low hum of grief that plays as familiar and low as a power line arcing overhead. The promise of death is grim as *The Fountain* opens with Conquistador Tomas on the verge of being disembowelled by a Mayan warrior as he comes into the presence of the Biblical Tree of Life—and transcendent in the end as astronaut (Major?) Tom merges an idea of Buddhist Zen with the cycles of suggested reincarnation that pull the picture through its survey of a thousand years of human yearning. It's more than a yarn about coming back, though—it's self-consciously the only story that Man has ever told Himself: the struggle, the journey, and the peace that comes with accepting that some truths surpass understanding. The Sanskrit word "shanti," invoked by T.S. Eliot for the coda to his "Wasteland" (and, as it happens, by Alfonso Cuarón's upcoming *Children of Men*, another accomplished 2006 sci-fi dealing with similar themes) is the articulation of that idea, and it feels as though Aronofsky means to surpass understanding in the final minutes of his film, opening the screen like Bosch's (like Dante's) multifoliate rose of the afterlife and challenging the audience to articulate what has been something like automatic writing.

*The Fountain* is about structures and patterns (within and without)—about love and loss and ambition and cost. It's impossible not to see in it something of the tale of its torturous creation (first as a Brad Pitt vehicle, then, years later, reborn with a budget-halved and a promising career stalled), though it's more fruitful to find in it a universal tale of the thirst for knowledge leading to the benevolent-in-hindsight denial of our right to literal immortality. A love scene in a bathtub is as intimate as the brush of a queen's hand on her champion's brow (accompanied with the promise that she will be his Eve upon his return from Eden) as a phantom's touch projected from the only living thing to another in the middle of an unimaginable gulf. For every moment I could only understand as an intention, there are commensurate moments that sing with sublimity; you leave with the feeling of having seen something that is at once inscrutable and inspirational. At the bottom, *The Fountain* is as elementary and as labyrinthine as a love story—as simple and as ineffable as a passage over water diseased with stars. Of all the things that it is, *The Fountain* is most a singular, ferociously-shepherded vision that, for all its production delays, for all its concessions to censors and producers, possesses a uniqueness and that quality of strangeness that marks great art. It's the product of the fever of ambition and its expression at any personal cost. (**WC**)

**FREE ZONE**
*/****
*st.* Natalie Portman, Hanna Laslo, Hiam Abbass
*w./d.* Amos Gitai

**THE SECRET LIFE OF WORDS**
*1/2/****
*st.* Sarah Polley, Tim Robbins, Javier Cámara, Julie Christie
*w./d.* Isabel Coixet

The not-at-all-hamfisted allegory of an Israeli woman and a Palestinian woman trekking across the disputed land to find an American who will settle some non-specific debt, Amos Gitai's tediously strident *Free Zone* opens with ten minutes, uninterrupted, of Natalie Portman weeping over what we discover to be the end of a love affair. It's showy and about as subtle as a kidney-punch— ditto the conception of Portman's passive Rebecca (Portman), the American on the sidelines, a matinee-beautiful beacon who stands by as impassively as Milton's God. That said, the device of a long, car-bound road trip narrated by flashbacks of the protagonists' separate journeys to this

journey is, at least for a while, intoxicating. The problem—and it's a doozy—is that Gitai's picture is so blatant an allegory that nothing any of the characters say comes free of dramatic distance or irony, making it impossible to take the film seriously as anything other than ventriloquism for Gitai's, let's face it, unsurprising politics. Nothing wrong with Wailing Wall lamentations about the state of the world, but watching someone shake a fist at a dead horse, long past the hope of resurrection, for upwards of two hours, is tiring and futile. Is there traction in proposing that the film merely mirrors the hopelessness of the Middle East conflict? I guess, but then how many people—specifically, how many people renting a film called *Free Zone* directed by Amos Gitai—are going to feel edified by that?

Rebecca hitches a ride with accidental cabbie Hannah (Hana Laszlo), taken along for a casual tributary trip to, oh, I don't know, Jordan, to make *Free Zone* the first Israeli production ever to gain permission to film in a Muslim country. Hostile border guards, suspicious gas station attendants, and lots of wiper blades accompany them on their endless quest for self-discovery, offering along the way a thick, sloppily-bound manifesto penned by Gitai for the benefit of the world of gaffed idiots Gitai imagines will be moved by Yankee Rebecca marvelling at things she's "only read about." It's the distaff equivalent of *Gunner Palace*, where being there lends some imagined power to simple positions already held by most sentient creatures, many of whom are surely gifted with a good deal more eloquence and shame. When Palestinian businesswoman Leila (Hiam Abbass) enters the fray to complete the unholy trinity of Holy Land hijinks, *Free Zone* becomes largely unbearable—and so schematic that without much effort you can imagine the corkboard littered with index cards mapping out the political clashes this cast is asked to act out in their robotic interactions. For me, my palms started tingling with the "slappin' bug" around the tenth time Rebecca complained of her (allegorically) insatiable hunger. Oh, I get it: America is a colonialist asshole made moronic for its greed because the world it covets is a suppurating sty.

More gloom and righteous doom from the indie set as *The Secret Life of Words* trundles centre stage with its closed-room tale of horribly-burned oil rig wildcatter Josef (Tim Robbins), bedridden and in need of the tender ministrations of pallid nurse Hanna (Sarah Polley). Spanish auteur Isabel Coixet casts the picture in a gratifyingly icy glow—would that she'd been content with drilling the opaque mysteries of two badly-damaged human beings forging a tentative, human connection in the middle of a black drink. Alas Coixet, like Gitai, can't resist the meaningful political backstory that will transform her characters into symbols—that is, into ventriloquist dummies rattling off humdrum rhetoric. Not one person in their right mind would find any controversy in the vilification of the Armenian genocide, and hand-in-hand with that, I'd argue that the treatment of the subject should be respectfully circumspect in the manner of Michael Haneke instead of shrill in the manner of Atom Egoyan. Bad enough to reward patience with inadequate epiphanies, what *The Secret Life of Words* does is lull with a certain *Breaking the Waves* tonal ode before reducing itself to a Phoebe Cates-in-*Gremlins* denouement all of unearned shock and awkward pathos. A *City Lights*-esque epilogue wherein blasted Josef, freshly-sighted (take note!), proceeds to *see* his heavily-accented ladylove by digging into her past and forcing her, and us, to endure another abysmal lecture, chiefly reminds that while you *think* you might be safe renting a UK-financed film with an American star (and a Canuck one, admittedly) and a Spanish writer/director, Canadian movies can be made anywhere in the world. (**WC**)

## FREEDOMLAND
**\*\*/\*\*\*\***
*st.* Samuel L. Jackson, Julianne Moore, Edie Falco, Ron Eldard
*sc.* Richard Price, based on his novel
*dir.* Joe Roth

Given that Joe Roth (*America's Sweethearts, Christmas with the Kranks*) directed it, Freedomland's first and biggest surprise is that it's not worse than it is. Maybe that has something to do with Samuel L. Jackson delivering his best performance since *Changing Lanes,* or a Richard Price screenplay (adapted from his own novel) that, while overwritten throughout and unforgivably histrionic by its end, manages to present its tensions with topicality and a passing familiarity, at least, with the complexities of race relations. It's deliberately set in 1999, just a few years after South Carolina mommy Susan Smith drowned her two children in a lake and blamed a non-descript "black man" in a knit cap for their carjacking/abduction, and the similarities to the Smith story continue through to incredulity in the black community and the involvement of activist parental groups. (Freedomland meanwhile takes place a decade after another case it seems to be based on: Bostonian Charles Stuart killing his pregnant wife and blaming a black guy, stirring nearby black suburb Roxbury to outrage.) Marc Klaas to the film's Susan Smith is child-safety advocate Karen Collucci (Edie Falco), while the New Jersey barrens—and, in its narrative fulcrum, a burned-out children's asylum called "Freedomland"—stand in for the wilds of the Deep South. The picture abounds with such similes and ironies, existing in a bizarre, terrifying version of the United States where iron-willed armies of the bereaved march through the blighted wastes of urban decay with sticks and resignation, looking for lost children they know, more likely than not, to be dead and, more, victims of their own parents.

You could call it a portrait of guilt, a war metaphor, or, broader, a journal of our divisive plague years stretching from the deaths of Malcolm X and Martin Luther King to Rodney King and O.J. Simpson. But at its heart, Freedomland is a dark fairy tale without a moral or, really, a resolution—a hopeless yawp offered up against the ruins of modern racial and cultural relationships. Those looking for an allegory of the Culture Wars could do worse, though by itself its fascination is in neither the martial lockdown of its underprivileged black neighbourhood Armstrong nor the quick, bigoted response of the wronged underprivileged white neighbourhood Gannon (detective Danny Martin (Ron Eldard) calls Armstrong a "jungle" where one of the "monkeys" got loose—all in front of his black superior officer), but rather in detective Lorenzo Council's (Jackson) role as sandwich meat stuck traversing the no-man's land between defender of his race and upholder of a broader, perhaps anti-black, public justice. He's a black man standing in the middle of lynch mobs on both sides (in place of the white men in the Wells and Stuart cases), trying to figure out whether coked-out, red-eyed charity case Brenda (Julianne Moore, losing another child in another melodrama) is telling the truth about her four-year-old boy getting carjacked by a nondescript black dude in the middle of something called "Martyr's Park." Sure enough, the first shot of the film is a wailing Brenda with stigmata on her hands, stumbling into an emergency room, the symbolism broad and lost on no one: Brenda will be put on the cross for this nation's ills though she almost certainly knows not what she does. Would that we were allowed the same level of ignorance, however, as Roth and Price conspire to underscore every nuance of their piece with fireworks and a brass band. A final monologue from Brenda in one of those pale green interrogation scenes stretches for close to ten interminable, unbearable minutes of Moore doing what she does best: playing hysterical. It's not a good performance, exactly, but it is an attention-getting one, and failing good, you might as well cause a racket to bully people into the belief that it's good. It's a philosophy Roth himself adopts with every superfluous camera motion and every antic edit, as well as one that Price takes to heart by having his characters wrestle with words like "over-abstain" and "unprecious." Jackson, though, is genuinely excellent (and supported by William Forsythe in a brilliant turn as Council's understated partner), and his scenes with a jailed son (upon whom he mistakes a Tupac tattoo for Buddha), if obvious for the fact of them, are unusually reverent in their execution. There's something broken in the world of Freedomland, just as there's something broken in the United States—enough so that relating an abandoned orphanage for neglected foundlings for this country pinioning between its series of critical junctures makes a certain kind of melodramatic sense. It's a film that would have starred Joan Crawford in another lifetime, doomed for the same cult appeal in a few years hence, yet for a moment in time, the clouds part and a movie like this strives for real significance. If it falls short, blame Moore's completely unsympathetic one-dimensionality, Roth's blazing incompetence, and Price's self-importance. Freedomland is the "Together We Stand" mural that stands in the middle of its Watts: unapologetic yet obvious. It's the Mildred Pierce of the new millennium—the world's loudest whimper. (**WC**)

## FRIENDS WITH MONEY
**\*\*/\*\*\*\***

*st.* Jennifer Aniston, Joan Cusack,

Catherine Keener, Frances
McDormand
w./d. Nicole Holofcener

Nicole Holofcener follows her marginal success *Lovely and Amazing* with the equally marginal failure *Friends with Money*, presenting a series of interpersonal apocalypses as awkward dinner parties and scenes made unwisely at Old Navy by super-successful fashion designers. It's not subtle in its broad strokes, and once the layers of Angelino self-mortification and obfuscation are plumbed, it's not subtle in its character strokes, either. What it is is a caesura in the middle of those pictures that don't care about their characters that's *only* interested in its characters—a film that might be shorthanded as "European" in that nothing much happens as words and glances billow in carefully ventriloquited clouds. It's about how people talk to one another among friends and then lover/confidants on the drive home, and as such it provides a clearer look at conversation in any single exchange than does the whole of *Crash*. *Friends with Money* is a comparison of our intimate with our open lives; in the comparison, it suggests a third persona, an interiority—though not entirely successfully, making it only as good, really, as the conversation that it may itself inspire on the ride home.

Olivia (Jennifer Aniston) is a pothead and maid (and former-middle-school teacher) who steals her upscale clients' beauty products and scams free perfume samples from weary retail clerks. Her titular friends with money, shocked at her fall from a poverty-level profession semi-respected and patronized by rich people to a sub-poverty-level profession patronized exclusively by rich people, endeavour to solve their own perceptual psychoses using her as the catalyst. Holofcener, of course, does the same, marking Olivia as a cipher and a repository (just like race in *Crash*) of upper-class guilt and phantom, retarded, self-satisfied attempts at liberal actualization: a Chauncey Gardener floating in and out of our collective consciousness as a character dumb to class, status, and cash. Finding irony in the casting of super-Friend Aniston as this metaphoric zephyr, one of the richest, most over-exposed people on the planet, is only natural, of course. (That's called "smug" in a certain lexicon—and sure enough.) Aniston's new "friends" are fashionistas Jane (Frances McDormand) and Aaron (Simon McBurney); screenwriters Christine (Catherine Keener) and David (Jason Isaacs); generally wealthy Franny (Joan Cusack) and Mike (Greg Germann); and potential love-interest/skeezeball Mike (Scott Caan), who habitually follows Olivia around on her jobs, screws her, then asks for half the cleaning money.

Holofcener has a way with the Algonquin chitchat in two long dinner sequences but betrays a definite weakness for the unearned fairy-tale ending in concluding *Friends with Money* in the one way that feels the least justified. Its very artificiality serves to cause a reassessment of its entire body, of how the picture has written its observations on behalf of badly-sculpted personality types and cast them accordingly for aging actresses deserving of better than these wax casts of Holofcener's "Sex and the City" icons aged accordingly and retrofit with class sensitivity. Accordingly, Jane's a brittle harridan on the verge of a nervous breakdown, Franny's a warm, big sister-type who takes the wayward "sibling" under her matronly-wing, and Christine is the castrating she-bitch with a *soupçon* of sublimated humanity. The men, though, define them still as gay cuckolds or frigid compulsives or air-headed house-moms—without a hint of irony, I should add, rendering the film a little confused as to what it could actually be better served to be about. *Friends with Money* is crippling narcissism and the Janus of interpersonal relationships at its best and the LA social strata and the sanctification of fecklessness at its worst. I believed Holofcener was on her way to creating something of real value by testing the strength of family bonds in *Lovely and Amazing*, but she takes a step backwards here by trusting the tactile fidelity of her assumed, imaginary daguerreotypes buzzing around one another in contrived, indecipherable orbits. (WC)

## DOCUMENTARY
### FUCK
½*/****
*dir.* Steve Anderson

I have no doubt that a first-rate documentarian could make a smart, provocative film about the sources and uses of the word "fuck." But the thing about first-rate documentarians is, they usually have better things to do. Thus it has been left to one Steve Anderson to do the legwork, resulting in a film that flaunts something far more obscene than the Seven Dirty Words: the self-righteous piety of comedians. Though I have been a lifelong user of the famous four-letter word, I found Anderson's *Fuck* almost completely unbearable, as it brings out a variety of non-experts left and right to get hot-and-bothered about something that almost certainly needs to be appended to a larger issue. Between comics who are all too happy to attack us with their hostile fuck-talk and right-wingers who counter with vicious, repressive hate, it would require a stronger man than I to sit through *Fuck* without feeling completely battered down.

As the title (typically referred to as *F\*\*k*) suggests, the film is overwhelmingly in favour of the expletive and its frequent deployment. Although it lines up several conservative witnesses for the prosecution (Alan Keyes, Michael Medved, Dennis Prager, Pat Boone), it's mostly a free-for-all in praise of the

word that keeps on giving. The problem that arises is one that George Orwell once defined: when it comes to obscenity, people act either more or less offended than they actually are. While I can't understand a nasty blowhard like Prager fearing that his children will hear a simple four-letter word, the rest of the usual suspects (Bill Maher, Ron Jeremy, Janeane Garofalo, Kevin Smith, Hunter S. Thompson) seem so attached to the expression that they've succeeded in completely missing the point. Alas, *Fuck* misses the point right along with them: instead of providing a genuine cultural history of the word, it merely fights to defend the right to repeat it *ad nauseam*.

To be sure, the film fumbles towards a thesis once it gets around to attacking censorship. Lenny Bruce's losing battle against the ever-encroaching Man is invoked, as are the scuffles with the FCC over a broadcast of George Carlin's "Filthy Words" routine; it's strongly implied that "fuck" is highly subversive, and thus prime territory for some first-amendment speechifying. Yet as the word appears to not offend most of the participants, one wonders what exactly they're protecting: surely the First Amendment is under fire for bigger issues than this. What happens is a typically libertarian confusion of personal freedom with actual activism—one is considered to be protecting the American Way simply through doing one's thing and never being challenged on the issue. This self-serving approach to politics is precisely the sort of thing that's doing the Left in: whereas the conservatives are at least proactive about their imbecilic horseshit, the freedom-lovers mainly erect monuments to their thoroughly toothless engagement in "freedom."

In-between, we have Anderson's attempts at "filling out" the interviews: Bill Plympton animations that don't rise to the level of his best work; "Fuck in the News" segments that offer stories on various idiotic censorship efforts; out-of-context quotes from Shakespeare and Voltaire; and assorted effluvia less informative or illustrative than thinly humorous. If one can agree that one shouldn't be restrained from saying "fuck" (and that it ought to be protected free speech), one also has to admit that Anderson and his pro-"fuck" rogue's gallery are a touch obsessed. A documentary entirely revolving around free speech and its opponents might have covered more ground and given a more complete view of obscenity and its discontents, but that's beyond Anderson and his quipster cohorts. What we have here is a dirty joke without a punchline, which might cut it in the clubs but looks a little flaccid in the face of the larger, more important issue. (**TMH**)

G

## GABRIELLE
***½/****

*st.* Isabelle Huppert, Pascal Greggory, Claudia Coli, Thierry Hancisse
*sc.* Patrice Chéreau & Anne-Louise Trividic, based on the novel The Return by Joseph Conrad
*dir.* Patrice Chéreau

It's official: the heritage movie is dead. Long the bane of young rowdies and middlebrow-haters the world over, the form breathed its last breaths earlier this century following a couple of decades of uncritical support. Witness Patrice Chéreau's outstanding literary adaptation *Gabrielle*, which manages to avoid the pitfalls of the genre while simultaneously critiquing its lesser examples. There is no comfort to be had in well-appointed houses or the tasteful appreciation of "the arts"—only, after Joseph Conrad's The Return, a vain and selfish man who uses such accoutrements for his self-aggrandizement. The film snatches away the cheap pleasures of heritage, blowing up its shallow comforts and rocking you in ways a mere "period piece" never could.

Jean (Pascal Greggory) is a puffed-up bourgie who pontificates in obnoxious voiceover. He's proud of his meticulously-culled group of friends, his popular and satisfying dinner parties, and, of course, his wife of ten years, Gabrielle (Isabelle Huppert), whom he gloats over like "a collector values his prized possession." We're consequently delighted to see him destroyed by a Dear John letter from Gabrielle that has him shattering glass and accidentally cutting himself. Of course, he's perplexed when she promptly returns in the hopes of retracting her missive, leading to a *tête-à-tête* that lasts the night and spills over into one of their blessed shindigs.

Right off the bat, the film sets you up for a moneyed letdown. In another context, Jean would be an unambiguous hero having comfortable torment over a romantic tragedy, but Chéreau has primed us that the background in which he luxuriates is about to be zapped. Indeed, Jean's fawning over his social set and smug reduction of women to property are exactly the things at which we must whittle away, making Gabrielle's puncturing a necessary act. After all of Jean's babbling, the film then dwindles into some of the most astoundingly nuanced writing (by Chéreau and Anne-Louise Trividic) ever to grace the genre: not only do husband and wife duke it out, but Gabrielle also has an encounter with panicked servant Yvonne (Claudia Coli) that further muddies the waters. It's best to enter the movie unaware of what goes on in said exchanges; I wouldn't want to ruin the best parts.

Suffice it to say, the director is just as brutal on the aesthetic level, laying waste to the gentle fluidity that is the heritage genre's stock and trade. Instead of indulging in unbroken streams of antiques and costumes, Chéreau jars you with aesthetic shifts: he changes stocks from tinted black-and-white to colour, slaps you in the face with enormous Godardian intertitles, and uses speedy tracking shots that hurtle past the standard-issue objects of desire. The camera is often crammed in the faces of the actors, or recording the skittering, frightened servants as they run to support them. (Like the dialogue, it's an emotional scrimmage that's as languid or brutal as the moment requires.) Watching it a second time, I was amazed at the nuances—in pictures and words—that I had missed the first time around; *Gabrielle* rewards repeated viewings as it does the patient viewer. So mourn not at the corpse of Heritage, for a better sort of adaptation has risen to take its place. (**TMH**)

## GLORY ROAD
½* /****

st. Josh Lucas, Derek Luke, Emily Deschanel, Jon Voight
sc. Christopher Cleveland & Bettina Gilois and Gregory Allen Howard
dir. James Gartner

## LAST HOLIDAY
* /****

st. Queen Latifah, LL Cool J, Timothy Hutton, Gérard Depardieu
sc. Jeffrey Price & Peter S. Seaman, based on the screenplay by J.B. Priestley
dir. Wayne Wang

There are two big laughs in Disney/Jerry Bruckheimer's African-American *Hoosiers*, *Glory Road*. The first comes when some white guy says derisively, "Can you imagine what basketball dominated by Negroes would look like?", while the sight of defeated Kentucky coaching legend Adolph Rupp (Jon Voight), vilified by history perhaps unfairly (though there's no question that he's vilified unfairly by this film), mourning the loss of the National Championship Game to an upstart team prompts the second. Both moments speak to the biggest problems in a film riddled with little ones: the former because it makes the audience complicit in—and comfortable with—the picture's callousness and casual blanket racism, and the latter because everything that happens in the film is already a foregone conclusion. The only appeal left is rooted in seeing the black players put on exactly the kind of degrading sideshow the picture suggests they're too human for. *Glory Road* is smug, offensive, and ignorant in the way that films with no self-awareness are ignorant—wrapped in a story designed specifically to make people cheer and believe that this one game in 1966 changed peoples' attitudes towards African-Americans in sports instead of simply bolstering the idea that the black athlete was

advantageous and alien rather than just merely alien.

The point illustrates itself early on as Coach Haskins (Josh Lucas) moves his ornamental reaction shot of a wife (Emily Deschanel) and kid (kids? Who knows) to the men's dorm of little Texas Western University in taking over the school's moribund men's basketball program. With no recruiting budget, resourceful Haskins resorts to acquiring seven young black men from across the country (out of his own pocket, it's suggested—so much is suggested and so little demonstrated that the picture's narrative outline must've looked like an ink blot) to institutional asides of "we don't want no nigger ball here," referring to the undisciplined playground style of basketball believed to be played by a race too stupid to learn the nuances of Dr. Naismith's game. Soon enough, after the requisite training montage that includes a lot of running and very little instruction, point guard Bobby (Derek Luke) says, "C'mon coach, you gotta let us play *our* game." Said "game," of course, proved to be superior and is augmented in true Jerry Bruckheimer-style (producer of this and the identically muddy *Remember the Titans*) by Magic Johnson/"Showtime" Lakers-era alley-oops off the glass, in-your-face theatrics, and reverse slam-dunks. It's the equivalent in knuckle-headedness of the heroine in the simultaneously-opening *Tristan & Isolde* somehow channelling John Donne poetry from hundreds of years into the future. These films don't know any other way to give their characters currency and figure that their targeted audiences won't know or care about the difference.

Supporters of *Glory Road* are interested in history insofar as it can be ground up and shoved into a sausage skin for ease of consumption, orally or otherwise. It suggests that once Haskins arrived at the El Paso campus, he brought with him the first black folks these crackers (other epithets used by the black heroes for their white teammates include "honkey" and "Green Acres" and "Jethro, Ellie May, and Uncle Jed" before their victims protest that at least on the team, *they're* the minorities) ever laid eyes on when the school had not only tentatively integrated in the fifties, but had already featured three black players on the basketball team, too. (The team that evil, monolithic Kentucky (which itself tried to recruit legendary, and black, Wes Unseld in 1964, two years prior to the events of the film) beat to play Western Texas in the finals, in fact, featured four-out-of-five black players in the starting line-up.) Important to few, Haskins won the title in his sixth year as coach, not his first—but important to me is a fictional pre-game pep talk that has Haskins expounding at length about how "everyone" thinks the team is a bunch of monkeys. That's pretty risky stuff in a film that itself skirts along the edge of being patronizing exploitation. Soft-sold is the way that the players were essentially imprisoned in their dorms so as not to disturb the rest of the campus: forward Dave Lattin (Schin A.S. Kerr in the film), a year removed from the Big Game, offered that "it's a funny place. On the basketball court you're groovy people, but off the court you're animals. Even the Mexicans look down on you." (Jack Olsen, "The Black Athlete," SPORTS ILLUSTRATED, July 15, 1968, pp. 30-43). (And speaking of Mexicans, there's one on the team so marginalized that he functions as befuddled wallpaper. Power to the people, my brothers.) The requisite ball-breaking earth mama figure is here, too, pushing her son to become a student athlete and scholar. In truth, Haskins received a lot of heat for the academic performance of his recruits:

*Winning the title focused national attention on the school, and what was discovered embarrassed Haskins. Most of the Texas Western players were either failing academically, or worse,*

*being carried by the school to keep them eligible. Haskins was publicly accused of exploiting his Black recruits for his own glory. For the first time the question of the intellectual cost of athletic integration was being raised. Yes, a basketball scholarship got these brothers into college. But what good did it do them if they made no progress to a degree?* (Nelson George, Elevating the Game, Harper Collins, 1992, pg. 137)

The problems solved by *Glory Road* are problems still. The NBA instituted a dress code this year in an unspoken effort to align the "thug" culture of modern basketball with the expectations of its largely white upper-middle-to-upper class audience. Philadelphia 76ers star Allen Iverson, tattooed, 'do-ragged, and the bane of conservative white culture, told the PHILADELPHIA DAILY NEWS that "just because you put a guy in a tuxedo, it doesn't mean he's a good guy." But more central to the issue are comments made by Rob Manfred, executive vice president of labour relations and human resources for Major League Baseball, when asked whether the MLB was considering following suit: "Because of the nature of our travel and the *makeup of our employees*, it has never been an issue that we had to centrally regulate." (Italics ours.) What *Glory Road* does is exacerbate difficult issues by blowing them into a sugared bauble of underdog sports clichés and, more damning, race caricatures and slapstick, sitcom misunderstandings and rapprochements, all excused as artifacts of some distant past. Whites are soulless and stiff, blacks are soulful and groovy; a scene on a bus where the whites compare music with the blacks is paid off with Lattin pulling out a giant speaker to demonstrate, what, that blacks liked their boomboxes even in the '60s? Between its wall-to-wall soundtrack of Motown-for-happy/Gospel-for-serious, its tacked-on love affair, its stock, gloriously-underwritten performances, and its badly-shot and context-less game re-creations, *Glory Road* is a mostly-fabricated feel-good flick about bigotry and the painful integration of America's public institutions.

Evil in a different way, Queen Latifah's latest turn as champion of the underclass is a remake of a little-known Alec Guinness starrer from 1950, *Last Holiday*. In it, find Guinness' George Bird transformed into sass-dispenser Georgia Byrd (Latifah), a house wares clerk in a department store (at least she's not wearing her house-mammy uniform from *Bringing Down the House*) who discovers that she has three weeks to live and proceeds to blow her savings at an exclusive resort in the Czech Republic, where everyone on the street speaks French. (French equals class and expense, Czech equals kidnapping and ransom, I guess.) The early part of the film is shot in pre-deluge New Orleans, lending the piece a good deal of gloomy irony as the very religious Byrd (she has a running monologue with God, throughout) thanks her maker at the end for allowing her to fulfill her dream of opening a restaurant in the Big Easy. The message of the piece is less Marxist, though, than it is confirmation that the best things in life aren't free, but in fact very, very expensive—and, moreover, worth it, baby. Byrd's initial repressed spinster-ism (she cooks a gourmet meal...well, an Emeril meal, takes a picture, and then pops in a Lean Cuisine instead) mutates into a sort of Bagger Vance font of down-home wisdom post-diagnosis, using her temporary wealth as the means through which to tug the ears of congressmen and business magnates with her brand of chicken soup for the soul. Georgia saves the world one Abramoff at a time.

It's a remake of not only the Guinness original, then, but also *Joe vs. the Volcano* and *Short Time*. A series of wailing protestations sees Georgia taking on the church, the government, the airlines, the broken healthcare system, and, curiously, the proletariat afflictions of having to wait in line. *Last Holiday* is one part self-defeating social commentary and one part *Being There* naïf tomfoolery as Latifah, her body-shape often the only punchline, snowboards and base-jumps for the purposes of inspiring rich people. Money can't buy love, except that it can—the picture's self-righteous message concerning the evils of capitalism in its palm-crossed politicos deflated utterly by its message that spending great amounts of cash on yourself is guaranteed happiness. After a night at the roulette table leaves Georgia one-hundred grand richer, the intention of the film is brought home with force as one remembers that she's at a charity event and that this hundred grand, especially in the hands of a terminally-ill woman about to die, would certainly benefit the less-fortunate more than another dress-up montage will. *Last Holiday* is the filmic equivalent of getting people to vote against their own fiscal self-interests—and if I can't be bothered to discuss the huge crush that co-wage slave Sean (LL Cool J) nurses for Georgia, leading to a weird climax wherein Sean appears to have frozen to death on a glacier, count yourself lucky. It doesn't make any sense (and neither does Gérard Depardieu as a smitten chef or poor Susan Kellerman as Frau Blücher), though what does strike a chord is the idea that to change the world, you gotta be loaded—and that once you're loaded, you're probably loath to change the system that got you there. Isn't that right, Ms. Latifah? You go girl. (**WC**)

## GOING TO PIECES: THE RISE AND FALL OF THE SLASHER FILM
\*\*\*/\*\*\*\*

My cardinal rule about documentaries:

they shouldn't just coast on the *gravitas* of their subject matter. They have to have some kind of perspective and work on their own terms. With that said, documentaries about movies are a bit of a blind spot for me, as I have a particularly strong difficulty separating my affection for the film and my affection for what it's about. I know that *This Film Is Not Yet Rated* isn't very good—it's childish and doesn't mount a terribly convincing case against the MPAA. But come on, I could talk for hours about the MPAA if I could find somebody who would want to listen. *Cinemania*? Yeah, the filmmakers didn't do much more than point and laugh at those guys. God help me, though, I had a little envy for them: I only *wish* I could theatre-hop in New York City, exclusively watching the films that interest me without worrying about money or having to review them. I could feel that my critical capacities were being tested in these cases, but I survived. However, when you have a documentary that isn't about merely the movies, but about *slasher* movies specifically—well, shit, any pretense of objectivity on my part has officially gone out the window.

*Going To Pieces: The Rise and Fall of the Slasher Film* (hereon simply *Going to Pieces*) is very information-oriented. There isn't any real intercourse between the subject and the filmmakers, who neither seek nor capture the bits of poetry that may exist between the lines. The film does seem to violate my cardinal rule about documentaries, though I'm beginning to question whether that's a meaningful way to approach non-fiction filmmaking. I feel obliged to tell you that *Going to Pieces* is not good art—not as good as, say, *Visions of Light: The Art of Cinematography*, or even *Midnight Movies: From the Margin to the Mainstream* (also produced by and for the Starz! Channel). Then again, does it really matter if it's good art? Is that what we're looking for when we watch a documentary?

Documentarians Rachel Belofsky, Rudy Scalese, and Michael Bohusz (the film doesn't appear to have a proper director, with Belofsky and Scalese credited as producers and Bohusz as editor) share an infectious love of slasher cinema. They successfully avoid the monotony of a conventional talking-head documentary by shooting their interviews outdoors in a dark alley or at a cemetery with a constantly-moving camera. There are tons of well-chosen film clips and a bunch of cheesy gags like quoting Ennio Morricone in cueing a "Spaghetti Slasher" title card. It's not much, but it gives the film a bit of a kick and shows that the filmmakers care enough about the material to not go on autopilot.

Criticism of the genre is answered with a certain amount of defensiveness. A special episode of "Sneak Previews" with Roger Ebert and Gene Siskel devoted entirely to slasher films is featured, wherein Siskel theorizes that the genre's misogyny is a reaction to the Women's Movement. Panel members counter that in slashers, women are oftentimes the killer and men actually make up the majority of the victims. Thing about this rebuttal is that it complicates rather than contradicts Siskel's assertion. Siskel is right that the iconology of the slasher film is inherently "pro-rape" and, yes, that the genre itself is a reaction to feminism. Yet it's a more sophisticated reaction to feminism than he thinks, since it indicates that we'll know women are truly equal to men once we have a female Ted Bundy. The female serial killer is a hypothetical, of course, but the icon is useful for systematically revealing the deficiencies of a cultural movement founded on liberation or, more disturbingly, "empowerment."

I'm not sure where they could have done so, but it would've been nice if Belofsky, et al had incorporated a moment from the "Sneak Previews" broadcast during which the two critics heap praise on *Halloween* and explain why it is exempt from their criticism.

"Artistry redeems any subject matter," Ebert offers. Evidently this is because the artful *Halloween* works on the "intended" level of a thriller. When a slasher film isn't done as well as *Halloween,* all that you pick up on is the subtext. Strangely enough, the film is done so well that it blinded Siskel and Ebert to the fact that it's as much about rape as any other film in the genre. Not too long ago, Ebert said that anybody who watches every selection on the AFI Top 100 Movies list would never want to see another Dead Teenager Movie, something he defines as "a movie that starts out with a lot of teenagers, and kills them all, except one to populate the sequel." I wrote in to point out that he awarded *Halloween* four stars. He graciously responded in his "Answer Man" column that *Halloween* isn't a Dead Teenager Movie, despite the fact that his definition of the genre fits it to a T.

Still, there's a definite distinction between *Halloween* and what followed. Belofsky, et al credit—correctly, I think—*Friday the 13th* for putting the emphasis on gore effects and implicitly encouraging audiences to empathize with the killer. They cynically deliver that which you came for, turning artistry into an unnecessary expenditure. After a few years of this, slasher fans grew bored and wanted something more. Enter Wes Craven's witty and adept *A Nightmare on Elm Street,* the film that revitalized the dying slasher genre and was such a phenomenon that it helped transform boogeymen like Michael Myers, Jason Voorhees, and Freddy Krueger into bona fide pop icons. From there the slasher genre grew increasingly silly. It died out and was then resuscitated by Craven's accomplished *Scream,* which understood precisely how silly the slasher had become. The film doesn't outline this quite so clearly, but thanks to *Scream,* the slasher was suddenly truly mainstream, and the typical fan now drank Zima and wore Abercrombie & Fitch. The sequels to *Scream* were literally about as scary as

an episode of "Dawson's Creek". We even started seeing slasher flicks with a PG-13 rating. As a reaction to this, we have the stirrings of the "torture porn" sub-genre, an attempt to be divisive within a genre that is now permanently in the public eye.

So who is responsible for the demise of the genre? Belofsky and co. don't really know. They love their subject so much that they're reluctant to assign blame. *Friday the 13th* demonstrated that films don't need to be stylish in order to be successful, they only need to have inventive kills. (The creators of *Going to Pieces,* mind you, unabashedly love *Friday the 13th* for what it is.) Post-*A Nightmare on Elm Street,* we get the "fall of the slasher film" montage. Indeed, *A Nightmare on Elm Street* did give us Freddy Krueger lunchboxes, but hey, that's pretty cool—and besides, it was a fine film made by a former professor of humanities attempting to explore the burden of consciousness.

*Going to Pieces* goes over the slasher genre's roots in the Theater of the Grand Guignol and moves on to the respective geneses of *Halloween, Friday the 13th,* and *Prom Night* (?!). There are segments on the "rules" of the slasher film, on how some producers actually looked through the calendar for a holiday to make a film about, and of course on the sociological underpinnings of the genre. John Carpenter's claim that *Halloween* was a product of the Carter administration is a real head-scratcher, but I loved his suggestion that the genre's extreme violence was a reaction to the "body culture" of the 1980s. The idea that the films were about youth paying for the sins of the '60s and that *Halloween* and the *Nightmare on Elm Street* films in particular were about the violation of suburban sanctuaries holds up especially well.

Ultimately, *Going to Pieces* lacks a coherent thesis. It basically throws up everything it can think of relating to the thirty-year history of slasher film and leaves it to us to sort out. There's an objectivity to the approach that protects the filmmakers not only from having to personalize their subject matter but also from exposing their arguments as naïve or possibly wrong. I can't say that it's a *challenging* moviegoing experience. And yet, with a genre as disreputable as this one, that might be the best approach. It's perhaps the perfect primer for those not familiar with slasher cinema in the sense that you can't help but wanting to fill your Netflix queue with nothing but slasher titles afterwards, and it provides you the fodder to form your own opinion of the genre. You can't ask for much more than that as far as I'm concerned. (**AJ**)

## THE GOOD GERMAN (see: *THE PAINTED VEIL*)

## THE GOOD SHEPHERD (see: *THE PAINTED VEIL*)

## A GOOD YEAR
½*/****
*st.* Russell Crowe, Albert Finney, Marion Cotillard, Freddie Highmore
*sc.* Marc Klein, based on the book by Peter Mayle
*dir.* Ridley Scott

## HARSH TIMES
**/****
*st.* Christian Bale, Freddy Rodriguez, Eva Longoria, Terry Crews
*w./d.* David Ayer

*The Fighting Temptations, The Family Man*—the list of sappy redemption flicks about terrible assholes is as long and lamentable as Ridley Scott's interminable *A Good Year*. Masquerading as a man-opause version of *Under the Tuscan Sun*, it is instead an incredibly cynical play for exactly the kind of audience Scott and Russell Crowe don't reach and,

apparently, shouldn't bother trying to seduce. Imagine a light, frothy romantic comedy written by Dostoevsky and directed by David Lean: every pratfall registers like a cattle stampede, every delightful romantic misunderstanding like a nuclear disarmament talk. Meanwhile, all around it, golden-drenched landscape shots of Provence play the part of the grinning idiot, dancing like crazy to distract the potentially-duped. (Scott at his best works in palettes drained of warmth and heat. Even the sunny *Thelma & Louise* plays like twenty miles of rough road compared to *A Good Year*'s pretty postcards and stultifying stereotypes.) With the whole mess paying off in the most unlikely and irritating sequence of happy endings in a film not directed by Garry Marshall (or his Limey equivalent, Richard Curtis), the choices are either that you believe Scott and Crowe to have lost their minds or that *A Good Year* is smug and strident for the very reason that its creators are supercilious jackasses long since detached from any notion of the possible. Moreover, the picture demonstrates a marked disdain for those poor sods who aren't millionaire stockbrokers or possessed of dead uncles with a sprawling villa to will to their heirs.

Said man-of-privilege Max Skinner (Crowe) gets a soul by mack'ing a hot local (Marion Cotillard) in a calendar panorama. Flashbacks to Max's bucolic childhood on the knee of his late uncle (Albert Finney) try pretty hard to humanize Max yet are more successful in pissing off anyone in the audience hoping their lives won't be bled through their eyeholes with a cash-baited hook. Max represents the modern fantasy of the emasculated male seeking redemption from a life of earning reams of money through discovering the value of rosebuds and gathering them while he might. It's the Oedipal detective story where the quarry is the hidden self; stories like this are at their heart puerile and indistinct, all the more so when the resolution is happy instead of a tragedy of regression and arrest. It's unfair to say that *A Good Year* is a failure at everything because the hard truth is that *A Good Year* — an excuse to visit a nice part of the world on someone else's dime — is every bit the misanthropic, remote bit of genre hijacking it intends to be. On a scale of scandal, it's not up there with Enron, I guess, but add it up and the money being siphoned off by people who know that they're making market-engineered bullshit for the almost-exclusive joy and admiration of their agents, bankers, and accountants is actually pretty damned scandalous. One thing to produce bad art with good intentions, another thing altogether to knowingly manufacture a broken product using someone else's blueprints for the express purpose of jilting old people and lonely women out of their money.

Look closely at David Ayer's L.A. story *Harsh Times* and you'll see a similar story of a man emasculated by the world who finds his actual self in the arms of a beautiful woman in a foreign country. But Ayer's has hero Jim (the ubiquitous Christian Bale) pull a gun on his pretty señorita (Tammy Trull, bound for stardom) after she makes the bad mistake of telling him she's pregnant and, worse, expressing hopes for a future with him. A former Army Ranger with a bad habit of getting fucked up, being a bad influence on his buddy Mike (Freddy Rodríguez), and having flashbacks to his own coming-of-age killing "hajis" indiscriminately and brutally in some vague Middle Eastern battleground, Jim is clearly insane and, as played by Bale, barely able to mask his fear and anxiety with a swig of liquor and sudden bursts of violence. Like Michael Mann's recent urban anatomizations *Collateral* and *Miami Vice*, *Harsh Times* peels away the layers of civilization we use to create a palimpsest of our simian natures. The cycle of action-reaction, culminating in an ending here that speaks of rough grace and what can only be a brief sanctuary, is punctuated with a poetic but authentic sense of how men talk each other into and out of things, of the dual Freudian temper of the masculine perception of women, and of how it's all just about roving tribes of apes intersecting one another to no good consequence.

*Harsh Times* is overblown melodrama. Bale's performance is ridiculous and sublime in the same moment while Ayer's screenplay and direction are hyperbolic to the point of genuine hysteria. It is in its way as much of a soap opera as *A Good Year*, as much the fable of man pinioned squirming on the end of a point. Still, at the heart of the piece is the reality that men can be really stupid, pumped full of sperm and vinegar, and retarded to the point of incoherence when goaded by one another into honouring imaginary codes and arbitrary rules of conduct. It's *noir* rewritten as chaos and decay, with the man looking for structure in the wasteland, an illiterate psychopath only really qualified to go into law enforcement. Too reductive to say that *Harsh Times* is just another *Training Day* for Ayer — better to identify the piece as a cartoon about what masculinity looks like in the first few years of the new millennium: unmoored and anxious at home, enraged and indiscriminately murderous abroad, and dreaming of quiet somewhere golden and impossibly far away. (**WC**)

# D O C U M E N T A R Y
## THE GROUND TRUTH
\*\* / \*\*\*\*
*dir.* Patricia Foulkrod

Too often I feel that critics and audiences place documentaries at the kid's table, refusing to critique them on the same level they do fiction films. Narration from the director, sit-down interviews with the subjects — in terms of filmmaking, we let documentaries get away with a lot of really primitive shit we probably wouldn't otherwise. Patricia Foulkrod's *The Ground Truth* is a pretty good rant, but not much of a movie; Foulkrod made it because she had a burning desire to say something, not because she had a burning desire to make a film. There's no excitement or joy in the aesthetics, it's all dreadfully utilitarian—just enough to illustrate her thesis without unduly affecting the audience. In part because there's no narrative, *The Ground Truth* doesn't have any dramatic high points, either: for the entire duration, it rumbles on the same low growl. Still, the film gets you good and angry, and because it's in that emotionally and cinematically vacant tradition of documentary-making called "objectivity," you know that you're getting angry off the ideas in it. The film is about how post-traumatic stress disorder is undiagnosed and untreated among veterans of the second Gulf War and how the media's whitewashing of the war's civilian casualties only exasperates the situation. If we were to truly "support the troops," we would have to acknowledge the damage they have caused the Iraqi people as well as the toll this has taken on their minds, hearts, and souls, to say nothing of their support for the actual war. To suppress the evil (necessary or otherwise) of the second Gulf War is an act of wilful naivety and a deflation of our troops' sacrifice. It's pitiful that a film like *The Ground Truth* had to be made, but it did. (**AJ**)

**THE GUARDIAN (see: *SCHOOL FOR SCOUNDRELS*)**

**A GUIDE TO RECOGNIZING YOUR SAINTS**
***½/****
st. Robert Downey Jr., Shia LaBeouf, Chazz Palminteri, Rosario Dawson

w./d. Dito Montiel

Dito Montiel's *A Guide to Recognizing Your Saints* (hereafter *Guide*) is exhibit A in the case against neophytes attempting the kind of blood-red braggadocio that Walter Hill brought to *The Warriors*. Unlike Hill, who's made a career out of examining male relationships and their place in the formation and evolution, such as it is, of society (suddenly, Hill is something like the quintessential director for the post-apocalyptic new millennium in American pictures; do *Miami Vice* or the *Bourne* flicks or even science-fiction laments like *Sunshine* or *The Fountain* find rhetorical counterpoint in their fully-furnished bleakness without Hill?), Montiel is all earnest overcompensation, molding wordy Bukowski out of his personal disasters. That being said, there are moments of real grace in *Guide*, chief examples a scene with a mentally-defective brother and an elevated train as well as a reunion between the Prodigal and his ailing, bellicose father. Indeed, it's hard to determine why there isn't more time spent with the crux of these moments: Channing Tatum as Dito's unbalanced childhood pal Antonio and Robert Downey Jr. as the adult Dito.

The problem with the film has a lot to do with its lack of balance—its inability to separate the tang of what's meaningful to nostalgia from the piquancy of what could be *true* in the story. You know what I really love? I love the scenes with young people in the middle of a hot New York summer, talking to one another like panthers circling. It's a short trip to *Guide* becoming a shot of religion like Coppola's *The Outsiders* (a film to which it bears a lot more resemblance than it does to the oft-cited *Mean Streets*): a blue trip down a melancholy byway. Not so good are those times when it puffs up its chest like its teen outcast toughs and starts acting like the movies it wants to be instead of contenting itself with the movie that it is. *Guide* is beautifully-shot and well-acted (sometimes extraordinarily acted (Tatum, Downey Jr.)) and it sports a lovely if obvious period soundtrack—yet there's a bluster to it that undoes its gorgeous discomfort. A more mature filmmaker makes a better film—though I don't know if a different filmmaker captures the moments of devastated human splendour Montiel captures here. (**WC**)

# H

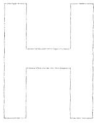

**HALF NELSON (see: *THE ILLUSIONIST*)**

A N I M A T E D
**HAPPY FEET**
***/****
sc. George Miller, John Collee, Judy Morris, Warren Coleman
dir. George Miller

For no other purpose, really, than that I loved its unabashed perversity and darkness, I used to make an annual ritual of watching George Miller's *Babe: Pig in the City*. The image of Mickey Rooney in full clown regalia, sopping at an ice cream cone, is the stuff of nightmares, as well as a marvellous example of how much Aussie director George Miller got away with halfway around the world from his financiers. As a kid's show, *Babe II*'s success has a lot to do with it recognizing how familiar is fear and isolation in the life of a youngster, and providing solutions to things that alarm instead of denying their existence. Watching the director's latest, *Happy Feet*, the moment Mumble (voiced by Elijah Wood, danced by Savion Glover) woke up in a zoo after an odyssey in pursuit of a commercial fishing vessel and was told by his inmate, a HAL-voiced fellow penguin, "Try the water, Dave. The water's real, Dave," I realized that we were down the same rabbit hole with Miller, seeing zoo animals as insane at best, made so by the drudgery of routine and the inability to communicate with their jailers. It's a fertile image amidst *Happy Feet*'s most fertile passage (and its connection to the Starchild sequence in *2001* is the second such allusion in a film this month (see also: *The Fountain*)), one that ends with Mumble tying the secret

of interspecies understanding to that old minstrel trick of tap-dancing for a very particular audience of otherwise disinterested aliens.

There's a great deal going on in *Happy Feet*. Social castes are flayed bare with a frankness unheard of in polite entertainment as the hero penguin—flawed (retarded, even) in his ability to communicate through song but gifted with funk and that loping, soulful gait of Glover's (an artist who by himself reshaped his medium)—befriends a quintet of "amigos" in the Antarctic barrio. The infant love story at its centre, with Mumble looking for another way to woo his beloved Gloria (Brittany Murphy, who can sing if she can't act), is in fact the MacGuffin of the piece (and an inoffensive, diverting one at that), a nod to convention like the first *Babe*'s struggle to not be eaten and the second's quest for reunion: it's the Latino sidekicks, the African-American leopard seal villain, and the surreal, voice-less killer whales that give the picture its jolt of contemporary maturity. Moreover, *Happy Feet*'s eco-politics are presented cogently and without the embarrassing scolding of mainstream fare like *Fast Food Nation*, while its ultimate hope for a free exchange of ideas in a world forum (the UN features prominently in its last half hour), coloured though they may be by entertainment media and our strange weakness for "cute," is actually genuinely inspirational.

There's a road map to saving ourselves in *Happy Feet* and it has something to do with revelling in difference rather than being repelled by it—of rolling ourselves up in alien culture so that a common language is rooted out. The climax of the picture reminds a great deal—self-consciously, I think—of the Devil's Tower sequence from *Close Encounters of the Third Kind* in that it, too, details the way that artistic expression can lead to a kind of joyous union. Pushing a message as frothy as this one with points scored along political lines and with an almost complete lack of syrupy sentimentality to gum up the works, the film's inevitable box-office victory (penguins are more of a sure thing nowadays than Harry Potter) is cause for celebration, in no small part because Miller is one of the few directors who deserves the freedom to do whatever the hell he wants. If *Happy Feet* is more pedestrian in its middle sections and clearly compromised (Robin Williams, anyone?), it still has more meat on its bones than any number of CGI fantasias from this year's bumper crop and, better, holds the promise that there's a *Pig in the City* waiting in the wings. **(WC)**

## HARD CANDY
**\*\* /\*\*\*\***
*st.* Patrick Wilson, Ellen Page, Sandra Oh, Odessa Rae
*sc.* Brian Nelson
*dir.* David Slade

## THE KING
**\*1/2/\*\*\*\***
*st.* Gael García Bernal, Laura Harring, Paul Dano, William Hurt
*sc.* Milo Addica & James Marsh
*dir.* James Marsh

SPOILER WARNING IN EFFECT. Arriving on DVD with its cult status in the bag, *Hard Candy* was inspired by a Japanese crimewave that found underage girls posing as prostitutes to bait wealthy businessmen they subsequently drugged, robbed, and in some cases tortured. I think I'd rather see that movie—in dealing more with entrapment than with vigilantism, it probably wouldn't want for integrity like this one does. *Hard Candy* pulls its punches too often for its own good (mainly, it would appear, in the interest of sustaining momentum, pendulum-like), and its literalmindedness only makes things worse. The picture's chiaroscuro *tableaux* brazenly paraphrase Edward Hopper, for instance, and lest there be any doubt about artistic intentionality, the two lost souls at the centre of this chamber piece arrange to meet at Nighthawks Diner. But then a T-shirt with Hopper's seminal "Nighthawks" silkscreened onto it turns up as part of the narrative, which is overkill and self-defeating besides, as in reducing Hopper to a decal, *Hard Candy* itself becomes kitsch.

Alas, highly-topical, overly-equivocating pseudo-satires are a little played-out. Not that *Hard Candy* is a snark-fest like *Saved!* or *Pumpkin*, but in its reliance on the *deus ex machina*, grotesque caricatures (see: Sandra Oh's soccer mom), and teenage ego-stroking, it's comparably puerile. In *Hard Candy*, an online flirtation between 14-year-old Hayley (Ellen Page, capturing a bit of Maria Falconetti in her close-ups), a.k.a. Thonggrrrl114, and thirtysomething shutterbug Jeff (Patrick Wilson), a.k.a. Lensman319, culminates in a rendezvous at Jeff's sanctuary, an Art Deco bungalow where he photographs—and maybe victimizes—his jailbait models. Hayley, a self-styled decoy in the "To Catch a Predator" mold, commits to emasculating Jeff (and all that that implies), steadfast in the belief that he has sufficiently incriminated himself through his passive-aggressive responses to her Lolita shuck-and-jive. Though name-checked Roman Polanski's violation of Samantha Geimer is indefensible, I'm loathe to the wellspring of adolescent sanctimony surrounding the episode; and for a while, Hayley is so insufferably self-righteous that the picture looks as though it will concentrate the brunt of its commentary on the hysteria attendant to allegations of child molestation, credibly channelling the worst tendencies of organizations such as Perverted Justice through that most moralistic of creatures: the pubescent female.

What has tongues wagging is the *tour-de-force* castration sequence, although it's hard to imagine a scenario in which a castration sequence *wouldn't* wind up being the focal point of the conversation. (We're not that jaded yet.) *Misery* by way of Miike, it earns every ounce of dread leading up to it, and the denouement of this set-piece—Hayley flushing a pair of testicles down a garbage disposal—left me crestfallen in a way that no movie has since the destruction of the figurines in *Dogville*. And yet I wasn't *offended* until Jeff subsequently groped at his nether regions and relievedly declared, "I'm all here!"—we've been punk'd. Perhaps with an eye on the Sundance brass ring, the film actively renounces its low-budget privilege to be either a serious meditation on the whole soliciting minors for sex over the Internet phenomenon or quasi-feminist grindhouse schlock; you can sense that it wants to be talked about more than it wants to actually say anything. Proof lies in Hayley's convoluted rationale for springing her commensurately Byzantine mousetrap: Jeff was an accessory in the slaying of a local girl—the revelation of which retroactively transforms every piece of circumstancial evidence that Jeff is a pedophile into stuffing for a straw man. It clears your conscience of any compassion you may have felt for this prisoner of a suburban Abu Ghraib, for however Jeff's persecution goes down, he's getting his just desserts. *Hard Candy* leaves us to contemplate the antiseptic act of murder and the propriety of biblical revenge.

No surprise that screenwriter Brian Nelson started out as a playwright—*Hard Candy* is not so much small-scale as it is proscenium-bound. That's probably why, as fearless as the two leads are, the theatre-trained Wilson plainly has the home-court advantage: having honed her craft on television, a medium that breaks performances up into mosaic tiles, former child star Page is hung out to dry a time or two by the choice to linger on idiosyncratically perforated

monologues so that the digital colourist (who receives an opening credit) can desaturate the image. Taking this virtual mood lighting into account, director David Slade apparently tried to compensate for the production's lack of resources by turning the staginess of the material into an aesthetic, even though he shoots in the defiantly cinematic Super35 format. It's a misstep, because the film looks all the more derivative of—and thus inferior to—landmarks in the hunter-becomes-prey genre like Ariel Dorfman's "Death and the Maiden" and David Mamet's "Oleanna" as a result. Re-reading Jonathan Rosenbaum's capsule review of *Oleanna*, Mamet's own underrated feature-film adaptation of his play, throws *Hard Candy*'s essential timorousness into sharp relief:

"[T]he two characters are so evenly matched by the dramaturgy that they become Strindbergian antagonists in a life-and-death struggle—equally odious in their authoritarian reliance on institutions to define their own identities and equally crippled by what might be described as their political impotence..."

How I wish *Hard Candy* had the same courage to be ambivalent.

A much less histrionic tale of reckoning, James Marsh's *The King* strives for the same Zen calm as co-screenwriter Milo Addica's similarly lurid *Birth* but comes off as merely protracted. Swallowing his Mexican accent so that he sounds like Pee-Wee Herman's masculine bellhop from *Pee-Wee's Big Adventure*, the overexposed, generally unpleasant Gael García Bernal plays Elvis—no, not *that* Elvis (the pic's cheeky title and scattershot allusions notwithstanding), but a sailor who takes his leave of the Navy and tracks down his deadbeat dad, David (William Hurt, who could only be Bernal's biological father in the same metaverse where Marc Anthony sired

Dakota Fanning), now a pastor living in Corpus Christi. Quickly turned away by the born-again family man, Elvis lures David's oblivious teenage daughter Malerie (the lollipop-like Pell James) into a clandestine affair, leading to a tragicomic *In the Bedroom* confrontation with Malerie's pious brother, Paul (Paul Dano).

When people accuse a movie of being made by a computer, they generally mean that it's drably conventional, prefabricated to a fault; *The King* suggests to me what a computer-generated movie would actually be like: discordant, amoral, and populated with Sims. While the picture has a defensible context for its Martian objectivity, tethered as it is to the sociopathic Elvis' point-of-view (and I suppose on one level, the absence of didacticism is laudable), its detachment doesn't seem entirely by design. It is, however, perhaps what a synthesis of documentarian Marsh's naturalistic impulses and Addica's manifest love for the taciturn cinema of the early-'70s was destined to yield. Text is swapped for subtext in *The King*; characters with implicit motives take implicit courses of action; and the whole thing washes out as a particularly leaden existentialist joke. Cast fruitfully against type as Paul's prim wife, Laura Harring paints a portrait of grief that provides fleeting moments of suture, but the filmmakers' stoicism finally proves insurmountable and indefatigable. (**BC**)

## HARSH TIMES (see: A GOOD YEAR)

## HEADING SOUTH (Vers le sud)
***1/2/****
*st.* Charlotte Rampling, Karen Young, Louise Portal, Ménothy Cesar
*sc.* Laurent Cantet & Robin Campillo, based on short stories by Dany Laferrière
*dir.* Laurent Cantet

*Heading South (Vers le sud)* represents such a departure from the milieu of Laurent Cantet's previous film (2001's brilliant psychological thriller *Time Out (L'Emploi du temps)*) that you can't really say it rounds out a trilogy he started with *Human Resources*. Nevertheless, it resumes his fascination with people in transience, people who've erected complex façades to avoid the repercussions of personal or professional failure; Cantet's pictures are screwball comedies played straight, and we see ourselves reflected in them like Athene saw herself in the water. Thanks to a chilling, if red herring-laden, prologue wherein a Haitian mother tries to "give" her endangered teenage daughter to a respectable-looking islander, a black cloud looms over the piece—and it's just one of the many ways in which Cantet shrewdly exploits Haiti's mystique without falling back on *Serpent and the Rainbow*-isms, paving a road to doom down which three middle-aged spinsters defiantly walk. Wellesley professor Ellen (Charlotte Rampling), willowy Midwesterner Brenda (Karen Young, who gets to deliver possibly the screen's finest erotic monologue since *Persona*), and earthy Montréaler Sue (Louise Portal) are returning guests at a kind of sex resort where they take turns patronizing Legba (Ménothy Cesar), a young gigolo who makes them feel not only beautiful but, critically, maternal, too. (When we first meet Legba, he's curled up in a foetal position on the beach, only to be 'awakened' by Brenda's touch.) Unfolding towards the end of Jean-Claude "Baby Doc" Duvalier's reign of terror, the 1978-set film relies a little too much on a working knowledge of Haiti's political history to sort out its narrative ambiguities, but by the same token, this seems to stave off noble-savage syndrome—of which the characters are guilty but the filmmaker, for a change, is not. (**BC**)

# THE HILLS HAVE EYES
*/****

st. Aaron Stanford, Kathleen Quinlan, Vinessa Shaw, Emilie de Ravin

sc. Alexandre Aja & Grégory Levasseur, based on the screenplay by Wes Craven

dir. Alexandre Aja

Alexandre Aja's follow-up to his hateful-but-effective *High Tension* is a hateful but not particularly effective remake of Wes Craven's *The Hills Have Eyes*. Opening exactly as *Dr. Strangelove* ends, with a montage of mushroom clouds set to soothing WWII-era croons (shock-cut with babies deformed by Agent Orange), the film all but declares itself a sardonic satire of the madness driving the United States' military policy where the original was pretty much a look at the country's simmering caste divide. Aja hopes to draw a line from the atrocities committed in Vietnam to atrocities committed in the desert against enemies of Our Own Making— and along the way, should a throwaway jab at the plight of subsistence miners be hurled and a few mutants get impaled by sharpened American flags, well, so be it. I'm not saying that there's nothing rotten in the state of Denmark, I'm saying that I don't care for a French filmmaker making a contemptuous, smug, proselytizing allegory about the legacy of Yankee colonial/expansionist violence. I don't buy Aja's outrage as anything more than practiced and ill-considered, the equivalent of those sick fuckers who drive around with pictures of aborted fetuses on the sides of their vans or set up haunted houses in their churches with any number of right-winger nightmares. As it doesn't teach anything new in any ways that are imaginative or truly horrifying, only the true believers are gratified, and then only by those same florid, ignorant little jabs.

It follows along the strictures established by the first *The Hills Have Eyes* and other splatter movies as a group of city slickers stop at the creepy last gas station, decide upon a shortcut, and wind up at the mercy of a band of degenerate hillbillies. The sons of the earth this time around are literally birthed from terrestrial wombs, the descendants of miners who refused to evacuate when the military tested nuclear weapons in the New Mexico desert and emerged, Sawney Beane-like, to eat the flesh of their un-mutated brothers. Some of the beauty of the original lay in the ironic paralleling of the family structure of the civvies with that of the muties, but that's jettisoned in this updating along with any kind of character development for the bad guys. (For a film wanting to portray the tragedy of the repressed, it sure does a lot of marginalizing of the repressed.) A rape, the gentle abduction of a baby, and the joyful immolation of head Republican paterfamilias (verily, he identifies himself as such) Big Bob (Ted Levine, seeing the other side in *Silence of the Lambs*) are each carried off with a remarkable lack of tension or investment. I can't say I was rooting for the Cirque du Soleil-ized miners, exactly, only that I was never nervous that the "wrong" good guys were going to get killed: something about the style of it feels squeamish and crowd-pleasing to me. I didn't like *Hostel*, but *Hostel* was at least lawless.

What does get the blood pumping (the end to which Aja both aspires and feels superior to), though, are the vicious murders of the villains in a sequence that can only be described as cynical and pandering. Aja knows that most of the young male (and dumb male) audience for this film will cheer, and sure enough, cheer they do as limp-wristed Democrat Doug (Aaron Stanford) takes up the axe (and that sharpened Old Glory) and does some Old Testament mutant-stomping as the score swells patriotically. But Aja also believes that the rabble being roused by his rabble-rousing is proof that America is driven by a degenerate Old

West manifest philosophy rather than evidence that he not only has not made his point to anyone who needs to hear it, but has become part of the problem, too. Consider when the hero dog kills a completely defenseless guy in a wheelchair, or when the red-riding hooded mutie Ruby (Laura Ortiz) sacrifices herself for the sake of the sadistic city dwellers in the most ambivalent moment in the picture.

Highlights arrive in the form of veteran character man Tom Bower as a guilt-ridden gas station attendant, young Dan Byrd as de facto man of the city family and steward of all the rage and gun issues (daddy has Dirty Harry's .45 used against his wife and daughter) implanted him by our culture of violence, and by the bald fact that Aja knows how to shoot a film when he has to. But *The Hills Have Eyes* is just a dumbed-down, ineffably watered-down *A History of Violence* sans character development, introspection, nuance, or maturity; the open hostility Aja harbours for his audience obscures its full-frontal assault on America. It reminded me of an adult teasing children into incoherent rages: the subtleties are lost and all that's left is one party that really needs to grow up. (WC)

## THE HOLIDAY
ZERO STARS/****
*st.* Cameron Diaz, Kate Winslet, Jude Law, Jack Black
*w./d.* Nancy Meyers

There are bad movies, and then there are Nancy Meyers movies (first *What Women Want*, followed by the similarly excrescent *Something's Gotta Give*): chick flicks in the most damning, insulting sense of the patronizing term and reason enough to question the wisdom of ever spending money to see a movie. If you go to Meyers' latest, not only are you about to watch what is easily the worst movie of the year—you're most likely going to do it in the company of people who'll actually like

it. *The Holiday* is appallingly written and icky besides in that familiar way of this brand of *Love Actually/The Family Stone* yuletide romantic refuse, casting Cameron Diaz and Jude Law as lovers fucking away the hours inside a Thomas Kincaid painting while Diaz's frumpy house-swap buddy, played by Kate Winslet, finds meaning in Santa Monica by propping up a fossil (Eli Wallach) and falling for a James Horner-esque composer of horrible soundtracks (Jack Black). Parliament on the Thames is featured as prominently as the Pacific Coast Highway to underscore either how vacuous the filmmakers are or how stupid they think the audience is while Hans Zimmer's soul-sucking, teddy bears-humping score saps away the last hints of credibility anyone has after participating in this gingerbread death march. If the opening voiceover narration by Winslet's lovelorn Iris isn't warning enough, consider that the narrative crutch used by Diaz's emetic movie trailer-editor Amanda is a series of fake movie trailers about Amanda's romantic imbroglios.

See, high-maintenance Barbie bitch Amanda meets her match in a man who seems a lothario but, wait for it, is in fact a loving family man with a pair of doe-eyed moppets Meyers uses in exactly the same way she does a little dog. (The real magic of Diaz's performance is that if you close your eyes, you can distinguish her from neither the whining of the dog nor the keening of the toddlers.) Seeking escape in the aftermath of a break-up with her good-for-nothing boy-chick (Edward Burns, of course), she heads to Google™ on her VAIO™ laptop and, like all retarded people do in retarded movies like this, proceeds to recite aloud everything she does and everything she reads. Meanwhile, her counterpart across the pond, Iris (Winslet), fed up with pining for her evil boss (Rufus Sewell—reaching his nadir at last as the British Edward Burns), agrees to exchange domiciles on the principle that exhausted, derivative crap such as *The Holiday* will appear less so with an infantile high concept. Jack Black (50% eyebrows, 50% gut) makes for the worst kind of love interest in that he's both physically unattractive and obnoxious, even turned down to a low simmer as he is here. That said, a scene in Blockbuster™ where he does his **Tenacious D**™ shtick to movie themes is, by that time, no more upsetting than a dinner party of the damned that accidentally recalls the card game from *Sunset Blvd.*, an entire subplot that has dinosaur-Jew <u>Tuesdays with Morrie</u> pathos scrawled all over it, and a two-second cameo by the once-promising Jena Malone as some girl her *Cold Mountain* co-star Jude Law is about to screw.

Between the constant product placement, the incessant telephone/Blackberry communications, the recurring glimpses of Jonathan Franzen's <u>The Corrections</u> (bizarre in and of itself but especially in a film full of illiterates), and an extended bit where Black's movie score aficionado doesn't know that "Arthur's Theme" was already composed by Christopher Cross for what is quite possibly the prototype for this kind of bullshit, *The Holiday* manages to be somehow worse than an Ephron sisters movie in that a fake trailer seen herein for a fake movie starring Lindsay Lohan and James Franco is something I felt I'd rather be sitting through. It's made by people so dumb they really think that references to *The Lady Eve* and *His Girl Friday* will augment their imaginary "discriminating" audience (let me break this to you gently: no one who respects film is voluntarily viewing *The Holiday*) while simultaneously mystifying the "broader" audience with a depth of movie knowledge. Even giving it the benefit of the doubt, *The Holiday* is the product of condescending census-takers who have dedicatedly watered down their script in order to avoid offending the people they hope will naturally be drawn to jellied tripe like

this. It manufactures uplift it doesn't deserve for inhuman ciphers shoehorned into situations so unlikely that any sad souls who identify with the "ugly" one and empathize with the "pretty" one (and you should've flipped the casting of Winslet and Diaz there, Meyers) will have a brief, nasty reality check. In a year already sparse in terms of great films, credit *The Holiday* for at least upholding the annual tradition of a dark horse sucking at the vein of seasonal warmth. (**WC**)

## HOLLYWOODLAND
**\*\*\*/\*\*\*\***

*st.* Adrien Brody, Diane Lane, Ben Affleck, Bob Hoskins
*sc.* Paul Bernbaum
*dir.* Allen Coulter

## THE BLACK DAHLIA
**\*\*¹/₂/\*\*\*\***

*st.* Josh Hartnett, Scarlett Johansson, Aaron Eckhart, Hilary Swank
*sc.* Josh Friedman, based on the novel by James Ellroy
*dir.* Brian De Palma

## FACTOTUM
**\*\*¹/₂/\*\*\*\***

*st.* Matt Dillon, Lili Taylor, Marisa Tomei, Didier Flamand
*sc.* Bent Hamer and Jim Stark, based on the novel by Charles Bukowski
*dir.* Bent Hamer

Deadening, dull, sepia-drenched *faux-noir* period hokum of a suddenly popular stripe, Allen Coulter's *Hollywoodland* casts lantern-jawed, wooden-countenanced Ben Affleck as his way-back literal and metaphorical doppelgänger George Reeves. An apparent suicide that has fostered a small measure of conspiracy theories, Reeves, television's original Superman, is shot in the head, naked in bed, on a summer night in 1959, briefly throwing a generation of kids into minor existential turmoil. But casting Reeves' death into suspicion is a far stickier wicket: even with the introduction of a woefully-underwritten fictional gumshoe (Adrien Brody) with his own crew-cut, wayward boy, and ice queen ex (Molly Parker) to match, the suggestion that someone in the portly statue's coterie (including his wife-of-a-studio-bigwig-mistress, played by the ageless Diane Lane) might have had a motive for slaying him is given a quick spin and then stabled without a whimper. What's left is the typical and unsurprising Hollywood fable of the high price of fame and the dreadful cost of its pursuit. The central irony that drives *Hollywoodland* is that, in its desperate attempt to make a mystery of Reeves' death, the only thing it succeeds in doing is cataloguing the myriad reasons Reeves had to justifiably cap himself.

Affleck gets high marks for—as he did in *Jersey Girl*—being self-aware enough to assay an exceptionally limited, traditionally handsome lucky duck who stumbled into the executive washroom only to find himself handing out towels and mints there a few years later. If his portrayal of a guy who doesn't know what he has until he shits it away by reaching for something of which he's not capable rings true, it's not because he's suddenly found a fountain of appeal, but because he's really just playing himself: too dumb to be interesting, too smart not to mourn that. The difference between Affleck and, say, Kevin Costner, is that Costner's limited in an amiable, folksy way while Affleck is limited in a mopey, sad bastard kind of way. Brody, then, is given the burden of manufacturing a magnetic performance in *Hollywoodland* (a film that's more interesting for the fact and timing of it than anything else), and, saddled with a stock character tracked in the usual scenario, he succeeds merely in highlighting how beneath him is all this perfunctory time-suck. If Affleck is the best thing about *Hollywoodland*, it

has something to do with the kind of symbol Affleck has become for this particular variety of Tinsel Town failure: to be great in *Hollywoodland*, unlike Brody, Affleck doesn't have to try.

The two fictional gumshoes in Brian De Palma's hotly-anticipated adaptation of James Ellroy's brilliant L.A. *noir* <u>The Black Dahlia</u> (and who better to join in holy matrimony than the insane Ellroy and the almost-as-insane De Palma?) are Bucky (Josh Hartnett) and Lee (Aaron Eckhart). Detectives, boxers, and best buddies, together with Lee's bombshell wife Kay (Scarlett Johansson) they form Ellroy's tarnished holy trinity. A tale of corruption and betrayal set against the backdrop of snuff films and the notorious murder and mutilation of Elizabeth "The Black Dahlia" Short (the always-unspeakably sexy Mia Kirshner), *The Black Dahlia* is the kind of De Palma plastic fantastic that renders his films candy-coloured genre dissertations. De Palma's *noir* is as slick as a Hollywood love letter should be, but gone is the auteur's sickness. *The Black Dahlia* is a lot more like his *The Untouchables* than the *Chinatown* to which it aspires—a technically-marvellous picture (its use of sound is astonishing) overburdened by a couple of actors simply incapable of saying the words.

Lee and Bucky, dubbed "fire" and "ice" for their respective demeanours in the ring, forge their bond in the squared circle in an energetic boxing scene that, like much of the first half of *The Black Dahlia*, bristles with the promise that De Palma is returning to his '70s and early-'80s heyday. Lee becomes obsessed with the lurid Black Dahlia murder, driven to distraction and—it's suggested in one of a few fumbled plotlines—paranoia about his best pal's friendship with his doll-like ex-whore of a wife. Eckhart is the best he's ever been, following up his career-turn in *Thank You for Smoking* with a role that finally frees him from the saddle of unctuous charmer. He's all virility and barely-restrained rage, filling the same role that Russell Crowe filled opposite Guy Pearce in another Ellroy adaptation, *L.A. Confidential*. Hartnett, though, seems lost inside the material, not so much "ice" as "gaffed"—a spectator who falls in with a hideously vamping Hilary Swank as a bi-curious *femme fatale* heiress so obvious in her machinations that you feel disdain as opposed to sympathy when Bucky falls into her web.

That being said, the scene where Bucky is introduced to his girlfriend's wacko blueblood family is one of the most satisfying moments of 2006, at once knowing homage to the first-person experimentation of Robert Montgomery's POV Phillip Marlowe flick *Lady in the Lake* and a delirious flip back to the mad, splitscreen-and-time-warp sensibility of vintage De Palma. It's almost worth the price of admission, but then there's Hartnett's befuddled glower and Johansson's second turn in a row that casts her most glaring weaknesses (glibness, eloquence, mystery) into sharp relief. Substitute Kirshner for Swank and a pulse for Hartnett and you'd instantly have visceral rationale for half the relationships in the film. Without some serious gravitas, *The Black Dahlia* flies apart under the strain of Ellroy and De Palma's complementary psychoses.

Maybe Hartnett's role should've gone to Matt Dillon, himself a revelation in Bent Hamer's *Factotum*—though the rest of the picture is deadpan in a way that left me wondering if both Dillon's Henry Chianski characterization and Charles Bukowski's source material weren't the butt of an absurdist joke. It's a movie at cross-purposes with itself, one hemisphere mocking the other with its own blank regard—but isn't it fair to offer that Bukowski can only really be taken with that proverbial grain of salt? Especially on film, where the internal monologues can undermine the actual torpor of the self-styled poet laureate of alcoholism and vagrancy.

*Factotum* is the successful version of Barbet Schroeder's *Barfly* in that it understands that what Bukowski is all about is the wry, maybe facetious, celebration of a certain kind of alcohol-aided inertia. It's too bad that a near-constant voiceover providing highlights from the book upon which the film is based distracts from the splendid absolute nothing of Chianski's existence. Without a hint that Chianski has a gift for turning his professional indolence (*Factotum* is essentially a series of vignettes depicting this loser pissing away a long line of menial jobs) into turns of phrase soaked in wounded machismo, this would play almost like a Chaplin picture. With it, though, Hamer appears to be apologizing for sticking a pin in Bukowski's inflated sense of self. There's a masterpiece in here somewhere—a film that redefines *noir* for our lost moment, adrift in the doldrums of our decades-long post-traumatic stress disorder, self-medicated and self-deluded into pie-eyed poesy. (**WC**)

**HOME OF THE BRAVE**
½*/****
*st.* Samuel L. Jackson, Jessica Biel, Brian Presley, Curtis Jackson
*sc.* Mark Friedman
*dir.* Irwin Winkler

**FLAGS OF OUR FATHERS**
*/****
*st.* Ryan Phillippe, Jesse Bradford, Adam Beach, John Benjamin Hickey
*sc.* William Broyles, Jr. and Paul Haggis, based on the book by James Bradley with Ron Powers
*dir.* Clint Eastwood

Irwin Winkler's *Home of the Brave* is just so much pussified hand-wringing and inflated self-importance—an updating of William Wyler's *The Best Years of Our Lives* to cover the toll of Iraq II on soldiers' families when their loved ones return. To say that it's hackneyed would be a considerable understatement, seeing as how the picture is intent on cramming real psychological and social rifts into cozy Oprah-isms and situation comedy. It's as predictable as a Quaker recipe for boiled potatoes. Still, there's something to be said for soda crackers, and *Home of the Brave* earns a little clearance for having its heart in the right place even if its brain is stuck in bromide-ville. Faint praise to be sure—so faint that it's largely the only praise the picture's been getting, suggesting that the collective effort to give this piece of shit a pass has a lot to do with what patronizing knob-cheesers we can be. Worse, it's not the film we're really patronizing, but the soldiers so broadly depicted herein and their plight before the unholy trilogy of obscenely devastating injuries being survivable now, an American health care system in the proverbial shitcan, and an administration (and its veterans' administration) that just prior to the war made getting aid almost impossible for the layman in one of history's most cynical money-saving ploys ever. See, if the paperwork is Byzantine, a lot of people won't be able to complete it correctly—and those same people will probably be too under-represented to raise sufficient complaint.

But, see, *Home of the Brave* doesn't delve very deeply into the pessimism of this war and its domestic aftermath—believing (as the powers that be do) that, apparently, people are too damned stupid to wade through a lot of complicated issues and thus simplifying the sacrifice of our volunteer army into a quartet of stock characters. There's the angry black guy (Fiddy, Fitty, Fifty-Cent, Curtis Jackson, whatever) who decides to knock over a drugstore; the handsome All-American Joe—er, Tommy (Brian Presley)—who re-ups after deciding he can't hack life on the outside; the athletic beauty queen (Jessica Biel)

who loses a hand but gains the poignant ability to not be able to catch a soccer ball (better for her to lose her facility in a sport that requires working hands for no more than one of its eleven players, but so be it); and the motherfucking doctor (Samuel L. Jackson) who loses his motherfucking mind during motherfucking Thanksgiving. I did like a jack-hammered scene in which Tommy and the bobby-soxer talk about the grim realities of the world in a theatre lobby packed with folks on their way to escape the grim realities of the world, but liked less the rest of the jack-hammering. A producer with a great track record (*Raging Bull*, *The Right Stuff*, *'round Midnight*), Winkler is a horrendous director (*The Net*, *Life as a House*, *De-Lovely*) given to safe, prosaic message pictures. The issue of what to do with mangled vets is as old as the amputee colonies set up after WWI—as old as the shambling cannon-fodder post-Civil War; pretending this is a new issue that's never dared speak its name in the modern conversation is disingenuous and another ironic example of the filmmakers (and the critics) thinking entirely too little of the audience. The ugly truth of it might be that stuff like *Home of the Brave* only really serves a purpose for people directly affected by the war in exactly the way depicted (in high, screeching melodrama) by the film. It's a sop to real activism to channel their outrage into these Pyrrhic catharses.

Only marginally preferable is tackling the basic nature of heroism in warfare—whether 'tis better to be Audie Murphy parlaying his medal of honour for a good decade of big screen humiliation or Sting's doomed soldier in *The Adventures of Baron Munchausen*, executed because his bravery has made everyone else feel badly about themselves. Clint Eastwood, along with the diseased homunculus sucking the life out of his last couple of Oscar-bait pictures Paul Haggis, gives the topic of heroism the old college try with *Flags of Our Fathers*, a picture essaying another troika of soldiers returning from the front: flat Rene (Jesse Bradford), drunken Injun Ira (Adam Beach), and stage-dad John (Ryan Phillippe)—half of the sextet immortalized on Iwo Jima, raising a certain flag over a blasted rock in the middle of a contested Pacific. The suggestion that soldiers think of themselves not as heroes but as the keepers of rapidly-draining war coffers and a general populace hungry for the Good News defines the narrow path plowed by this single-issue epic. Haggis' signature credit is as sometime writer for "The Facts of Life", and his dimwit devotion to burning away all the tasty fat around the gristle of a difficult issue renders *Flags of Our Fathers* both inert and ridiculous. Its usefulness as allegory for our current dire straits (and draining coffers, government-manufactured heroes (I'm looking at you, Jessica Lynch), and so on) is deflated by its obviousness in precisely the same way that *Crash's* reprehensible simplification of race relations made a happy fairy tale out of one of the essential questions of our leap over civilization, straight from birth of a nation to fall of the Roman Empire with no Golden Age in-between. Judging *Flags of Our Fathers* against its companion piece *Letters from Iwo Jima*, find Paul Haggis removed as principal screenwriter for the latter and, miracles, an Eastwood masterpiece about the toll of violence on the innocent (and not so innocent) that completes a loose trilogy of such things begun with *Unforgiven* and *A Perfect World*. All *Flags of Our Fathers* does is complete a different, crap-packed kind of trilogy with *Million Dollar Baby* and *Crash*. (**WC**)

## HOOT
*\*¹/₂/\*\*\*\**
*st.* Luke Wilson, Logan Lerman, Brie Larson, Tim Blake Nelson
*sc.* Wil Shriner, based on the novel by Carl Hiaasen
*dir.* Wil Shriner

On the subject of keeping young people away from R-rated movies, Pauline Kael once remarked: "How are kids supposed to appreciate movies if they only see the crap that's aimed at them?" That "crap," of course, is usually stuff that's been interrogated for controversial subject matter and aesthetic interest alike, as if a sweeping camera or a finely-tuned *mise-en-scène* would disturb the kiddies. And on past performance, Walden Media is a leading exponent of this kind of subdued mediocrity: not only did they issue that ultra-bland C.S. Lewis adaptation from last winter, but they also cranked out the thoroughly innocuous *Hoot* to disastrous box-office this spring. It's a movie that treats potentially charged material like No Big Deal—which is the supposed position to take with young minds in the room.

At first, I found it strange that a conservative organization like Walden would adapt such tree-hugging material as Carl Hiaasen's source novel. After all, the subject is rescuing burrowing owls from an evil fast-food company, complete with a transient junior-high eco-terrorist (Cody Linley's "Mullet Fingers") trying to stop the encroachment of big business. But, of course, Mullet Fingers isn't the main event. That honour belongs to Roy Eberhardt (Logan Lerman), dutifully providing as the new-kid-in-school of yore the milquetoast underdog to which kidpix so often gravitate. It's his mission to vacillate on whether to support Mullet Fingers' mission to save the owls from the pancake franchise or be a nice boy and try to dodge the school bully—a subplot that eats up time while going nowhere.

It turns out that the environmentalist theme is barely noticed by the filmmakers—to say nothing of the desperate circumstances of off-the-grid Mullet Fingers, who lives by his wits without home or country. I could mention the distinctly homoerotic overtones of Roy's initial infatuation with this golden-haired rebel boy who runs really fast, but it's fruitless: denial of any disturbing content is the film's primary goal, in the name of not upsetting the children and, more importantly, their parents. This means the machinations of evil corporations seem comical, while the poverty of Mullet Fingers makes him a frisky Twain figure whose sister/fellow traveler Beatrice Leep (Brie Larson) thinks nothing of hiding out under Roy's bed when she fights with her parents. If anyone thought twice about what was going on, we might have an actual movie, but everything is so scrubbed clean there's hardly any meat on *Hoot*'s bones.

I can hear the sound of somebody screwing up their face, ready to bellow, "But it's a movie for kids!" And indeed, something called "Film Advisory Board, Inc." has thoughtfully sanctioned *Hoot* to ward off suggestions of low quality. But though the standards by which films for kids are judged are considerably more lax than those for adults, that doesn't mean you shovel whatever at your moppets and call it a day. I'd like to believe we want to awaken some sort of curiosity and conscience in our offspring instead of frightening them away from thinking, and while *Hoot* may entertain them, it won't exactly set their imaginations ablaze. It's mind control in the form of thinking for yourself, ultimately, and it can't be recommended to parents who want to raise sentient human beings. (**TMH**)

## HOSTEL
** /****

st. Jay Hernandez, Derek Richardson, Eythor Gudjonsson, Barbara Nedeljakova
w./d. Eli Roth

I had a fair share of affection for Eli Roth's writing-directing debut *Cabin Fever*, seeing in it a refreshing honesty about his love for traditional spam-in-a-cabin flicks that I thought carried it over some of the (perhaps)

intentionally shoddy filmmaking and a layer of *Jackass* crudeness and hostility. *Hostel*'s a middle-finger flipped at every single thing that makes films like this worthy of deeper examination and, more importantly, the carriers of genuine unrest and discomfort. It lurches along with a wilful rejection of intelligence and sensitivity for fear of emasculation—"pussy" and "faggot" the two words its heroes use most often in *Hostel*'s and thus, as Dr. Phil would tell you, the two things author Roth probably most fears that he is. The result of that puerility in its creation (maybe creator) is a film that bends over backwards to punish women and homosexuals; *Hostel* is unrepentantly, unselfconsciously leering, and so ugly on the topic of gay men that it reserves its nastiest, ugliest punishments for quiet schlep Josh (Derek Richardson) and the older Dutch man (Jan Vlasák) in whom he may be interested. Tellingly, the one vivisects the other before encountering his personal Waterloo in a train station's public water closet, his pants around his ankles and his head in a toilet full of his own waste. It's where queers go to die in movies made by homophobes. For more eloquent commentary than I'm capable of providing of the damage done by this kind of image, look to a bathroom murder scene in *Hellbent*.

It begins as the *Last American Virgin* remake Roth's been threatening us with as a trio of college-age hedonists, on a budget and armed with a europass, frequent the ganja bars of Amsterdam just prior to going window shopping in the Red Light District. The usual suspects: the wild party guy is Icelander Oli (Eythor Gudjonsson); the devil-may-care daredevil is Yankee Paxton (Jay Hernandez); and the delicate, budding writer recovering from a break-up is fellow Yankee Josh (Derek Richardson). After getting locked out of their hostel, they find themselves in the apartment of a seamy Russian who advises them to take a train to

Bratislava, where the women are beautiful and desperate. Sure enough, once they're in a gothically-appointed hostel, a pair of Russian beauties (and why are Russians staying at a Russian hostel? Who cares, right?), Natalya and Svetlana (Barbara Nedeljakova and Jana Kaderabkova), accidentally (oops!) flash their tits, invite the boys to a spa, and then flash their tits on purpose. Yet apparently these girls have more on their minds than fucking (but fuck they do, don't get me wrong)—seems they're paid a lot of money to deliver young men to a shadowy network of flesh peddlers who sell rich international businessmen the opportunity to torture someone to death.

Japanese girl Kana (Jennifer Lim) has an eyeball plucked out in slow-motion, quails at her appearance, and kills herself by jumping in front of a train. Yeah, she's vain, but is there anything to the notion that the loss of her eye is speaking to an objectification subtext? I doubt it. *Hostel* revels in its venality and arrogance, rubbing it all over itself like the gouts of blood it uses to soak every non-victim in the picture. It's posed itself as a piece owing a debt to the Japanese shock cinema of Takashi Miike (himself a bit player in the film) when it really owes more to the gore/schlock cinema of Herschel Gordon Lewis. For whatever you can say about Miike's pictures, not a one of them (and he's been known to churn out up to five a year) would you describe as empty, sadistic capering. *Hostel* can't be a commentary on sexual tourism because it *is* sexual tourism; it can't be a commentary on exploitation of women and virulent gay-bashing because it's those things, too; and, ultimately, it's neither as scary nor as funny as it wants to be, because it's just a cheap bit of garbage and everyone, even or especially the people who'll like it best, knows it.

But there's a catch—and the catch is the torture scene of anti-hero Paxton, whose humiliation Roth shows in bald, intimate detail. There's a suggestion in this lead-up that Paxton is "unmanned"—turned into the "pussy" he cavalierly calls his dead friends in bonhomie and goading. And so, in the calculus of his lizard brain, he's been degraded in a more significant way than dissection. He delays his own demise (and facilitates his escape) by showing off his bilingual ability, confusing his German tormentor with pleas for his life in his native tongue and, in the process, identifying a theme of ugly-Americanism that works as a weak undercurrent in the film. If *Hostel* fails to add much to the conversation about voyeurism and sexual identity in the slasher genre, at least it manages in spite of itself to suggest in a meta way how Americans piss off the rest of the world not just with their politics and their arrogant ignorance (note that in *Syriana*, another film with a disgusting torture sequence, one of the emir's men says of the Chinese that at least they learn Arabic to deal with them in business), but with their affluence and sense of entitlement, too. It doesn't make *Hostel* a good film—but it does make it worth a conversation. (**WC**)

## HOUSE OF SAND (see: *ONLY HUMAN*)

## DOCUMENTARY
## HOW TO EAT YOUR WATERMELON IN WHITE COMPANY (AND ENJOY IT)
\*\*\*/\*\*\*\*
*dir.* Joe Angio

Director Angio takes the traditional documentary route in this loving, comprehensive look at the life and career of maverick jack-of-all-trades Melvin Van Peebles, which intersperses interviews with archival footage. Moving to Paris as a young man and teaching himself French while earning a living as a street performer, Van Peebles—novelist, film director, playwright, artist, lothario, musician (his son Mario describes dad's singing style as a "frog on acid"), professional gadfly—is a man of steadfast individualism with a gift for knowing what buttons to push with the society at large. The documentary does a good job chronicling his evolution from urchin to icon even as it leaves the contextualization to scholars, ex-Panthers, and Spike Lee. Still, a lot of the clips are rare and Angio lets them run long enough for us to gain an invaluable insight into how Van Peebles was stirring the pot before *Sweet Sweetback's Baad Asssss Song* changed the conversation for everyone. For a more uncompromising look at Van Peebles, consult the excellent *Baadassss!*—but for a curriculum vitae, you could do a far sight worse. (**WC**)

**IDIOCRACY (see: *MY SUPER EX-GIRLFRIEND*)**

**THE ILLUSIONIST**
*½/****
*st.* Paul Giamatti, Edward Norton, Jessica Biel, Rufus Sewell
*sc.* Neil Burger, based on a story by Steven Millhauser
*dir.* Neil Burger

**HALF NELSON**
***/****
*st.* Ryan Gosling, Shareeka Epps, Anthony Mackie
*sc.* Ryan Fleck & Anna Boden
*dir.* Ryan Fleck

Out of the gate, Neil Burger's *The Illusionist* threatens to become the Viennese magician version of *Amadeus*, with Paul Giamatti's Inspector Uhl subbing for Salieri and Eisenheim the Illusionist (Edward Norton) his rabbit-hatted Mozart. But the film resolves itself in no time into something a good deal more mundane: a twisty crime drama complete with gauzy Guy Maddin visuals that cements Norton as the gravitas-heavy young actor most likely to be cast as Heathcliff in a badly-considered community theatre adaptation of <u>Wuthering Heights</u>. It's tedious and protracted, if not otherwise offensive—an elaborate piece of fluff that does its little tricks to the medium-delight of its tiny, undemanding audience before fading into the wings. Though it's tempting to laud it for having no pretensions to greatness, it's equally tempting to stay home and laud it from there.

Giamatti and Norton are facing Janus heads of actors, the homely/less-homely versions calved from the same school of over-emoting and scenery-chewing. Their dry-humping exchanges relegate the eternally-misused Rufus Sewell to evil Crown Prince Leopold, who molders in swaths of opulence and in-breeding while slavering over his aloof lady-love, Sophie (a largely mute Jessica Biel). When Giamatti and Norton square off in a fit of Method technique, the urge to knock their heads together in a cathartic spasm is overwhelming. A nickelodeon-hued flashback shows young Eisenheim the commoner courting young Sophie the highborn, telegraphing their reunion over a special locket, eventual tragedy, and even more eventual triumph in broad, self-satisfied strokes. It's easy to see the cinematic allure of the piece (which began life as a Steven Millhauser short story)—not so easy to appreciate the literary possibilities of a story free of any ambition beyond allowing its A-list character actors the opportunity to work their mouths around stilted dialogue in an awkward bit of Victoriana. The irony of a film called *The Illusionist* sporting no discernible magic is just too choice to ignore.

With pretensions to be something meaningful, *Half Nelson* is another movie anchored by a mad Method performance by an insane character actor (this time Ryan Gosling, the new Ed Norton). It talks about Harvey Milk and the <u>Communist Manifesto</u> and the Civil Rights Movement and the CIA installation of Pinochet and the madness of a majority that still believes there were weapons of mass destruction in an Iraq...and it does so as backdrop to the disintegration of privileged white boy Dan (Gosling), a teacher at a rough inner-city school nursing a crack habit. Until it gets too obvious about itself (somewhere around the halfway mark (like an addict nursing a jones, as it happens)), that sense of futile outrage at the fruitlessness of trying to affect change in a world that has never been more informed yet remains incapable of avoiding (recent) history's harshest lessons lends a nice feeling of indignity

104

to what is already a pretty fair genre inversion.

I have to admit to feeling dismay when I heard we were in for another white teacher/black student piece, but *Half Nelson* manages to sidestep the standing-on-desks bullshit, replacing it with something that feels like *The Big Chill* in its throwback to good old-fashioned Flower Power outrage. (In its way, it's a nice, unexpected, companion piece to this year's *V for Vendetta*.) Name-dropping Rosie Grier's "It's All Right To Cry" from Marlo Thomas' well-remembered but horrifically obsolete *Free To Be You and Me* (and **Marshall Tucker Band's** now-rhetorical "Can't You See") suggests a genuine sadness over ideals left castrated and bleeding beneath an avalanche of depressing truths about the state of our eroding union. The voice of its outrage is married to the nihilism of the modern age.

The story of a basehead befriending a girl (Shareeka Epps) headed for the wrong side of the law feels appropriately like doom—*The Wizard of Oz* reconfigured for the Wasteland. Maybe not surprisingly, what damages the film for me to some extent is its hopefulness: I don't even think it's cynical anymore to be unhopeful and I do wonder if I'm actually embarrassed that *Half Nelson* pulled my strings. What saves the film is the character of poor, conflicted, nuanced Dan as the new face of the American liberal. He's among the finest explanations we've had thus far of why the Left can't seem to muster a compelling resistance: in the face of all this outrage and insult, under the weight of almost four decades of poisoned passion, the voices of our best intentions find themselves tongue-tied and thunderstruck, sick on smack with their heads against a toilet—as slow in coming to our defense as the punchline that serves as this picture's surprisingly understated grace note. *Half Nelson* suggests that our stupor might be wearing off. I hope it's right. (WC)

DOCUMENTARY
**AN INCONVENIENT TRUTH**
***½/****
*dir.* Davis Guggenheim

DOCUMENTARY
**WHO KILLED THE ELECTRIC CAR?**
*½/****
*dir.* Chris Paine

Spend much time mining the cultural divorce in these delightfully divided United States and you'll discover that the stereotypes governing our perceptions of either side (bellicose vs. pussified) tend to be by and large accurate. Given the choice between violent and dogmatic or simpering and equivocal, the American electorate has erred badly on the side of a unified message, no matter how dangerous—and who can blame them? I mean, shit, whatever the leadership qualities, Custer didn't die alone. The mess of our national politics (and the mess that it's made of our standing in the international community) inevitably must inspire a spate of left-wing documentaries and, judging by last year's Clooney-fest, a handful of well-intentioned (if simpering and scattershot) partisan fictions. It's a strange world out there, and in it find Al Gore (did he lose office to a *coup d'état*?) as the breakthrough star of the non-fiction summer, following the path ploughed by Michael Moore and Penguins before him. It's not strange because he's uncharismatic; it's strange because in *An Inconvenient Truth*, he's both charismatic and on-topic. He's become that rarest of beasts: a democrat in the public eye who's not afraid to make strong statements and take his shots at obvious targets without indulging in self-abnegating ambiguities.

Some have equivocated that *An Inconvenient Truth* is akin to a concert movie (going so far as to compare it to Jonathan Demme's *Neil Young: Heart of Gold* or, more laughably, *Stop Making Sense*), when the naked truth is that *An Inconvenient Truth* is a PowerPoint presentation captured faithfully on film with a few segues to a pensive-looking Gore gazing over photographs or riding along in a car to another speaking engagement. The irony isn't lost on anyone, I'd gather, that Gore has expended countless units of irreplaceable fossil fuels spreading his message of global warming—yet the point that holds water, so to speak, is the idea that we just don't have any choices right at this moment. The question of why there aren't viable alternative energy options (particularly when the electric car was not only more popular than the gasoline engine once upon a time but was also shown as recently as ten years ago to be a working technology) is raised subtly by *An Inconvenient Truth*. The rest of it—the pictures of glaciers shrinking into nothing, the graphs demonstrating the massive increase in greenhouse gasses in the last few decades—ties in cozily with the sudden hurricane-destruction of New Orleans and the evacuation of a lot of Pennsylvania due to fears of flooding. You're alarmed by it only if you don't think that, to crib from "The Daily Show", Adam and Eve rode a brontosaurus to church and, perhaps more divisively and to the point, that evolution is a theory and that two men who want to get married spells moral and spiritual Armageddon more neatly than does invading a Muslim country for their oil.

The inconvenient truth here for me is that I'm recommending what is essentially a non-film because I agree with its politics and I'd like for more people to agree with me than disagree—it's a slideshow, but it's a good one, and unlike Michael Moore's flicks, it's cogent and filled with a preponderance of scientific fact. It's tempting to wish that *An Inconvenient Truth* had something like a narrative, but then there's Chris Paine's *Who Killed the Electric Car?*, which opens with a mock-funeral for the titular GM-produced EV-1 staged by the A-list of insufferable character actors (Ed

Begley Jr., Peter Horton) to mourn the recall of their electric cars. Title cards tick off the possible suspects in the demise of the technology (OIL! BIG AUTO! CONSUMERS!)—it's like *Murder on the Orient Express*: everyone's guilty. But the victim isn't the car so much as it's the environment. Sound difficult to champion? It is. The film is well-meaning but so desperate to *entertain* that it begins to grate like the left-wing message has begun to grate on even the left wing. Smug and self-satisfied (if only, like "The Simpsons'" dig at Begley Jr., "self-satisfaction" could be tapped for energy), I learned a lot from *Who Killed the Electric Car?* (mainly that all the auto companies crushed their perfectly functional machines despite wide protest and demand), but can't be the only one cringing in the choir. (**WC**)

## INFAMOUS
**\*\* /\*\*\*\***

*st.* Toby Jones, Sandra Bullock, Daniel Craig, Peter Bogdanovich
*sc.* Douglas McGrath, based on <u>Truman Capote</u> by George Plimpton
*dir.* Douglas McGrath

Just as Milos Forman's *Valmont* was doomed to live in the shadow of *Dangerous Liaisons*, so, too, will Douglas McGrath's *Infamous* always be the poor relation to the Oscar-winning *Capote*. This is no mean feat: while *Dangerous Liaisons* was a very tough act to follow, *Capote* is an average-to-decent TV movie with a mugging central performance. Toby Jones manages to best Philip Seymour Hoffmann in seeming like someone named Truman Capote, but aside from a couple of peripheral turns, the film fails completely to suggest real life: whatever your feelings on *Capote*, it managed to give a sense of the psychology behind the *bon vivant* while being far more damning of his handling of the case that became *In*

*Cold Blood. Capote* may have been a little square, but *Infamous* pretty much amounts to starfucking—and unconvincing starfucking at that.

We all know that something funny went down when Capote, itching to invent his "new form of *reportage*," investigated the murder of the Clutters in rural Kansas and came in contact with the killer Perry Smith (Daniel Craig). Until that fateful meeting, *Infamous* features a half-hour of what people expect from a Capote movie: that is, the author cutting up. A seemingly endless array of publishing types (presumably culled from George Plimpton's oral history, credited as the screenplay's source) are invited to his audience, with counterfeits ranging from Diana Vreeland (Juliet Stevenson) to Bennett Cerf (Peter Bogdanovich) and Babe Paley (Sigourney Weaver). Vreeland/Stevenson has her own grotesque moment when she admits, in one of a tedious number of *faux-*documentary talking-head inserts, to ironing her money, but mostly, this section of the film is devoted to the novelty of the British Jones deploying an accent and spitting out the witticisms—which to be fair, is the box in which he and the rest of the performers are hopelessly trapped.

Of course, it all has to come to an end: after the writer worms his way into the lives of Kansas natives (an occasion for more so-Capote behaviour), the killers are captured and Capote finds in Smith his rendezvous with legend. The film, which has until this point strictly skimmed the surface of the events at hand, really doesn't know how to deal with the mixed emotions that their meeting creates: though Craig nails his turn as the would-be artist who drifted into poverty and then murder (and though Jones manages to lend credibility to his caricatured role in interactions with Craig), there's no denying that the relationship had to be more complicated than the way it's presented here. *Capote* at least tried to show the cynicism behind the author's

exploitation of Smith, the crime, and anyone who was within hailing distance—*Infamous* refuses to put Tru under too much scrutiny beyond depicting the occasional "outrageous" indiscretion. It doesn't make him an angel, yet it forgives him far too much.

This, of course, is the trap into which many Capote recreations fall. Like Andy Warhol, everybody yearns to be anointed by the artist's presence; we don't necessarily want to hear reasons because that would shatter the image of the perfect surface that both artists managed to project. Thus it becomes increasingly difficult to render Capote with anything like psychological detail, since everyone, the author included, was working overtime to either fabricate or sustain that image. True, his childhood friend Harper Lee is on hand to say otherwise (and in Sandra Bullock, the film has another actor who soldiers on, script be damned), but the film can't—or won't—entirely surrender the fiction that destroys genuine reflection. However half-baked *Capote* is, it showed cracks in the attention-craver and sometimes-vampire that was Truman; *Infamous* is rightly doomed to second-banana status. (**TMH**)

## INLAND EMPIRE
**\*\*\*\*/\*\*\*\***

*st.* Laura Dern, Jeremy Irons, Justin Theroux, Grace Zabriskie
*w./d.* David Lynch

Nikki (Laura Dern) is an actress landing her dream role opposite Devon (Justin Theroux) in a film directed by the great Kingsley Stewart (Jeremy Irons). Alas the project, "On High in Blue Tomorrows", has a history in which a previous, doomed production ended as reality seeped into its fiction and the film's onscreen/offscreen lovers were killed. For a moment, it seems as though David Lynch's *Inland Empire* might be as straightforward as a haunted Hollywood genre exercise—but time slips, it's suddenly the next day, and as one character says to another, you're sitting over there. Displaced, distracted, the picture is a masterpiece that, for the patient, the active, and the curious, may be the most literal definition of "dread" captured on film. That feeling you get when Henry Spencer contemplates his feral baby in *Eraserhead* is the same species of disgusted, familiar fascination that infects this film like a murder of maggots.

Lynch's exploration of love, betrayal, and identity inundates *Inland Empire* with an ineffable, existential quagmire. It's glorious, defiantly individual, and an untidy mess of loosely-connected vignettes that manage to coalesce over the course of the film's three-hour runtime into something like an *avant-garde* telling of the myth of Eros and Psyche—the girl-child of the myth Nikki, fully-grown and in a profession that makes her as visible as the Psyche of the story (who earns the unwelcome attention of rival-in-beauty Aphrodite), confronting her sexual anxieties as they manifest in a potential affair with notorious lothario Devon. On the surface, it appears that Lynch is revisiting the Tinsel Town, notoriety-fuelled identity nightmare of *Mulholland Drive*, but, freed of the *Persona* dynamic of woman/woman (and of the Hitchcock dialectic of blonde/brunette), *Inland Empire* is grounded in the friction between two men: the bestial husband and the potential lover.

Like the interchangeable personae of Lynch's two women, the two men of *Inland Empire* are, if the Eros and Psyche read carries, likewise antipathetic aspects of the same character. They are the romantic and the horrific, perhaps something so simple as the emotional and the intellectual parts of what should in essence be interpreted as one functional archetype. To complete the transformation of full-grown woman into a child inexperienced in love, Lynch employs regression tropes like

alienation, confusion, misunderstanding, and inconsequence. Take the circular Theater of the Absurd conversation of a family of bunnies on a stage, or the overlapping realities of the film-within-a-film (within-a-film), or the death scenes enacted before mental incompetents and social orphans; the ability of Lynch's films to discomfit can be drawn from this ability to winnow all the existential nightmare of being small into little pockets of forlorn isolation.

*Inland Empire* feels like a Charlie Kaufman movie at times as Nikki evolves through the indignities of childhood while coming to flower in a series of very public deflowerings: first on a ridiculous talk show (curiouser and curiouser, Dern's real-life mother Diane Ladd plays the host), then through the shooting of a cursed screenplay. Lynch seems conscious at least of establishing the premise as something timeless, with an off-the-reservation Polish gypsy woman (Grace Zabriskie) relating Nikki's story as an old folktale before revealing that the script Nikki's so pleased to be shooting had been attempted before with tragic results. Nothing new under the sun and all that, it follows that Eros and Psyche represent only one of multiple potential avenues for unlocking this text.

Allowing for that, *Inland Empire* jibes particularly well with the story of the young woman, Psyche, spirited away to a castle of shadows by a wind to be the bride of Eros, where her attendants are disembodied parts and where her continued existence is contingent on her agreement to not know her lover. Consider, too, that in the tale—one that is ostensibly employed to demonstrate the epic difficulty of bridging the divide between the head and the heart, the two aspects that the two men in Nikki's life could be said to represent—Psyche mortally transgresses and dooms herself to a series of impossible tasks to earn her way back into the sweet embrace of the bliss she enjoyed in ignorance. Like Psyche, Lynch provides Nikki with animal helpers of a sort—and to compound the complexity of any analysis of Lynch's films, at some point the idea that Lynch is in fact providing proverbial bread crumbs for his audience proves inescapable. Dreams are nonsense, too, until they're held up against the candle of archetype.

I don't think that Lynch is difficult; I think it's possible to regard Lynch's films fairly simply as directed at the collective unconscious, given that they're uniformly sticky and unpleasant despite rarely making conventional narrative sense. Clocking in at just under three hours, *Inland Empire* makes the case, by its gut-impact alone, that there's something huge and nameless roiling in its belly. For my part, I'd offer that the picture completes the loose trilogy begun by *Lost Highway* and *Mulholland Drive*: examinations each of identity and sexuality, as well as perception and the slipperiness of existence. If *Lost Highway* and *Mulholland Drive* are relatable as extrapolations of themes proposed by Hitchcock's *Marnie* and *Vertigo*, think of *Inland Empire* as Lynch's *The Birds*, wherein the indomitable *femme* is reduced to domesticity at the end not by any supernatural source, but by her agreement to be assimilated into the patriarchal norm. Writing about it is perhaps, to paraphrase Frank Zappa, like dancing about architecture, but *Inland Empire* is a fascinating, terrifying document of the machinations of the lizard brain and even the instinct to represent it in story and image—of how all the intricate steps in the waltz of love and jealousy (and art and expression) might just be the product of millennia of biological hardwiring. (WC)

## INSIDE MAN
***/****

*st.* Denzel Washington, Clive Owen, Jodie Foster, Christopher Plummer
*sc.* Russell Gewirtz
*dir.* Spike Lee

## THANK YOU FOR SMOKING
***/****

*st.* Aaron Eckhart, Maria Bello, Adam Brody, Sam Elliott
*sc.* Jason Reitman, based on the novel by Christopher Buckley
*dir.* Jason Reitman

You make mistakes as a film critic sometimes and, unlike a lot of professions, when you flub, you do it for the record. I underestimated Spike Lee's *25th Hour* badly upon its release a few years ago, misunderstanding it, fearing it, seeing it as a mediocre film when, in fact, subsequent viewings have revealed it as possibly Lee's tonal masterpiece. My inclination, then, is to overcompensate with *Inside Man* by offering it every benefit of the doubt beforehand, during, and now—by trying hard to overlook the first bad Jodie Foster performance I can remember as well as a mishandled denouement that stretches the picture past the point of recoil. But even with a jaundiced eye, *Inside Man* cements Lee as one of the few filmmakers with the brass ones to comment on the race schism, and to shoot (with assistance from ace cinematographer Matthew Libatique) a post-9/11 New York with the gravity of a heart attack. In his individualism, though, that almost-shrill dedication to pumping fists up familiar channels, Lee raises a few eyebrows (and elicits a couple of grins) for posing his Nazi villain in various desktop-photo *tableaux* with other twentieth century profiteering, conservative ogres like George and Barbara Bush and Margaret Thatcher. It's an interesting companion piece to *V for Vendetta* in that way, at once a melodramatic throwback and a progressive scalpel. It's blaxploitation, seventies paranoia, and the latest Spike Lee Joint from Ground Zero.

Detective Keith Frazier (Denzel

Washington) has been implicated in an evidence embezzlement probe, but when a New York bank on financial row gets knocked over by a band of eurotrash commandos led by garrulous Dalton Russell (Clive Owen), Frazier's on the case, *Dog Day Afternoon*-style, partner Bill (Chiwetel Ejiofor) at his side. *Inside Man* drops that film's title (*Serpico*'s, too), decking Frazier out in a cheap white suit and raffish hat that segue brilliantly into the closing shot of a black man in a wife-beater, standing in front of a vanity while in the foreground, a luscious lady in recline dangles that hat off some manicured, impatient toes. That somewhat reductive instinct to simmer the bones of complexity until it's all a thick soup of familiar saturated flavours makes the picture post-modern in its self-conscious shout-outs to Lee's video library and body of work—and evocative, too, in the surprisingly cheesy desire to honour the double-meaning embedded in its title. There's not so much an "inside man" in the caper of it, see, as the film is about the contents of a man: the various indignities and desires, compromises, and moments of pyrrhic revolt that make the rest of the surrenders a little easier to stomach.

Consider the interrogation of a Sikh teller who complains of being called an Arab and having his turban arbitrarily confiscated by the police, but who agrees to cooperate once Frazier defuses the situation by joking that he probably doesn't have any trouble getting a cab. Or the bit where the identity of one of the robbers hinges on her "exquisite tits" and, after a detainee takes umbrage at too close a scrutiny of said rack, Lee cuts to a woman's sweaty cleavage as she tries to poke a hole in the bank's floor. "You can't hide that kind of quality," says one witness, referring to her shapeless jumpsuit. In this leering and practiced nudge-nudge misogyny, there's suddenly here another statement on the impossibility of disguising a truer nature beneath not only clothes,

certainly, but also the veneer of civilization. She is what she is and he is what he is. And lest the naturalistic fallacy be indulged, I don't think Lee is excusing us our animal natures, but rather illustrating—as he always has, in his way—that things are hooked in there a helluva lot deeper than skin and tits.

It's not terribly deep as insights go, but when Spike connects on one of his roundhouses, it feels like the gospel. You look at Christopher Plummer getting a haircut in a "gentleman's club" manned by black men in pastel suits as Foster's frigid, shadowy information broker lays down the law and it plays a lot like a paranoid fantasy of ten Jews in a luxury cave in the Bahamas, rigging Wall Street and the Super Bowl. But then there's Willem Dafoe's weary SWAT captain, or the bank manager whose cell phone is programmed to ring with hardcore gangster rap. Lee's simplicity is as knotty and dense as the tangled thrush of race and gender relations, and by being so bold as to proclaim this shitty, meandering genre picture to be about Nazi gold (no kidding) and the importance of being Shaft, suddenly *Inside Man* becomes vital and engaging in a way that doesn't end in the scrotum, even if it starts there.

Aaron Eckhart's tobacco lobbyist Nick Naylor also visits an exclusive, plantation-era gentleman's club in Jason Reitman's indie *cause célèbre Thank You for Smoking*, an adaptation of Christopher Buckley's arch novel about a few weeks in the life of one of the most despised people, engaged in one of the most despised professions on the face of the planet. Like the surface revelations of *Inside Man* (that men look at women's chests and that we notice that people are of different races), the revelation of *Thank You for Smoking*—that cigarettes aren't good for you—is notably beside the greater point that we're seeing a lot of movies now in which people in positions of power at every level are portrayed as venal, ineffectual, opportunistic liars desperately in need of (and/or deserving of) being put down with extreme prejudice.

The obvious problem with *Thank You for Smoking* is that it's at least a decade past its sell-by date for satires of how we're manipulated by media messages (certainly by the evils of Big Tobaccy); the virtue of it is that it's a tight, slick piece of amoral black comedy centered around an asshole (and Eckhart hasn't been this good since his last great asshole turn in *In the Company of Men*) who doesn't spend a lot of time rationalizing the evil that he does. It's a film, then, for word junkies and spin-doctors who get off on semantics and out-smarting debate opponents even when they're defending the weaker flank. Its wider appeal, though, is ironically predicated on the extent to which much of its audience gets off on thinking they're gaining some sort of insight into anything other than how deliciously wicked is this yuppie Mephistopheles. (Meaning, essentially, that most have been seduced by the bad guy, which Reitman neatly underscores by portraying the Media as the ogre for Just Telling the Truth. Meaning that for all the liberal drum-beating, Truth is still the bad guy.) So the Devil is attractive. As messages go, Milton told us that in the seventeenth century. We could argue that Eve learned it some time before that.

But *Thank You for Smoking* is slippery as hell. It identifies the last smokers in mainstream movies as the "RAVs" (Russians, Arabs, and Villains) on its way to manipulating its audience into hissing at an opportunistic young reporter (Katie Holmes) who trades on her—there's that phrase again—"exquisite tits" in order to write an extremely frank, entirely accurate story on the life of a tobacco lobbyist. In so doing, the picture demonstrates that if the last smokers in entertainment are bad guys and Europeans, the last irredeemable wrongdoers are journalists. We're slaves to conventions and images and saucy turns of phrase (another subplot involves the campaign of fey, Birkenstock-wearing Vermont senator Finistirre (William H. Macy) trying to get a skull and crossbones printed on every pack of cigarettes), the film tells us, and then it proceeds to use images and conventions and saucy turns of phrase to manipulate our sympathy with this self-proclaimed shark. The lobby of a Hollywood production company features a big-screen playing killer whales exuberantly playing with dying seals, and the head of said company (Rob Lowe) is reverently said to "really love Asian shit" in the middle of sand gardens and silk kimonos. It's loony-tunes and it's exactly the tenor of Los Angeles, just as the rest of it is exactly the tenor of the Beltway, just as Eckhart (and J.K. Simmons as his cigar-chewing boss, Robert Duvall as a julep-slurping tobacco baron, and on and on) are exactly the tenor of unctuous power brokers, rigging Wall Street and the Super Bowl from a luxury cave in the Bahamas.

*Thank You for Smoking* is a beauty: an honorary Neil LaBute picture about how easily we fall into moral ambiguity that exposes your own moral ambiguity. Light on the contemporaneous insight, it is instead, like *Inside Man*, doing the you-Nietzsche/it- Abyss polka. Although there's a lot that's wrong with both, each is saved by this *meshuggah* audacity regarding the function and potential of film to be genuinely lawless, even ebullient, in describing the ways that monkeys don't ever change. Why fight it? (**WC**)

## IRAQ IN FRAGMENTS
\*\*\*/\*\*\*\*
*dir.* James Longley

Aesthetically-speaking, *Iraq in Fragments* isn't all that fragmentary. Although director James Longley essentially divides the country into thirds (according to Sunni, Shiite, and

Kurd), the film is really quite fluid and harmonious. This has its drawbacks: we're released from the take-a-step-back God's-eye approach familiar from countless documentaries and thrown into what appears to be the scrum of social life in Iraq, sink or swim. A little context would be useful, as it would be if we were in the middle of the war zone itself. Whatever the shortcomings of this approach, however, *Iraq in Fragments* takes a necessary swipe at the idea that the eponymous country was a mass of undifferentiated Oppressed yearning for a conquering hero to release it from bondage. It suggests that Iraq is at least as complex as that of its invading "liberators"; and if Longley's three snapshots can contradict each other, that's to be expected from any nation with more than one cultural faction.

The film is carved up into three sections: "Mohammed of Baghdad", which follows the story of an 11-year-old boy juggling school and a job (with a bully of a taskmaster in the latter); "Sadr City", which talks of attempts at free votes competing with Muqtada al-Sadr's Shiite resurgence; and "Kurdish Spring", in which a Kurdish man and his son discuss their hopes now that the Americans have removed the source of their persecution. There is no reconciling these segments. Part one is a concentrated expression of cynicism over American benevolence that ultimately fails to express the relevance of the child's plight in a coherent thesis. Part two is a more detailed exploration of the fallout of Saddam's fear of Shia after the Iranian revolution, but still a bit of a snarl as to who's doing what and why. Finally part three is a fairly cut-and-dried affair whose main flaw is that it could perhaps go into further detail.

Still, Longley is not interested in feeding you a line. His more lyrical approach to Iraq and its politics makes you feel like a bystander in the political no-man's-land of the nation instead of a distant observer with godlike powers of self-righteousness. If one doesn't get a solid sense of the undercurrents driving the main action (and that's a fault Longley should have addressed), neither does one get a sense that such undercurrents are easily mastered. Implicitly, the film is saying that the absolutism and reductionism involved in the ideal of "regime change" are bound to fail due to the infinite complexity of Sunni vs. Shiite and the Kurdish skeletons in the closets of both. While *Iraq in Fragments* closes on the idea of America as a sort-of saviour for the Kurds, it's more of a wrinkle than a total position; Longley is interested in challenging assumptions, even of those well-meaning leftists who may make sweeping generalizations of their own.

As a stylist, Longley proves more proficient than astute. The pictures are attractive, yet one doesn't see a cinematic expression of Longley's ideas so much as a visually-pleasing framework for the same. As the only Western film about Iraqis (as opposed to American soldiers in Iraq) to crack the public consciousness, though, the situation could be a lot worse. The director isn't always articulate enough to expand our consciousness, but at least he shows us the shape of the problem and alerts us to how little we actually know about it, thus insinuating that careful consideration must be taken before blundering into partisan bluster that may talk around the problems. And despite that an unambiguous position never comes to the fore, one surmises that Longley's sympathy isn't that of a faker or a poser. His compassion is as obvious as it is refreshing in light of a certain administration's fear-mongering. **(TMH)**

J

## DOCUMENTARY
## JACKASS NUMBER TWO
***/****

*dir.* Jeff Tremaine

I myself feel like a jackass saying it, but there's something invigorating—almost rejuvenating—about *Jackass Number Two*. It could be as simple as my being there in a communal setting, before a democratic medium, bearing collective witness to a gang of good-looking guys doing their best to die creatively. It's all based on the Marty McFly call to action when manhood is challenged; if this results in stunts disturbingly homoerotic, then so be it and, more than so be it, now it all makes sense. Like that thing about how girls mainly dress up to impress other girls, so it is with the *Jackass* franchise that it's mainly guys doing stupid shit to impress other guys. Stupid's not the half of it, though: there's also the chugging of horse spunk (bestial bukkake?), which is probably harmless but existentially disturbing; and fishing for snakes with a dick in a sock dressed to look like a mouse—which, however stupid, is sort of brilliant for its theological perversity. Having been inoculated against most offense by *Borat* and of course the rest of the Jackass library, the only thing that really bothered me was a brief—almost interstitial—sequence where a fat guy farts into a tube that leads to a face-mask worn by an unfortunate who, almost instantly, pukes like a firehose. What is it about this experience that got under my skin when a running gag about public ambush comedy and Spike Jonze wearing old-woman boobs didn't? I think it's that something about it seems degrading instead of touched with brilliance.

It follows, then, that *Jackass Number Two* is about male friendship. It's ramped to a ridiculous degree, of course, marinated in dangerous levels of testosterone—but the heart of the piece is an almost touching demonstration of how men show love for one another. You don't haze someone like this whom you don't like. It works as anthropology, too, begging ultimate questions about why certain behaviours are learned—why this testing instinct among males is favoured evolutionarily, and why other humans observing said behaviour don't find bile and mean-spiritedness but *bonhomie* and high-spiritedness. It's "puerile," but "puerile" in the sense that theirs are child-like pursuits (many of the gags utilize children's toys: skateboards, brightly-coloured rockets, dollhouses). *Jackass Number Two* also has up its sleeve a fairly serious conversation about the nature of filmic reality vs. stuntwork and whether there's really any difference between the nasty surprise of a hornet's nest on your lap and carefully choreographing a stunt-filled, Busby Berkeley singing and dancing extravaganza. The possibility for chaos is equal when the camera neglects to edit what it captures—it's no more or less staged, it suggests, than any other documentary, but its sense of risk is greater because the reality of the piece is buried in the native intelligence of its gag-design. It's true, *Jackass Number Two* is smart and subversive, an acid test for the viewer and a portal to deeper conversations about socio-political interactions, the cult of masculinity, the nature of leadership, and the difficulty that boys encounter on their way to becoming men. **(WC)**

## DOCUMENTARY
## JESUS CAMP
**½/****

*dirs.* Heidi Ewing & Rachel Grady

It's hard to not be moved by the

horrors of *Jesus Camp*. A record of one Pastor Becky Fischer's far-right Christian summer camp, it's loaded with stuff any compassionate person would decry—usually the cruelty and intimidation of adults, who are often seen scaring children shitless. But even as we may despise these guileless sadists as they reveal themselves to the camera, at some point it all begins to ring hollow. The film has nothing beyond the image of children being bullied while their parents natter on about hateful fundamentalism; perhaps most regrettably, there's no discussion as to why, in the 21st century, 80 million Americans willingly believe in such corrosive nonsense.

Still, the emotional impact of what's caught by Heidi Ewing and Rachel Grady's camera is undeniable. The early scenes are easy enough: Fischer proves to be a humourless true believer who has decided that you have to start recruiting early, thus allowing for a variety of juvenile, "visual" faith metaphors that are more hilarious than horrifying. But though a bit with two Barbie dolls and a balloon must be seen to be believed, the indoctrination sessions are the main event, with an array of speakers putting their young charges on the spot by leading them into confessing their sins—real or imagined—against God. Some parrot back what they're told without thinking; some, like the poor kid who has to admit that he doesn't feel the presence of the Lord, just go along with it; and some weep in terror as the music swells and the orders to witness reach a crescendo.

I started out laughing (and, remembering my Lutheran past, wincing in embarrassment), but by the end I was crawling out of my skin. At my most reactively atheistic, I've never experienced anything like the monstrous pro-life rally in which the kids have duct tape scrawled with the word "LIFE" placed over their mouths, as if to silence everything within them. (So the message will take?) The casual disregard for the feelings of these children, who in interviews clearly have no idea what's happening (including the adolescent preacher who's under constant pressure for a sermon), is appalling, and after a while even YOU feel beaten down. The idea of an existence with these vile parents—who encourage their young to scream out "This Means War!" over and over again to the Devil and predictably espouse anti-evolution rhetoric—is intolerable, and will make you grateful if you managed to escape such a fate.

And yet, the film is as evasive as it is effective. Nobody bothers to ask the irritable Fischer what led her to her downbeat view of humanity and the need to seize upon children—in fact, nobody is terribly well-drawn in the Ewing/Grady universe. There's little sense of inner life for any of the film's subjects—they are viewed from afar, be they the crazed evangelists offering horrifying spectacle or the confused children offering exquisite suffering. When *Jesus Camp* tries to feebly stave off accusations of Christian-bashing with a more levelheaded Christian radio host who decries the evangelicals, the viewpoint that emerges is almost as unsophisticated as (albeit a lot less brutal than) that of the simpleminded Christian crazies. If this Oscar-nominated documentary is useful in defining the extent of the damage caused by certain religious groups, it has no ideas on how to act on it; you're left in the middle of the highway with the fear of a semi bearing down on you. In that sense, the film's exploitation of the kids' panic is not so different from Fischer's. (**TMH**)

**JET LI'S FEARLESS (see: *THE SCIENCE OF SLEEP*)**

**JUST MY LUCK**
ZERO STARS/****
*st.* Lindsay Lohan, Chris Pine,

Faizon Love, Missi Pyle
*sc.* I. Marlene King and Amy B. Harris
*dir.* Donald Petrie

A movie as ill-conceived as the original *Bring It On* (yeah, let's root for the privileged white chicks against the...all-black inner-city cheerleading squad?), Donald Petrie's *Just My Luck* fatally hitches its wagon to the miniscule charms of Lindsay Lohan. The migraine begins to form as soon as Lohan makes her grand entrance as PR chick Ashley Albright, striding out into the pouring rain without an umbrella knowing full well that the weather will clear up to accommodate her. (It does.) After scraping his jaw off the sidewalk, her Stepin Fetchit of a doorman hails a taxi, and while climbing into it Ashley notices a five-dollar bill stuck to the bottom of her boot. Does this cosmically-pampered princess tip the doorman with it? LOL! She's admiring the creases in Lincoln's beard as the cab peels away. Later, Ashley will receive two barely-provoked, if wholly deserved, punches in the face from a jailed black woman, while a Suge Knight-type record company overlord (Faizon Love) will declare: "I used to be [an idealist and a purist]...but then I decided to become filthy rich." I'm as surprised as you are that D.W. Griffith didn't write the treatment for this thing.

But inciting darkie panic may be the least of *Just My Luck*'s myriad offenses. Although Lohan has no comedic instincts and delivers every line of dialogue in that laryngitic monotone of hers, it's not merely her phantom appeal that gets her into trouble here. With her ubiquitous presence in the media for all manner of pop-tart transgressions, she simply brings too much baggage to the proceedings; at the risk of equating a stick of Disney jerky with a bona fide screen siren (or a steaming turd with a masterpiece like *Cat on a Hot Tin Roof*), this must be what it was like to watch Elizabeth Taylor movies back in the day. In *Just My Luck*, Ashley's lifelong lucky streak comes to a crashing halt when she kisses an accursed stranger, Jake (pod person Chris Pine), at a masquerade ball, thus passing her good fortune onto him and inheriting his bad in return. Yet because of Lohan's offscreen sense of entitlement (those tales of truancy that Morgan Creek founder James G. Robinson exposed have real half-lives), the early scenes ring insufferably true, while her subsequent string of *Final Destination*-style torments inspires nothing but schadenfreude. In other words, postmodernism insinuates itself through Lohan's casting, but both the actress and the movie go about their business with blissful ignorance.

*Just My Luck* whitewashes, for example, the uglier implications of its Cinderella allegory in pinballing Ashley around New York City in search of the man who infected her[1] by having her taste-test each suspect. (She then scratches a lottery ticket to see whether her luck has returned.) While the filmmakers have skewed young by reducing the paraphernalia of adult sexuality to mistletoe, they've contradictorily equated kissing with unprotected sex and promiscuity. (What is Ashley's predicament but a fairytale simile for venereal disease?) Taking this into account with Lohan's coquettish reputation, a moment where Ashley complains that one of the potential culprits bit her tongue registers as particularly skeezy: she's French'ing them?! While we're at it, why doesn't she swap fates as well as spit with any of these other guys? I guess that's a rhetorical question, since I've essentially just said that the movie is sorely lacking in foresight.

There are a few actresses in Lohan's age bracket who could've made Ashley's self-centeredness a little more innocuous, a little less soulless—*Just My Luck*'s own Bree Turner, for instance. (Like Rachel McAdams and Alison Pill before her, the unspeakably cute Turner renders Lohan an even more inexplicable sex object simply by being in her orbit.) Conversely, if there were a female equivalent to Bill Murray out there to endow Ashley with a puckish swagger, it might've at least transformed that section of the film where she's unbearably lucky into a genuine guilty pleasure—there are few greater vicarious thrills than watching old-school Murray reign supreme over us unsuspecting mortals—as opposed to an aggravating reminder of Lohan's unearned, unappreciated cachet. But, of course, the script is so shallow as to be irredeemable. Fitting that Sarah Jessica Parker is invoked at some point (Ashley receives her dry-cleaning by mistake and, without compunction, wears it instead of returning it), since *Just My Luck* is to "Sex and the City" as Brownies are to the Girl Scouts.[2] One of the screenwriters actually worked on "Sex and the City" and it shows, not only in the amoral veneration of Ashley's "That Girl" smugness, but also in the scrupulous annotation of her footwear.

As for Jake: a struggling music producer repping four hobbits collectively known as **McFly**[3], he's saintly before he inherits her luck and remains uncorrupted by the riches visited upon him thereafter. If anything, his newfound success only facilitates a latent desire to be charitable. Recognizing the newly-disaster-prone Ashley's breed of embarrassment—though not, curiously, her greasy, liver-spotted countenance—at a diner, he rescues her from a hairy situation, gets her his old job at the bowling alley, and basically invites her to convalesce from her reality-check at his tricked-out pad.[4] (It's *The Apartment* for the T-Mobile generation.) To be perfectly reductive, affluence humbles Jake, whereas going back to square one turns Ashley into a barnacle. So what is the desired outcome of Ashley's predicament? Waiting for her to kiss Jake is a lot like waiting for Dracula to bite Mina Harker; wouldn't it make more sense to have Jake be the venal one?

After all, *Just My Luck* isn't interested in redeeming Ashley. Sure, she makes an overture ("You deserve my luck, you put it to better use than I ever did," she tells Jake), but as with any remotely human gesture on the aforementioned "Sex and the City", it registers as passive-aggressive bait—she's a narcissist fishing for compliments. I might add that after reclaiming her luck on a knee-jerk whim, Ashley ditches her patsy to go shopping and is wholly unsympathetic upon hearing that her friend's song has been dropped from **McFly**'s set as a result of Jake's bad luck. (She's really kind of a sociopath.) I suppose that secularizing the film's high-concept hook would've helped: because luck is explicitly shown to be a product of divine intervention rather than a state of mind, it leaves accountability out of the equation. But then, that's what attracted the starlet with the biggest...martyr complex in Hollywood to the project, isn't it? OMG! It's *The Passion of the Lohan*! (**BC**)

1. It took me a while to remember where I'd seen this before: Larry Clark's Kids!

2. Star Wars for COSMO GIRL subscribers, "Sex and the City" has been sanitized for syndication, making it more virulent than it ever was. See, the T&A was always far less offensive than the superficiality of the show's central quartet, and now their materialistic, misanthropic doctrine has the potential to seduce a much broader audience. Having bought a white suit in sixth grade, circa the heyday of "Miami Vice", I don't doubt that it's pretty tempting for tweener girls to emulate Parker's dynamic Carrie Bradshaw.

3. Although this is a kind of "origin story" for the real-life musicians, Lohan is probably not cloaked in as much fiction as they are.

4. *Isn't it a little, um, lucky that she runs into him again? And the bad that results from trying to extinguish a sparking hairdryer under a tap while it's still plugged in, or waxing a floor in stiletto heels, or pouring an entire box of soap into a washing machine has fuck-all to do with chance, for these are the actions of a spaz. When you get right down to it,* Just My Luck *is one mouse shy of becoming a reverse <u>Flowers for Algernon</u>.*

# K

## KEEPING MUM
½* /****
st. Rowan Atkinson, Kristin Scott
Thomas, Maggie Smith, Patrick
Swayze
sc. Richard Russo and Niall
Johnson
dir. Niall Johnson

With Patrick Swayze no longer in the
public eye as anything but a pop-
cultural toss away on one of those VH1
retrospective shows, his entry into the
conversation these days is as a shade
of his iconic man-mentor. He's not
entirely unlike guys like Robert De
Niro in that way, though unlike De
Niro, I don't think Swayze is
disrespectfully cashing in on his
legacy. Sadly, that respect is tested by
*Keeping Mum*, an insufferable British
dark comedy in the tradition of other
happy-horseshit classics *Waking Ned
Devine* and *Greenfingers* and *The Full
Monty* and on and on into quirky
geriatric hijinks purgatory. Dame
Maggie Smith stars as Grace, a well-
meaning sociopath who becomes the
housekeeper in the house of schlub
priest Walter (Rowan Atkinson), his
frustrated wife (Kristin Scott Thomas),
and his nymphomaniac daughter
(Tamsin Egerton). Swayze lampoons
his beefcake mentor persona here (as
he does much better in *Donnie Darko*)
as the golf pro lothario Walter's wife is
banging on the side. Spoiling nothing
because no one is going to rent this
film (just as no one went to see it in
theatres), Grace kills him in a moment
of mercy for everyone involved:
audience included. *Keeping Mum* is an
unfortunate crossbreed of *Saving Grace*,
a Tom Ripley novel, and *Monkey
Shines*—an unbearably fey tea-and-
crumpets opera mixed with a serial
killer machinations that suggests that
carefully-calculated murder is the way
to social order and real happiness. I
like the idea, I must confess, that the
only way to truly walk the Christian
walk is through the acceptance of
greater atrocity, but the picture is way
too dim-witted to be a satire of
organized religion or, better yet, man's
eternal struggle with its Old Testament
self. No, *Keeping Mum* is best regarded
as a smug, self-satisfied bit of ugliness
perpetrated by guys who should know
better. (**WC**)

## THE KING (see: *HARD CANDY*)

# L

## LADY IN THE WATER
ZERO STARS/****
st. Paul Giamatti, Bryce Dallas Howard, Bob Balaban, Jeffrey Wright
w./d. M. Night Shyamalan

## SYMPATHY FOR LADY VENGEANCE
****/****
st. Lee Yeong-ae, Choi Min-sik, Kim Shi-hoo, Kwon Yea-young
w./d. Park Chanwook

The creeping, inescapable feeling is that M. Night Shyamalan would like to be known as "M. Christ Shyamalan": a guy who wants you to drink the Kool-Aid; a messiah with a shrinking flock preaching a platform that his increasingly deluded, astonishingly arrogant fables are actually themselves the secret to world peace. He claims to hear voices—the first couple of times he did so (here in the stray interview, there in *The Buried Secret of M. Night Shyamalan*, that abhorrent mock-documentary he did for the Sci-Fi Channel), I thought he was kidding. Hell, the first couple of times he did it, he probably *was* kidding. But I don't think he's kidding anymore. And there's no longer any currency in playing this ethereal shaman card. Prancing about like a mystic while shitting away millions of other people's money isn't a pastime with longevity: it's something only a zealot would do. I think he's gone off the deep end, hubris first, overfed to bloating on a steady diet of his own press and the tender ministrations of yes-men too afraid to set off Shyamalan's diseased persecution complex by telling him that while he might be good at a few things, *Lady in the Water* was unsalvageable. When Disney executives did approximately

that, Shyamalan took his ball and went across the street to Warner Brothers.

Thing is that everything Disney told Shyamalan about this film (that he needed not to take such a big role for himself, that he needed not to have an officious asshole of a film critic be the victim of an animal attack, that the script begged another pass through the typewriter at least) turns out to have been pretty fair, and temperate, criticism. What they also should have told him—if they didn't—is that, as an Asian himself, he should resist the urge to indulge in the two most damaging stereotypes this culture harbours for Asian women: the first the "me ruv you rong time" pidgin-shouting gook whore (poor Cindy Cheung, whose character Yung Soon is introduced from behind as two men try not to gape at her tits), the other the wizened non-English speaking Dragon Lady, spitting and cursing hilariously while offering the Ancient Chinese Secret, introduced by "regend say." No, I'm not kidding. Pair them with the Mexican family featuring five howling girls (who, in the film's prologue, hysterically identify a bug under their sink as a creature sent from the devil) and find in *Lady in the Water* a picture distasteful not only for its creator's raging God complex, but also for Shyamalan's abandonment of narrative, film craft, and shame. Put aside all of the film's philosophical pomposity and *Lady in the Water* is still boring, embarrassingly stupid, humiliatingly transparent, notably un-thrilling, and able in its one feat of enchantment (and only discernible twist) to make the low-brow decision-makers at Disney look like fucking geniuses.

Opening with a simple animation in the vein of *Watership Down*'s prologue (if not nearly as cool), *Lady in the Water* tells of the sea-bound narfs, who once upon a time had a deep spiritual connection with Man—but Man was so consumed by an overwhelming need to "own everything" he lost contact with the narfs. Yet the narfs didn't give up on Man and thus send their daughters— in this case Story (Bryce Dallas Howard), an apparently-exceptional *madam* narf—to track down people they hope to "awaken" with some kind of Man-saving inspiration. Beginning its life as a bedtime story Shyamalan elaborated upon nightly for his kids, *Lady in the Water* succeeds, if nothing else, at putting us to sleep, and in record time.

Opposing the narfs are scrunts, dogs with grass for hair, while narfs successful in spreading their blank message of non-specific hope are ferried home by giant eagles that, in Shyamalan's wondrous fantasia, are called Giant Eagles. There's also a trio of monkeys made out of trees called the "Tartutic," completing a cycle of nonsense noises. I've been speaking an Asian tongue for thirty-plus years now and I'm pretty confident that noises like "narf" and "tartutic" and "scrunt" and "giant eagle" just don't occur. That's one place to poke a hole in this abortion—others include a scene where apartment superintendent Cleveland Heep (Paul Giamatti) holds his breath for twenty minutes, or the question of how if the narf is only in peril from the scrunt when it's out of the water, why not get back in the water? In fact Story, despite having a luxury cave at the bottom of the pool, hardly spends any time there—they should've called it "Lady in Schneider's Apartment". I wondered, too, why a girl dragged around by her head and neck by a giant grass dog would have scratches on her legs alone, and how Shyamalan could have possibly thought that it was okay to cast himself as the to-be-martyred author of a new Bible from which a future President will take cues to save the universe.

The message of the film seems to be that it takes a village to save the narf that will reveal M. Christ Shyamalan as a true prophet. (I only wish it were ridiculous that the leader of the free world would be guided by a compromised mythology.) When the inevitable cheap sentiment section of the proceedings unfolds, with Cleveland using his high hanky-wringing past to heal Story in a ritual resembling one of those collective-sharing workshops, take a moment to mourn the exploitation of all these real actors (Jeffrey Wright, Mary Beth Hurt, and Jared Harris are likewise snared in this thing) doing their best to avoid looking their deranged master in the eye. It's the would-be emotional epiphany of the movie, the moment where Cleveland exorcises his demons and embraces the idea that everyone's life has value no matter how worthless they are, and it comes off like a sadistic parlour trick. I should mention that Method stuttering explosions aside, this is the first film in which I've liked Giamatti; that Howard would make a wonderful decorative candle; and that if Shyamalan has any friends left who still have his best interests at heart, it might be time to stage some sort of intervention before Philadelphia's favourite son's voices instruct him to climb a water tower.

Where Shyamalan envisions Grace as a group hug, South Korean auteur Park Chanwook sees it as an animal slippery and savage and prone to biting the hand that holds its leash. Park completes his vengeance trilogy (*Sympathy for Mr. Vengeance*, *Oldboy*) with *Sympathy for Lady Vengeance*, wherein, for arguably the first time, he contemplates a real psychic cost of avenging unimaginable losses, discovering, at the end of three films' worth of perverse bloodshed and genuinely Greek atrocity a better definition for the idea of Grace. Just the possibility of Grace in Park's world is something that verges on horrible, a reminder eloquent that the last and most terrible thing released by Pandora's box is Hope; credit Park for crafting a beautiful picture that takes the moral middle. Lee Geum-ja (Lee Yeong-ae) is hope personified in *Sympathy for Lady Vengeance*: convicted of abducting and murdering a five-year-old boy, she spends her time in prison championing the downtrodden, going so far as to donate one of her kidneys to an antagonist as down-payment on a future favour. It seems like it's going to be a distaff <u>The Count of Monte Cristo</u>, but like ducks in a row, Park mows down routes to redemption (through atonement, through religion, through reunion, through traditional social structures, through violence) for his heroine, who is so attractive that no matter her actions, we wish her satisfaction.

Identification with the monster is nothing new in cinema, but *Sympathy for Lady Vengeance* is out to ruin you. After a first half that thrills with the audacity of its technical acumen, Park presents a second half that touches on the claustrophobia of *Sympathy for Mr. Vengeance*, climaxing in a scene before a video monitor in a children's classroom that counts as among the most sadistic and wrenching in a director's portfolio notorious for eliciting like emotions. The laughter in the film is of the delighted variety — like almost every other emotion elicited by the piece, it's designed to provoke a reflexive revulsion in our delight. When a wronged woman pauses before plunging a knife into her tormentor, our desire to see her to skewer the pig gives us pause in a way that any number of revenge pictures simply do not. Gruelling in the best sense of the word, *Sympathy for Lady Vengeance* embodies all the artistry, introspection, and courage to which something like *Lady in the Water* can only pretend. It's the product of an actual artist with an actual vision, shaping a piece with the same spring-loaded barbs as later, bitter Hitchcock masterpieces like *North by Northwest* wherein the heroes are villains and the villains are equally insupportable. More to the point, like Hitchcock again, *Sympathy for Lady Vengeance* is a self-parodying genre picture that does no disservice to pictures of the genre; an exhilarating exercise in the never-more-topical balancing of the ethics of man vs. the ethics of man as beast; and

the umpteenth example of how the spirit of the age impregnates hack and master alike. (**WC**)

## THE LAKE HOUSE
**\* /\*\*\*\***

*st.* Keanu Reeves, Sandra Bullock, Dylan Walsh, Christopher Plummer
*sc.* David Auburn
*dir.* Alejandro Agresti

I couldn't help but conjecture, while watching the trailer for Alejandro Agresti's inexplicable *The Lake House*, that when Keanu Reeves' character is poring over a letter, a little thought bubble above his head would say, "Dude, I totally can't read." Continuing to think that is the only thing providing much of a distraction during the laggardly-paced, sloppily-scripted, hilariously-acted proceedings, which, as that same preview gives away, concern the romance of two people separated by two years, exchanging letters through the providence of a magic mailbox. Argentinean director Agresti's visual compositions are meticulous and his eye for architecture is almost as good as that of his protagonist, Alex Wyler (Reeves), but it's cold comfort against the raging inferno of illogic attending this scenic, stupid, Nicholas Sparks-ian shipwreck. Not helping things is Agresti's lamentable penchant for cornpone, exhibiting itself most stridently in the piano-tinkle, magical-elf-opening-a-treasure-chest score and a series of whimsical wipe-edits and dog reaction shots. Among its dedicated sub-genre of time-warp kiss-face (*Somewhere in Time, Happy Accidents*), *The Lake House* is a dud, too, frustrating first because its big gushy epiphany is solved by everyone with a working pre-frontal within a second of it happening, and second because Wyler, lagging two years behind his beloved Kate (Sandra Bullock), never once thinks to ask for a lotto number or a World Series winner. Even within the logic of the film, when Alex misses a date with Kate (he makes a dinner reservation two years in advance of Kate's next night), everyone in the audience not only knows why he doesn't show, but also wonders why Kate doesn't just pick up a phone book and ask what's keeping him. Two years isn't two hundred years, after all, and in this era of shrinking time, it isn't really two years, anymore, either. Just within the rules the film establishes for itself, nothing that these characters do to achieve their inevitable moment of suck-face makes a lick of sense. It's a one-trick pony and that pony is tortured near to death. Worst might be the casting of Reeves (whose romantic films—like the legendarily stupid *Sweet November*, in which he slings a dish-washing machine over his shoulder and carries it up a fire escape through a second-story window, or the also stupid, if dishwasher-free, *A Walk in the Clouds*—should be screened in conjunction for a good understanding of pop surrealism) against Bullock: he with his drugged incomprehension, she with her fussy, animated-pig voice (like a non-drag-queen version of Kathy Griffin) constantly chewing itself around the same romcom treacle that should by now belie the perception of her as a smart cookie. Agresti uses tricks to suggest the two are talking to one another, their gentle (some would call it boring) repartee impossible to conceptualize as correspondence left in a mailbox—but there you have it. As a film, then, it's more like a dinner party idea rushed to the drawing board without a middle or a resolution.

Genuinely insipid, *The Lake House* is home to profession-/dialogue-as-character development, like Alex saying he's an architect because "I like to build things." (Meanwhile, Kate is a doctor because she's "dedicated to caring for the sick.") Alex's sidekick is a ghostly sketch of a brother (Ebon Moss-Bachrach) while Kate is saddled with poor, thankless Shohreh Aghdashloo as her no-nonsense, tough-talking surgical resident—both

second bananas are invested with the picture's perfunctory skepticism, and both are shuttled off into the atmosphere as soon as they've given the star-crossed lovers a chance to ooze on about how "Dude, she's like more totally real to me than a real girl... Dude." I liked the sick little black girl who introduces Kate (and us) to the idea that the love story in *Notorious* is the ideal model for Kate and Alex (brought to us by people who either have a really sick sense of humour or have never seen *Notorious*), because, truly, what other purpose is there for ailing minority children than to facilitate a date for two upper-class white folks (see also: *The Interpreter* and its million dead black people). I liked how Alex plants a tree in the past and it materializes, suddenly and terrifyingly, right next to Kate in the future (lucky that it doesn't appear under her or through her). And I really liked how the picture introduces Jane Austen's <u>Persuasion</u> not once, not twice, but thrice, I guess to give the picture a little literary juice. The final nail, though, is a ten-minute finale that tries like hell for inscrutable reasons to transmogrify this trudge through Moronville into a rip-snorting suspense flick (which hinges, of course, on Alex being able to read something and—aye, here's the rub— *understand it* as well), wrapping it all up package-neat without also resolving how it is that this thing is at all like <u>Persuasion</u>, *Notorious*, or even *Kate & Leopold*. (**WC**)

**LAST HOLIDAY (see: *GLORY ROAD*)**

PREVIOUSLY UNPUBLISHED
**THE LAST KING OF SCOTLAND**
*/****
*st.* Forest Whitaker, James McAvoy, Kerry Washington, Gillian Anderson
*sc.* Peter Morgan and Jeremy Brock, based on the novel by Giles Foden

*dir.* Kevin Macdonald

## THE QUEEN
**\*\*/\*\*\*\***

*st.* Helen Mirren, Michael Sheen,
James Cromwell, Sylvia Sims
*sc.* Peter Morgan
*dir.* Stephen Frears

Because he's black, there's no way that anyone in their right mind could be interested in a straight biopic of one of the most notorious genocidal maniacs of the twentieth century. Insert, then, a fictional white protagonist (see also: *Men of Honor*)-cum-foil to dilute the Afro-aversion. It's a storied trend in Hollywood to send bwana into the darkest continent to save the savages from themselves—fuck, it's a storied trend in the Christian world: be saved or be crucified, am I right? If it's not Jennifer Connelly and Leonardo DiCaprio essaying the troubles they've seen in Sierra Leone, it's James McAvoy in Uganda, playing personal doctor to Idi Amin (Forest Whitaker) and engaging in an adulterous affair with one of the madman's wives. Why? I don't really know, except to provide drama to what already couldn't be more dramatic, or to add a weird racial/jungle feverish element to the proceedings the film doesn't have the wit or the balls to follow through on. Maybe to attract a provincial, high school-educated, middle-American audience that wouldn't be caught dead in an arthouse in the first place? I'm reminded of newspapers trying desperately to court the "Joe Lunchbox" demographic—and I'm reminded of how quickly newspapers have made themselves obsolete. *The Last King of Scotland* is dreadful, formula pabulum buoyed by one virtuoso performance from the oft-underutilized Whitaker that conveys a terrifying *bonhomie*, which if nothing else clarifies Amin's ability to earn followers with one hand and fill mass graves with their bodies with the other. It's quite a shame that the performance gets recognition from the Academy because its mode of delivery is this colourless, shapeless, gelatin suppository of a movie.

It's quite a shame, too, that *The Last King of Scotland* is so fucking racist. Amin is a cartoon bogey, and because he's more gorilla in the room than fleshed-out man, his victims are the charnel in a slasher pic instead of real live folks who had the misfortune of living in Uganda during this time. While there's a certain temporal synergy in any tale told today about people captive beneath a charismatic (to some—and by "some," I mean "redneck assholes") leader who's making their lives miserable, that's really grasping for wheat from this chaff. McAvoy's fictional doctor is first tasked with relieving the dictator of his pent-up flatulence, then with assuming the national dilemma with his own acts of selfishness and hedonism. If he becomes Uganda under Amin, his final uplifting acts of semi-heroism are the crucifix and nails through which the country can be remade—namely in the image of a white saviour, white role model, white white white. What I'd like to see one day is a story about Queen Elizabeth told through the eyes of a fictional Chinese diplomat who, through his noble example, teaches Britain a little something about the value of Confucianism and building great big walls, the better to keep the Huns at the gates. Insulting, right? Fascination blossoms accidentally here in Amin's real-life declaration of himself as the King of Scotland—a conceit that sublimates the picture's existence, its Scottish director and star, and this broad consent to the idea that the only way towards importance for an African story is through a Caucasian scrim.

Despite coming from the same screenwriter, no such concerns mar Stephen Frears' exceptionally ordinary docudrama *The Queen*, again featuring a virtuoso central performance (from Helen Mirren as Queen Elizabeth) and a set of real-life events that give an otherwise lightweight, meaningless actor's studio the whiff of importance and grit. Essayed here are the days following the death-by-fame of Princess Di, a period that, because the monarchy is entrenched in the belief that a certain distance is what's expected of them, nearly led to the fall of the throne in our emotionally-exploitative media wonderland. If it's not on tape, it didn't happen—so grief has nothing to do with privacy, but with the perfectly modulated soundbite. As small declarations go, it's not a bad one to chat about. Politely. Over tea, perhaps. *The Queen* is the very definition of serviceable and workmanlike. It's easy to praise, not so easy to get excited about; the kind of movie that knobs you don't trust declare to be the antidote to the alleged dreck in the cineplex, betraying their awesome debt to dinosaurs like Vincent Canby in the same breath. Who gets boners from dead-on impersonations of Liz and Tony Blair (Michael Sheen) talking about what's best for the Royals? Who gets thrills when Liz beaches her car in a river and sort of mutters a swear word under her breath? What's left for the rest of us is to applaud the performances, compare the representations to personal perceptions, believe that we've learned something of interest or not, and hurry on to movies that don't wear their pedigree like a condom. *The Queen* is a prophylactic to real edification—it feels good while it's going on, but nothing's getting alive as a result of it. (**WC**)

## THE LAST KISS
ZERO STARS/****
*st.* Zach Braff, Jacinda Barrett, Casey Affleck, Tom Wilkinson
*sc.* Paul Haggis, based on the screenplay for L'Ultimo Bacio by Gabriele Muccino
*dir.* Tony Goldwyn

## TRUST THE MAN
½*/****
*st.* Billy Crudup, David Duchovny, Maggie Gyllenhaal, Julianne Moore
*w./d.* Bart Freundlich

Zach Braff's auto-elevation into the rarefied air of Ed Burnsian self-satisfaction has required a fraction of the smarmcoms, if a meaningful assist from an obscenely-popular TV show that's running on fumes at this point. *Garden State* is dreadful, of course, swarming with awkward, overwritten, creepy alt-folk montages and pocket epiphanies (just like "Scrubs", albeit with half the rage and exploitation of frailty), but team up former "The Facts of Life" scribe (and Oscar-winning screenwriter) Paul Haggis with instant-brand Braff—he's like sea monkeys: just add grease—for *The Last Kiss* and discover in the alchemy a more pungent, twice-as-stale vintage of a type of picture that used to be done with grace and wit by people like Whit Stillman and Hal Hartley, cheapened by noxious voice-overs and skeezy dialogues obsessed with the female orgasm without having the honesty to actually show one. What we get instead is the idea that this shit sells to a privileged "indie"-craving hipster demographic oblivious to the fact that "indie" films are as homogenous a ghetto as any other now. (Independent of what? Alternative to what?) There's nothing genuine about these "relationshit" flicks (thanks to blogger John Landis for the term); they're a sloppily-baited hook dangling in a waitlisted stucco bistro.

Braff is prototypical emo yuppie Michael, who, on the eve of tying the knot with lovely Jenna (Jacinda Barrett), meets a free-spirit skank (Kim (Rachel Bilson)) and almost (or successfully) ruins everything in the pursuit of fresh tail. Inevitably, *The Last Kiss* will be about either learning that what's really important is a stale monogamous existence (*My Best*

*Friend's Wedding*) or learning that the fiancée is a bitch/whore much better off with an accountant than with our architect/ad exec/artist hero, thus freeing the latter to commit adultery as he pleases (or, more likely, retroactively excusing his infedility). If it's wish-fulfillment, it's a pretty ugly variety of it—but more often than not, the relationshit pic boils down to endless pop-culture/pop-psych conversations punctuated by *faux*-emotional spikes and walking/shopping/raining montages scored with the tops of the vagina charts. Count *The Last Kiss* as a film that treats its women characters as the entire Greek pantheon of hysterical goddesses, from a flat-crazy mother (Blythe Danner in a series of ironed housecoats) pining after an old flame to our collegiate temptress (who, for no earthly reason, is mightily attracted to thirtysomething milquetoast Michael), to finally our damsel in distress Jenna, three months pregnant (her hormones blamed more than once for her behaviour—and she agrees!) and ready to pull a knife on Michael when he cops to snogging his clueless stalker.

It's inauthentic, to say the least. Not a scene of it plays quite right, and as *The Last Kiss* couldn't be considered obscure, the only thing left to think is that it's incompetent—a failed test of a limited writer trying on quirk and once again proving most at home with facile characterizations and pat, hermetically-sealed traps that pose unlikely scenarios with predetermined outcomes. Hyperbolic, epic, screeching disintegrations are the spine of this soppy melodrama, the winner of which is the eternally-slumming Tom Wilkinson, cast as a cold fish for being a grown-up in what used to be an adolescent coming-of-age set-up (Michael does everything short of lifting a boombox over his head to win back his lady fair): a grown-up with a normal speaking voice, a reluctance to feel sorry for himself, and a paucity of Byronic one-whiners. Based on a bad-

but-not-this-bad Italian film, *The Last Kiss* distinguishes itself as unusually poor because its metaphors for arrested adolescence range wide and slapdash. A subplot involving slut Kenny (Eric Christian Olsen) and his acrobatic single-guy sexual exploits rings indescribably lecherous—it's like you're watching an awful Noah Baumbach ripper when suddenly Cinemax soft-porn breaks out. Exactly like. And by the time chinless, overcast Michael finally shtups bat-faced cyborg Kim, you've developed such a dislike for both of them that it's not merely unerotic, it's downright irritating. A literally sodden finale is likewise so aggravating that the only thought that crossed my mind as it unfolded was if or where Michael was taking a piss during his interminable, creepy, **Coldplay**-narrated vigil.

Say this for Bart Freundlich's *Trust the Man*: even if you wonder about the pissing habits of Billy Crudup's Tobey, it's not at the climax/resolution of the picture. The eternally-arrested adolescents in this particular morose fit of compulsive yak are Tobey and his brother-in-law Tom (David Duchovny, at least not writing/directing this one), who through childish inclinations sabotage their relationships with women they don't deserve in the first place before rescuing them with equally childish demonstrations. Tobey doesn't want to get too serious with aspiring children's-book author Elaine (Maggie Gyllenhaal) and Mr. Mom Tom wants constant intercourse with his glamorous actress wife Rebecca (Julianne Moore, Freundlich's glamorous actress wife). The two couples separate and find unfulfilling love in the arms of joke paramours because real contenders for affection and respect are complicated to write and resolve; and in the end, all these people we've decided we don't like, much less identify with, end up back together so as to breed adorable, *Annie Hall*-dressed, poop-obsessed moppets. Freundlich isn't as poor a writer as

Haggis, though he does suffer from the same sick desire to patly resolve his romantic frictions. It makes *Trust the Man* (and *The Myth of Fingerprints* and *World Traveler*) almost more disappointing because the clouds unerringly part for a moment or two in Freundlich's pictures, offering a glimpse of a guy who may not be a complete snag but still can't resist chasing the path of least resistance whenever a scene gets tangled. That feeling is called "betrayal," as you're led to feel confident about a director's ability to guide a ship to a far, strange shore only to discover, amid an Ephron sisters chain of *faux*-delightful contrivances, that the hull's been compromised since leaving port. **(WC)**

**LETTERS FROM IWO JIMA (see: CHILDREN OF MEN)**

**LITTLE CHILDREN**
*\*¹/₂/\*\*\*\**
st. Kate Winslet, Patrick Wilson, Jennifer Connelly, Gregg Edelman
sc. Todd Field & Tom Perrotta, based on the novel by Perrotta
dir. Todd Field

Kate Winslet is a joy if no longer a revelation, and in Todd Field's *Little Children*, she demonstrates the kind of courage that has made her the most essential actress of her generation. Aside from Winslet, *Little Children* feels like a burlesque of deep-feeling pictures: the lesser of two possible sophomore efforts from the guy who brought us *In the Bedroom*, which was, in 2001, my since-regretted pick for best of the year. (I can be a sucker for well-played big emotions, I guess.) But *Little Children* is icy, stentorian, and patrician in its staginess and self-consciousness, and its disdain for its subject matter is front and centre. The picture presents its tale of suburban woe as the world's most condescending fairytale, inserting an omniscient narrator in a way that,

along with the upcoming *Stranger Than Fiction*, makes me wonder what it is about unseen movers that is so seductive in the modern conversation. I also wonder how Field and co-screenwriter Tom Perrotta (adapting his own book) could have rationalized the amount of bile mustered in reconfiguring *American Beauty* to include a raincoat perv (Jackie Earle Haley, the heart and soul of the film—if also its patsy and mule) and a sweaty adultery punctuated fatally by a winking nod to Madame Bovary.

The suspicion inescapable, however, is that Perrotta, who penned the source novel for one of the better social satires of the '90s, *Election*, has in fact fashioned a script intended to play like the ultimate snark-fest, complete and sneering in its shiny, polyester skin. When this material finds the hand that feeds in a hyper-real melodramaturgist like Field, the resulting concoction is a weird tension between someone playing it for tears and someone playing it for barbs. *Little Children* can only really be read as the goat in the satire: bearded, teeth-bared, and fast at ladling abuse upon itself as its audience readies to pounce. Take the nattering sewing cotillion that is the picture's chittering Greek Chorus of Stay-At-Home-Motherhood: they gather at the local playground, micromanage their children's playtime, and swoon like French ladies in waiting when Stay-At-Home Dad, Brad (Patrick Wilson), wheels his tyke in for a turn on the swings. Field sucks the air out of their scenes—where the other performances are alive and complex, theirs are stage-bound and mannered. And their queen, Mary Ann (Mary B. McCann), is so rigid in her small-minded villainy that what could she be but an allegorical every-bitch?

The same fate befalls too-educated Sarah (Winslet). In baggy sweaters and ugly mom-pants and with a daughter she doesn't seem to love in tow, she moons over dimwit loser Brad and her own adolescent dream of disaffected disassociation. She's less a carefully-

126

drawn character than a cautionary tale, just as there was never anyone as doofus-y as Brad (a key point comes when he's transfixed by teens jumping off steps on their skateboards—this film's plastic bag in the wind)—just as there was never any mother (May McGorvey) as Ma Kettle as indecent-exposure artist Ronald's (Haley). The caricatures are so vicious and uni-dimensional that *Little Children* suddenly if briefly becomes unique in that it actually has the balls to attack the bread and butter of the indie dysfunction genre. It's only a satire upon deep reflection, though, the same way *In the Bedroom* might be read as the world's sneakiest satire of over-wrought prestige pieces: by being almost the perfect example of that which it seeks ostensibly to overthrow. Imitation is the sincerest form of flattery *and* the most devastating form of criticism, it's true—but where *Little Children* loses itself is in trying to keep one foot on both bases. Meant as profound in some way, it's profound in no way. (**WC**)

## LITTLE JERUSALEM (La Petite Jérusalem)
**\*\*/\*\*\*\***
*st.* Fanny Valette, Elsa Zylberstein, Bruno Todeschini, Hédi Tillette de Clermont-Tonnerre
*w./d.* Karin Albou

The deck of *Little Jerusalem (La Petite Jérusalem)* is so obviously stacked from the very beginning that it's not much fun to actually play the game. We know from the outset that its philosophy-student heroine, Laura (Fanny Valette), is going to fly the coop from her stifling Orthodox Jewish home. (A few stern words from her married sister Mathilde (Elsa Zylberstein) are deemed sufficient grease for the wheels of antagonism for the full 94 minutes.) Laura's fall from vacillation between the two stools doesn't feel like much of a struggle, even though her Kantian

walks upset her proper family (they'd rather see her hitched and making babies); it's hard to rally much enthusiasm for the film's foregone conclusions, which are telegraphed at that. *Little Jerusalem* is painless enough, but there's no *there* there, and the whole thing evaporates minutes after you've sat through it.

Laura's transformation doesn't offer many surprises. Of course she falls in love with the wrong non-Jew—in this case, Arab co-worker Djamel (Hédi Tillette de Clermonte-Tonnerre). Of course her mother (Sonia Tahar) is predisposed towards her daughter giving up her studies. And of course ultra-pious Mathilde gets disappointed by straying husband Ariel (Bruno Todeschini), leading to a marriage counsellor's eye-opening revelation that coital pleasure is not against God's law. All very obvious story beats, all very obviously leading up to a moral that stands for freedom from a stifling religion. That the screenplay won a prize at Cannes is amazing: however writerly, it's really quite broad.

Writer-director Karin Albou tries to sell the rather mechanical script with a Bazinian realist style. No matter how forced or expository the exchange, the camera does not cut in, simply observing the action "naturally." This has the effect of loosening up what could have been stifling, though it can't actually cover up the deficiencies of the text. The more the style keeps cuing you to the reality of the action, the more you're reminded that it's not terribly convincing: far from hiding the wires, it exposes them as part of the machine. The talented cast also does what it can with the situation, but again their unforced approach to the roles underlines the forced nature of the situations. Nothing peripheral can triumph against a screenplay that's at once the main event and the kiss of death.

Aside from the occasional intrusion of anti-Semitic attacks (a synagogue is torched; masked thugs attack Ariel at a soccer field), *Little Jerusalem* fails to give a charge to any of its hugely painful events. This is most apparent when Djamel brings Laura home to meet mother and mother is scandalized by her son's choice of mate: it's an obligatory scene with a "Degrassi"-sized tin ear that only serves to embarrass you when it ought to be breaking your heart. (Bazin doesn't help in this case: the approach defuses the tension when it should be ratcheted up). The film is hardly disgraceful, but it's only "worthy": if it's not exploitive or melodramatic, neither is it very creative or insightful. We don't learn much more about Orthodox Judaism than we already gathered, and we leave entirely unmoved. (**TMH**)

## LITTLE MAN
*/****

*st.* Marlon Wayans, Shawn Wayans, Kerry Washington, John Witherspoon
*sc.* Keenen Ivory Wayans & Shawn Wayans & Marlon Wayans
*dir.* Keenen Ivory Wayans

An adult male the size of a baby masquerades as a toddler in order to retrieve a diamond he's stolen and secreted in the purse of a young suburban wife (Kerry Washington) who happens to be contemplating starting a family. This sets the stage for man-baby mistaken for baby-baby jokes, man-baby resenting being mistaken for baby-baby jokes, man-baby trying to suck tits, man-baby raping his adopted mother, and getting-pissed-on gags; meanwhile, a crotchety old man character (John Witherspoon) suspects foul play but, as he represents the other demographic no one listens to (besides black people), no one listens to him. That's it. Gut the Wayans machine's latest, *Little Man*, and all that slops out is a Möbius strip of high-concept sketch-comedy garbage that isn't really objectionable (save for the happy rape and the infantilization of a grown man

and all that) in any way while actually managing to know itself as owing a debt to *Baby Buggy Bunny en route* to offering a few nightmarish, surreal images. Marlon and, I think, Shawn are the key instigators of this one, with Keenen (I bet) the man behind the flat, uninvolved camera set-ups and pacing. On the scale of such things, it's not as bad as *Son of the Mask, Are We There Yet?*, or *Problem Child*, though it's vastly inferior to *Marci X*.

The worst thing I can say about the Wayans' body of work is that, for the most part, it dedicatedly avoids offending anyone of any race or creed—to make a film about a pair of black FBI agents masquerading as the Hilton sisters takes a special kind of genius for appeasement and assimilation. The much-publicized supremacy of the Wayans family's entertainment empire strikes me as a direct product of how easily they're embraced by the white culture as black people who don't threaten them with dangerous observations on racism, homophobia, and misogyny. Keenen, et al are a throwback, is what I'm saying, peppering their flicks with little mini-uplift vignettes, backhands to communal bruised targets (gays, women), and a vision of African-American culture that's completely rounded, often laughable, and vanilla. What's most remarkable about *Little Man* is when pint-sized felon Calvin (Marlon Wayans, why not) experiences his suburban domestication, it points to all the stereotypical ills of urban youth (broken family, poverty, lack of education, criminality) as salvagable by the magic bullet of a rambling ranch house, Amana appliances, and birthday parties with live entertainment. Hooray! To help this tiny hint of ugliness go down, and before it devolves into a cartoon complete with spring sound effects and a Dave Sheridan cameo, *Little Man* slathers itself in scatology, crotch-punching, hilarious elder/child abuse, and a brutal ration of unearned sentiment. (**WC**)

## LITTLE MISS SUNSHINE
**\*\*¹/₂/\*\*\*\***
*st.* Greg Kinnear, Steve Carrell,
Toni Collette, Paul Dano
*sc.* Michael Arndt
*dirs.* Jonathan Dayton and Valerie
Faris

## WORLD TRADE CENTER
**\*\* /\*\*\*\***
*st.* Nicolas Cage, Michael Pena,
Maggie Gyllenhaal, Maria Bello
*sc.* Andrea Berloff
*dir.* Oliver Stone

I laughed a little during *Little Miss Sunshine*, a piffle of a movie that boils down to that **Blind Melon** music video where the chubby girl in a bumblebee outfit finds joy at the end of three minutes of kicking ant piles by dancing in a field of misfits also wearing bumblebee outfits. It's a smarter, less-angry version of *Transamerica* while featuring the same number of depressed gay people and *Harold & Maude*-esque teenage boys; it's got the Wes Anderson stamp of approval for its coterie of sage oddballs, deadpan surrogates, and family decompositions; it has a stellar cast doing extremely predictable work at a stellar level; and it comes with the Sundance stamp of approval predestined for it because *Little Miss Sunshine* is a summary of every independent film since "dysfunction" became a hot-key button on critics' keyboards.

It's no wonder that the film is the new indie sensation because, in its way, *Little Miss Sunshine* is the *Scream* of its genre. If you were to bring a checklist, you'd tick off every quirky character box, from the foul-talking senior citizen (Alan Arkin) through to the reptilian father (Greg Kinnear), the wistful daughter (Abigail Breslin), the suicidal gay uncle (a winningly reserved Steve Carrell as the world's premier Proust scholar), the mop-topped, Nietzsche-reading teen too smart for this world (Paul Dano), and the tough-talking, big-loving, long-

suffering mom (Toni Collette). It's a road trip movie that ends in the "Big Competition," layering in a disappointment for each of the main characters. Dad's 9-step program to self-empowerment doesn't get the book greenlight he's been promised; Gramps learns the real cost of snorting heroin and reading roadside porn; teen's elaborate plan to undertake a vow of silence until his acceptance into the Air Force Academy hits a roadblock; and suicidal gay uncle touches us all, but in a welcome way. Targets include insensitive assholes who tell their young daughters they're fat and former beauty-pageant participants who pimp out their toddlers in hooker-wear for the express purpose of crippling them with self-esteem and performance issues for the rest of their trailer-bound lives. The ultimate message is that you should make lemonade and blood is thicker than water.

Saving grace for *Little Miss Sunshine* is that, despite its essential triteness, barnside targets, and a phenomenally misguided ending, its parts are more than the effect of its whole, with Dano's smart, soul-sick suburban philosopher (a giant, hand-sketched portrait of Nietzsche hangs on a bedsheet in his room) providing a Greek Chorus that's free, somehow, of rancour or judgment. The film walks that line and walks it well: you're not often left with the impression that it's hanging its characters out to dry for the sake of a joke at their expense. The weight of the world piles on this collection of pathological losers, and *Little Miss Sunshine* admirably decides against adding to it with our derision and condescension. I do wish that it didn't seem so inconsequential when all's said and done, because, in truth, everyone does such a nice job (Breslin, in particular, is fast becoming a reason to see a film by herself) with what they're given that I felt kind of badly that they weren't given something less threadbare and obvious.

The same feeling troubled me

following Oliver Stone's static, workmanlike retelling of the true rescue of two Port Authority policemen trapped in the ruins of the Twin Towers. Afraid of stepping on toes and stung, I have to think, by the reception that greeted Stone's hilarious rummage sale *Alexander*, *World Trade Center* is Stone at his most well-behaved. One senses the conspiracy maniac champing at the bit in the stray shot across the bow at how we're going to avenge this blow against our country (by taking down a Middle Eastern nation because its despot once tried to kill our current leader's daddy, apparently), or in recycled footage of Bush Jr. jetting across the country, pausing long enough at the stray landing strip to deliver robot platitudes and promises of vengeance—yet Stone resists politicizing the events of 9/11 by presenting what can most delicately be described as an entirely unexceptional film about completely familiar events. Nicolas Cage is twenty-one year vet McLoughlin while *Crash*-saint Michael Pena is rookie Jimeno; Maria Bello and Maggie Gyllenhaal, respectively, are their wives, and the events of the day play out in the style of an Irwin Allen disaster movie. McLoughlin and Jimeno hustle through the early chaos of lower Manhattan on that fateful morning, glimpse flashes of something or another momentous happening, demonstrate courage and resolve, hear resounding thuds that we might presume to be bodies falling to Earth, and then get buried in a series of theatre-rattling cave-ins and collapses.

Fairly gripping, Stone's foxhole instinct pairs well with this story, what with its militaristic uniform roll call and camaraderie between men under extreme duress. Once the buildings collapse, however, *World Trade Center* becomes a long time in the dark with actors pinned beneath tons of *faux*-rubble and the standard guilt about things not said to their loved ones before the sky fell. It's a *carpe diem* film, in its way, with Stone providing a few

quiet flashbacks to happier times, many of which involve McLoughlin beaming like an idiot over his children while his adoring wife looks on. Controversy is scrubbed from their lives (though it's suggested by Bello's wide-awake missus listening in silence to her husband going off to work) to the extent that no clear picture of who these men are emerges from the wreckage. What's left is a curiosity in Stone's career: a film that's afraid to suggest friction and that regards issues ripe for satire and examination (like the looney tunes Marine Staff Sgt. (Michael Shannon) who goes debris-diving at the advice of the Lord) with a straight, crowd-pleasing face.

For all his faults, Stone never much seemed to care what anyone else thought of his pictures before, making *World Trade Center* his most compromised-feeling picture as well as his most conventional. It's hard not to be apathetic towards a story with a pre-determined outcome (especially one that compacts Cage into a monosyllabic ball), and there's something un-serious about a film centered around two survivors of an event that claimed three-thousand lives. It's a READER'S DIGEST "Drama in Real Life" composite picture, its epiphanies minor and its execution pure movie-of-the-week. Maybe that's where Stone's buried his edge: in the idea that the reason we've turned 9/11 into an uplifting greeting card is that we've become too sissified as a nation of passive observers to be able to assimilate such an offense without an Oprah/Dr. Phil strategy of platitudes and soft-focus montages firmly in place. It's "always look on the bright side of life" as our new national slogan of mental illness and denial; at least *Little Miss Sunshine* knows it's about losers. (**WC**)

## LONDON
*¹/₂/****

*st.* Chris Evans, Jason Statham, Jessica Biel, Joy Bryant

w./d. Hunter Richards

SPOILER WARNING IN EFFECT. I'll say this for Hunter Richards' *London*: it's compelling enough that you want its "hero" to get his. Whatever the (obnoxious, belligerent, self-absorbed) nature of main character Syd (Chris Evans), he's a well-drawn example of a common macho type, meaning the more stupid things he does the more you crave to see his comeuppance. But "payback" in this case would mean rejection by his ex-girlfriend London (Jessica Biel), whose going-away party he's just crashed—and no matter how many flashbacks we get to him behaving like a jerk in her presence, the film's total commitment to his point-of-view gives us the sinking feeling that he's not going to receive the brush-off he deserves. And sure enough.

A more astute or perhaps objective writer-director would have found Syd's behaviour amusing—that is, the Pinter claustrophobia created by his barging into a party uninvited and then holing up in the bathroom the entire time. But in the heavy, inexperienced hands of Richards, this is occasion to have massive sub-Eric Bogosian exchanges while doing lines off a Van Gogh reproduction. Flanked by his trusty coke-dealer Bateman (Jason Statham), who's been dragged there against his better judgment, Syd proceeds to go through the motions of a) complaining about how much he misses London (the girl, not the city), b) professing half-considered beliefs tending towards atheism, and c) relating the rocky relationship he's desperate to rekindle. A relationship, I might add, that involves the belittlement of the woman to whom he can't even say "I love you."

Yet the detail in which Richards sketches Syd's quirks makes it irresistable to rubberneck. One isn't quite sure how to take his ranting: it could be a satire of a drug-addled hipster's mentality or it could be a vindication of same, and you stick around to see how it'll all shake down. Still, he's a hard character to take. The flashback scenes involve his ridiculous possessiveness and pseudo-intellectual bullying as London tries desperately to reason with him; after a few of these, you wonder why the hell she stuck around in the first place. There's another movie to be made about why some women tolerate a drip like Syd, but that's not on Richards' mind. Mostly, he's interested in elaborating upon the protagonist's self-martyrdom—which, while fascinating, only has the effect blotting out any reason we might have to sympathize.

True, the older Bateman (his name an allusion, perhaps, to one of the snort genre's pioneers, Bret Easton Ellis)—who has an Edward Albee sexual dysfunction that renders him "tragic" as well as a variety of sexual peccadilloes that at least make his getting-serious act funny—exposes Syd's callowness for what it is. But an about-face by London at the end is as puzzling as it is unlikely—unlikely, at least, for the assertive, no-nonsense woman we glimpse throughout the picture. We're assured that the young man has grown wiser, more chastened, but I wasn't buying it for a minute: nothing in that bathroom suggests that Syd was ready for a committed relationship with anything other than the asthmatic dog from whom he pinches barbiturates. (**TMH**)

## LOOKING FOR COMEDY IN THE MUSLIM WORLD
*/****

st. Albert Brooks, John Carroll Lynch, Sheetal Sheth, Fred Dalton Thompson
w./d. Albert Brooks

## D O C U M E N T A R Y
## WHY WE FIGHT
**/****

dir. Eugene Jarecki

The most frustrating thing about Albert Brooks' crushingly boring, infuriatingly unfunny *Looking for Comedy in the Muslim World* (hereafter *Comedy*) is the possibility that such was the intention all along. 'Lost in Arabia' (well, India and Pakistan—let's not get crazy, here) finds Brooks doing a high-wire act with post-modernism—the same one he's been doing his whole career, as it happens. At some point, though, it's fair to wonder how long you can push self-awareness before it finally flies apart in a storm of narcissistic deconstruction. Mull over, if you will, a moment where Brooks (as Brooks) recreates one of his classic gags—involving the world's most ironically-tragic ventriloquist—in the middle of an interminable stand-up routine staged in a New Delhi auditorium, closing his act with the dummy (the wooden one) drinking a glass of water. It's Brooks, and Brooks' film, in microcosm: a man who returns the term "mortification" to ritual and religion while being incapable of subsuming the belief that he's still the smartest guy in the room. The trick of *Comedy* is that in making a movie that isn't very funny about a man who isn't very funny in the middle of a gulf of cultural misunderstanding that's especially not very funny, Brooks hopes to draw a corollary between how the troubles of the world boil down to everybody's inability to communicate. As revelations go, it's not earth-shattering. Guess it goes without saying that it's also not worth the effort to get there.

*Comedy* opens with Penny Marshall in a casting session for her hopefully-fictional remake of *Harvey* (not that *Harvey* couldn't stand to be remade—what's scary is the thought that Marshall might still have a directing career), blasting Brooks' remake of *The In-Laws* just prior to Brooks showing up for an obligatory cup-of-coffee and a thank-you-very-much. It establishes the premise of the film (an aging, unpopular Jewish comic really needs a job) as well as that Brooks is possibly trying to make another clever point regarding his own alleged inadequacy by shooting the picture like a blind longshoreman, dropping boom mikes into the frame and lighting everything in a flat, "documentary" style. Once Marshall rejects Brooks for a role in a remake because he starred in a remake she doesn't like, it all gets so thuddingly, obviously, pleased with its wooden intellectualism that it could've been written by John Kerry. I do understand nuance and the kind of social satire that allowed Brooks' *Lost in America* to soar—and I also understand that *Comedy* is about as nuanced as a barium enema.

Summoned to Washington DC and given an assignment to infiltrate India and Pakistan to figure out what tickles the Muslim funny bone, Brooks complains about his airplane ride, his office, his handlers, and the impossibility of his ever producing a five-hundred page report for the State Department. The United States' bureaucracy is on the chopping block initially and we laugh good-naturedly at an old joke told again (if not particularly well), while a call-centre Mecca where dozens of Indians answer questions on behalf of American corporations threatens to be interesting. But then the general shittiness of India is brought into the crosshairs, and the laughter, without enough of a connection linking globalization to said shittiness, turns ugly. Brooks' bad time stops being a result of his State Dept. goons and starts being a result of the Third World. It could be that Brooks is illustrating how "Brooks" can only see the troubles of the world through the prism of his own deadly inconsequence in the public eye (certainly this is inferred when a spy overhears him going on about a bomb—referring to his show, naturally), but ultimately *Comedy* doesn't have any identity more dominant than this exhausting, plangent, pathetic vanity piece for a guy who once turned self-immolation into an art—and is now trying to stay current by turning it into a screed.

The way that Eugene Jarecki's *Why We Fight* (winner of the Grand Jury Prize at last year's Sundance Film Festival) fails isn't entirely different in that although it's a neo-Errol Morris montage documentary rather than a "*faux*-documentary," it likewise stumbles into its own navel and fatally loses its way. The logical companion piece to Jarecki's more—here's that word again—*nuanced* documentary *The Trials of Henry Kissinger*, *Why We Fight* examines America's hopelessly incestuous military/industrial complex (after all, as retired air force colonel Karen Kwiatkowski offers, "We elected a defense contractor as vice-president") through the veil of misinformation that led to our involvement in trying to quell a costly insurgency in the Middle East.

Featuring, initially, a nice mix of talking heads—including an outspoken John McCain—in addition to infuriating archival footage of the powers that be contradicting themselves habitually (maybe pathologically), the picture eventually leans too far on certified wacko Gore Vidal and the heartbreaking testimony of Vietnam Vet and ex-cop Wilton Sekzer, who lost a son in the fall of the WTC. Both the man's grief and the film itself start out affecting and end up Strangelove-ian, with Sekzer relishing his boy's name gracing a bomb dropped on a clearly not-responsible country and the film similarly indulging in dropping its own bombs on a hapless administration. Perhaps the very victim of outrage fatigue, I feel on the one hand glad that *Why We Fight* takes a strong stand from a political party that hasn't exhibited a backbone since before it was too late— but on the other, I can't help but be bugged by propaganda, no matter its point-of-view. Neither *Comedy* nor *Why We Fight* deals with the act of discovery, self or otherwise, instead sticking to the process of madly justifying conclusions (personal, popular, or pointless) with increasingly Byzantine tactics. (**WC**)

## LOOKING FOR KITTY
*/****

*st.* Edward Burns, David Krumholtz, Max Baker, Connie Britton
*w./d.* Edward Burns

This is Edward Burns' fifth feature. Wouldn't you think he'd have learned a little something about filmmaking by now? If Burns were a complete unknown outside the margins of the industry and this were his directorial debut, maybe we could pat him on the head, tell him good job, and stick *Looking for Kitty* on the refrigerator door, all the while assuming that now that he's proven he can make a movie and get it seen, he'll move on to something he actually cares about. But this is his *fifth* film. *Looking for Kitty* feels like the first attempt at narrative storytelling by a young, inexperienced screenwriter who's just glad to have finished something. It's the kind of thing you write before you've found your voice. This is where you start out, not where you end up.

*Looking for Kitty* is so simple it makes *The Adventures of Elmo in Grouchland* look like *Chinatown*. For starters, it's entirely without subtext. The problem isn't that Burns spells out everything for the audience, it's that he rarely has anything that needs spelling out. There's never an ambiguous moment where we might be forced to rely on our own subjective interpretation. It challenges my idea that a film should not require any prior experience on the part of the viewer: to understand *Looking for Kitty*, it's not necessary to have seen a movie before, much less been out in the real world interacting with people. It's one of the least demanding films I've ever encountered, about as taxing as a mug of warm skim milk.

I had wondered how this could possibly represent an evolution for Burns as an artist, but evidently it doesn't. In the DVD's audio commentary, he says that if he were a novelist this would be a novella, if he were a musician this would be his B-side. Burns had wanted to make a different film for six million, but when he had trouble raising the funds, he decided he was going to say "fuck Hollywood" and wrote a little something he could do on the cheap. He shot *Looking for Kitty* on digital video for around $200,000 with industry friends willing to work for little if any compensation. Remarkable. Why would they sacrifice a few weeks of their time for this? Did they actually believe in the project so much that they were willing to act in it during a cold New York winter? I wonder sometimes whether I truly understand the artistic process. Don't you always want your best film to be your latest one? If it's not going to be, why bother?

Apparently, Burns encouraged the cast to improvise, though you'd never know it by looking at *Looking for Kitty*. It has none of the advantages or disadvantages of improvisation. At 87 minutes, pared down from a 95-minute version that premiered at Tribeca, the film is taut and fast-moving, lacking in fatty self-indulgence. At the same time, it feels very artificial and trite. I heard and saw nothing that couldn't have been scripted by a novice screenwriter. Burns' characterizations are very shallow: as SLANT MAGAZINE's Nick Schager observes, the two central characters have a couple of personality quirks to conquer as an index of their personal development. (One won't drink coffee or eat "international foods" while the other won't eat indoors.) And there is a bizarre abundance of baby boomerisms. For example, the villain is a rock star named Ron Stewart and all the characters ask why he doesn't change it to avoid confusion with Rod. A woman in a bar (Rachel Dratch) unsuccessfully attempts to seduce/befriend our hero, Abe (David Krumholtz), by singing "Just the Way You Are." Is Burns condescending to his characters, or is he simply a dinosaur?

Okay, let's talk about the plot. Abe's wife Kitty has abruptly left him without a trace. Somebody sends him a newspaper clipping that shows the aforementioned Ron Stewart with a woman who resembles Kitty. He figures that she's living with him in New York, as she couldn't possibly afford to be there by herself. Hoping to get an explanation and maybe even reunite with her, Abe hires Jack (Edward Burns), a former cop turned private investigator, to locate her. Jack works alone, but Abe insists on tagging along, as he's desperate to confront Kitty. From there, *Looking for Kitty* turns into a buddy picture, the antagonistic relationship blossoming into friendship and the Kitty mystery driving the narrative.

Before seeing the film, I had pegged Burns as a misogynist. This was mainly residual hatred for the Butler Brothers' unholy *Alive and Lubricated*—an entry into the "let's-me-and-my-friends-drink-beer-and-talk-about-women" genre so popular among filmmakers lacking in talent, money, intelligence, and insight—as well as a suspicious reaction to the title, which reads like an obvious double entendre. Turns out I was casting aspersions: Edward Burns does not hate women at all. He's as meek as a pussycat. I'm not sure this is exactly an improvement, however.

What Kitty does to Abe is pretty reprehensible. At first we are led to believe that Abe had it coming for spending too much time with his job as a high school baseball coach and ignoring the fact that his marriage was coming apart. Surely, he would learn over the course of the film to put her ahead of his career, or to show her better that he loves her. Yet he says he feels guilty about spending so much time at work, thus there was apparently no lesson to be learned there. The blame, then, boomerangs back on Kitty. Abe loved his job and was making a difference. Whenever one of the players was having trouble at home and couldn't deal, Abe let him spend the night in the garage, annoying Kitty to no end. Plus, she never came to any of Abe's games and never showed any interest in baseball. So now Kitty is a selfish bitch. But wait: when Jack finally locates Kitty, Burns' characterization of her is sympathetic. He doesn't hold her accountable for her selfishness and cowardice.

The idea would appear to be that people grow apart, it's nobody's fault, and if you lose somebody you just need to move on. Jack uses his encounter with Kitty to come to terms with his wife's death, suggesting that having a wife who dies and having a wife who leaves you to shack up with a rock star are essentially the same thing. Neither Kitty nor Abe have any accountability for the dissolution of the marriage, because the success or failure of a relationship is apparently attributable more to fate or "chemistry" than to the participants' inability to communicate with one another or identify their wants and needs.

Again I stress that Burns is not a misogynist and *Looking for Kitty* is not a misogynistic film. Still, I do think he harbours some *fear* of women and sees platonic male camaraderie, surrogate father relationships, and baseball (a breeding ground for both, obviously) as at least a temporary substitute for healthy romantic relationships. What's more, he's terrified of this sort of introspection. Afraid to come to terms with his fear of women and possibly be labelled as misogynistic, he censors himself and buries his insecurities to the point where they're no longer objectionable. *Looking for Kitty* is a very mild adherent of the "bros before hos" philosophy, but it is an adherent all the same; the film may have been improved by Burns mustering the courage to confront this and see the film to its logical end. Kitty can't leave Abe without being the bad guy, and if that means the film's central female character is a backstabbing bitch, well, so be it. Anybody who had completely resolved his issues with women in general would never write a film like *Looking for Kitty* in the first place. (**AJ**)

## LUCKY NUMBER SLEVIN
\*\*\*/\*\*\*\*

*st*. Josh Hartnett, Morgan Freeman, Sir Ben Kingsley, Lucy Liu
*sc*. Jason Smilovic
*dir*. Paul McGuigan

I wonder if it's not ultimately a little too pat for its own good, but Paul McGuigan's *Lucky Number Slevin* is another slick, Guy Ritchie crime-manqué to pair with the director's breakthrough *Gangster No. 1*. It stars his muse Josh Hartnett (great in McGuigan's underestimated Hitchcock shrine *Wicker Park*) as the handsome Roger O. Thornhill/Wrong Man archetype—and it finds for Lucy Liu the first role that didn't make me sort of want to punch her mother. But the real star of a film that finds supporting roles for Bruce Willis, Morgan Freeman, Stanley Tucci, and *Sir* Ben Kingsley is McGuigan's restless camerawork: an intricate lattice of matching shots and glittering surfaces that becomes almost an impressionistic projection of the mad, labyrinthine interiority of a mind bent on vengeance. Flashbacks and CGI-aided swoops and zooms are woven into the picture's visual tapestry, so that *Lucky Number Slevin* is read best as a lurid, comic-book send-up of a genre—every scene is played with a good-natured nudge, and when it overstays its welcome with a round-up that verges on sickly, its only real crime is that it's less a grotesque than a screwball romance. Hitchcock did it like that sometimes, too.

Slevin (Hartnett) is mistaken for a friend he's visiting—a friend in deep with crime lords Boss (Freeman) and Rabbi (Kingsley), leading to a few congenially-violent meetings in their facing glass high-rises, kings in conflict in castles sharing the same thoroughfare moat. Boss and Rabbi have both hired killer Goodkat

(Willis)—one to kill the other's son, the other to kill the other to prevent the murder of said son, Fairy (Corey Stall), so named because he is, of course, gay. Slevin has a twice-broken nose and a fondness for argyle sweater vests and the Asian-coroner neighbour, Lindsey (Liu), of his missing pal. But there's more: a flashback where a guy and his whole family are wiped-out after he bets on a fixed horse race and loses more than he can afford to lose; some inconsistencies in Slevin's story about his first broken nose; and then the Jew jokes and the fag jokes and the black jokes and Goodkat in a wheelchair and twists and contortions. So many convoluted avenues, in fact, that it both wears you down and announces itself in blazing neon as a beast that understands its prey enough to craft a pretty fair facsimile of it from itself on its way to excess.

It might be too kind an assessment of the picture on its own, but looking back on McGuigan's films, there's a trend emerging of romantic movies flowering out of masculine genres to be explored in his punk depeche modes. *Lucky Number Slevin* displaces as a throwback and a pomo in the same way that Kevin Williamson's scripts used to—the way that Joss Whedon's seem to, now. You either spend all your time or none of it trying to follow it—both tactics resulting in the same kind of involved junk appreciation to which genre seems to always aspire and only rarely achieve. The focus on errata is the stuff of which cults are made, after all. A number of critics have compared screenwriter Jason Smilovic's pop references to Tarantino's (foreplay herein involves the tangle of actors portraying Bond and Blofeld), but they strike me more as a pastiche of Tarantino, just as the rest of the picture plays as commentary beneath mod British gangster flicks and the more operatic of the *films noir*. It's not a sophisticated film, it's a sarcastic one— which is not to say that it's without sophistication, but rather that all of its bramble is MacGuffin, and the real interest here is in the relationship between Slevin and Lindsey (and Slevin and his mystery dad), making *Lucky Number Slevin* a witty little lark about a boy completing his Oedipal split—and falling in love in the process. **(WC)**

# M

## MAN PUSH CART
**/****
st. Ahmad Razvi, Leticia Dolera,
Charles Daniel Sandoval, Ali Reza
w./d. Ramin Bahrani

As far as subject matter goes, *Man Push
Cart* couldn't be more needed. A movie
about an immigrant Pakistani coffee-
stand operator is just what the doctor
ordered in an American film culture
devoted to the bourgeois angst of Wes
Anderson and Noah Baumbach (when
it's not padding Tom Cruise's wallet,
that is), and it could have been a real
antidote to the same's anti-political
"Crisis? What Crisis?" mentality.
Unfortunately, writer-director Ramin
Bahrani's feature debut falls into the
most obvious pitfall of social realism
by treating its central character,
Ahmad (Ahmad Razmi), like a lost
puppy. There's no real dimension to
Ahmad beyond his social-pariah status
and the many indignities he suffers—
and things only get worse when he
gets a sort-of girlfriend named Noemi
(Leticia Dolera), who makes him seem
more a bashful teenager than a grown
man stripped of his dignity. Though
Bahrani doubtless understands the
invisibility that Ahmad and co.
endure, his idea of a credible hero is a
protagonist treading water.

Ahmad is closer to a laundry list of
suffering than to a fully-functioning
person. We know he was a rock star in
his native Pakistan who fled with his
wife only to see her die; that he mans a
lonely coffee cart and does odd jobs on
the side; that his son is in the hands of
his dead wife's parents, whom he
rarely sees; and that Noemi, the
beautiful young Spaniard working the
nearby newsstand, is his one oasis of
hope and respite. *Man Push Cart* thus
comes loaded with potential, but

Bahrani appears to believe the mere
assembly of these parts has him made
in the shade. Not quite: the character is
so under-drawn that all we really
know about him is that he's sad. And,
far from restoring dignity to Ahmad,
the constant use of his situation to coax
"awww"s from the audience makes
him look even smaller. All hell breaks
loose once Noemi shows up: instead of
proposing a meeting of two adults in
the same boat, the film treats Ahmad
like he's never seen a girl before and
Noemi like she's some squeaky-clean
honours student who's got him
tongue-tied.

Bahrani is young, so maybe he's
interpolating his naiveté onto that of
his character. Still, that's no excuse for
the nuance-free depiction he's given us
here. Though many critics have
invoked the Italian neo-realists in
describing this film, it's only neo-
realist in superficial ways: the
melodramatic aspects of the genre are
here imported without the strong
sense of setting, society, and
economics, while the tortured
innocence depicted by Rossellini, et al
decidedly belongs to another time and
place. To slap what's credible in *Bicycle
Thieves*—from which Bahrani jejunely
swipes his climactic moments—onto
the bukkake-download Babylon of
early-21st century New York is to court
madness. *Man Push Cart* is in love with
the romantic elements of neo-realism
to the point that it can't create its own
identity, swooning over them to such
an extent that it blows the finer points
of forming an argument and sketching
a social process.

Most telling among the film's many
loose ends is Ahmad's relationship to
Mohammed (Charles Daniel
Sandoval), the successful Pakistani
businessman who hires him to work
on his apartment. The obvious irony is
that Mohammed recognizes Ahmad,
raves about his music, then goes about
exploiting him—yet the matter of how
these two immigrants wound up
occupying completely different
stations in life is left up in the air.

Although Bahrani gets that the gulf between rich and poor is wide and daunting (and ultimately, who *doesn't* get that?), the mechanisms by which some people end up on top and others on the bottom—especially within the immigrant context—are left invisible. *Man Push Cart* is in a position to fill in some gaps about how things work but instead settles for tritely devastating stuff like the hero finding a lost kitten and not knowing how to care for it. The film offers no insight into social engineering and even less into simple human behaviour; it seems to think the mere mention of life on the bottom is daringly political. Perhaps *Man Push Cart* is exceptional in the context of Hollywood liberal condescension and *demimonde*-hipster heroin chic, but this well-meaning botch hardly seems like much of an alternative to those shallow approaches to life on the margins. (TMH)

## MAN OF THE YEAR
½* /****

*st.* Robin Williams, Christopher Walken, Laura Linney, Jeff Goldblum
*w./d.* Barry Levinson

Notorious dullard Barry Levinson's second try at *Wag the Dog*, the Robin Williams vehicle *Man of the Year* is a limp wrist waved weakly at no more pathetic a target than new voting technology. The story, such as it is, involves a late-night political comedian/talk show pundit (in the Jon Stewart mold, I guess, if Jon Stewart were stupid, unfunny, and irritating) named Tom Dobbs (Williams) who carries his antiquated shtick all the way to Pennsylvania Avenue on the back of a faulty computerized voting system. Frail egghead techie Eleanor (Laura Linney, too good for this shit) discovers her company's HAL-like flaw (hardly godlike in her erudition, she puzzles out that the digital voting booths choose winners alphabetically), and then promptly goes on the lam after an inexplicable and out-of-tune assault hays her wires and inspires her to seek out the freshly-minted POTUS-elect to inform him of the error. Meanwhile, Dobbs keeps acting like that asshole Robin Williams, desperately in need of a strong hand at his reins lest he run roughshod over his co-stars, the script, sense, respectability, plausibility, and so on down the line.

Williams gets to be sad, gets to be righteous, gets to do his bad impersonations of gay people—gets, most importantly, to be the lone truth-teller in a world of vicious un-truths. He poses here as the voice of the people (positioning the picture he ostensibly anchors as somewhere between *Dave* and *The American President* in terms of fluffy pinko politics), believing, along with Levinson and the other dimwits guffawing at his Mork-from-Ork histrionics, that mortal wounds are being inflicted on partisan politics by declarations that special interest groups are corrupting forces and that televised presidential debates are ridiculous spectacles. If you need *Man of the Year* to tell you the kinds of things that *Man of the Year* tells you, then everything that's wrong with this country and our bellicose, arrogant leadership is probably your fault, anyway. Its obviousness doesn't prevent the film from exuding self-satisfaction, though, marking it as the "comedy" version of Steve Zaillian's disastrous *All the King's Men* (in truth, the two films are equally funny), complete with bad casting decisions, poor direction, and a screenplay that needs not another run through the typewriter, but a first run through the shredder.

Lewis Black appears as a comedy writer, Christopher Walken appears as a sometimes-wheelchair-bound manager, and Williams' Dobbs, at one point, appears before Congress dressed like George Washington. That's when I lost all willingness to play along with the slack premise driving *Man of the Year*, because while you can spit all you want on the man, once you start mocking the actual institution it's not fun anymore. Dissent is indeed the essence of true patriotism, but being a disrespectful clown is something of which the villains of any political piece should be guilty, not the hero. That's the tragedy of the film, really: that although Levinson could write this crap, he couldn't conceive of it as a dark comedy in which this obvious buffoon is obviously a buffoon in the eyes of everyone in the picture, yet nonetheless poses a threat for the simple reason that he knows just enough to influence people with the strings of garbage trailing out of his ass. *Man of the Year* should have been about an undeserving guy who squeaks into office, delivered there by malfeasance, ignorance, and the un-checked/un-balanced providence of our Judicial Branch—only to proceed to ruin the economy and the country's reputation in the world theatre, kill off thousands of American soldiers and tens of thousands of Middle-Eastern folks, engage in acts of illegal domestic espionage, and sanction the torture of enemy combatants without giving them the benefit of bedrock American values like due process and proper representation. Now *that* would've been hilarious.

Instead, Levinson steers *Man of the Year* into a dopey subplot involving an evil computer magnate's hunting and attempted murder of one of his ex-employees (already discredited in the public eye, by the way) while encouraging Williams to exhume his exhausted riffs to the orgasmic admiration of countless cutaway reaction shots. 'Williams must be funny,' Levinson sledgehammers, 'look how hard the whores I've hired for this film semi-capably pretend to find him amusing.' (The picture is a half-step away from installing a running laugh-track.) The only thing educational about the piece is its stunning revelation that some people must

actually still think Williams is hilarious; and the only thing entertaining about it is watching other people in the audience actively deserve more movies like this starring more performers like Williams and directed by people like Levinson. If not for Linney and what is actually a powerhouse turn buried under tons of flab, I'd actually hate *Man of the Year* more than *All the King's Men*. And that's a lot of hate. (**WC**)

## DOCUMENTARY
## MANUFACTURED LANDSCAPES
\*\*\*\*/\*\*\*\*
*dir.* Jennifer Baichwal

There's something about Jennifer Baichwal's profiles of artists. After debuting with a nicely-modulated piece on writer Paul Bowles, Baichwal heard her muse with *The True Meaning of Pictures*, a profile of Appalachian portrait photog Shelby Lee Adams that, without overtly politicizing the subject, digs gratifyingly deep into the question of where representation becomes exploitation and, trickier still, how the audience might have as much to do with that difficult equation as the essayist himself. With *Manufactured Landscapes*, Baichwal looks at the work of Canadian photographer Edward Burtynsky, an artist who shoots landscapes of industrial wastelands that reveal men to be astonishingly productive beasts—and destructive, too, in the same procreative stroke. It's hard to imagine the industry necessary to manufacture the scale of the freighters getting dismantled in the ship-breaking yards to which Baichwal travels with Burtynsky (I've heard a similar sense of awe attends a visit to the Vehicle Assembly Building at NASA)—hard to assimilate the amount of Nietzschian will-to-power necessary to even contemplate the construction of titans.

It's harder, though, to appreciate the toll on human life that the industry around the deconstruction of giants takes on underdeveloped nations, which, unencumbered by such niceties as individual liberty and the Environmental Protection Agency, accept the corpses of unimaginable technological achievements for the purposes of an often very toxic repurposing. The opening eight-minute tracking shot of *Manufactured Landscapes*, pulling laterally across an infinite assembly plant somewhere in China (they're producing steam irons, I think, though it hardly matters), is humbling, but a moment later, it's revealed that the factory's work-force, carefully sorting through old scrap metal and transistors for reusable materials, has most likely been mortally contaminated by lead.

Burtynsky's photographs turn the ugly business of industrial waste into dazzling gestalts: patterns the eye makes into a kind of terrible, beautiful sense. The first reaction to a picture of several thousand abandoned microchips is that there's sense to it: the instinct is to try to understand the insect who created it. By putting a frame around waste, chaos, ruin, Burtynsky forces philosophy on it; and by exhibiting it in galleries in the middle of the affluence and privilege — the main benefactor of these wastelands — he forces irony on it. Then Baichwal comes with her own camera and set of invisible prejudices and artistic predilections and suddenly the true meaning of these pictures is hopelessly muddied by the layers of representation that separate us, the audience, from the subject. I'm reminded of Christian Frei's *War Photographer*, a documentary about another photographer, James Nachtwey — in particular, I'm reminded of how Frei captures a scene with his camera that we revisit later in the film through Nachtwey's stills, and of how Frei's and Nachtwey's documentation of the same events couldn't be more disparate upon critical consideration. Why film should be so much different from still photography — why watching an event unfold in real time buggers analysis while a snapshot of the same event is thick with critical throughways — is the type of question that serious defenders of art in any medium should be asking.

*Manufactured Landscapes* goes farther, however, because in choosing Burtynsky as its subject, it forces the viewer to consider more than the morality of taking photos of an Appalachian for the pity/piety of the Manhattan literati. You're forced to consider, for instance, that you're watching this film about several pieces of machinery, itself pressed/burned/developed by several other pieces of machinery, in the sort of material comfort afforded by the exploitation and waste documented by Baichwal and Burtynsky. The picture, in other words, questions its own existence. In so doing, *Manufactured Landscapes* also questions the means through which one assimilates data and, vitally, how film as a medium disseminates information. Not exactly entertainment, this is more like a master's course in critical theory. It's not a shock to learn that humans are badass evolutionary killing machines wired to thrive on the misery of others, but it is something of a shock to be confronted with the extent to which we fail to challenge our filters. Take the film's closing shots of a blasted Shanghai, wherein a woman with a red veil over her face cycles through the post-apocalyptic cityscape, challenging the very notion that there is a more "natural" environment for man.

There's a comfort with the presence of Baichwal's and Burtynsky's cameras — there's nothing anomalous about them and it's questionable that any of the people documented in the film have altered their behaviour appreciably for the camera's presence. Without the usual problems of representation provoked by the popular documentary fallacy (that it's Truth), the film offers the thornier suggestion that there might not be anything left "outside" — that *Blade Runner*'s utopian "offworld" is as much the fantasy for us now as it was for that film's synthetic humans. The corollary to the title *Manufactured Landscapes* is that it's populated by manufactured people, something Baichwal hints at with aerial shots of beehive suburbia connected by miles of mousetrap overpasses—the saving grace of all that nihilism being that the film betrays a gratifying faith in the audience's agility. It's active viewership as the modern conduit to Descartes' notion of being human. (**WC**)

## MARIE ANTOINETTE
**\*\*1/2/\*\*\*\***
*st.* Kirsten Dunst, Jason Schwartzman, Judy Davis, Rip Torn
*sc.* Sofia Coppola, based on the novel Marie Antoinette: The Journey by Antonia Fraser
*dir.* Sofia Coppola

## TIDELAND
**\*\*\*1/2/\*\*\*\***
*st.* Jodelle Ferland, Jeff Bridges, Brendan Fletcher, Jennifer Tilly
*sc.* Terry Gilliam & Tony Grisoni, based on the novel by Mitch Cullin
*dir.* Terry Gilliam

In going from *The Virgin Suicides* to *Lost in Translation* to *Marie Antoinette*, Sofia Coppola appears to be charting the arc of her own soft, unstructured dive into the morass of melancholia and regret, discovering her voice along the way in the bell tones of Kirsten Dunst, who plays a fourteen-year-old in *The Virgin Suicides* and, at the start of Coppola's latest film, a fourteen-year-old again, the Austrian Archduchess Marie Antoinette. Coppola's "Fast Times at Palais Versailles" opens with Marie loping through her Austrian palace, just another sleepy, stupid girl with a tiny dog, one poised to have the fate of two countries riding on her ability to produce a male offspring. Betrothed to nebbish French King Louis XVI (Jason Schwartzman), she's put into a French court ruled by gossip and bloodline (in one of the film's few literal moments, Marie offers that her waking ritual attended by what seems the entire family plot is "ridiculous") and, while crowned with the mantle of governance, thrust into the role of most popular girl in school, sprung fully-grown as the captain of the football team's best girl. It's impossible for me to not see something of Coppola's own premature coronation as the emotional centre of her father's own royal court, the third *Godfather* film—and to see in the intense media scrutiny afforded her in the wake of that fiasco the source of all these films about lost youth and the pain of hard choices made on her behalf. *Marie Antoinette* isn't a historical film so much as it's a dress-up picture; and like most any work of honesty, it's autobiographical (as indicated by its selection of '80s punk-influenced pop) and intensely vulnerable—at least for most of its first hour.

The moment that vulnerability turns to defensiveness—when Marie declares that she would never suggest the starving proletariat eat cake—is the same moment *Marie Antoinette* loses its hustle and flow. Best left a confection of surfaces that climaxes during a shoe-frenzy montage following the rival birth of a sister-in-law's male heir, the picture has as its strength the ability to find common ground in the plight of teen girl-dom eternal and to see spending sprees and personal shoppers as an extension of some subsumed coital frustration. Versailles is a high-school battleground complete with favourite teachers, cruel principals, dreamy boys, meddling mothers, best friends to cry with, and outcast unfortunates (Asia Argento, finding her dream role as the floozy mistress of Louis XV (Rip Torn)) to humiliate. Marie's is a life of masked costume balls as well as, in a delirious picture's most delirious moments, gambling, playing stupid parlour games, and staying up to watch the sunrise, drunk and drunk on the romance of sleep deprivation and youth at its terminus. You can see the little girl lost in these reckless moments—they're like the karaoke montage from *Lost in Translation*. It's fun and it's mortal. But Coppola isn't content to let that delirium ride through to its known conclusion, giving her teen-queen alter ego the burden of existential grief before giving her the edge of the guillotine blade. Empathy eventually wanes for this party-girl martyr.

The hero of Terry Gilliam's <u>Alice in Wonderland</u> by way of Andrew Wyeth (and Flannery O'Connor) is a little girl lost of another sort. The daughter of twin junkie caricatures Noah (Jeff Bridges, cranking The Dude up to "11") and Queen Gunhilda (Jennifer Tilly, doing Nancy Spugnen), Jeliza Rose (Jodelle Ferland) is left to fend for herself in a burnt autumn landscape alive with fireflies and overturned schoolbuses and patrolled by mental defectives (Brendan Fletcher) and Red Queens (Sally Crooks). Jeliza whiles away her lonely hours providing voices for disembodied dolls' heads and imagining white rabbits and mad tea parties; meanwhile, her father's rotting corpse is embalmed and tanned to sit at the head of a family reserve. There are elements in *Tideland* of Gilliam's aborted *The Man Who Killed Don Quixote* (the equation of a train that slices through the Grant Wood-side with a mighty beast to be slain its most complex image of transportation, arrest, and romantic madness), especially in the character of a hero who is heroic only in her dreams, making a heaven of a her hell. Elements of *Fear and Loathing in Las Vegas* surface, too, in its canny deployment of magical realism and, in truth, its long stretches of unwatchability.

It's southern gothic—a literal train wreck of a film that relies entirely on mood and the performance of a little girl miraculously occupying every frame of the film. Except for its excessive canted angles and camera movements, it's the least *cluttered* of Gilliam's films—and even those times where the picture seems prepared to delve into necro- and pedophilia speak to a child's perspective on death and love. It's almost a pastoral, coloured of course by a feeling of pervasive dread. *Tideland* is a terrifying picture because there's a real sense that there's no law in it that would discourage Gilliam from venting his spleen and carefully-tended garden of neurosis all over little Jeliza Rose. And so he does. A diary of pain and a chronicle of the armour of mythology an imaginative mind expels to salve it away, it's a film so personal, so vulnerable, that it becomes Gilliam's own emotional history of rejection and isolation. (**WC**)

## MATERIAL GIRLS
**\*/\*\*\*\***
*st.* Hilary Duff, Haylie Duff, Anjelica Huston, Lukas Haas
*sc.* John Quaintance and Jessica O'Toole & Amy Rardin
*dir.* Martha Coolidge

There's a paper to be written on the significance of our current obsession with rich young women. One generally doesn't append Brad Pitt or Tom Cruise with the "rich" tag or corral them by age-bracket and gender—it's the notion of young *women* (Paris/Lindsay/Britney, et al) conspicuously consuming that causes the flashpoint for mania and complaint. They're held up as standard-bearers whether they ask for the job or not, and they're absurdly lionized or demonized depending on your demographic. Though Hilary Duff has cleverly managed to sidestep the trainwreckery of the Lindsay/Paris/Britney sideshows, she's still taking on the ambiguous symbolism of Girl Rich in her latest vehicle, the execrable *Material Girls*. If you're looking for meaningful discussion, this ain't the place to find it—but the film manages to say symptomatically damning things in spite of itself.

The rather narcissistically-tailored plot sees the Duff sisters (Hilary and Haylie) playing celebutantes Tanzie and Ava Marchetta, heiresses to a cosmetics empire that's going south following the death of the visionary father who started the company. Imagine the girls' surprise when they discover that the "all-natural" products responsible for their fortune are causing massive skin damage, thus cutting them off from the cash flow. Compounding matters, the sisters set their house on fire AND mistake some roughnecks for valets, meaning they're without home or transportation. Lucky for them, their servant Inez (Maria Conchita Alonso) agrees to put them up; not so luckily, the whole scandal is apparently a stock fraud engineered to obtain competitor Fabiella (Anjelica Huston) the keys to the company. To defeat the evil that has deprived them of their birthright, Tanzie and Ava must depend on their wits, their wiles, and a hangdog pro bono lawyer (Lukas Haas, frighteningly well-cast).

The film is placed right on the knife-edge between people's yearning to live large and their loathing of those who do. In one corner is the basic promise of *schadenfreude* in teaching young doyennes a lesson about living hand-to-mouth, while in the other is the fact that nobody actually wants to watch living hand-to-mouth in a movie where they can watch a fantasy projection of being rich. *Material Girls* therefore becomes a sad trade-off — and as Hilary and Haylie Duff are so clearly wedged in the public eye as both rich and grateful (unlike the gross displays of Lindsay/Paris/Britney), it would be too much to punish them harshly — or even give them much to be punished for. Although our heroines realize the plight of their Columbian housekeeper and the travails of pro bono legal agencies, the point is to restore them to wealth a little wiser as opposed to upsetting the whole social order.

The concessions made for the sake of fantasy are a little hard to take. Poor Alonso is forced to play the biggest sap of her career as a woman who by all rights ought to slap her clueless charges around. Instead, she's a smiley-faced mother doll wheeled in to keep our heroines out of homelessness. (It's a shamefully patronizing role for an actress who used to be powerful and implacable.) Worse is that she's the only major representative of the underclass in the entire film: aside from Haas as the lawyer and a few bit parts, *Material Girls* is almost totally taken up with aristocrats. By the time of the Marchettas' inevitable redemption, the girls have learned practically nothing — but they've gone through the motions of learning, which in the movies is almost as good. (**TMH**)

## DOCUMENTARY
## MATTHEW BARNEY: NO RESTRAINT
**\*\*/\*\*\*\***
*dir.* Alison Chernick

Full disclosure: my exposure to Matthew Barney extends solely to his whales/Björk/petroleum jelly extravaganza *Drawing Restraint 9*, and to say I didn't get it would be putting it mildly: it sailed so far over my head that it may still be in orbit somewhere over Mercury. Yet I was game for Alison Chernick's *Matthew Barney: No Restraint*, if for no reason other than that it might decode said production and provide a framework for appreciating Barney's other work. On this score, the film only does half the job. Running an abbreviated 71 minutes, it offers a rather rushed assessment of the artist's métier, with various critics and performers peppering the roughest outline of Barney's *modus operandi* with soundbites of approval. When all's said and done, it's a teasing, fitfully interesting suggestion of a mindset but far from key to understanding Barney's peculiar dream logic.

Barney, of course, has courted

controversy ever since his fast acceptance into the art elite. Landing an ARTFORUM cover nearly immediately after graduating from Yale, he's inspired jealousy and scorn for his apparently frivolous career as a model and for bypassing the season of neglect that upstart artists generally endure. But the main criticism has been the man's apparent obscurity, his cultivating in the *Drawing Restraint* and *Cremaster* cycles a personal symbolism that is all but impenetrable to the layman. No strident political issues or austere frustrations of narrative: his portfolio (as excerpted in the film) is just pure, hardcore insanity to anyone who exists (as I do) outside the art world. To be sure, *No Restraint* offers several intriguing rationales for everything from Barney's choice of seldom-used materials to his lingering on physicality. The "drawing restraints," for example, are about him setting tasks that literally restrict his ability to create; the enormous effort is effectively what each piece is about.

That being said, we learn more about Barney's influences (athletics play a big role) and original aspirations (plastic surgeon!) than we do about his output proper. Though interspersed with expert witnesses stating the case for Barney, the film is mostly devoted to the making of *Drawing Restraint 9*, interviewing the artist as he enthuses about Vaseline and the musculature of whales and the particular, less-than-obvious symbols he embeds in the work. The man spends more time worrying about the meaning of the makeup on a shaman's face than most people lavish on entire movies—and while he has a noble attention to detail, the significance of his choices remains largely uncommented-upon. There's no directorial voice—Chernick trains her camera on Barney and barely imposes order on what she shoots. It's not even a précis of a man whose complexity has defeated critics and viewers better versed in these things than I.

As I say, the length is an issue. I don't know why *Matthew Barney: No Restraint* is so short: to an outsider, that brevity is maddening, and I believe the film barely scratches the surface for anybody looking for even an introduction. Furthermore, it's opaque about what it does delve into: one learns little from the set of *Drawing Restraint 9* beyond the vagaries of petroleum jelly use and other technical ephemera. There's no point-of-view beyond a vaguely-defined cheerleading that may be touching tribute but doesn't get down to the meat and bone of *what is this thing Matthew Barney*? Although I haven't written the man off and do intend to access his stuff in the future, the mediocre nature of this documentary didn't bring me much closer to a place where I could approach him without some trepidation. (**TMH**)

## MIAMI VICE
\*\*\*/\*\*\*\*

*st.* Jonathan Rhys Meyers, Brian Cox, Matthew Goode, Scarlett Johansson
*w./d.* Woody Allen

Slot Michael Mann's *Miami Vice* in there alongside other millennial films about the disintegration of society and its subsequent renewal along tribal, exclusively masculine lines. It's a film from whose nihilism I would've recoiled just a few years ago, but now I see that as perhaps the definitive trend of the first six years of this brave new world (first five after 9/11, the inciting event of this love affair with apocalyptic cultural reset) and not entirely divorced from our reality besides. The best illustration of how we've gone from the voodoo of self-esteem of the Reagan '80s (for which the Mann-produced "Miami Vice" television show has become something of a cultural roadmark) to the blasted, self-abnegating, divided wasteland of Bush II's America might be the difference between the white suits and socks-less loafers of the previous incarnation to the flak-jackets and high-velocity splatter head-shots of this one. WWI introduced irony into our lexicon with the advent of long-range, impersonal murder—and 9/11 deepened it in the popular culture in the United States with an existential fatalism borne of the idea that not only is sudden, arbitrary destruction from above a possibility, but most likely an unavoidable eventuality.

With the United States declaring itself the world's militarily-enforced morality behind a Texas cowboy and his insular retinue of yee-haw Major Kongs, there is no better entertainment to tickle that identification nerve in the public at large than this dark, dank portrait of modern life as a series of compromises against idealism made in the name of male bonding through rites of gun love, violence against brown people, and the steady acquisition of flashy cars and flashier women. If hope is lost, discover cold comfort in hedonism. Read Mann's *Collateral* as his ice-blue dissection of sharks at play in the divorced wonderland of Los Angeles, locating *Miami Vice* as its border-town brother, where good guys (like Jamie Foxx's cabbie from *Collateral*) don't need to be told to look for their inner predator: they've been nurturing that bastard for years on a rich diet of righteousness, impotence, and rage. There's no fire to the combatants in Mann's nightmare dreamscape, just a flat-eyed hunger that plays out as the dull thuds of bullets splintering bone and impacting on concrete along industrial waterways; and nights spent in sweaty nightclubs, working out the kinks in walls of anonymous flesh and light. Our earliest glimpse of vice detectives Crockett (Colin Farrell) and Tubbs (Foxx) is in just such a strobe-lit box, the two cruising through the insensate bacchanal, meting out violence in short, impersonal bursts and meeting on a rooftop against an impossibly bright, DV panorama to mumble tough words and promises into satellite phones while the rest of the world falls apart.

Mann joins Paul Greengrass and Doug Liman as one of the finest visual poets of the fall, able to sketch in brash, reptilian movements the ways that violence is ultimately as doomed an endeavour as love, loyalty, faith, or vigour. Note how Mann alternates cold sex with cold bloodletting—cementing the pieces with a mess of blather and a cops and robbers heist plot that works only because it's confusing enough to keep your attention. Law is arbitrary and in the hands of psychopaths, and for the wreckage grapple these men with guns, at war in liminal spaces (border towns and beaches) for uncertain gains. It's like trench warfare, in a way, in that *Miami Vice* doesn't offer possibilities for resolution, just minor pushes and pulls in the outlines of wholly capricious lines.

At its best, the picture is like Robert Altman's *The Long Goodbye*: a story of a world torn apart and reordered under the terms described by the animal logic of pissing contests. (At its worst, it's every bit the self-indulgent fever dream Mann's detractors always accuse him of making.) But there's a real, intoxicating idea burning in Mann's films: his end-of-civilization masterpieces like *Heat, Last of the Mohicans*, and even *Collateral* are science-fiction about the last real men in a spiritual vacuum, surrounded by their booty of playthings. If the film feels Old Hollywood in that the stars are pretty, the heroes are tough, and the sex is good but the brutality is better, then excavate the ways that this period in our history dissolves into period *noir*: shells of men entrusted with the rebuilding of our society, with dangerous women and effete men (abortion rights and gay marriage vs. the evacuation of civil rights and ground wars in the Middle East) embodying the greater peril. *Miami Vice* isn't a great film, but it's ours. (**WC**)

## MISSION: IMPOSSIBLE III
*/****

*st.* Tom Cruise, Philip Seymour
Hoffman, Ving Rhames, Billy
Crudup
*sc.* Alex Kurtzman & Roberto Orci
& J.J. Abrams
*dir.* J.J. Abrams

SPOILER WARNING IN EFFECT.
That classic combination of a film that
doesn't make any sense with one that
doesn't inspire anyone to invest an iota
of emotion in giving a crap, J.J.
Abrams' *Mission: Impossible III*
(hereafter *M:i:III*) isn't convoluted like
the first two instalments so much as it's
just incoherent and loud. It's the
camera-in-a blender-school of action
filmmaking: there's so little
understanding of spatial relationships
that the whole thing plays like that
*Naked Gun* gag where the gunfight is
taking place between two people
within arm's reach of one another. An
extended heist sequence set in Vatican
City, for instance, features the four
members of IMF ("Impossible Mission
Force") hotshot Ethan Hunt's (Tom
Cruise) team (Ving Rhames, Jonathan
Rhys Meyers, and the requisite hot
Asian chick (Maggie Q)) running
around in completely anonymous
locations, sticking doodads to walls,
and confirming to one another that
they're "ready" and "in place." But
without knowledge of their plan, their
location (respective to one another and
their goal, whatever that might be),
their peril, or the stakes, you're left
with four people doing something for
some reason, necessitating our
willingness to play along with the
charade that we know who these
people are, what their goal is, and why
we should care. Consider a helicopter
chase through a wind farm, too, and
the many lovely visuals that such an
enticing premise suggests—then look
to the end-product, which is a lot of
tight shots of helicopters in the middle
of the night, parts of giant windmills, a
bad soundtrack, and multiple decibel
screaming about "incoming" and

"they've got a lock on us." Who does?
And where are they going on that
wind farm? And why does the promise
of an instrument-factory explosion
induce yawns?

They've taken the *On Her Majesty's
Secret Service* route this time around,
with Ethan marrying poor
screamer/hostage Jules (a thanklessly
cast Michelle Monaghan), who, in the
prologue, appears to be shot in the
head by evil something or other Owen
Davian (Philip Seymour Hoffman,
looking more than a little like a wax
effigy of himself). Davian wants a
MacGuffin from Ethan and his mates
and is willing to do a little over-acting
to get it, causing much globe-trotting
to exotic (and curiously deserted)
locales where Ethan can do wind
sprints while his buddies talk to each
other on headsets and stare at
computer monitors. A Q-figure
emerges in British comedian Simon
Pegg's lab-bound Benji while Laurence
Fishburne plays Morpheus again and
Billy Crudup is Ethan's immediate,
ineffectual successor Musgrave. If
nothing else, maybe you'll be pleased
to see Keri "Felicity" Russell have a
bomb go off inside her head in one of
two moments in the film where
someone you'd like to see cranially-
defibrillated actually is cranially-
defibrillated.

To say there isn't a hint of character
and/or plot development in *M:i:III* is to
imply that some was attempted and
that the attempt failed. From the looks
of things the picture was always
simply meant to be a series of
spectacular action set-pieces—and in
the staging of said set-pieces, television
director Abrams forgot that he had the
option of shooting in something other
than extreme close-up or respectful
medium. There's a nifty-seeming stunt
where Cruise slides down the side of a
building, yet the way it's shot suggests
that he's either going down vertically
or, alternately, horizontally, and
without knowledge of the particulars
(how high? how dangerous?), all you
have is a stunt man sliding across a

blue screen: something you could simulate by throwing an action figure across a slip-and-slide. More, if you don't care who Ethan is (and are acutely aware that he's indestructible, anyway), and if you don't know what he's doing, for whom he's doing it, and what the time frame of his actions are (though he's given forty-eight hours to accomplish a mission, we don't get back to the countdown until there are two minutes left), then how could you possibly care about anything that happens as a result of his derring-do?

Perhaps all would be forgiven if *M:i:III* were competently-directed (while *M:I-2* is one of the stupidest films ever made, as John Woo is one of the best action directors of the past twenty-five years, damn if it's not beautiful, coherent, *auteurist* stupidity), but it's a glassy-eyed, dead thing complete with superfluous flashbacks to events we don't care about involving characters we don't recognize, an interminable party sequence in which Cruise trots out his smile like it was a weathered, beaten-down trophy wife, and a smug, self-congratulatory conclusion full of high-fives, victory arms, and shit-eating grins. What they believe they've accomplished is anyone's guess (seriously: anyone have a guess?)—all I know is that *M:i:III* made me want to take a nap in almost the same way that *Episode III* bored me to tears. Basic math to say that lots and lots of strobe-lit business multiplied by nothing is still nothing, as well as that the only thing more boring than nothing happening is a lot of nothings happening. Let's see if *Casino Royale* can do any better. (**WC**)

## MONGOLIAN PING PONG
**\*\*/\*\*\*\***

*st.* Hurichabilike, Dawa, Geliban, Badema, Yidexinnaribu
*sc.* Gao, Jianguo, Xing Aina, Ning Hao
*dir.* Ning Hao

There's no arguing with the absolute beauty of the Inner Mongolian landscape captured by Chinese filmmaker Ning Hao (I used to say of *Brokeback Mountain* that you could send a donkey with a disposable camera into that kind of landscape and it would come back with a calendar), but from the condescending English title *Mongolian Ping Pong* (the original translates as something closer to "Green Grasslands") to the story that justifies it, I found the picture boring at best, a confused mess at worst. It's a cross between *The Gods Must Be Crazy* and *Travellers and Magicians*, perhaps—a farce about culture clash and impossible naivety wherein three little Mongolian boys find a ping pong ball, are told that it's a magical glowing pearl from the heavens, and then, upon discovering that it's "the national ball of China," endeavour to return the ball to Beijing, where they must be missing it. Insightful about neither childhood nor the Mongolian people (nor the collision of tradition with modernity; nor the influence of sports in a Communist country fixated on "face"; and so on and so on), the picture's really about transferring our own desire for an impossible Eden onto the faces and experiences of fictional children in a prelapsarian state. If only puerile wish-fulfillment didn't so often feel like patronizing bullcrap onscreen. (**WC**)

## PREVIOUSLY UNPUBLISHED
## MONKEY WARFARE
**\*\*\*½/\*\*\*\***

*st.* Don McKellar, Tracy Wright, Nadia Litz, Marya Delver
*w./d.* Reginald Harkema

The best thing about *Monkey Warfare* is that it seems like somebody wanted to make it. Most Canadian films exist in a snarl of cross-purposes, so obsessed with pleasing culture-crats or aping Americana that they cease to know what they are. By contrast, this sardonically funny twilight-of-the-Left riff is in touch with its self, its body, and its sad sense of regret at the world not turning out as planned. Though the film is yet another exercise in destroyed hubris and failed ideals, one doesn't come away from it emotionally maimed à la Atom Egoyan's movies; *Monkey Warfare* is about recovering people instead of self-righteously punishing them, and creating a life after the defeat instead of saying "game over." It's also very, very entertaining—hip without being smug and quite surprisingly sexy. Given the national imperatives, this could very easily have been screwed up, but the film turns out to be terrific on its own terms and not just in comparison with other CanCon.

Anarchists Dan (Don McKellar) and Linda (Tracey Wright) are living off the grid in Toronto, making their living picking through garbage and garage sales for collector's items to hock on the internet. The savage irony is that two left-wing desperadoes are reduced to selling commodities with inflated value, the antithesis of their Marxist ideals. But the busting of their pot connection sets the stage for the entrance of Susan (Nadia Litz), a young dealer who takes a shine to bored Dan and uses him to learn about radical politics (and radical terrorists). Unfortunately, Susan proves entirely less responsible than Dan and Linda: while they're living down a terrible secret (and subsequently refining their stance), Susan proves to be one of those irresponsible Baader-Meinhof types who use left rhetoric to justify conscienceless adventuring. As the two poles drift apart, Susan is about to commit a terrible act.

Godard has clearly been an influence on writer-director Reginald Harkema: his previous film, *A Girl is a Girl*, transplanted the master's early, youthfully-romantic movies to millennial Vancouver, but with the sense of fun that Godard supplicants usually miss. This combination of serious intent and genuine irreverence places him to the side of most other

Canadian directors—unlike them, he doesn't appear to be apologizing for his existence. His characters might (especially in light of the disaster that drove his heroes underground), but his own position is impious even as it pays homage to the icons of terrorist chic. It's also surprisingly merciful to the frustrated heroes: Dan's barely-suppressed lust for Susan is treated for comedy but not derision, with the mid-life-crisis-ness of his interest backdropped by the growing rift between the once-intimate radicals. It's a movie about inappropriate expressions of very real feelings, and just because the outcome screws up doesn't mean the intention is denied.

Harkema also knows his neighbourhood. I live in the film's setting, the rapidly-gentrifying West Queen West, which went from skanky to upscale and sent property values through the roof; thus, I've seen first-hand the damage done by well-heeled hipsters driving out lower-income households. The heroes' crash pad is about to be sold under those circumstances—thus threatening their under-the-radar existence and taking their one comfort zone away from them. Yet Harkema doesn't underline this with social-realist piety; he's pissed-off and accepting at the same time, infuriated at the marketplace steamrollering human values (cross-referenced with the silliness of the collector's market) as well as understanding of the fact that time moves on and nobody can expect to stay still when all that is solid melts into capitalist air.

Harkema has taken the particular circumstances of what I assume is his personal milieu and brought to them his own intellectual interests, resulting in something far more revealing and specific than anything produced by those trying to please everybody but themselves. And he's brought to the film a nose-thumbing formal intelligence that's brimming with a wit and irony that prove he's no pretender. Though clearly made for no money (even by Canadian standards), *Monkey Warfare* is so cleverly and pleasurably shot that it makes bigger-budget movies seem inadequate: there's no moment where you feel the seams show and the man behind the curtain is visible; you keep waiting for the dead spots to materialize, but they never do. Swift, sexy, humane, outraged and informed, it's a model of what Canada ought to be doing instead of the stiff, merciless martinet it has become. **(TMH)**

# A N I M A T E D
## MONSTER HOUSE
**\*\*\* /\*\*\*\***

*sc.* Dan Harmon & Rob Schrab
and Pamela Pettler
*dir.* Gil Kenan

There's a lightness to the heroes of *Monster House*, as well as a certain callous insouciance in the way the film handles itself as a metaphor for puberty, but the effects for the titular monster and the care with which it sketches the human monster living inside it make the picture fascinating. When it's humming, above and below, the contraption identifies the malady of adolescence as loneliness, as becoming an outcast caste of one ("*This* is why we sit by ourselves at lunch"), if in mind only. It knows the sudden, emboldening rush of recognizing a girl's charms, and it sees in friendship the bonds and courage that time hasn't yet had the chance to disdain. None of this is surprising, particularly, especially since its executive producers are Robert Zemeckis and Steven Spielberg—who, between them, have fashioned some of our finest monuments to the cult of childhood. But then *Monster House* throws a curveball and makes its bad guys...tragic. And not just tragic but *unbearably* tragic—tragic enough that they become ennobled through their tragedy; by the end of the film, with its surprising declaration of "freedom," what could have been a trite

affirmation of the ironic swap of the fears of childhood for the anxieties of the teenage years is transformed into a more ecumenical discussion about how life is sacrifice and love is sometimes unrequited, and about loyalty to causes in which we believe and the people in whom we invest ourselves.

It plays especially like a Ray Bradbury story (or like Stephen King's It or Dan Simmons' Summer of Night), a tale from a carnival in the October Country of the house on the block that's home to the crazy old guy who keeps the kites that stray into his yard. Our boy DJ (Michael Musso) and his portly pal Chowder (Sam Lerner) have an encounter with said crazy old guy, Nebbercracker (Steve Buscemi), who, in the picture's most surprising moments, develops a backstory and manifests a wife (Kathleen Turner) encased in concrete in a caged tomb sealed with a heart-shaped padlock. Dark stuff (Jungian, too), with the house/monster's innards a jumble of skeletal ductwork and pilfered toys and its maw a swirl of peristaltic planks. (After the Sarlacc throat of *Pirates of the Caribbean: Dead Man's Chest*'s Kraken, the curious synchronicity of vagina dentatas swallowing heroes whole announces something like a new variety of *femme fatale* in 2006.) As for real women, there's a teenage babysitter whose personality is authentically that of a teenage girl (Maggie Gyllenhaal, fantastic) and an ally (Spencer Locke) given the chance to show some stones before being reduced to the kiss-dispenser and object of desire.

That carelessness with the relationships between its central trio— dorky hero, fat goofball, girlfriend—is *Monster House*'s weakness, and we find ourselves straining to see the secondary characters (including a Renaissance Fair loser who plays video games in convenience stores). A pair of slapstick cops don't offer much to the authority figure sweepstakes, while DJ's parents (Fred Willard and

Catherine O'Hara) are essentially absent, meaning that the references to the inability of the adults to comprehend the enormity of the kids' peril feel perfunctory and slight. There are a lot of missed opportunities in the picture, most of them falling on the one side. Visually it's awesome, though, the conclusion especially impressive and frightening (the film as a whole is surprisingly scary, even with a placating curtain call)—and though the characters are motion-captured using the same technology Zemeckis employed for *The Polar Express*, the design itself is pleasantly stylized. But when all's said and done, you wish the film had been about Nebbercracker and his girl, because no one is interested anymore in this thing about the skinny kid who gets the girl and the sloppy comic sidekick along for the ride. Including the filmmakers. (**WC**)

**MUTUAL APPRECIATION (see: *THE PIANO TUNER OF EARTHQUAKES*)**

**MY SUPER EX-GIRLFRIEND**
½* /****
*st.* Uma Thurman, Luke Wilson, Anna Faris, Wanda Sykes
*sc.* Don Payne
*dir.* Ivan Reitman

**IDIOCRACY**
***½/****
*st.* Luke Wilson, Maya Rudolph, Dax Shepard, Anthony 'Citric' Campos
*sc.* Mike Judge & Etan Cohen
*dir.* Mike Judge

Ivan Reitman has a pretty good reputation based mainly on being the producer of *Animal House* and the director of *Ghostbusters*—a reputation, as it happens, that's persisted through stuff like *Evolution* and *Kindergarten Cop* and *Six Days Seven Nights* and,

good fuck, *Fathers' Day* and *Junior* and *Kindergarten Cop*. The idea that Schwarzenegger could be a comedian on purpose is just freaking ridiculous and largely the fault of Reitman. What I'm trying to say is that *Jingle All the Way* is, in some way, Reitman's fault. The only reason I don't trash him more often is because he also had a hand in launching the career of the most consistently fascinating filmmaker in North America by co-producing David Cronenberg's *Shivers*, thus earning him no end of good karma. But let's face it: when he's not producing abortions like the *Beethoven* pictures, he's excreting garbage like *My Super Ex-Girlfriend* on his own; and if *Ghostbusters* was one of the films that defined my childhood to a certain degree, I'm not sure that one camp masterpiece is enough to justify the continued goodwill Reitman has enjoyed and now passed on to son Jason, who, with the middling *Thank You for Smoking* and the dreadful *Juno*, is threatening to continue a decades-long legacy of bad flicks. The usefulness of *My Super Ex-Girlfriend* has a lot to do with how much a survey it is of Reitman's failures: flaccid pacing, fumbled high concept, flat execution, non-specific bloat, and milquetoast miscasting.

Uma Thurman is Jenny "G-Girl" Johnson, the titular former beard who puts a twist on the standard psycho-bitch/geek-uprising plot point by having the ability to throw a shark at her schlubby ex (Luke Wilson, typecast hardcore) before launching his car into outer space. Indeed, it's amusing mainly in the way that unimaginative people trying to be funny is amusing—you feel embarrassed and itchy a lot of the time and that "exit" sign hums really loudly. It's certainly possible to make a statement about power dichotomies in the picture—about how society treats women and how that's so often at odds with comic books (a medium that's allegedly the epicentre of puerility). Failing that, the hope is that it's at least funny. Alas, watching a guy get sort-of raped by his super-

150

sexually-aggressive girlfriend isn't the same as being hilarious and provocative. And because it's locker room cliché already to suggest that your friends are faggots and that their girlfriends and wives are testosterone freaks, you have the right to hope that there's more to *My Super Ex-Girlfriend* than exactly the kind of misogyny and childishness for which comic books are accused in the first place. The picture is a wet towel to the ass, and the expectation that all will nod in caveman agreement that 'bitches is crazy,' just because it's clothed in hipster cred, should probably get it a wet towel to the ass in return. The ex's new girlfriend Hannah (Anna Faris) is super nice, of course, fulfilling her only real function as an extra pair of incredulous eyeballs—and arch-villain Bedlam (Eddie Izzard) is the type of bad guy who fights Condorman and Inspector Gadget. Completely buffed of any sharp corners, *My Super Ex-Girlfriend* is as supple and inoffensive as a suppository.

The real deal is Mike Judge's scabrous *Idiocracy*, a satire so spot-on that it's like a documentary—so perfect in outrage that despite a good deal of studio interference post-production, it still comes across as among the angriest, most hopeless comedies ever made. Making the film's lack of subtlety its central point, Judge imagines a future where our disastrous hijacking of Darwinian evolution results in the least fit, intellectually and civilly, out-reproducing the theoretically more-fit in geometric multipliers. The end result is a culture that makes a guy getting hit in the groin the top-rated television program, and a film showing an endless loop of an ass being the Best Picture winner. (We're not that far away.) Starbucks dispenses lap dances and blowjobs and big business has so infiltrated all levels of society that it has, in a direct way, led to the collapse of humanity's ability to sustain itself. When an ordinary modern man (Luke Wilson, typecast again)—frozen in a secret army experiment to be thawed as by far the most intelligent person in the future—visits a hospital, he's diagnosed by picture touch-screen and treated like the obscure answer to a multiple choice questionnaire. Best is his (by twenty-first century standards) average vocabulary branding him in the eyes of these Morlocks an effeminate dandy. *Idiocracy* hits close to home repeatedly, brutally, remorselessly. As for Judge, it feels like a parting shot, a middle finger from the bottom of the abyss; there's no hope of solution in his passion play, this reverse *Being There* where the idiot is the smartest man in a world of graceless, post-literate slugs. It's so good, so prescient, that the strongest complaint could be that it's not very funny. (It's the highest praise, as well.) *Idiocracy* is the best comedy of its kind since *Dr. Strangelove*—the kind that's existentially humbling and already too late. (**WC**)

# N

## NACHO LIBRE
½*/****
st. Jack Black, Ana de la Reguera,
Héctor Jiménez, Peter Stormare
sc. Jared Hess & Jerusha Hess &
Mike White
dir. Jared Hess

Nearly unwatchable from an aesthetic perspective, *Nacho Libre* is also invasively offensive and cheap-feeling in its gags, its performances, and its targets. Lampooning Mexican professional wrestling seems an onanistic pursuit at best insomuch as, clearly, the sport is already busily in the process of self-parody—but letting Jared Hess (single-handedly bringing the Special Olympics to Wes Anderson) tackle it along with Jack Black doing an "oh Ceeesco" accent in skin-tight tights is a particular kind of torture. The film's going to have its defenders (Uwe Boll has his defenders, too, I hasten to add, as does Hess' *Napoleon Dynamite*), and I'm thinking that it's going to be along the lines of "Well, sure, it's not *Citizen Kane*." But does anyone go to anything expecting it to be *Citizen Kane*? Moreover, have people who like this bullshit actually seen *Citizen Kane*? It's germane to talk about this because sooner or later it has to be pointed out that pictures like *Nacho Libre* exist because pictures like *Napoleon Dynamite* were popular: mean pictures about small-minded folks picking fun for no profit at slow-witted caricatures of racial groups and social classes. Pictures like this exist because people are used to lowering their expectations so much that they're actually irked when someone doesn't. It's most instructive to take a minute to look at how low we go now to construct the straw dogs we mock.

The Hispanic-loathing subtext of *Napoleon Dynamite* finds full flower in *Nacho Libre*, naturally, as Nacho (Black), the cookie at a monastery that harbours sadsack orphans, dreams of the riches and women that come with being a top-flight *luchador* on the Mexican wrestling circuit. The film also loathes fat, though it takes an ambiguous stance on midgets and beautiful nuns (represented by Ana de la Reguera), and it can't be too bothered to give Nacho a heart in that mighty chest of his to forgive his sins of lust and greed. It's a movie without a hero (and even Cheech & Chong were the heroes of their own films), a lot more like Hess' *Napoleon Dynamite* than like co-screenwriter Mike White's *Chuck & Buck* in that regard, but its one saving moment is ineffably *Chuck & Buck*-like: an amorous senorita (Carla Jimenez) pursues Nacho's sidekick Esqueleto (Héctor Jiménez) through a series of "secret tunnels" unaccountably burrowed into the walls of a palatial villa. The image of it is so delightfully bizarre that all at once the forced, almost Brechtian, artificiality of the piece comes clear as intent rather than sloth—if only for a moment. The rest of it (Nacho passing wind when he leaps, Nacho clenching his ass, Nacho drawing childlike pictures, Nacho taking a dump, Nacho blowing raspberries, Nacho replicating the eagle-egg gag from Chris Farley's *Almost Heroes*, Nacho calling his shirt a blouse) is unimaginative juvenilia marked by a strange obsession with loud foods and a peculiar preoccupation with eye violence. If you're the kind of person who thinks it's funny that a person with a pidgen Mexican accent sounds like she's saying "poopies" when she's saying "puppies," have I got a movie for you.

A "Battle Royale" towards the end of the film features a tall black wrestler named "Snowflake" and a Chinese guy named "El Chino"—satire, if you want to call it that, of either the lubricated showiness of pro wrestling or the callow stupidity of the audience for the same. It's an umbrella that stretches broadly enough to envelop the audience for the film, too. See, I suspect that *Nacho Libre* is a film that imagines itself as somehow above itself, as commentary on the ugliness of its conception and execution instead of just a pig wallowing in its own slop. I like to think that because it's more reassuring to think it than to suppose that in the year 2006, there are still assholes who believe that making a film that essentially gives idiots the permission to say stupid things in a revolting, derisive accent without a healthy dose of self-awareness and intelligence is okay. (Take this flick with the *Hills Have Eyes* remake as pictures in 2006 that hate all over their audience.) It's disheartening to try to explain to folks that *Napoleon Dynamite* is comedy sprung from our basest bullying instinct—and it's that much more disheartening to have to point out that *Nacho Libre* is about how funny our musty stereotypes of Mexicans are because of the way they talk and the things they like to watch. The joke's on us, though, because we're the ones lining up to throw our cash at *this* piece of shit. Oh Ceeeesco. (**WC**)

# NANNY McPHEE
**\*\*¹/₂/\*\*\*\***

*st.* Emma Thompson, Colin Firth, Angela Lansbury
*sc.* Emma Thompson, based on the "Nurse Matilda" books by Christianna Brand
*dir.* Kirk Jones

Often as garish and shrill as it is magical and enchanting, Kirk Jones' *Nanny McPhee* throws into sharp relief the difficulty of describing the tightrope so artfully navigated by *Babe: Pig in the City*. In its favour, there are strong, fairytale-sinister undercurrents to it that feel authentic where the darkness of the slick *Lemony Snicket's A Series of Unfortunate Events* felt, on the whole, manufactured and arch, and the film finds its surest footing in an idea essential to children's

entertainment: that every action has a consequence. The answer to the question of what, exactly, is Nanny McPhee (Emma Thompson), or what generator produces these Mary Poppinses like sexless, befrocked clergy attending wayward British moppets, is that Nanny McPhee is stuffy consequence personified—the element of parents and/or society that, often with something like a supernatural hand in the eyes of a child, embeds itself in a growing moral conscience. There's something grand and mysterious about these figures, and Jones allows Nanny the freedom to be as enigmatic, omniscient, and omnipotent as a superego on the wax.

Undertaker Brown (Colin Firth), mourning the recent passing of his wife by making her armchair a creepy totem to which he narrates his thoughts, has exhausted every nanny at the agency with his nasty yet adorable brood of seven when the mysterious Nanny McPhee materializes on his doorstep, snaggletoothed and carbuncular. Nanny quickly outlines several steps the children must follow in their forced civilization, while the usual subplots involving seeking out an appropriate mate for daddy dearest, sabotaging evil Austen aunts, and "freeing" (through the beautifaction of?) McPhee round out the British-ness of the fable between bouts of terminal cuteness and starchy intimidation. In the end, it's all *Auf Wiedersehen*, good night, into the Technicolor sunset, of course.

It says a lot more about the state of children's entertainment that a mildly diverting, almost apologetically barbed trifle like *Nanny McPhee* seems so much the fringe element. Thompson is infernal and appears to be having a blast with the screenplay she wrote using Christianna Brand's series of "Nurse Matilda" books as inspiration; Firth is workmanlike in the besotted romantic clod role he's made his stock and trade; and the children are saucer-eyed in reaction shots, sleep frocks, and Isles uniforms. Beyond its familiar efficiency, though, there's not a lot to be mined here besides the broad backhand that it at least has something to recommend it unlike most of the rest, as well as its justification of the nostalgic, old-man complaint that things were better once upon a time. (No matter that the "time" is somewhere in the eighteenth century with the Brothers Grimm.) Not a bad try, *Nanny McPhee* rattles when it mistakes cacophonous for whimsical kid's wonderlands, marking wide swaths of it as a distaff, if obviously vastly superior, version of *The Cat in the Hat*. (WC)

## PREVIOUSLY UNPUBLISHED
## NATHALIE...
**\*\*¹/₂/\*\*\*\***

*st.* Emmanuelle Béart, Fanny Ardant, Gerard Depardieu
*sc.* Anne Fontaine, Jacques Fieschi, "with the collaboration of" Francois-Olivier Rousseau, from an original screenplay by Philippe Blasband
*dir.* Anne Fontaine

*Nathalie...* director Anne Fontaine seems genuinely invested in her story of an apparently-cuckolded wife and her bizarre plan to gain control of her husband's extramarital sex life. There's real fascination when pleasant but unromantic Catherine (Fanny Ardant) discovers a provocative phone message on her husband's cell and learns he's been straying. In response to the aloofness of hubby Bernard (Gérard Depardieu), she approaches a prostitute named Marlène (Emmanuelle Béart) to pose as an interested party and then report back to her on their erotic goings-on. Fontaine gets right the disturbing nature of the revelation and the mixed emotions of the apparent victim, while simultaneously coming up with an elaborate acting-out scheme that could go so many ways. Catherine's plot could be an attempt to gain control of the sex Bernard isn't having with her;

she could be masochistically punishing herself for failing to keep her mate, or she could be exacting revenge that even she doesn't understand. There are so many reasons she might have for engaging in this ruse that the possibilities beggar the imagination.

Alas, our imaginations have to do all the legwork. As the movie progresses and Marlène keeps describing wild sexual encounters, it becomes clear that Fontaine hasn't got a clue as to why she or her heroine are doing what they're doing. Though the director has a real attachment to the material, it's an unexplained attachment—she's staring at something that fascinates and horrifies her, without ever considering what causes her mixed emotions. This isn't a teasing ambiguity that lets us draw our own conclusions—it's a conceptual confusion that leaves us completely in the dark as to the significance of the exercise. And while it's sometimes hot to hear Marlène ramble on about what she's doing with Catherine's husband, that shouldn't necessarily be the point of the exercise. The film is never less than watchable, but it also never crystallizes into something we can use. What's left is more a sex-talking melodrama than a coherent take on human behaviour.

Moreover, the film's ill-defined fear and loathing of the main throughline is accompanied by a similarly mystified attitude towards Marlène. The relationship between the two female leads is again teasingly ambiguous, but it mostly breaks down in Catherine's favour: we're assumed to know her boring bourgie existence and be fascinated by, but never understanding of, the question mark that is Marlène. Soon, Catherine's shtick involving her husband becomes a somewhat-condescending sympathy towards the young prostitute, again without a full understanding of what exactly she's contemplating. Béart responds by playing her cards as close to her vest as her character would, giving a remarkably nuanced performance for someone who's supposed to be an erotic mask until the film's big twist reverses the power dynamic. Although one could argue that that twist explodes the whole stupid concept on which Catherine has been operating, it doesn't make Catherine a more understanding person—it just makes her retreat back into what she always knew. As a series of unexamined premises, the film is suggestive, engrossing, and sneakily erotic, but I never felt I knew what it was driving at, and I don't think Fontaine does, either. (**TMH**)

## THE NATIVITY STORY
* /****

*st.* Keisha Castle-Hughes, Oscar Isaac, Hiam Abbass, Shaun Toub
*sc.* Mike Rich
*dir.* Catherine Hardwicke

## 3 NEEDLES
½* /****

*st.* Shaun Ashmore, Stockard Channing, Olympa Dukakis, Lucy Liu
*w./d.* Thom Fitzgerald

The nativity, consigned primarily in my imagination to bad children's pageants and gaudy lawn displays, gets a third image in my own private trinity with Catherine Hardwicke's *The Nativity Story*: a thunderously boring film so circumscribed in scope and crippled in execution that it's destined to be a minor hit fuelled by the line of buses stretching from your local bible chapel. It's another teen melodrama from Hardwicke, complete with disapproving adults and pregnant little girls batting doe-eyes at rough-and-tumble shepherds; you see Hardwicke occasionally attempting an anachronistic *Fast Times at Golan Heights* à la Sofia Coppola's *Marie Antoinette*, but Coppola, for all her dips into self-pity, is a filmmaker of note while Hardwicke is just beating someone else's drum on someone else's dime. (Proof positive is that despite the uniformity of Hardwicke's output across three identically-non-descript flicks, there is still no sense that decisions are being made, or that anything more than a sickly colony from a thin scrape across the John Hughes petri dish has been born.) Mary is played by young Maori actress Keisha Castle-Hughes—her race of note because if there's something important about the instantly forgotten pic, it's that its cast is comprised of people who look like people might have looked in Nazareth around two thousand years ago and not like Andy Gibb. A shame that Castle-Hughes is dreadful (and not helped a bit by another dreadful, pop-eyed screenplay courtesy Mike Rich of *Radio* and *Finding Forrester* fame) and that Oscar Isaac (as Joseph)—who is not dreadful—is trapped in this prosaic sinkhole. Tempting to use terms like "sanctimonious" and "smug," but *The Nativity Story* is more accurately dissected with the observation that it's a faithful telling of a story that has as its only purpose the drumming up of ecstatic anticipation for a foregone conclusion.

It's absolutely game to call Thom Fitzgerald's films sanctimonious and smug, however, and *3 Needles* is their self-important messiah. Three parallel tales of Third World woe, each of them infected with a secret, unnamed viral ailment (it's AIDS, stupid), the non-stunning film offers as its most non-stunning revelation that Fitzgerald equates his native Canada with Africa and China, though it doesn't play as self-deprecating so much as it plays as evidence that Fitzgerald has levitated himself above the plight of not only the "little people" of the rest of the world, but of his homeland and beyond as well. The struggle of *3 Needles* isn't between man and ignorance, it's between Fitzgerald-as-Saviour and everyone else. The Great White North segment (which he calls, tongue poking through cheek, "The Passion of the Christ") involves a porn star (Shawn Ashmore) who uses his father's blood as his own during mandatory disease screenings while passing the love bug around like a bad penny. No rape in this one, but gang rape is the loathsome catalyst (rather, the only catalyst loathsome enough for this filmmaker) of the other two: one with Lucy Liu as a dedicated government worker inadvertently decimating an entire Chinese village before giving allegorical birth alone by the side of a dusty road; the other with Chloë Sevigny as a Catholic missionary in South Africa, selling her body for a few precious capsules of a miracle pharmaceutical.

It's a nasty, misanthropic film, the only kind someone with a dangerously misguided and inflated sense of self can produce—yet what really nails 3 Needles to its cross is the hollowness of its constant, deadening, non-illuminating moralizing. (I'd love a peek at the keyboard Fitzgerald uses to conjure his screeds: I've never seen one sledgehammered into dust and splinters before.) Olympia Dukakis provides grandmotherly narration, reminding us that these three stories are but three out of ninety-million—and when it all wraps up, the picture reminds of that guy at the cocktail party who gathers a crowd for his passion only to gradually lose it with his arrogance. Without criticizing the AIDS epidemic or, even, the importance of a film on the topic, what most rubs about 3 Needles is the same thing that offends about similarly self-important message flicks like Fast Food Nation (and, hell, Crash and Babel): that no amount of crouching behind the major issues of our day can hide a general lack of insight and eloquence. One would think that films like 3 Needles would make you care, but generally they just make you angry about being spoken to as though you were an idiot in need of all the wisdom an Emilio Estevez or a Thom Fitzgerald is able to impart. Praised in some circles for providing no real answers, 3 Needles merely substitutes thoughtful ambiguity with hand-smacking and lumpish metaphors. For those keeping a tally, other things Fitzgerald's film shares with The Nativity Story include nice scenery and an overpowering score. (WC)

## DOCUMENTARY
## NEIL YOUNG: HEART OF GOLD
***½/****
*dir.* Jonathan Demme

Not long after the death of his dementia-stricken father and in the four days preceding an operation to fix a potentially fatal brain aneurysm, Young recorded "Prairie Road", then called Jonathan Demme post-operation to say that he was taking some time off and interested in making a movie. Demme's best film is still a tossup between *Swimming to Cambodia* and *Stop Making Sense*—his forays into mainstream filmmaking (*The Silence of the Lambs*, *Philadelphia*) tending towards exactly the kind of slick populism his documents of performance pieces never seem to. His latest, *Neil Young: Heart of Gold*, is a return to form for a filmmaker who might be our best chronicler of the glorious syncopations of rhythm and flow: a deft, evocative film that finds new poignancy in Young's voluminous back catalogue while allowing cuts from "Prairie Wind" the kind of metaphysical room its title promises.

The new songs are plaintive touching on maudlin—repetitive and circular in the Young style (to the extent that he ever had an identifiable hallmark). But Demme and cinematographer Ellen Kuras (who photographed *Eternal Sunshine of the Spotless Mind* and *Bob Dylan: No Direction Home*) manifest the melancholy in Young just as Demme and the late great Jordan Cronenweth made literal the scattered, discursive madness of **The Talking Heads** more than two decades ago. It's the perfect companion piece to Jim Jarmusch's couldn't-be-more-different Neil Young documentary *Year of the Horse*: place the two side-by-side to find a chronicle of the maturation of an artist who ploughs a demilitarized zone between his "Old Man" and that twenty-four-year-old hippie with a guitar, growing now into the twilight of his mortality.

The first hour of the piece is predominantly new material, the highlight for me a number called "Here For You" that Young dedicates to his daughter turning twenty-one ("An empty-nester song. Maybe a new genre," he deadpans), augmented by Demme with a shot of the Memphis Strings backup players standing after their contribution to the song then filing off the stage. It's subtle in the way it's edited and composed of medium shots—and it just breaks your heart. Unobtrusive, Demme's gift—and his greatest contribution—is in comprehending the song and, moreover, the language of images in such a way as to critique the moments as they occur. *Neil Young: Heart of Gold*, then, is a piece of performance art that's constantly in the process of critiquing itself and, in the examination, revealing parts of itself hidden or, in its best moments, old songs transformed by new events by the alchemical agent of terrible experience. When Young wails "I want to live" at the beginning of his classic "Heart of Gold," continuing into "And I'm getting old" as the song's repeated affirmation, it's melancholy where it was once defiant, with no "better to die young than to fade away" anywhere in the set list.

Young performs his junkie dirge "The Needle and the Damage Done" acoustic, alone in the spotlight on Ryman Auditorium's darkened proscenium in much the same way that "Psycho Killer" opened *Stop Making Sense*. But the caesura occurs towards the end, now, not in the metronomic calm before the storm but in a contemplative breath, taken and held for a minute before blowing through an encore of Young's most wistful selections. The only song missing that I would have liked to hear

is "Differently"—but maybe that makes the point too broadly. The fact is that *Neil Young: Heart of Gold* suggests an artist at peace with his decisions. The mad monk, eternally dissatisfied with the world and at war with his demons, has become an old man with a grown daughter he loves and misses, at enough ease to write a song about his guitar—which used to be Hank Williams' guitar, and will someday be someone else's guitar. His roadie talks with amazement as he tunes it at the beginning of the film ("Do you know the songs that were written on this?"), and Demme finds all the major players in means of conveyance on their way to the two nights melted together in the picture. The film is about the journey; if the art is good, it illustrates the past with the same intensity and brilliance as it bounces off the present. *Neil Young: Heart of Gold* is immediate and timeless. What I'm saying is that you don't have to already be a fan. (**WC**)

PREVIOUSLY UNPUBLISHED
## NIGHT AT THE MUSEUM
ZERO STARS/****
*st.* Ben Stiller, Carla Gugino, Dick Van Dyke, Mickey Rooney
*sc.* Robert Ben Garant & Thomas Lennon, based on the book by Milan Trenc
*dir.* Shawn Levy

PREVIOUSLY UNPUBLISHED ANIMATED
## CURIOUS GEORGE
***/****
*sc.* Ken Kaufman, based on the books by Margret Rey and H.A. Rey
*dir.* Matthew O'Callaghan

Based on a picture book, I guess, Yale scholar (just like Dubya) Shawn Levy's obscenely popular *Night at the Museum* is Exhibit A in the increasingly compelling observation that the average IQ is around 100—and that most chimps are smarter than that.

Explanation for a scene where Ben Stiller gets into a bitchslap contest with a monkey after it pisses on him, it's also another example of why we keep getting the same kind of shit over and over again in our popular culture. Don't blame the idiots who support movies like this—blame the idiots who *don't* support worthwhile pictures. (Make no mistake, these idiots are not interchangeable.) The smug, elite festival audience that clucks their tongues at garbage like this tends to avoid it like the plague—just as they tend to avoid every other film save the handful that the same critics they ignore the rest of the year promise will win devalued trophies during awards season. No, *Night at the Museum* is a guided missile aimed straight at the "family audience" demographic, meaning it comes armed with a payload of expensive special effects, kid-friendly comedians, scatological humour, and unearned sentiment. There are at least one of these things a year—and a sequel to *Night at the Museum* is already in the works— because the business of pandering is, as it's always been, booming.

Larry (Stiller) is the new night watchman for the local natural history museum, taking the proverbial keys to the kingdom from crusty Cecil (Dick Van Dyke) and his sidekicks Gus (Mickey Rooney) and Reginald (Bill Cobbs). What Larry doesn't know is that when the sun goes down, all the exhibits in the museum bloom to life courtesy some Egyptian doodad, with the stupid caveat that should anything thusly animated find itself outside at sunrise, it'll turn to dust. (Once suggested, this peril is quickly relegated to perfunctory, late-game plot expedience.) Larry's obligatory love interest is Rebecca (a ravishing Carla Gugino); his new pal Theodore Roosevelt (Robin William) has an obligatory love interest in Sacajawea (Mizuo Peck); and miniature diorama-ite Jedediah (Owen Wilson) meets cute with Roman Centurion Octavius (Steve Coogan). Tension, such as it is, arrives

in the form of the ex-watchmen's scheme to steal said doodad for its spry-enhancing properties (the opposite is arguably needed for Rooney), leading to third-act chase slapstick ended by a completely arbitrary button-push that renders everything A-OK in as syrupy, noxious a way as possible. Lest one forgets to mention, the *faux*-emo stakes are augmented by a *Mrs. Doubtfire* divorce resulting in a kid who needs a daddy to make some grand parenting gesture in order to earn his kid's love; and there's an epilogue with dancing to disco music because *Shrek* has forever decreed that lowbrow family effluvium should end just like it.

The grooves that *Night at the Museum* runs along are so deeply-etched and travel-worn that its box-office success is not exactly unprecedented. More of a surprise is the relatively poor take for something as inoffensive and charming as Matthew O'Callaghan's *Curious George*. Blame the lack of characters pissing on each other. Based on H.A. and Margret Rey's beloved children's book series, the animated film gives the Man in the Yellow Hat a name, Ted (Will Ferrell), and a regular vocation as a museum curator. His boss is played by Dick Van Dyke again in a really curious bit of typecasting for 2006, while the boss's son is, in a stroke of genius, a snag voiced by David Cross. There's a touching bit about the son trying to please the father, and obligatory romantic interest Maggie (Drew Barrymore, adorable in this form) is, in a pleasant twist, a ditz with a crush on distracted goofball Ted. The animation is lovely: warm and deceptively simple, it takes a cue from both the illustrations of the original books and the ethic that drives Warner's Art Deco superhero franchises. If nothing about the piece strikes as particularly original, the whole of it proceeds with an agreeable energy that connects its non-sequitur slapstick sequences and is made with obvious love for its source material and respect enough to not turn George into a shit-throwing, farting, face-slapping monster. Damned for being gentle, *Curious George* addresses issues of family, friendship, and romance; builds its character-based humour with clever dialogue and none-cutesy cuteness; and does it all with cheerful goodwill. Sometimes what's wrong with us as a society is hard to put a finger on. Sometimes it's not. (**WC**)

## THE NIGHT OF TRUTH (La Nuit de la vérité)
**\*\*¹/₂/\*\*\*\***

*st.* Naky Sy Savané, Commandant Moussa Cissé, Georgette Paré, Adama Ouédraogo
*sc.* Marc Gautron and Fanta Régina Nacro
*dir.* Fanta Régina Nacro

Watching the thoroughly detestable *Blood Diamond* recently, I wondered what it would take to get something approaching the process of suffering in the Third World without the added distraction of stupid white people and their irrelevant angst. But it turns out there are other ways to water down the story, too: *The Night of Truth (La Nuit de la vérité)* would apparently do away with Hollywood's fondness for outsiders looking in, yet in many ways, it has its own simplistic solutions and vague sentiments. Whatever the film's good intentions, its depiction of fictional warring peoples enjoying a shaky truce leaves out much of the important data needed to understand the original conflict. Though fitfully moving in terms of the breadth of atrocities on display, it doesn't say much more than "war bad"—which, though true, doesn't bring anyone any closer to good peace.

The fictitious West African peoples are the ruling Nayak and the rebellious Bonandes. After years of fighting, the two tribes—headed by Le President (Adama Ouédraogo) for the Nayak and Col. Theo (Moussa Cissé) for the Bonandes—are settling down for a cessation of hostilities. A ceremonial feast is prepared, and ranking members on both sides are invited. Trouble is, many aren't so sure this is going to work out. Theo's wife Soumari (Georgette Paré) and the President's wife Edna (Naky Sy Savané) have less "noble" concerns than their statesmen husbands, each of whom remembers the violent acts committed against them and their children. Neither trusts the opposition; even local eccentric Tomoto (Rasmane Ouédraogo) is all but wishing for the war to continue. Nevertheless, the two sides get together at the President's residence, lay down their arms, and approach one another despite the rancour of years and countless dead.

*The Night of Truth* never gives us a real sense of either side or how the fighting started in the first place. Wars are generally fought because somebody wants what someone else has—and nobody seems to want anything in this particular situation. We're not fed any information on what was being fought over, or the origins of the conflict, or any colonial influence that might be involved. All we know is that there was a war, and it's gotta stop. The film is often chilling in its evocation of people wearily used to war (a scene where youths recount how they lost various limbs is hard to forget), and the apparent impossibility of forgiving and forgetting bubbles to the surface in vivid ways. At the end of the day, though, it's not analytical enough to come up with anything beyond "Can't we all just get along?" Peace here is not brokered, it's just sort of declared.

It would be nice to be able to wave one's hand and bring "Adam's sons" together in harmony, but the kind of hatred that influences the Nayaks and Bonandes of the world comes with serious economic stakes and historical precedents that make reconciliation a tad complex. To be fair, *The Night of Truth* isn't trying to avoid these problems: it's often moving and unpleasant, especially in dealing with the psychic fallout of endless ethnic strife; and it places most of the burden on the women, who are left helpless as their sons and husbands abuse them. Unfortunately, the film isn't just gunning for an evocation—it appears to believe that it can put its foot down and get enemies to come to their senses. Where someone like Ousmane Sembene would have sketched the mechanisms that allow oppression to exist, director/co-writer Fanta Régina Nacro simply jumps to the last step of freedom and omits the long process that would climax at such a moment. This is understandable, but it doesn't teach much in the long run. (TMH)

## NIGHT WATCH (Nochnoi Dozor)
*/****
*st.* Konstantin Khabensky, Vladimir Menshov, Valeri Zolotukhin, Mariya Poroshina
*sc.* Timur Bekmambetov and Laeta Kalogridis
*dir.* Timur Bekmambetov

When it's not frantically whipping up arbitrary rules in its supernatural universe like the world's most convoluted (and expensive game) of Calvin-ball, Russian sensation Timur Bekmambetov's epileptic fusion of *Highlander* and *The Matrix*, *Night Watch*, comes off as every bit the puerile lightshow that such a union would imply. Consider the premise: light and dark "Others" live amongst humans, sometimes not knowing that they're not human, frozen in a centuries-old truce policed through night and day watches (and a dusk watch, too, judging by the proposed title of the third film in this planned trilogy) that ensure both sides refrain from killing one another. They're all vampires, I guess, though some are also shapeshifters (or instead are shapeshifters, who knows?) and some are those Indian fakir surgeons who used to pretend to reach into human body cavities and yank out chicken guts. It's telling that no positive review of this film is complete without a mention that there's a sequel and, with it, the rationalization that the many narrative crimes of *Night Watch* are explicable within the need for extended exposition in the first chapter. (See also: *The Phantom Menace.*) Telling, also, that the best proof presented for the quality of the film is that it's the top-grossing film in Russian history—that is, until its sequel recently eclipsed its $16M gross with a $33M haul of its own.

I wonder if it wasn't Russian whether *Night Watch* would be getting any kind of attention at all—but because it's the product of a national film industry that's been moribund since Eisenstein (or maybe Tarkovsky), there is attached to it a sort of patronizing "Boy, I didn't even know they had theatres in Russia!" benefit of a doubt afforded it. You feel like you want to treat it as you'd treat your kid's Christmas pageant. And, likewise, it's fair to call *Night Watch* a mess bordering on unwatchable and written with the mindless conviction of a kid's first attempt at writing a comic book. It's the kind of film that's widely appealing, doing most harm by confirming the belief held by most studio moneymen that the best way to attain crossover appeal is to jettison "difficult" elements like dialogue, character development, and quiet. Consider the scene where an owl-pal (like the clockwork Bubo from *Clash of the Titans*) transforms into a comely Russian lass (Galina Tyunina) who doesn't remember how to use a faucet, yet has been achin' for a shower for sixty years. (A shower she doesn't take, opting for a bath instead.) She also doesn't appear to have a problem remembering anything else during the course of her human-hood, leading me to assume that a fratboy nitwit cobbled the whole thing together using the "cool" parts of his favourite flicks. Oh, and there's something to do with a "chosen one" kid that plays a lot more like Eddie Murphy disaster *The Golden Child* than like *Star Wars*, which couldn't be, I don't think, what Bekmambetov intended.

One might argue that *Night Watch* grapples with issues of free will and personal identity, but let's be serious: anything resembling subtlety or subtext is most likely residue from the myriad sources the film has joylessly ripped off. Not content with the usual bloat, there's also something about how the Dark Others can apply for licenses from the Light Others to harvest humans for food except something or another then happens, leading to milquetoast protagonist Anton (Konstantin Khabensky) accidentally killing a Dark Other in self-defense, resulting in a vampire broad wanting revenge. And then, in a subplot related in ways that are a total mystery to me, there's a cursed vestal virgin Svetlana (Mariya Poroshina) therefore destined to bring about the end of the world in a really bad CGI vortex unless Anton and his yellow raincoat Night Watch cohorts can find out who cursed her and get the curser to uncurse the cursed. It goes on and on like this for what seems like an eternity, scenes of people walking down a street afforded multiple jump-cuts, cacophonous Russian-metal noise, stylized subtitles that comprise the film's niftiest effects, and finally an impossible-to-follow splice of the prologue's *Highlander* furry costume stupidity, with at least one person wielding a light(ed)saber. A downloadable trailer compresses the entire film into a two-and-a-half minute time lapse, and I won't be the first to say that, viewed at light speed, there's no appreciable loss of clarity nor, in truth, in quality of experience. (WC)

## NOTES ON A SCANDAL
**/****

*st.* Judi Dench, Cate Blanchett, Bill Nighy, Andrew Simpson
*sc.* Patrick Marber, based on the novel by Zoë Heller
*dir.* Richard Eyre

## CANDY
**/****

*st.* Abbie Cornish, Heath Ledger, Geoffrey Rush, Tom Budge
*sc.* Neil Armfield, based on the novel <u>Candy: A Novel of Love and Addiction</u> by Luke Davies
*dir.* Neil Armfield

When Judi Dench's brittle enunciation breathes life into the prologue of Richard Eyre's *Notes on a Scandal*, there's a hope, however fleeting, that the film will deserve the performance. Her tweedy, support-hosed teacher Barbara Covett is set up as a distaff Richard III, looking to subvert the beautifuls acting as the royals in her school's social strata—the newest member of which, Sheba Hart (Cate Blanchett), attracts the greatest amount of envy and desire. The characters' names are embarrassing (why not call them "Barbara Lust" and "Sheba Love"?), and it's not long before the picture follows suit, becoming as obvious and stillborn as its first half hour is scabrous and dangerous. Adapted from the Zoë Heller novel, it reminds of screenwriter Patrick Marber's *Closer* and how Mike Nichols' film adaptation similarly suffered from a gradual slackening of shock with the realization that its umbrella of misanthropy doesn't cast a dark shadow on all of us so much as it provides a vicarious thrill, like watching a cockfight, say, or a mantis eating its mate: though foul, its pungency is isolatable.

There's fascination here, but not much nasty, lingering insight, turning the experience of the film into something closer to spectacle. *Notes on a Scandal* contorts so awkwardly to paint its players as merely different shades of insufferable and pathetic that its misanthropy loses its edge. I don't know that Marber's wrong about the vile primate state of man, but I do know that the revelation—we're vile primates—isn't instructive in its pornographic exploitation. (I wonder if it doesn't seem like a better, more daring movie just because the perception is that the British wear their knickers tightly.) *Notes on a Scandal* doesn't have conflict but rather a series of damnable events illustrating nothing particularly shocking in a world that's already lapped it in terms of atrocity and subterfuge. The speed with which the story of a 53-year-old man breaking into Colorado's Platte Canyon High School to sexually assault six girls before killing one (and then himself) disappeared from the headlines speaks volumes about first the dustiness of *Notes on a Scandal*, then how the trappings of "class" in this awards-season prestige piece verges itself on the precipice of appalling. The only ones who don't agree are also the only ones interested in the film for anything beyond the weary laying of odds on the Oscar race.

Marber seems invested in fairytales with neither morals nor heroes. The evil queen of the ruined kingdom is Covett, her eunuch coterie composed of various forms of middle-aged teachers crippled by their station. Free-spirit princess Sheba, married to an older man (Bill Nighy) and mother to two children, one of them disabled, earns her stalker while searching for her own lost youth in the arms of one of her young prep-school Prince Charmings (Andrew Simpson). As the film takes us into Barbara's confidence by peeks into her diaries ("I"s dotted with hearts) and by her withering voiceover, we're to assume her point-of-view, but doing so casts the film's relationships with her travel-worn worldview. Dench unleashed is a marvel, the perfect counterpoint to Blanchett's effervescence, yet both are shoehorned into the restricting mold of Eyre's stuffy direction that handily neuters any audience indictment. It occurs to me that this film was done better by Liliana Cavani's *Ripley's Game*.

It seems to me that Neil Armfield's *Candy*, another superbly-acted bit of completely familiar melodrama, was done definitively as *Requiem for a Dream*. (Best of the genre, though, for me: the one-two punch of Gus Van Sant's *Drugstore Cowboy* and *My Own Private Idaho*.) Enough so that this endless iteration of pretty-people-taking-a-shit-bath in a film about the unsurprising dangers of drug-taking feels like a death march from the opening credits. Which is not to say there aren't moments of titillation in the hungry addict-sex between burnouts played by Heath Ledger and Abbie Cornish. Supplied with helpful title cards denoting its triptych narrative as Dante's "Heaven," "Earth" (i.e. purgatory), and "Hell" and opening with a ride on a centrifuge that's almost as embarrassing as far as allegory goes as the names in *Notes on a Scandal*, *Candy* manages to distinguish itself, however briefly, by letting Ledger and Cornish loose with their dangerous charisma and chemistry. If it's all nothing more than Samuel Fuller-lite in a post-grunge can, and if, generously speaking, the reasons for us watching it have more to do with seeing hotties get fucked literally and figuratively (by sticking themselves with hollow metal phalluses, the better to inject life- and body-altering liquid) until they're dead, at least *Candy* can claim Geoffrey Rush's dizzy boho cameo as our heroes' father enabler. Now there's something you don't see everyday. (**WC**)

O

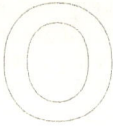

PREVIOUSLY UNPUBLISHED
## OFF THE BLACK
\*\*\*/\*\*\*\*

*st.* Nick Nolte, Trevor Morgan,
Rosemarie De Witt, Timothy Hutton
*w./d.* James Ponsoldt

PREVIOUSLY UNPUBLISHED
## PEACEFUL WARRIOR
\*\*/\*\*\*\*

*st.* Scott Mechlowicz, Nick Nolte,
Amy Smart, Tim DeKay
*sc.* Kevin Bernhardt, based on the
novel by Dan Millman
*dir.* Victor Salva

It comes as something of a surprise to report that Nick Nolte has weathered his way into the role of crinkle-eyed mentor. He remains at the vanguard of the last generation of American movie stars to demonstrate some level of shaggy virility—no little-boyness about him: his appeal wasn't to the TIGER BEAT set in ascendancy since *Dirty Dancing* (and popping its collective cherry against *Titanic*), but to bad old whiskey broads who like it rough. Nolte's best film is possibly Paul Schrader's devastating *Affliction*, which could also mark the last time Nolte played, without irony, a guy with the gun and all the phallic connotations that implies. In feel-good pics *Off the Black* and *Peaceful Warrior*, however, Nolte has become something like Mr. Miyagi—or, in the case of the former, Matthau in *The Bad News Bears*: the sometimes-inebriated, always scary papa bear (see: *Over the Hedge*) catalyst to the development of his winsome, dark-haired young wards. A natural progression, perhaps, in the hellraiser-to-role-model Darwin chart of men's evolution, it still represents a kind of uncomfortable castration for someone who remains among the most compulsively watchable people in movies.

James Ponsoldt makes his hyphenate debut with *Off the Black*, the best Richard Russo adaptation not based on a book by Richard Russo, chronicling the last days of a miserable old fucker who finds a brief purpose in the eyes of others through the auspices of a young buck wandering onto the reserve. The buck in point is Dave (the endlessly appealing Trevor Morgan), a pitcher in a game umpired by Nolte's Ray Cook, who, on a hotly-contested pitch, walks in the winning run, knocking his team out of summer-league playoffs. Caught in the act of vandalizing Ray's house later that evening, Dave strikes a bargain that he will pose as Ray's son at Ray's upcoming high school reunion, thus giving Ray some scrap of dignity and Dave, who's recently lost his mother and, in the psychological fallout, his father (a great Timothy Hutton), a surrogate dad. It's best described as a nice little indie, occasionally well-observed and laudably free of most of the expected appeals to sentimentality. It boasts of a tremendous performance by Nolte and uniformly excellent turns by everyone else (Sonia Feigelson as Dave's little sis, in particular, steals the movie with one scene where she sings a couple of refrains from "My Darling Clementine" *a capella* in the middle of a Wyeth field), and Ponsoldt earns a lot of respect by trying to approach the subject of death and fort/da with sobriety and intelligence. If anything, it reminded me a lot of a jellying moment in the first season of "Rescue Me" where the Denis Leary character talks to his father in a series of grunts that are subtitled to reveal the depths of love and regret conveyed by an essential inability to communicate until it's just too damned late.

Not so good is Victor "*Jeepers Creepers*"/convicted pedophile Salva's magic-realist, sports-movie uplift melodrama *Peaceful Warrior*, wherein Nolte plays a Zen mechanic named Socrates, oracle to a young gymnast,

Dan (Scott Mechlowicz), who has shattered (in CGI-fanciful literalism) his leg, and his confidence, in a disastrous motorcycle accident. Packed with bromides and saddled with adapting a semi-autobiographical self-help book (The Celestine Prophecy for jocks), the picture mistakes stuff like "live in the moment" for "wax on, wax off"—lines that not even Nolte can deliver with conviction, much less spine-tingle. Predictably, the film follows Dan's journey from shell-shocked survivor of a near-amputation to Rocky-like climb back into Olympic contention, all under the gnarly wing of mystical Socrates, who has the power to float to the rooftop canopy of his service station and promote his policy of clean-living (wow, Nolte really *is* a great actor) and meditation to cure Dan of the asphalt-inspired demons that haunt him. Montage sequences? Check. Love interest (Amy Smart), long suffering and gone when the film doesn't know what to do with her? Check, check.

What distinguishes *Peaceful Warrior* from any number of identical pictures is Salva's own ugly past as a pederast and maker of movies that fawn over their young boys like that guy with the van looking for his puppy. (I say this as someone who liked *Jeepers Creepers*.) Posed like a horror movie and packed with horror-movie tensions and, occasionally, images, Salva's mortification of his celluloid flesh is made manifest as Socrates turns Dan (a real asshole, truth be told) into a pommel-horsing machine. Salva's triumph is in keeping the tone of the film oblique. He's hidden his self-hate beneath genre picture trappings, offering up what seems like shame in a story about a guy giving up what he truly wants in favour of pursuits ennobling and socially acceptable. It's The Confessions of St. Augustine in cheesy, leotard form—and true to tradition, the first bits are more interesting than the last. Holding our fascination, though, is witnessing Nolte finally getting to play the role he's been groomed for: God. (**WC**)

**OLD JOY (see: *THE DEATH OF MR. LAZARESCU*)**

**THE OMEN (see: *AKEELAH AND THE BEE*)**

## DOCUMENTARY

## ON NATIVE SOIL
***/****
*dir.* Linda Ellman

I know I'm beating a dead horse here, but I think the documentary too often gets a pass as cinema. All of the focus is on the subject matter and next to no interest is paid to technique. The core audience for documentaries might be the same one Pauline Kael described in her infamous essay "Fear of Movies", i.e., the people who refused to see *Carrie*, *Taxi Driver*, or even *Jaws* because they "don't like violence" (read: they don't like anything that is going to take them out of their comfort zone). The larger problem isn't simply that films, on a visceral level, ought to be pleasurable or, at minimum, interesting, but that the lack of filmmaking excitement in most documentaries is intended to approximate objectivity, which is poisonous to art. "Objectivity," almost by definition, eliminates values and any perceivable human element, and once art eliminates values and any perceivable human element, it ceases to have any utility.

But as the line between news and entertainment—or real life and "reel" life, if you will—has been blissfully blurred in the age of Michael Moore, reality television, and "The Colbert Report", it may be time to retire this rant. Non-fiction films are now aesthetically similar enough to fiction films that the two can sit down at the table of brotherhood together. The traditional granola documentary, at least when it comes to feature-length films, is very nearly extinct. Nevertheless, I found myself pleasantly surprised by Linda Ellman's under-publicized *On Native Soil*. The film is actually pretty good cinema, worthy of comparison to the year's other September 11th films, *World Trade Center* and *United 93*. It was adapted directly from <u>The 9/11 Commission Report</u>, an ominous sign indeed—and yet Ellman has given the material some kind of point-of-view and endued it with passion and intensity.

What needs to be understood about September 11th is that the whole thing took place over the course of a couple of hours on a lazy Tuesday morning. For all intents and purposes, the attack materialized out of thin air without warning and without reason. As hard as people like Sean Hannity may try, it cannot be thought of as another Pearl Harbor and what followed as a result cannot be thought of as World War III. The accused perpetrators are as varied as Osama Bin Laden, Islam, "the Jews," God, feminists, homosexuals, and, incredibly, the Bush administration. It seems to have been an act of war, but with whom are we at war? September 11th is closer in nature to the Columbine shootings than to something like Pearl Harbor. The historical context is painfully indistinct and the attempts to make sense of it are borne of conflicting political agendas, suggesting that there is no sense to make.

Between *United 93*, *World Trade Center*, and *On Native Soil*, only *United 93* is a bona fide masterpiece. That film is told in real time, a decision that feeds our dread to an unbearable level. In focusing on the story of United 93, its attitude towards 9/11 is surprisingly nihilistic. It's saying that we are all going to die, the real question is are we going to die with dignity. In the end, the passengers of United 93 are rotting in the exact same earth as the hijackers, not to mention those trapped in the towers. They went out fighting and they possibly saved several other lives, but they are still dead. They did not willingly sacrifice themselves (they would be dead whether or not they rushed the cabin) and so they cannot properly be called heroes or martyrs. They died with dignity and that is a meagre triumph.

In a sense, *On Native Soil* is a mean between *United 93* and *World Trade Center*. (To paraphrase Stanley Kubrick's oft-quoted summary of *Schindler's List*, if September 11th was about three thousand people who died, then *World Trade Center* was about two who didn't.) It analyzes and re-analyzes exactly when and how the attack happened and all the ways in which the United States was vulnerable. Several Americans died and the film is, in part, a fitting memorial to them. The heroes are the victims' families, who pushed Congress to form a commission to investigate what happened that day and, in a moment that rather inexplicably makes me teary-eyed in the recounting, prompted former NSC counterterrorism coordinator Richard Clarke to apologize to the deceased's families and admit, "Your government failed you, those you entrusted to protect you failed you, and I failed you."

Port Authority police officer David Lim was evacuating Tower I when it collapsed. He survived. "You have to imagine a straw on a pancake," he says, "we were in that straw." In this passage, *On Native Soil* reveals itself as more *The Pianist* than *Schindler's List*. Survival is ignoble, random, and meaningless. There is no fate and there is no divine intervention. The universe is governed by chaos and so it is only natural that in a catastrophe like the World Trade Center attacks, someone will be left standing. There was absolutely no good reason that a select few wound up in the straw instead of under the pancake. Lim, for what it's worth, is a bit on the odd side. The "straw on a pancake" metaphor paints a vivid picture, but who puts a straw on a pancake? He describes the ensuing wreckage as being like "the beginning of *Terminator*." Lim also slightly overanthropomorphizes his dog, Sirius. He told Sirius he was going to come back for him, but he was unable to deliver on that promise. "At this point, I already knew, he passed on. 'Passed on,' I make it sound like he went in his sleep. But he was killed. He was murdered." Just a tad odd, saying that his dog was "murdered."

Understand that Ellman doesn't condescend to Lim in the least and brazenly accepts his odd way of speaking. One imagines that this oddness is part of the point: human beings don't come out of a box. If you're going to discuss September 11th on a microcosmic scale, you can't iron out behavioral idiosyncrasies. As the universe is governed by chaos, not all the pieces fit together perfectly and sometimes the Port Authority officer who survived is the type of guy who compares the wreckage to the beginning of *The Terminator*. It almost goes without saying that Lim is more interesting, sympathetic, and *human* than anybody in either *United 93* or *World Trade Center*. Strangely enough, he's too out there to be anything other than utterly authentic.

The film's strong visceral wallop is attributable primarily to the wide variety of source material. While *On Native Soil* utilizes talking-head interviews and an omniscient narrator (alternately Hilary Swank and Kevin Costner, the latter of whom has little talent in this arena), there is a sufficient amount of archival footage here for Ellman to be able to tell the story in mostly cinematic terms. We see and/or hear airport surveillance video of the hijackers getting through security, C-Span coverage of the Commission Report hearings, air traffic control's audiotapes, and, of course, the actual attack on the World Trade Center, which is covered from an astonishing number of angles. Ultimately, there is too much information for us to take in and Ellman doesn't organize it in a way that's easy to follow. Some could justifiably conclude that she is

therefore incompetent at documentary filmmaking, but this shotgun approach is, in itself, a meaningful way of looking at September 11th. THE ONION wisecracked at the time that American life had begun to resemble a bad Jerry Bruckheimer movie, but *On Native Soil* more or less legitimizes this observation. This onslaught of information reminds us that the attack happened in the media age—that 9/11 has had the ever-living shit documented out of it; and this lends it a certain hyperrealistic quality. I'm beginning to think the very act of photographing something somehow renders it less "real," which may be why I'm so disdainful of distinguishing fiction from non-fiction film.

Though *On Native Soil* is a triumph on an artistic level, I nevertheless find myself having strong reservations about its merits. While I might've been wrong in expecting documentaries to be more like fiction films, I'm not quite sure what I would prefer instead. Something appears to be missing—*On Native Soil* doesn't stick to the ribs like it should. It's forgettable. All that cinema kind of sugarcoats it and renders it too palatable; a boring anaesthetic documentary about September 11th may paradoxically yield more power. The film is rather politically naïve, too. The premise is essentially that the United States became vulnerable to a terrorist attack through failures of both the Clinton and Bush administrations. Clinton refused to retaliate against previous Al-Qaeda attacks, in effect "emboldening" them, and Bush refused to follow up on CIA reports that an attack was imminent. Airport and border security were lax. We see the actual approved student visa used by one of the terrorists: his address is listed as "hotel." Essentially, the film is saying that the United States should've fostered its current culture of fear long before September 11th, 2001.

For the sake of ideological continuity, liberals need to decide if they hate Bush for not defending the United States against the 9/11 attacks or for cultivating a society in which we lose the right to bring bottled water onto airplanes. They cannot have it both ways. *On Native Soil* chooses the former and this, in my eyes, is the wrong choice. There is little comment on the potential threats to civil liberties and, moreover, there is little comment on the terrorists' motivations for attacking. Ellman seems unwilling to consider that surrendering to their demands and adopting a foreign policy of isolationism could prevent another attack. I'd like to claim that this is why the film doesn't have much staying power, but Michael Moore's *Fahrenheit 9/11* was just as dumb, probably dumber, and still it lingers.

Moore's film undoubtedly benefited from a sense of communal synergy, nay, urgency. This was more than hype: *Fahrenheit 9/11* came out the summer before the last election and I saw it at the Century 16 in Salt Lake City, Utah, where audience members screamed "Fuck you!" whenever Bush came on-screen. These factors certainly gave *Fahrenheit 9/11* a primal power that is lacking in *On Native Soil*. But I also believe that Moore is more comfortable as a pop filmmaker. (The use of **Go-Go's**' "Vacation" during a montage of the President golfing is the sort of trick that is finally beneath Ellman.) *On Native Soil* is political but non-partisan, and this is a problem. Although Ellman's ideas are not substantial enough to sustain a "real" documentary treatment, she maintains a sense of *faux*-objectivity, softening the film's primal emotional impact. Neither fish nor fowl, *On Native Soil* is a worthwhile curiosity but hardly indispensable. **(AJ)**

## ONLY HUMAN (Seres queridos)
**\*\* /\*\*\*\***

*st.* Guillermo Toledo, Marián Aguilera, María Botto, Fernando Ramallo
*w./d.* Dominic Harari & Teresa Pelegri

## HOUSE OF SAND (Casa de Areia)
**\*\*\*¹/₂/\*\*\*\***

*st.* Fernanda Montenegro, Fernanda Torres, Ruy Guerra, Seu Jorge
*sc.* Elena Soárez
*dir.* Andrucha Waddington

Married hyphenates Dominic Harari and Teresi Pelegri craft a screwball comedy (which has the audacity to end with the final line of Billy Wilder's *Some Like it Hot*) about what happens when good Jewish girl Leni (Marián Aguilera) brings Palestinian nebbish boyfriend Rafi (Guillermo Toledo) home to meet her *My Big Fat Greek Wedding* ethnic cartoon family. There's the blind, rifle-toting old fossil fond of recounting his days of potting Arabs along the Gaza strip; the short, hysterical Jewish mother; the slutty older sister who only fucks anything with a dick because mama loved little sister more; the younger brother who's newly fanatical about the Koran and the observance of the Jewish Sabbath; and the niece who's a monster because, well, who wouldn't be in that household? Discomfort turns into farce when Rafi drops a cube of frozen soup out a window, killing someone who might be Leni's father (said father later mistaking a black prostitute for Leni's mother) — this event also leading to the discovery that Leni's mother has never had an orgasm and the *tableaux homorte* where grandpa is caught groping Rafi during a trip to the loo.

Yet *Only Human (Seres queridos)* is somehow not terrible. There's warmth to Toledo's performance (as well as a wide-eyed earnestness to Aguilera's) that forgives the tedious proselytizing and forced slapstick to a degree, making for a few surprised laughs even if a late-in-the-game argument about Jerusalem thuds with all the grace of an Ayn Rand screed. I liked these people in the same way I like people I've met at Human Rights festivals and screenings for Al Gore documentaries—people so enlightened that they've thoroughly repressed their innate racism, sublimating it into something that resembles the beatific self-satisfaction of the holy idiot. *Only Human* would like to be more than a Stanley Kramer film about the Intifada, but alas, the only lesson it has to impart is that a gifted, charismatic cast can elevate the most tired material into something closer to mediocrity. Its ultimate shrug and a prayer, then, carries with it—unintentionally, I think—the message that there's actually hope in being resigned to our essential hopelessness.

Hopelessness also rules the day in Andrucha Waddington's ravishing *House of Sand (Casa de Areia)*, a distaff *Lawrence of Arabia* married to Nicolas Roeg's *Castaway* in which two sets of mothers and daughters find themselves adrift in the vast nothing of the Brazilian desert. Shot with real genius by Ricardo Della Rosa, Waddington's film is pregnant with silence and emptiness. It's like a Portuguese Carroll Ballard film where nature serves as the first testament to the actions of man, or like Hiroshi Teshigahara's *Woman in the Dunes* (indeed, Hiroshi Segawa's cinematography in that picture is the precursor to Della Rosa's in this) as another telling of the Sisyphus myth, whereby, if Kirkegaard is to be believed, man can only find solace in the knowledge that all his tomorrows will be identical to all his yesterdays. Aurea (Fernanda Torres) is dragged to the frontier by her mad husband (Ruy Guerra), Aurea's mother Maria (Fernanda Montenegro) in tow, when the husband accidentally kills himself and the rest of their settlement flees to less desperate climes. Over the course of the next six decades, Aurea, Maria, and Aurea's daughter struggle to carve out an existence in a harsh, implacable landscape that seems solely interested in swallowing up every trace of them should they ever take a moment to rest.

*House of Sand* is about the nobility of the human animal, desperate to leave its mark in the shifting sand and made mute and numb by the effort. It sees triumph in ambition—it's truly the journey and not the destination (oblivion), marking this as one of the more existentially graceful arthouse pieces in years. Without pretense, without trickery beyond the decision to forego trickery, it tells its story as an idyll, and in its ornate, hyper-detailed structuralism it reminded me a lot of Stanley Kubrick's *Barry Lyndon*. The most beautiful-looking film of the year so far, *House of Sand* also happens to be the best Roeg film since *The Man Who Fell To Earth*. There's steel in the three generations of women depicted in the film (real-life mother/daughter actors who, poignantly, switch roles as time rolls on), and there's poetry in the revelation that the whole film was inspired by one photograph of a lonely shack standing against entropy and the inexorable wilderness. (**WC**)

## A N I M A T E D
## OVER THE HEDGE
**/****

*sc.* Len Blum and Lorne Cameron & David Hoselton and Karey Kirkpatrick, based on the comic strip by Michael Fry and T Lewis *dirs.* Tim Johnson & Karey Kirkpatrick

It's just a largely inoffensive, vaguely environmentalist (inasmuch as being anti-sprawl is pro-environment) assembly-line animation featuring the usual passel of aging and/or second-run celebrities subbing for trained voice performers as anthropomorphic CGI animal bodies engaged in slapstick, stink jokes, and other interchangeable ephemera for the delight of our toddlers. If you feel as though you've seen *Over the Hedge* a hundred times already, that's because it's been cobbled together from a hundred other identical pictures; and if you have a little trouble afterwards remembering a thing about it, well, it's only natural that something with no nutritional value would pass right through you. That's not to say there's no fertile ground to be mined here in exploring the line between the natural-natural and the human natural (a line that the Japanese puzzler *Pom Poko* attempts to describe to similar effect)— safe to say, in fact, that a great satire lies in the suburban morass as viewed through the eyes of the "un-civilized." But *Over the Hedge* is a slave to the theoretical peanut gallery, resorting to manufacturing a villain and then staging a series of boom/crash operas. Though Pixar's *Cars* can pretty fairly be described as awful, it's Pixar's legacy of brilliant children's entertainments that DreamWorks has tried to ape with its puerile, art-destroying, post-pop *Shrek* series, and if *Over the Hedge* at least resists the scatology that marks *Shrek* as low entertainment for the lowest common denominator, it still can't quite make that jump from loud noises to real insight and value.

RJ (voiced by Bruce Willis) pisses off a bear fresh from hibernation (Nick Nolte, typecast), who makes him an offer he can't refuse by ordering him to restore his winter stash, toot sweet. So our hero enlists a gaggle of good-hearted, dim-witted wildlife (including a skunk (Wanda Sykes, typecast); a frenetic squirrel (Steve Carrell); a hilarious, William Shatner-voiced possum; and turtle/conscience Verne (Garry Shandling)) to infiltrate suburbia, liberate various and sundry foodstuffs, and generally put their hides on the line to save his. RJ is to learn a lesson, of course, and comeuppance to is to be had by not only the bear but also the evil head of the local HOA, Gladys (Allison Janney), and the *Wallace & Gromit*-borrowed ace exterminator, The Verminator (Thomas Haden Church). Both truisms lead to the downfall of a picture that simply did not need a villain besides the encroachment of Man into the wild.

An early sequence is spot-on brilliant as RJ introduces his charges to the excesses of human existence, which lie in stark contrast to their own subsistence, hardscrabble lives. Humans are seen as worshipping at altars of food; if only the picture had followed these observations through to the big box marts and gas stations, it might actually have had something to say. Alas, all it ends up doing is tap-dancing around a Persian character and setting up the skunk with a cat so inbred it's lost its sense of smell. When the film is funny, it's funny that way: not insightful, just sort of grotesque, leading to the inevitable conclusion that it's fun to watch animals do people things and almost get smeared by propane tanks, and not as fun to consider how many opportunities they're missing in a film with this premise. Consider especially the usefulness of junk food as a Pavlovian prod (and how Dr. Phil might be junk food for the soul)—how completely these animals give themselves over to the sway of trans fat, carbonation, and processed sugar. (More, how these trifles are packaged in lovely arrays of irresistibly intoxicating packages and colours.) There's a real movie in there somewhere about pods and the food industry. Shame that *Over the Hedge*'s only real presence is that it's part and parcel of the same excreted legacy. (**WC**)

# P

## THE PAINTED VEIL
*** /****

*st.* Naomi Watts, Edward Norton,
Liev Schreiber, Diana Rigg
*sc.* Ron Nyswaner, based on the
novel by W. Somerset Maugham
*dir.* John Curran

## THE GOOD SHEPHERD
** /****

*st.* Matt Damon, Angelina Jolie,
Robert De Niro, Alec Baldwin
*sc.* Eric Roth
*dir.* Robert De Niro

## THE GOOD GERMAN
*1/2/****

*st.* George Clooney, Cate
Blanchett, Tobey Maguire, Jack
Thompson
*sc.* Paul Attanasio, based on the
novel by Joseph Kanon
*dir.* Steven Soderbergh

One of seemingly dozens of
pretentious, self-produced vanity
pieces from the Edward Norton grist
mill, *The Painted Veil*, John Curran's
adaptation of Somerset Maugham's
story of colonial malaise, is a pleasant
surprise. Naomi Watts and Toby Jones
are fabulous (and Norton is steady);
it's not terribly paternalistically racist
despite being another Western film in
which white people exert their magical
influence in foreign lands; and even
though it's all about prestige and
hedonism, it manages now and again
to actually be about prestige and
hedonism. But like the simultaneously-
opening Soderbergh *noir The Good
German*, it's mostly interesting in the
meta. What keeps this updating of the
old Greta Garbo weeper from being
literally better is the lack of immediacy
in its tale of emotionally distant
scientists and their flapper wives,
adrift in the boiler pot of 1920s
Shanghai. Not timeless in its remove
but instead ineffably dated by it, it's an
Old Hollywood production in both
epic scale and lack of subtext, making
the picture a lovely trifle not unlike
other well-done bits of instantly-
forgotten prestige (see: Philip Noyce's
*The Quiet American*).

Walter Fane is a bland, emotionally
distant research scientist specializing
in infectious pathogens. "How
fascinating," says socialite and object of
Walter's affections, Kitty (Watts). "No,
not really," Walter responds, yet Kitty
marries Walter, anyway, moving to
Shanghai following a whirlwind
courtship largely meant to throw her
mother's Jane Austen-tatious
disapproval back in her face. (A
mistake, safe to say.) Kitty finds respite
from her subsequent boredom in the
arms of diplomat Charlie (Liev
Schreiber), an act of adultery the
cuckolded Walter avenges by spiriting
them away to a cholera outbreak in the
middle of the country. Chinese legend
Anthony Wong Chau-Sang has a juicy
part as a military man who expresses
that the troubles of his country are the
responsibility of his countrymen and,
in what's probably the film's most
satisfying scene, demonstrates exactly
how culturally specific are the
problems that white imperialists like
Walter try in vain to solve. Refreshing
to say that this version restores
Maugham's original ending (mangled
in the Garbo), thus allowing for a final
shot of the Chinese countryside that
encompasses its vastness and beauty
along with its essential mystery. In
terms of how spoilers bleed, Curran's
take has a lot more in common with
Scott Smith's well-received penny
dreadful <u>The Ruins</u> than with things
like Edward Zwick's appalling *Blood
Diamond* or Kevin MacDonald's
similarly horrendous *The Last King of
Scotland*. No matter the number of
proofs given for silly Kitty's
redemption, no matter the number of
times it invokes a *carpe diem*
worldview, *The Painted Veil* works

thanks to its pessimistic belief that people can never carve out more than a moment or two of happiness for themselves in the middle of such a beautiful, insensible mess.

Robert De Niro's plodding *The Good Shepherd* is a different kind of insensible mess. The emotional centre of this semi-fictional account of the founding of the CIA (grounded by a stoic, monotone Matt Damon) hinges on another ill-conceived marriage (to another socialite, played this time by Angelina Jolie) infringed upon by the cloak-and-dagger of the newly-minted Cold War. There's some nice masculine bonding ritualized in the top-secret, homoerotic spanking/pissing/Greco-Roman wrestling of ultra-secret frat Skull & Bones (where Bush Jr. first learned to be a spook) that only occasionally elicits giggles, as well as snatches of interrogation and espionage that make *The Good Shepherd* a Bletchley Park presentation of a James Bond intrigue, i.e., a spy flick as filtered through the sort of secrecy and emotional reserve required by the profession itself.

Damon's spymaster Wilson is a cipher—made such, the film suggests, by the suicide of his stentorian father, which he witnessed firsthand. We get a boilerplate psychoanalysis of the toll his reticence takes on his life through a parade of treacherous father figures (a gay, Red teacher (Michael Gambon), an FBI man (Alec Baldwin), a military muckety-muck (De Niro)), women wronged (Jolie, a luminous Tammy Blanchard, Martina Gedeck), and finally a boy of his own (Eddie Redmayne in the film's best performance), whose pillow talk might undermine daddy's most important mission. It's the birth of a covert nation allegorized as the dissolution of a traditional family structure; there's no trick in discerning the message of the film as similar to that of *Apocalypto* (the fall of a great nation facilitated by corruption from within) and, in so doing, figuring out that beyond skewering the cult of masculinity in

general and the Skull & Bones in particular lies *The Good Shepherd*'s grand design of indicting the Bush administration's shameful legacy of illegal surveillance and dirty tricks abroad as the culprit behind America's global loss of face. Hardly a lightning bolt, and hardly one that deserves 160 deadening minutes of misdirection and repetition, and hardly anything to justify casting Jolie as the jilted wife of a disinterested husband.

Steven Soderbergh's *The Good German* is meant as a film set in the 1940s that looks as though it were released in the 1940s, too. Inasmuch as a self-consuming experiment can succeed, it succeeds, though proof of Soderbergh's ability to emulate Guy Maddin proves very little indeed. *The Good German* is ultimately a slack *noir* with an oft-beaten anti-hero Geismer (George Clooney), a hissing *fatale* in the Dietrich mold Lena (Cate Blanchett), and a pseudo-Lorre toad in army driver Tully (Tobey Maguire). It all amounts to not much as Geismer rekindles his wartime flame with turned-out Lena in post-war Berlin while Soderbergh builds a visually-arresting shrine to Weimar filmmakers and expats like Michael Curtiz.

A journalist who's seen more than he should, Geismer wanders around in a wide-eyed gape that skirts on the perilous edge of Clooney's *O Brother Where Art Thou?* moron performance. He's too smart to be this far behind, and all that's left for us to do during the downtime is contemplate how the picture is really about moral relativity in the pre-Cold War machinations of the Russians and Americans and their German scientist pawns. It wouldn't pass muster in the company of John Huston, Jacques Tourneur, or Jules Dassin; this is less *Out of the Past* than it is mired in the meta, its only import located in the furious exculpatory labours of critical admirers and, ironically, the one or two viewers still titillated by ugly words and brief flashes of doggy-style sex. For as much as Soderbergh's *Solaris* was a wonderfully intimate update of Tarkovsky's canonical vision, *The Good German* attests that any act of critical mimic experimentation (Gus Van Sant's *Psycho*, for instance) requires the same core of human failure and desire, lest it come off as just so much masturbation and self-congratulation. (**WC**)

## PAN'S LABYRINTH
****/****
*st.* Ariadna Gil, Ivana Baquero, Sergi López, Maribel Verdú
*w./d.* Guillermo del Toro

Brutal and ignoble, the antithesis of romantic, the violence in Guillermo del Toro's *Pan's Labyrinth* slaps metal against flesh like the flat of a hand against a steel table. It's the only element of the picture that isn't lush, that isn't laden with the burnished archetype of Catholic superstition as it exists in eternal suspension with the pagan mythologies it cannibalized. By itself, this seems a metaphor for the pain and the magic of how fable turns the inevitability of coming-of-age into ritual. An early scene where hero girl Ofelia (Ivana Baquero)—a storyteller equal parts experientially innocent and allegorically savvy, making her the manifestation of del Toro's ideal avatar—tells her prenatal brother a story about a rose that blooms nightly on a mountain of thorns touches in one ineffably graceful movement all the picture's themes of immortality, aspiration, isolation, and the promise of escape held, sadistically, just out of reach. There's something of the myth of Tantalus in Ofelia's tale, as much as there is of Lewis Carroll's Alice and the sagas of parental absence by the Brothers Grimm, which surface in the premise of a young girl traveling, as the film opens, with her pregnant mother into the war-torn Spanish countryside during Franco's rule to join her wicked stepfather Captain Vidal (Sergi López) at his remote outpost. Ofelia will be reminded repeatedly throughout the film that there's no such thing as justice or innocence left in the world, and that the best intentions are crushed by cynicism and rage. The question left as the picture closes has to do with whether Ofelia's taken the lesson to heart, to say nothing of del Toro—or us.

It comes down to what you decide the film is about—what, in fact, film itself might ultimately be about. There's telling stories, then telling stories with substance, then telling stories with resonance; and linking it all together, there's the promise of immortality once the story you tell is illuminated by the crackle of firelight. Still, *Pan's Labyrinth* is the kind of familiar that astonishes with our inability to imagine it better than the way del Toro has. Ofelia escapes into a fantasy-world (of her own creation or not, it's ours to decide—for the filmmaker's part, he's expressed that no element of the picture is a phantasm), led into a hedge labyrinth by an insectile pixie to speak with a faun (Doug Jones), who assigns the girl three tasks to prove her worthiness for inclusion in the faun's world. Del Toro's obsessions with insects and clockwork figure prominently in the piece (the latter coming into focus with Vidal's careful ministration of his dead father's pocket watch, a bit of ticking legacy he hopes to pass on to his unborn son)—likewise the director's interest in the underground and the fecundity of it as a signifier of both potential and the repressed. The first task has to do with confronting the beast in its belly, in the roots of a gnarled tree; the second with a candlelit banquet hall that imagines the Mad Hatter's tea party as something uniquely unstrung; and the third with the spilling of blood and the choice between the destruction or preservation of innocence. Ofelia is tasked with discovering her courage, her self-control, and her judgment as del Toro parallels her quest with Vidal's merciless persecution of guerrilla rebels and casual abuse of his servants and Ofelia's mother.

Each storyline complements the other without becoming confused; when the narratives converge in the final reel, they do so with sense and poetry. Vidal undermines Ofelia's attempts to save her mother, precipitated not just by the nature of his solipsism but by Ofelia's inability to manage her own appetites as well. And when Ofelia is given a chance at the end to explore again the ideas of sacrifice and selflessness (already embodied in the parallel of her nanny's loyalty to the insurgency), *Pan's Labyrinth* suggests that conscience—native, infant conscience—is the key to change. Though it couldn't be more different, the film shares its optimism with Michael Haneke's *Caché*, placing its faith in the next generation to rediscover, not invent, resourcefulness and the hopefulness to employ it to affect a more positive outcome. *Pan's Labyrinth* addresses the "sins of the father" not as a death sentence, but as an opportunity to correct what's been broken: the bridge from the Old Testament's antisocial savagery to the New Testament's covenant to honour civility in the body and suckling morality of a child. Easily del Toro's best film in a portfolio of fantastic pictures, it's timely and timeless (the foremost prerequisite of any useful parable); as beautiful and obscene as anything beautiful must carry the potential for; and as horrible and hopeful—often in the same breathless moment—as life can be. Del Toro's films are uncompromising and very much his own, and *Pan's Labyrinth* is a masterpiece. (**WC**)

**PEACEFUL WARRIOR (see: *OFF THE BLACK*)**

**THE PIANO TUNER OF EARTHQUAKES**
*½/****
*st.* Amira Casar, Gottfried John,

Assumpta Serna, César Saracho
*sc.* Alan Passes and The Quay Brothers
*dir.* The Quay Brothers

**MUTUAL APPRECIATION**
***½/****
*st.* Justin Rice, Rachel Clift, Andrew Bujalski, Seung-Min Lee
*w./d.* Andrew Bujalski

**UNKNOWN**
½*/****
*st.* Jim Caviezel, Greg Kinnear, Bridget Moynahan, Joe Pantoliano
*sc.* Matthew Waynee
*dir.* Simon Brand

The Quay Brothers, Stephen and Timothy, are marvellous animators, having shepherded stop-motion and a disquieting biomechanical ethic into a series of notably discomfiting shorts, more than one of which pays tribute to their hero/mentor Jan Švankmajer. I met their 1995 transition to live-action features (*Institute Benjamenta*) with equal parts excitement, curiosity, and trepidation—I believed they'd be a little like either fellow animator-turned-director Tim Burton or those masters of a form who overreach by switching to a different medium, à la Michael Jordan. The truth is somewhere in-between, as the Quays have retained a bit of their glacial patience and a marked affection for created environments but have miscalculated the extent to which our fascination with animate clockworks translates into a commensurate fascination with people sitting around, staring at a wall. The former inspires existential thoughts on the nature of sentience; the latter generally inspires boredom. No question in my mind that something's lurking in the Quays' underneath, but it's important to mark that fine line distinguishing fascination from obtuseness for the sake of itself. Exploring the waking/dreamlife divide is interesting—but it's neither original nor terribly useful when the main tactic seems to be to conjure up pomposity-inspired sleepiness.

Piano tuner Felisberto (César Saracho) is summoned to the secluded forest manse of evil genius Droz (Gottfried John) to "tune" a series of arcane machineries (which look to have been designed by, well, the Brothers Quay) for use in an elaborate revenge plot involving the culturati and dead/reanimated/doppelgänger opera ingénue Malvina (Amira Casar). The bulk of the picture is composed of long, wordless, largely action-less shots that allow the viewer to take in immaculately-conceived environments played forwards and back. It feels like the intent is to draw relationships between our programming and the programmatic process of watching, then analyzing, film. Beyond that? Not much. *The Piano Tuner of Earthquakes* is an impenetrable, deep-arthouse version of Gaston Leroux's The Phantom of the Opera that prizes its one timeworn conceit above all other considerations. It owes an allegiance to *avant-garde* in that sense as a relic more interesting to discuss than to actually experience. To that end, it's interesting to me that I'm more enraptured by the bits of string and nails the Brothers Quay animate than in the people they ossify. I don't mind films that require a lot of heavy-lifting—what I do mind are the ones that don't pay off the effort.

Going in the other direction, Andrew Bujalski's exuberant *Mutual Appreciation* feels like, so help me, a product of John Cassavetes' kitchen-sink aesthetic and Michael Winterbottom's dizzy brinkmanship. It hums along on improvisational energy and Larry David awkwardness as it essays the lives of new-hipster boho Brooklyn rockers putting on shows in empty warehouses, meeting over radio broadcasts at independent stations, and having endless conversations structured around puffed-up intellectual braggadocio and Bujalski's genuine observational gift. These are people drunk on quirk and the gilded cachet of saying "chin chin" as a toast in a futon-centric loft larded with coffee table books and French café posters silkscreened onto grape trays. It's the dark side of a Waldorf education. I see *Mutual Appreciation* as presenting the kind of brainy discomfort that Woody Allen used to do so well—this idea that too much rounded equals too little edge. Passion is at a premium in Bujalski's world, to the extent that inarticulate distress is the norm instead of the exception. "We should do cocaine!" exclaims cute girlfriend Ellie (Rachel Clift), and boyfriend Lawrence (Bujalski) offers a long pause before blurting an "Okay!" that dances that delicate wobble between being cool and being scared in front of someone you want to impress.

The star is promising alt-rocker Alan (Justin Rice)—he reminds of Jonny Polonsky—and it's his struggle to reconcile an affair with the sister of his drummer (Lee Seung-Min) and his attraction to his best friend's girl that leads the picture to its graceful, unexpected, perfectly-metered resolution. *Mutual Appreciation* isn't about their mutual appreciation, though—its title refers to a more general sense of affectedly-insincere sincerity. Everything feels like a euphemism for real emotion: a downward-spiralling nightcap party (where the guests are wearing wigs and talking about feminism) featuring Alan standing in a doorway with a frozen rictus painted on his face captures all those tongue-tied post-grad moments where you just wish someone would break out the chips and turn on the football game. Here's a deeply independent—and smart and observant and funny—picture that doesn't have much time for the people most likely to see it.

Neither opaque like *The Piano Tuner of Earthquakes* nor energized like *Mutual Appreciation*, Simon Brand's *Unknown* is an excruciating piece of shit making a play for mainstream credibility by being a glorified trailer reel for mainstream thriller detritus. As such, it's a sub-par facsimile of the lowest rung of soggy, self-loving, *Saw*-like fare. Enlisting familiar faces Jim Caviezel, Greg Kinnear, Joe Pantoliano, Barry Pepper, Jeremy Sisto, Bridget Moynahan, and Peter Stormare to go through the paces of a heist/*Memento* wheezer, the picture opens with five men in various states of physical disrepair waking up in a destroyed warehouse without any memory of who they are or how they got there. The only thing the film has going for it, free as it is of anything resembling suspense, intelligence, direction, or interest, is the cozy assurance that nobody's likely to try this particular gambit to reach the big-time again any time soon. (As even higher-profile cult disasters like *The Boondock Saints* spelled the end of careers, safe to say that *Unknown* looks more and more like a director's tombstone.) Suffocatingly stagy, appallingly- written and plotted, the picture is all epileptic flashbacks and a parallel exculpatory plot that does more to diffuse the tension a truly closed-room drama might have eventually manifested. It's hard work of an entirely different kind: if you stay with it, you do so by pretending you don't know how it ends and, moreover, that you care. (**WC**)

## PIRATES OF THE CARIBBEAN: DEAD MAN'S CHEST
**\*/\*\*\*\***
*st.* Johnny Depp, Orlando Bloom, Keira Knightley, Stellan Skarsgård
*sc.* Ted Elliott & Terry Rossio
*dir.* Gore Verbinski

I've liked almost everything Gore Verbinski's done up to this point—he's treated genre pictures with a degree of sobriety that's refreshing when snarky post-modernism seems the golden mean. But *Pirates of the Caribbean: Dead Man's Chest* (hereafter *Pirates 2*, though "*Pirates Reloaded*" is perhaps the more appropriate paraphrase) carries with it the taint of desperation that comes with impossibly raised expectations and a burgeoning "known" director who—for lack of a better idea—devotes himself to the notion that magnification is the same thing as inspiration. A giant budget and a franchise tag is an effective snuff to that alchemical combination of energy and brilliance that has thus far typified Verbinski's output, and *Pirates 2* is exhibit one of just how boring an unimaginably expensive a blockbuster can be when it jettisons character and story in favour of gimmick and state-of-the-art-for-now special effects. The first of two consecutively-shot sequels, the movie has the added difficulty of being entrusted (like *Episode II*, *The Two Towers*, and *The Matrix Reloaded*) with the exposition third of the tripartite narrative arc. *Pirates 2* is a middle without a beginning or end that tries to compensate for that deficiency by throwing money at the problem. Yo ho-hum.

Stiff as boards Will (Orlando Bloom) and Elizabeth (Keira Knightley) are due to be nailed together in holy matrimony as the redcoats come calling at the beck of evil bureaucrat Beckett (Tom Hollander), sending the pair off on another swashbuckling adventure on the heels of Captain Jack Sparrow (Johnny Depp) and a few magical trinkets. The heavy this time is half-man/half-delicious Davy Jones (Bill Nighy), a pirate with the face of calamari and the elocution of a Shakespearean ham. Jones captains the Flying Dutchman ghost ship and its crew of similarly mutant minotaurs (the best a hammerhead first mate), as well as controlling the mighty leviathan the Kraken with some doohickey screwed into his deck. Jones has a bone to pick with Jack, Jack wants a key Davy has to a box that, *Bloodrayne*-like, holds Davy's evil heart, and Stellan Skarsgård appears with barnacles stuck to his face as Will's woebegone father. That makes two martyred fathers; an awkward and unbelievable love triangle between our three principals; two Kraken attacks; two scenes where everyone rolls down a hill in a giant contraption; and two visits to a Creole swamp and voodoo priestess Tia Dalma (Naomie Harris). Thankfully, there's only one visit to booga-booga Cannibal Island, where all the racial outrage misdirected at Peter Jackson's self-knowing *King Kong* can finally find a deserving target.

Ditto the trepidation accompanying the first film: that it is of all things an adaptation of a mouldering theme park attraction, so how good could it be? *Pirates 2* is gruesome to no good end and dead in the water where the first showed a spark of playfulness and invention. Maybe the only difference is that Depp's trick performances now strike me as sort of selfish and arrogant (he's the weakest part of Tim Burton's *Charlie and the Chocolate Factory*) instead of inspired as they used to. Even at that, Depp isn't in nearly enough of the movie to counteract the feeble pacing and flat scripting, which, in one interminable scene, lets an embarrassing drivel of doublespeak drool on forever without one laugh and, worse, without advancing the action of the film in any significant way. Everything stops, often and completely, in order for you to, along with the rest of the cast (including Depp), gape at the special effects—it's a mighty thing to ask that such a giant contraption stop itself and then lumber back to life every few scenes. The chief insult is that you feel each of these 150 minutes, giving you plenty of time to consider that this is the first time Depp and Verbinski have consented to film a sequel and that the only shiver the picture offers your timbers is that next summer they'll do it all over again. (**WC**)

**POSEIDON**
ZERO STARS/****
*st.* Kurt Russell, Josh Lucas, Jacinda Barrett, Richard Dreyfuss
*sc.* Mark Protosevich, based on

the novel The Poseidon Adventure by Paul Gallico
*dir.* Wolfgang Petersen

Sort of like *Ghost Ship* without the gore (and it promptly loses the points it earns for being *sans* Julianna Marguiles by featuring Kevin Dillon), Wolfgang Petersen's soggy underwater soaper *Poseidon* starts with a theoretically exciting (but just unintentionally hilarious) set-piece and limps the rest of the way on the standard old slogging-through-wet-hallways bullroar that may be the very definition of "un-exciting." Kurt Russell is Robert, an ex-fireman/ex-New York mayor who appears to have a gambling problem and a contentious relationship with his daughter Jennifer (Emmy Rossum), which will of course be resolved, Mark Twain-style, by a late-in-the-show heroic action. Josh Lucas is Dylan, the rogue ex-Navy man with a plan; Jimmy Bennett is the buck-toothed little idiot who wanders off a lot (and Jacinda Barrett is his long-suffering mom, Maggie); Richard Dreyfuss plays Richard, a suicidal queen planning on leaving his pals with a hefty bill by leaping from the mighty Poseidon luxury liner's galleria after dinner; and all people of colour are meatbags to be fed to the mill whenever someone needs an example of what could happen to the rich whiteys not unfortunate enough to be in steerage.

I like when Jennifer's boyfriend Christian (Mike Vogel) sends stowaway Elena (Mia Maestro) off to get electrocuted early on—just as I enjoyed Richard kicking Elena's boyfriend off his foot and onto a bed of spikes inexplicably sprouting from the top of an elevator shaft. It's not a good thing to be reminded of Sylvester Stallone's appalling *Daylight*, but *Poseidon* does so often with its story of insufferable wankers negotiating their way through a flooded obstacle course, following an inarticulate alpha male (Dylan) and suffering predictable—and highly-melodramatic—fatalities along the way. *Poseidon* ups the ante by including a couple of vocal performances from the **Black-Eyed Peas**' torso Fergie that make the audience start rooting for the "rogue wave" that eventually capsizes the titular tub to hurry up and sink the damned thing already. Said terrible-CGI event occurs at around the fifteen-minute mark—which is sort of amazing both for its ridiculousness and because I'd already checked my watch about a dozen times by then. The only time the film is funnier is when Lucky Larry the Lounge Lizard (Dillon) gets hit by a train. Don't ask.

Mark "*The Cell*" Protosevich's screenplay is unspeakably terrible, matched step-for-step by Petersen's increasing inability to shoot anything in a way that generates interest, energy, or heat, much less sense. Take the example of Richard's ferocious Mexi-cide (or is it Blue Collar-cide? You de-cide), and of how the script tickles around the idea that since he does find out that it's Elena's boyfriend he offed to save his own life, in later offering her his foot to grab, it's probably meant as a means towards personal redemption (if mainly reminding me of the identical race/power dynamic in Dreyfuss' shrimping scene from *Down and Out in Beverly Hills*). But the narrative is such a stripped-down, anaemic thing that even this eye-rolling pass at character development is sad and withered, leaving only the ugly after-image that on the hierarchy of *Poseidon*'s moral compass, rich white gays rank just above poor Argentinean beauties.

It's a feckless parsing of rank stereotypes that ultimately allows the filmmakers to skip past all that messy plot stuff, making way for the bad action scenes, the thundering score, and the worse special effects. *Poseidon* is a waste of life, a waste of cash, and a step backwards somehow from the original waste of life upon which this is based. Russell steps into Shelly Winters' shoes here, something the film seems to make fun of when someone asks Russell's character how he managed to squeeze through a tight spot; meanwhile, emotionless cipher Lucas earns his action hero stripes by setting his jaw and growling his lines. Take this with *M:I:III* as examples of why people stay home in droves. It's not the experience, it's the films—and *Poseidon* is as dumb, inept, and boring as they come. (**WC**)

# THE PRESTIGE
**\*\*\*/\*\*\*\***

*st.* Hugh Jackman, Christian Bale, Scarlett Johansson, Michael Caine
*sc.* Jonathan Nolan and Christopher Nolan, based on the novel by Christopher Priest
*dir.* Christopher Nolan

It's possible to say that Christopher Nolan's perplexing chimera of a film, *The Prestige*, has something on its mind about not only the nasty, zero-sum game of vengeance but also the belief that if you cut one head off a malevolent beast it will, hydra-like, sprout another. It's a costume drama that feels like the world's darkest, dour-est, most inappropriate thriller serial, placing a series of increasingly complicated and unpleasant revenge-scenarios in chronological order and reminding of, if anything, just how bad Nolan's *Memento* makes you feel. *The Prestige* shares a heart of darkness, after all, with that film: a belief that men are essentially callow opportunists and liars who will misuse the people in their lives in order to maintain an illusion of command, however tenuous, over entropy. The manipulation of illusion is arguably the auteur mark of Nolan, who played with the idea of the manipulation of fear as a weapon in *Batman Begins*, the practical purpose of dream sleep in his remake of *Insomnia*, and of course of identity as fluid, ephemeral, and dangerously malleable in *Memento* and *Following*. Matching this director with a strange, campy film about turn-of-the-century magicians engaged in mortal combat makes a lot of sense.

Angier (Hugh Jackman) and Borden (Christian Bale) are aspiring magicians as the film opens—apprentices, along with Angier's wife Julia (Piper Perabo), in some hack's tired stage act. When Julia dies, Borden is blamed, and Angier begins a campaign to bring Borden to some hazily-defined idea of Old Testament justice. His weapons are humiliation and professional one-upmanship (and guns and hatchets and booby-trapped boxes and stolen cushions); when Borden begins to respond in kind, the fallout before the last act's disquieting resolutions involves Angier's girl Olivia (Scarlett Johansson, testing my faith with a terrible accent) in addition to Borden's wife Sarah (an exceptional Rebecca Hall) and daughter Jess (Samantha Mahurin). It's hard to watch—and Nolan takes pains to confuse our allegiances in ways that suggest a very British class tension (Borden and ace engineer Cutter (Michael Caine) share a Cockney brogue while Angier, a Yank, is cut from different cloth), a certain nationalism, and, in the figure of Nikolai Tesla (David Bowie) at play mad-scientist-like in a mythical Colorado Springs, a clearly delineated duel between magic and the notion that technology before its time is a kind of witchcraft.

Long stretches in fact threaten to turn The Prestige into a Grand Guignol melodrama not unlike David Cronenberg's extraordinary version of The Fly. Tesla's declaration that a machinery he designs for Angier needs a different kind of material (a cat, as it happens, instead of Cronenberg's unfortunate baboon) for proper testing, in particular, inspires a thrill of dread at the midway point. But The Prestige seems more interested in prestige as we currently define it, falling back at moments of consummation on its extraordinarily dedicated cast's careful characterizations as opposed to the full potential of the madness that its first

hour establishes in earnest. Often campy, the movie isn't, until its end, campy enough, turning its final sting into more a confirmation of the sobriety of its build than the release of revulsion that I suspect was the intention. Still, the picture is one I rooted for, that I wanted desperately to work just a little better. Tesla at war with Edison's gang of hired goons in a wintry Overlook wonderland is a wondrous fantasia; a story told through twin diaries and a voiceover narration by consummate artist Caine shouldn't work as well as it does (and yet doesn't quite work as well as it might). The aggregate affect of The Prestige is that you can't believe what you're seeing, yet you wish that its most fascinating wickednesses were allowed more room to fester. What's left is a handsomely appointed exercise in filmmaking and performance and a lingering aftertaste that creates no little excitement for Nolan's upcoming Batman sequel The Dark Knight, even as it lodges itself as not much more than a (perhaps shockingly) bitter little pill. (**WC**)

**THE PROMISE** (U.S. version)
*/****

*st.* Hiroyuki Sanada, Jang Dong Gun, Cecilia Cheung, Nicholas Tse
*sc.* Chen Kaige and Zhang Tan
*dir.* Chen Kaige

Any fad reaches its nadir in due time and the Western *wuxia* infatuation, which started somewhere around *Crouching Tiger, Hidden Dragon* and more or less peaked with Zhang Yimou's exceptional *Hero*, has found its basement in the truncated version of Chen Kaige's already-pretty-embarrassing *The Promise*. Somewhere, King Hu is spinning in his grave. An abomination just about any way you slice it, this ultra-expensive, CGI'd-to-exhaustion wire-fu epic—especially as sanitized for North America's consumption—suggests the world's saddest public display of penis envy.

Chen, hailing from the same Fifth Generation school as Zhang, produces a show-offy, self-indulgent bit of flamboyant one-upsmanship destined to become a queer camp classic. When the Crimson General (Hiroyuki Sanada) trades in his fabulous duds for a lavender muumuu in which to trade barbs with archenemy Wuhuan (Nicholas Tse, suspended somewhere between pretty girl and Japanese anime hero), a bad guy garbed in white feathers who wields a gold staff topped with a bronze hand, index finger extended in proctological menace, the homoeroticism of the piece—already distracting in the subtext—suddenly becomes the main event. It's probably this unfathomable cut of the film's Rosetta Stone, in fact, pared down to some half-assed companion piece to Chen's own *Farewell My Concubine*. Without much strain you can see *The Promise* being transformed, in all its kitsch excess, into a Broadway pop-opera: *Memoirs of a Geisha: The Musical*.

Opening with a really bad deal—one that, incidentally, spoils the rest of the film's plot—a little urchin strikes with a goddess (Chen Hong), the picture immediately betrays itself with more canted angles than *Battlefield Earth* and a long, computer-generated shot of a tasty biscuit sinking into a bog. The green underwater light dimples as Chen and his merry band of hyperactive technicians turn in a feature-length rendition of one of those "Final Fantasy" interstitials. From there, we skip forward a few decades to find the Crimson General taking a Thermopilian stand against a horde of barbarians by sacrificing a few hundred slaves in what must be one of the stupidest moments in, let's face it, a frequently-stupid genre. One slave, Kunlun (Jang Dong-Kun), survives because he's crazy-fast; a weird scene transpires in which Kunlun begs to be the General's slave, followed by a series of misunderstandings as Kunlun rescues a pretty girl (Cecilia Cheung) from an evil king, falls in love, does the

Cyrano, grows a pair, gains a backstory, and bores us to distraction: we don't think to ask why, for instance, a captive girl in a gilded cage comes to greet her emancipator descending from a staircase leading from nowhere.

The U.S. edition of *The Promise* is a debris field. Without proclaiming the original a masterpiece (it's bad, but not quite a boondoggle), the redux is a disaster of the gaudiest kind, the sort of spectacle that's almost as effective as a lobotomy in neutralizing thought processes—enough so that the peculiar bits of homoeroticism (not even counting the feather boas and mascara that act as character development for our boys) that erupt now and again in lieu of anything else happening generally only register in the rear-view. It was never really about anything—now it's also mainly an attempt to piggy-back on the "crossover" hit parade, meaning that it mimics everything, going about it so indiscriminately that the picture's inherent imitation registers as cynical and aggressive. (At the risk of acknowledging too much, it reminds me a lot of that episode of "Star Trek: The Next Generation" called "Samaritan Snare," wherein a race of pig-like aliens appropriate technology without understanding, nor wishing to understand, anything beyond the rudiments of function.) Meanwhile, the things that wouldn't have been instantly obsolete, like story and character, are shuffled off to the wings.

As a fan of the genre, one who took a certain comfort in its power of cultural diffusion despite its perpetuating certain Asian stereotypes, I found *The Promise* particularly disappointing. It isn't an expression of artistry and vision that's true to its roots in Chinese myth, stage, and screen, it's an expression of a distributor's desire to earn boffo box-office while regaining the attention of foreign financiers on the back of the genre's own cultural legacy (and its recent renaissance abroad)—an object of derision that substantiates criticism of the *wuxia*. Worse, it justifies a specific type of racism whereby you write off all manner of ignorance and vulgarity simply because it's foreign. *Borat!* takes advantage of that paternalism to prick us where we're vulnerable; *The Promise*, intentional or not, takes advantage of it for different reasons altogether. (**WC**)

## THE PROPOSITION
*/****

st. Guy Pearce, Ray Winstone, Danny Huston, John Hurt
sc. Nick Cave
dir. John Hillcoat

In his review of Rene Cardona's exploitation quickie about the Jonestown Massacre *Guyana: Cult of the Damned*, Roger Ebert describes how Cardona ends the film with photos of the real-life victims while the audience is solemnly reminded "that those who forget the past are doomed to repeat it," prompting Ebert to crack, "So remember, don't drink cyanide." I only wish that John Hillcoat's *The Proposition* were that lucid in delivering its Important Lesson. This is a movie at least as gory and brutal as Eli Roth's *Hostel*, the highlights being an exploding head and an extended, Gibson-esque flogging of a prisoner. And Hillcoat loves flies: they're always buzzing over the carrion, the human corpses, the gourmet meals, and the sweat of the film's grotesquely hairy Australian men. I don't have a problem with gore per se, but I do have a problem with the self-important joylessness with which it's depicted here—and frankly, *The Proposition* hasn't any justification for its austere tone. The proposition of the title is offered by Captain Stanley (Ray Winstone) to Irish criminal Charlie Burns (Guy Pearce); Stanley has captured Charlie's 14-year-old brother Mike and is prepared to hang the two of them for the murder of a family that included Stanley's pregnant sister-in-law. If Charlie can find and kill his second brother, the truly evil Arthur (Danny Huston), then both he and Mike will be absolved of their crimes. This sounds like a fairly standard western plot, but Hillcoat treats the material like *Schindler's List*. While I can't readily identify who we're meant to sympathize with, the characterizations aren't particularly nuanced: Mike is a victim; Arthur is a bastard; Stanley believes in justice; and Charlie, as played by straight-arrow Guy Pearce (a persona cultivated in *L.A. Confidential* and subverted in *Memento*), is a reluctant hero. The violence is moralistically ugly and we derive no vicarious pleasure from identifying with the anti-heroes, though in light of the equally moralistic finale, violence is shown to be just, too. *The Proposition*, then, can't be called either anti-violence or particularly nihilistic in its viewpoint. Good guys die horribly, bad guys die horribly, neutral guys die horribly— yet the ending shows that some deserve to die horribly more than others. (**AJ**)

## THE PROTECTOR
***/****

st. Tony Jaa, Petchtai Wongkamlao, Bongkoj Khongmalai, Xing Jing
sc. Kongdej Jaturanrasamee & Napalee & Piyaros Thongdee and Joe Wannapin
dir. Prachya Pinkaew

## THE COVENANT
½*/****

st. Steven Strait, Sebastian Stan, Laura Ramsey, Taylor Kitsch
sc. J.S. Cardone
dir. Renny Harlin

Tony Jaa is a bad motherfucker. There's a moment in his latest export *The Protector* where it appears as though he's killed someone with his penis (lo, how I would love to avoid *that* epitaph), and in the meantime, he dispatches foes with the heedless joy of obvious predecessor Jackie Chan (who has a cameo in the film shot so ineptly that it suggests a Jackie Chan impersonator smeared with Vaseline). Alas, there's a plot (something about the kidnapping of two elephants, one of which is turned into a gaudy tchotcke in an evil dragon lady's den of inequity), too, told through a lot of howlingly incompetent narrative chunks you could seemingly rearrange in any order with no tangible disruption of sense. (The Butchers Weinstein may of course be partly to blame.) The film is easily the funniest, most exhilaratingly ridiculous picture in a year in which *Snakes on a Plane* aspired to the same camp/cult heights, and it does it the only way that you can: by being deadly serious.

It's serious when a giant white man-hammer throws a baby elephant; serious when Jaa's titular elephant keeper has an inopportune flashback while a band of baddies pummels his teary-eyed body; even serious in imagining a Sydney, Australia with an all-Thai-speaking police force and media. It seems to mean it when it shows Jaa stalking around with a baby elephant *sans* uproar through a major, Western metropolis, when that same elephant somehow sneaks up on him in the dark, and when a clarion rings through the metal canyons to summon a tribe of rollerblading/BMXing delinquents—thus once it finally comes time for Jaa to kick some serious ass in a sequence of orthopaedic upset protracted to the point where I actually started wishing mercy on Jaa's victims, the only response possible is a hysterical combination of tears of joy and tears of shame.

Two scenes make the film an instant classic. The first is a SteadiCam sequence up the stairs of a tiered edifice (shades of Matthew Barney's ascension of the Guggenheim in his *Cremaster* epic), the second the abovementioned gallery of calamitous joint trauma. They're showcases for the humourless Jaa's specific brand of Muy

Thai mayhem—and so intensely pleasurable that they turn the bug-eyed horror of its purported storyline into just the chantilly on this violent sundae. I confess that I haven't had this much fun watching—nor in truth harboured this much affection for—a film in ages; this is a picture that thinks it logical to have its hero strap elephant leg bones to his forearms for a little extra oomph—a picture *so* clueless in its misogyny and racism that it's almost adorably naïve. *The Protector*'s protectors post-pubescent are probably all coming from a similarly patronizing perspective, sadly, but there's no head-patting Jaa's prowess as an emerging martial arts legend. Only time will tell if he evolves into Jet Li's introspective, serious artist or Chan's gracelessly-aging also-ran, but for now, *The Protector* feels like a little of the old religion.

*The Covenant*, on the other hand, feels a little like a cross between *The Lost Boys* and *Zapped!*, replicating the boy-band evil superhero vibe of the former and the flip a girl's skirt up with your dirty telekinetic mind of the latter. (I'm not kidding.) In fact, we're introduced to arch-villain Chase (Sebastian Stan—and if you think this is a spoiler, you're not able to read this anyway) when he transforms himself into gas to spy on gorgeous love interest Sarah (Laura Ramsey), who, bless her heart (and her roommate's heart), goes to bed in a selection of Victoria's Secret workout gear. There's a moment where schlock pulp maestro Renny Harlin pans through the exclusive New England prep school providing the film's central setting that I wondered, briefly, if he wasn't attempting some sort of allegory about Aryan perfection and the Third Reich's courting of the occult arrayed against a curly-haired heartthrob protagonist (Steven Strait). But that moment passed.

*The Covenant* is, sadly, just another fallout from the *Titanic* blast of programming garbage for the babysitter demographic; it's packed to the gills with pretty boys doing their best not to be forgotten in the next wave of pop-cultural irrelevance. Imagine a film that frames its climactic showdown between two *Highlander*-infused warlocks as a duel that features as its weapons of choice the kind of pestilential plagues and possessions of classic witchcraft (which this film invokes through arcane references to Salem—making it the second dud in as many weeks to do so after Neil LaBute's *The Wicker Man*) instead of what *The Covenant* does, which is have its antagonists throw digital force balls at one another. Of all the modern American authors namedropped in one of its dour classroom sequences (Cormac McCarthy has never been this egregiously misused), the one notably missing is John Updike and his The Witches of Eastwick. There's not one smart moment in *The Covenant* (though opportunities for intelligence abound), not even unintentional hilarity in its daft awkwardness—but the real reason it sucks is because it's as boring as a pine weevil. (**WC**)


# THE PUFFY CHAIR (see: *QUINCEAÑERA*)


# THE PURSUIT OF HAPPYNESS
\*/\*\*\*\*
*st.* Will Smith, Thandie Newton, Jaden Christopher Syre Smith, Brian Howe
*sc.* Steven Conrad
*dir.* Gabriele Muccino

They should pass out insulin plungers with the purchase of a ticket to the new Will Smith vehicle *The Pursuit of Happyness*, which sports a subtle tickle of plantation politics that's overwhelmed by a sense of smug entitlement and ugly elitism. Inspired by the true story of eighties Wall Street bootstrap wizard Chris Gardner, it's a telling in a way of the Hercules legend, complete with insurmountable, fickle tasks and divine inheritance. Our mythological hero solves the Rubik's Cube in the back of a taxi for the bemused delight of potential employer Jay Twistle (Brian Howe); deals with the abandonment of his frustrated wife (Thandie Newton); and figures out a way to retrieve a pair of the bone-density scanners (the sale of which were his profession pre-Dean Witter) stolen by the homeless peers he disdains. It's true: the picture—even with its ghetto-cred misspelled title and restroom-to-boardroom fable—is intolerant of people consigned to the impoverishment the film contorts to assure us will be Chris' plight for only the time it takes his uplift to ripen.

Although the story wants you to believe that it's about hard work, it spends more time establishing Chris as a Beautiful Mind savant who could "go through a math book in a week" when he was a precocious kid yet didn't, we fill in the blanks, have the privilege of college because of his background and maybe the colour of his skin. I don't mind the message that it's only hard work in combination with natural ability that leads to success, but what of the boardroom scenes in which a panel of old white men deciding Chris' future at the brokerage (a doddering James Karen the worst caricature among them) speak to him as though he were a child, stopping just short of patting him on the head and sending him back to the cotton fields? It's hard to know if *The Pursuit of Happyness* has gauged the complexity of its racism, much less the extent to which it's a satire of how blacks view whites (all of Chris' pre-trader clients are white doctors; almost all of his clients post-trader are white executives) and of how whites view blacks (i.e., as sometimes-precocious children). I did, however, marvel that the two transients who steal Chris' precious devices are white: no black-on-black crime here—*The Pursuit of Happyness* is as clear-cut a case of Man-phobia as a film that also wants to eat its cake can be. (A bit where Chris bluffs his way into a 49ers game and then proceeds to shuffle and charm his way into a pocketful of business cards strikes that same discordant chord with gusto.) In the picture's most troubling irony, much of its delighted whimsy (to which we're cued by self-deprecating Maya Angelouvian voice-over) is predicated on Chris' entertaining ability to bounce back from a series of perverse, Job-like setbacks.

If we're honest, the only reason Chris isn't a villain is that we know the outcome. His wife is angry because her husband appears unwilling to get a job that actually pays a salary so she can stop working double-shifts at an industrial laundry, pay the rent and utilities, and keep their child in daycare—what a bitch! *The Pursuit of Happyness* is great for the minute or two it talks about how hard it sometimes is to come up with the pennies for a hot meal for your family in a single-income household—the rest of it's just such glad-handing garbage. The trailer-friendly tableau of father and son (real-life Smith-spawn Jaden), sleeping in subway can with Smith squeezing out the Denzel Washington-in-*Glory* Teardrop of Oscar Gold is the perfect counterpoint to its parade of Stevie Wonder and Ray Charles anthems and is, again, so affected as to be a single-panel political cartoon. The final equation of *The Pursuit of Happyness* is that happiness is a job that can support your family, no matter what indignity one suffers in its pursuit and execution—a message that should bring tears to the eyes of The Man everywhere. What I left with is this idea that the three men positioned as Chris' superiors (after Chris goes through his unpaid internship as a boiler-room cold-caller) are each, in turn, shown to be officious, condescending, and racist, leading one to justifiably wonder whether the real message of the film isn't that smart, hard-working minorities should shut up and be grateful for whatever scraps the gentry deigns to toss out. Way to get your mind right, Will. (**WC**)

## THE QUEEN (see: *THE LAST KING OF SCOTLAND*)

## THE QUIET
\*/\*\*\*\*
*st.* Elisha Cuthbert, Camilla Belle, Martin Donovan, Edie Falco
*sc.* Micah Schraft and Abdi Nazemian
*dir.* Jamie Babbit

Laden (leaden?) with melo-tragedy, Jamie Babbit's *The Quiet* is a burlesque of high school and incest, and though I don't doubt that there's a great movie in the intersection of the two, this ain't it. The film stars Elisha Cuthbert as the wounded "Heather," Nina, whose reputation as the perfect girl (read: the head cheerleader) is stained by a home life dominated by a zombie mom Olivia (Edie Falco) and an all-too-loving pedophile nice guy dad Paul (Martin Donovan). It wanders into the mind listlessly a time or two that Nina's backstory is identical to something the crazed Christian Slater character from *Heathers* would manufacture to justify the "suicide" of some teenage girl he's just murdered. The only way to really up the ante in *The Quiet* is through the introduction of deaf-mute orphan Dot (Camilla Belle), taken in by Paul and Olivia to act as the shadow/doppelgänger to our damaged-goods protagonist—and sure enough. But Dot can play Beethoven's "Appassionata" and "Moonlight" as the situation demands, and she provides treacly narration throughout in her piping, irritating lilt. She even goes so far as to attract chronic masturbator Connor (Shawn Ashmore) away from Nina's cartoon of a queen bitch pal Michelle (Katy Mixon).

Search hard for satire and you'll discover ham-fisted solemnity instead. I miss Donovan's collaborations with Hal Hartley; every indie credible project in which he finds himself (though, honestly, I don't know if I'm more horrified that he's in *Agent Cody Banks* or *The United States of Leland*) only widens the gap between what a gifted artist with no budget can accomplish and the sincere "message" movie that passes for Sundance-certified nowadays. The question with heat has to do with the nature of *The Quiet*'s message, anyway—I mean, surely it can't be a searing indictment against fathers banging their daughters and mothers medicating themselves into oblivion, can it? More likely, *The Quiet*—in title and, ostensibly, in title character—is a hopelessly sincere metaphor for the pain of societal and personal repression. Enough so that it's not unfair to wonder whether Dot began life as a psychotic split from the good ship Nina, or if the script was originated by a high-schooler during a particularly intense hormonal episode.

It's not a fairytale and it's not a fable. Moreover, it's not recognizably anything of real value at all. The only thing the film succeeds at is the unfortunate feat of creating a work of prurience whereby twenty-three-year-old Cuthbert in a cheerleading uniform and less becomes an object of true distraction. *The Quiet* produces the disquieting effect of being naturally interested in seeing a grown woman pretending to be a high-school cheerleader in various states of sexual compromise. Though Cronenberg made some hay with this sort of thing in the contrasting sexual fantasies that bookend the exposition of *A History of Violence*, Babbit, dipping her toe into the same psychosexual pool, just doesn't have the water wings to make it float. But what ultimately sinks *The Quiet* is that it's ridiculous. Not that such a thing could never happen, but that these words, these people, that character, create a perfect storm of overheated improbabilities. It's the world's most inappropriate Harlequin romance novel: a heavy-breather of a potboiler for Judy Blume's audience of babysitters and old men in long coats. (WC)

## QUINCEAÑERA
**\*\*½/\*\*\*\***

*st.* Jesus Castanos, Araceli Guzman-Rico, Emily Rios, Alicia Sixtos
*w./d.* Richard Glatzer & Wash Westmoreland

## FALL TO GRACE
**½\*/\*\*\*\***

*st.* René Alvarado, Ricardo Azulay, Bill Johnson, Cassidy Johnson
*w./d.* Mari Marchbanks

## THE PUFFY CHAIR
**\*\*½/\*\*\*\***

*st.* Mark Duplass, Kathryn Aselton, Rhett Wilkins, Julie Fischer
*sc.* Mark Duplass
*dir.* Jay Duplass

The Gentrification is the inciting phenomenon of Richard Glatzer and Wash Westmoreland's *Quinceañera*, only the second film to land both the Grand Jury Prize and the Audience Award at Sundance. Its celebration at the festival—which, like most festivals, prices itself culturally and financially out of most of the subjects its films exploit—should be regarded as something of a foregone conclusion: if it's not a product born of self-flagellation, *Quinceañera* at least owes its existence to an instinct towards the atonement of its two white, privileged creators, shooting a quasi-documentary/half-improvised character drama in the Echo Park neighbourhood where they found themselves the land-investor fixer-uppers. But it's even more complicated than that, owing to Glatzer and Westmoreland's homosexuality and the specific insight that an unpopular, oft-misrepresented minority engaged in the creation of a non-traditional family unit might bring to a story of another unpopular, oft-misrepresented minority (Mexican working class) looking to create a haven of kinship in a sea of cultural turmoil. Inserting themselves into the story as unkind spoiler-avatars in the piece (a gay, white couple acts as *Quinceañera's* bogeymen)—the set for their tasteful duplex serves as Glatzer/Westmoreland's real-life digs—is as thorny a po-mo entanglement as these two otherwise successful guys interpolating themselves in their neighbour's lives, homes, and rituals with movie cameras and an evangelical mission.

Magdalena (Emily Rios) has a prettier sister and a looming date with her own Quinceañera: a traditional celebration (sort of debutante "coming out" ceremony) that marks a Mexican girl's fifteenth birthday. Her cousin Carlos (Jesse Garcia) is the very image of a Mexican gang-banger, fulfilling the *papi chulo* fantasies of his gay landlords when he's forced to move in with his old uncle Tomas (Peckinpah fave Chalo González) while managing through the sympathies of the filmmakers and Garcia's affecting performance to transcend either stereotype with grace and intelligence. Much of *Quinceañera* is a surprise in that vein; the opening scenes of partying teens speaking in that impenetrable patois of youth tests the patience of the most sympathetic viewer, yet as the picture proceeds, it becomes clear that the prejudices that threatened to push me into the lobby were my own and that the strength of the piece is in the care with which Glatzer and Westmoreland handle their characters. It reminded me of Nir Bergman's *Broken Wings*, that Israeli film from a couple of years back about a small family that avoided almost any mention of the turmoil of their surroundings and, in the process of sketching a detailed, human portrait, spoke volumes about it. You might be tempted to roll your eyes and say that of course Magdalena gets pregnant, but *Quinceañera* challenges this stereotype as well with a series of strong insights into the fundamentalist religion that serves as the backbone of the culture. Too strong, some might say, and the picture's transparency of purpose erodes its usefulness as a social auger. We know what's on its mind, but the trip might be worth taking, anyway.

Gentrification of a different kind infuses two Austin-bred projects hitting the arthouse circuit almost simultaneously in herky-jerky rollout releases. Russian clowns, Russian gangsters, Texan drug-dealers, *Some Kind of Wonderful*-era hairdos, hunky-jock exchange students treated like the nerd class, manufactured tragedies, hackneyed social critiques—the lot of it brought together in *Fall to Grace* by first-time hyphenate Mari Marchbanks with an unspeakable screenplay and a collection of performances that veer from awful to just run-of-the-mill bad. The picture is hopeless: hopelessly earnest, hopelessly well-intentioned, hopelessly bad. The folk ballad soundtrack by local rock heroes says all there needs to be said, really, the dirge unspooling beneath its melancholic opening credits promising more to come.

Consider the scene where hulking drug dealer Auggie (Bill Johnson) proclaims that a kid "looks like a punk," only to have Marchbanks, *sans* any hint of irony, cut to a close-up of a kid with a spiked mohawk and leather jacket. Hilarious and not on purpose (think "That kid looks like a clown" and then a pan to Bozo in red wig and nose), the description goes for every exchange between the adults in this roundelay melodrama (which steals from everything from *The Killing* to Austin bible *Slacker*), locating the demiurge to the preciously-titled *Fall to Grace* as a corn factory fertilized for about twenty years with the cream of the indie dysfunction crop. If there's a function for this film, it's to give everyone quick to jump on the arthouse bandwagon a reminder that lack of talent, budget, and distribution

is often—brace yourself—an indication that the product stinks to high heaven. No one should have to tackle a line like "You know inside of me," and more to the point, no one should have to listen to it. Blame Sundance.

Though actress Kira Pozehl threatens a time or two to overcome the script and staging, the rest of her compatriots are swallowed whole by flat camera set-ups and thrift-store production design that has a crystal chandelier in a country kitchen hung so low that its giant denizen would be banging his nut on it roughly every three minutes. Or blame editing that gives every last dialogue exchange the frantic, extreme-close-up/chop cut energy of a monumental plot point when, point in fact, they just seem to be talking burgers and fries. Without a lot of squinting, you could view the piece as a primer on how not to make a movie—even a satire of bad cinema, maybe. The only place this kind of unleavened hysteria makes sense is in a *telenovela*.

To be fair, *Fall to Grace* might best be described as a season of "Dos Mujeres, Un Camino" smashed from two decades of histrionics into feature-length form. The style of the picture is so out of tune with its "deep meaning" intentions that it actually made me itch. If it achieves any kind of success, it'll be because *Crash* made this type of overlapping liberal handjob briefly prestigious and not because every word Julia Polozova drops as a long-suffering Russian mommy sounds like a community theatre audition for a Georgian dinner theatre version of "The Roman Spring of Mrs. Stone". Add overlit to the picture's list of technical difficulties; defenders of the "spirit" of these indie pics, be aware that Austin prodigal Richard Linklater made silk purses out of the same no-budget sow's ears with an unerring ear for dialogue, gift with *mise-en-scène*, sense of character and rhythm, and an actual desire to do something new instead of simply something.

At least *The Puffy Chair* uses

Cassavetes' laconic, loquacious love stories as a template, following the relational travails of ex-failed-Austin-rocker Josh (writer Mark Duplass—brother Jay is the film's director) and girlfriend Emily (Kathryn Aselton, Mark Duplass' real-life fiancée) as they take a van and Josh's brother Rhett (Rhett Wilkins) on a road trip to pick up the titular eBay-acquired furniture item and deliver it for their father's surprise birthday party. As the road trip genre is best when it's used as a catalyst for a metaphysical journey of discovery engaged in by our protagonists, the narrative of *The Puffy Chair* is not nearly so important as the rambling, improvised conversations (arguments and pillow talk) engaged in by its trio of twentysomething slacker pilgrims. There's a little Linklater in the stew, too, of course, and the Duplass brothers extract similar broth from the modest bones of their premise and cast of unaffected players. A breakfast the morning after the sort of moonstruck spectacle that most of us remember from that one night from our lost youth stands as the highlight of the piece: terse and hopeless but at the same time melancholic, breathless, and sweet. At its best moments (and there are a couple of great ones in here), *The Puffy Chair* makes you want to shake some sense into the kids struggling mortally with what appears small-time in the rear-view—but then there's the realization that poetry is woven from these threads of wilfulness and the courage of being naïve in love. (**WC**)

# R

## REQUIEM

***1/2/****

*st.* Sandra Hüller, Burghart Klaussner, Imdgen Kogge, Anna Blomeier

*sc.* Bernd Lange

*dir.* Hans-Christian Schmid

Like most pop epics, *The Exorcism of Emily Rose* was all about being sure. One had to throw down for the concept of the physical manifestation of Satan—any human considerations were swept aside in the affirmation of God's merciless will. And if certain college girls were crushed to pulp (a sentiment which extends to the general expendability of humankind), so be it. Thank goodness, then, that there's a movie like *Requiem*, based on the same case that inspired *The Exorcism of Emily Rose* but comparatively merciful in its mission. It wants to salvage the blighted life of an epileptic tossed around from doctor to doctor—one who, once presented with the beginnings of psychosis, had only religion and a mistrust of medicinal practice to fall back on. She's a victim of other people's indecision rather than of the Devil himself.

It is perhaps the natural inclination to milk the particulars for melodramatic excess: surely the notion of a frail, unhappy girl battling epilepsy, depression, and a confusing, pious upbringing should be the springboard for sensational shock entertainment. But Hans-Christian Schmid proves to be an extremely subtle director, capturing Michaela Klinger (Sandra Hüller) and her journey—first to university, then to madness just as she's about to define herself as a person—in unobtrusive yet pointed master shots. The film is without the sledgehammer of shrieking violins and the punch of rapid montage—instead, it gazes with sad powerlessness on Michaela looking sheepish when she declares for God at her first pedagogy lecture, looking uncertain at a dance, and twisting with fear whenever the voices start in her head. *Requiem* betrays an immense compassion as she tries to stake her claim and falls in a hail of confusion.

It's also quite complex in delineating the environment that leads her to her doom. Though she's granted a hometown friend named Hanna (Anna Blomeier) and a gentle boyfriend, Stefan (Nicholas Reinke), it's true that her heart belongs to home and church. She wants to break free from some of the more oppressive directives (embodied by her mother (Imogen Kogge), with whom she clashes on more than one occasion), but it's inevitable that her helplessness in the face of mental illness will pull her away from her new friends and into the arms of overbearing religiosity. Despite the attempts of her father (Burghart Klaussner) and a moderate priest (Walter Schmidinger) to sway her onto a psychiatrist's couch, they're overruled by Mother and a rapacious younger priest named Borchert (Jens Harzer) who firmly believes in the mighty, literal God and Devil that taint *The Exorcism of Emily Rose*.

Borchert comes off a little creepy and a bit too intense—it's a bit of caricatural shorthand and *Requiem*'s only real misstep. Otherwise, this is a remarkably nuanced film. I can't remember the last time a movie was this intent on sitting and watching what people do; it telegraphs nothing, and barely foreshadows its tragic trajectory while setting up the characters and letting them be themselves. Whereas the Hollywood version programmed us for a foregone conclusion, this incarnation of the Anneliese Michel story, set in a West German village in the early-'70s, refuses to claim anything as predetermined. It allows and emphasizes choices based on circumstances and interpersonal interactions as opposed to the requirements of narrative practice.

Hüller's heroic turn must also be singled out. Her quietly-controlled hysteria is crucial for the film to work as well as it does: it needs extremely vivid behaviour to witness in order to convince us of its veracity. And Hüller rises to the occasion magnificently in what may be the single best performance of 2006. Her range is astounding as she goes from tense and withholding to a screaming mess at the sound of the Lord's Prayer. Her collaboration with Schmid (and her interpretation of the excellent Bernd Lange script) is the kind of harmonious relationship that gives *Requiem* its naturalistic street cred. Hüller provides a spectrum of behaviour that the filmmakers can release into the flow of other peoples' lives—the screen on which other people can make decisions, informed or not. She's the capper to a brilliant film that you simply shouldn't miss. (**TMH**)

# D O C U M E N T A R Y
## THE RITCHIE BOYS
\*\*\*/\*\*\*\*
*dir.* Christian Bauer

*The Ritchie Boys* is an exploration of the contribution of some unusual heroes: the titular immigrant German Jews, drafted into the US army as an elite intelligence unit and so named because of their schooling at Camp Ritchie, MD. The team had been selected for their intimate knowledge of the German mind, and their memories of both their lives and their methods are by turns hilarious and disturbing. Aesthetically, the film is hugely conventional, alternating interview recollections with stock footage and voice-overs to such middling effect that I wasn't surprised to see the History Channel listed in the credits.

But there's no denying the fascinating nature of the recollections as they interrogate POWs (where the German fear of the Russians was their biggest tool), take part in the Battle of the Bulge, and find themselves stunned at the liberation of the concentration camps. (**TMH**)

# D I R E C T - T O - V I D E O
## ROAD HOUSE 2
ZERO STARS/\*\*\*\*
*st.* Johnathon Schaech, Jake Busey, Ellen Hollman, Will Patton
*sc.* Johnathon Schaech and Richard Chizmar
*dir.* Scott Ziehl

Set in the Louisiana bayou (they could've called this *Wild Things 4* and no one would've been any the wiser), *Road House 2* stars rent-a-cipher ~~Billy Zane~~ Jonathon Schaech (who also co-wrote the screenplay (!)) as Shane Tanner, the Patrick Swayze character's own private immaculate conception, a DEA agent so badass (read: off-puttingly cocky) that he goes undercover in a T-shirt with "DEA" splayed on it. When bad guys led by Jake Busey—who began his screen career in earnest by playing the Grim Reaper and now all but embodies said harbinger of doom—put Shane's uncle Nate (Will Patton, still protesting his gay bureaucrat from *No Way Out* too much) in the hospital for not selling his bar, Shane takes over Nate's establishment The Black Pelican, which involves continually fending off Busey's goons, following a trail of breadcrumbs back to his dad Dalton's murderer (! and keep reading), and flirting with an SUV-driving woman (Ellen Hollman) as narcissistic as her name, Beau, would imply. *Road House 2: Bouncer Boogaloo* is too chaste and tedious and not organically or consistently campy enough to facilitate a good MST3K'ing; it sits there like a dead frog waiting for the electrodes. According to a cross-promotional featurette on the new Deluxe Edition

DVD of *Road House*, the filmmakers believe they've pimped the ride of the previous film, but it's the original's old-school charms that have endeared it to legions of fans.

Confession: for the longest time, I've been jotting down ideas for a sequel to *Road House* (think *Shane* meets *The Color of Money*) in the vain hope that they would one day fall on receptive ears; if you ask me, it's among the few catalogue titles Sony has chosen to stigmatize with a dtv prostitution that's more than earned—through an ironic but devoted cult following (it retroactively became the *Snakes on a Plane* of its day)—the merit badge of a big-screen continuation. (The prestige of which just might have lured Patrick Swayze back into the fold, à la *Dirty Dancing: Havana Nights*.) Part of the problem is that any and all of *Road House*'s franchise potential is wrapped up in Swayze's mulleted frame: take him out of the equation and you're crediting the original's popularity to that great American pastime of bouncer'ing. The absence of the palpably-charismatic Swayze in *Road House Reloaded* leaves a crater that only dilates thanks to the lip-service paid to his iconic Dalton, whom we learn went out like some punk (shot to death in his living room, Bugsy Siegel-style, after borrowing his son's car—in one sentence a mythic figure is totally and thoroughly emasculated) in the interim, thus tainting the movie with a youthful arrogance it fails to justify time and time again. And it's one kind of presumptuousness for Schaech to try to fill Swayze's steel-toed boots, another altogether to get Thomas L. Callaway and Edgar Burcksen to pinch hit for cinematographer Dean Cundey and editor Frank J. Urioste, respectively. **(BC)**

**PREVIOUSLY UNPUBLISHED**
**ROCKY BALBOA**
***½/****
*st.* Sylvester Stallone, Burt Young, Antonio Tarver, Geraldine Hughes

*w./d.* Sylvester Stallone

The *Rocky* movies have been a memoir in progress for hyphenate Sylvester Stallone, a *roman à clef* equal parts self-flagellating and self-aggrandizing, with his alter ego's boxing career charting much the same rollercoaster course as his own. Generally treated in the popular discourse as a shorthand for Hollywood's propensity to beat dead horses ("Coming up, Pongo's review of *Rocky 5...thousand*," went the joke in Mel Brooks' *Spaceballs*), the franchise is actually more vital and, it goes without saying, more *personal* than other long-distance runners like James Bond or *Star Trek*, both of which get off comparatively easy.[1] Scoff if you will, but the six-film *Rocky* saga is probably the closest American analogue there is to Francois Truffaut's 'Adventures of Antoine Doinel.' Aside from the fact that Antoine is Rocky's physical and intellectual opposite, the crucial difference between them is that Truffaut never became trapped in the hermetic seal of fame quite like Stallone, and so for us, Rocky's arc—unlike everyman Doinel's—grows progressively fantastical as the sequels accumulate.[2] In other words, somewhere along the line Stallone turned into Superman, whereas Truffaut never exactly stopped being Clark Kent.

Yet the almost embarrassingly heartfelt *Rocky Balboa* is decidedly earthbound. Stallone doesn't condescend to the character here like he did in the previous film, which always felt like an ersatz comeback to me. (*Rocky V* came out *after* the smash hit *Tango & Cash* and *before* that one-two punch of *Oscar* and *Stop! Or My Mom Will Shoot*; maybe it was intended as a pre-emptive strike.) It's a cashing-in of a meal ticket, no question, but for Stallone it stopgaps a period that saw him doing dtv dreck and reality-TV—a spiritual sister, I reckon, to the days he spent as a struggling actor, dreaming up the screenplay for the first *Rocky*. Inspired in part by John Glenn's last hurrah in the space program, *Rocky Balboa* is about how we presume our living monuments to victory—and/or our elderly—have nothing left to prove, least of all to themselves. Rocky's former glory casts a long shadow, eclipsing the life he's currently living as the proprietor of an Italian restaurant ("Adrian's," natch) where he's effectively reduced, on a nightly basis, to regaling his customers with blow-by-blow accounts of matches past. (Like his creator, Rocky has matured into a hell of a raconteur.) He's a ghost, especially without a proper support system in place: Adrian's dead (of "woman cancer," as Rocky so delicately puts it); Rocky, nay, Robert Jr. (Milo Ventimiglia) has estranged himself out of resentment for the burden of his father's legacy; and Paulie (Burt Young) is...well...Paulie.

A couple of things finally allow Rocky to, in Paulie's words, "change the channel from yesterday." First, he is reunited with Little Marie (Geraldine Hughes, a compellingly naturalistic performer who brings out the best in Stallone), the tough-talking girl he walked home in a beloved bit from *Rocky*. She's a single mother now working as a bartender, and in an astonishingly brave, beautifully-observed scene, Rocky picks out her son from a group of kids and she cautiously corrects him that, No, hers is the black one. Although they forge a friendship and maintain a healthy flirtation, she's less a replacement for Adrian than she is the cyclicality of life personified, alerting the Italian Stallion to the sound of opportunity knocking when ESPN pits heyday-Rocky against current heavyweight champion Mason Dixon (Antonio Tarver, sadly floundering to flesh out an underwritten Clubber Lang clone) in a computerized bout—and Rocky wins. "Keep moving forward," Rocky implores Robert; misinterpreted as an act of regression, sixtysomething Rocky takes his own advice the best way he knows how by accepting the

challenge of a real-life exhibition fight with Dixon. Rah-rah moment of the year? Gotta be the call to arms from Rocky's long-time cutman (Tony Burton): "Let's start buildin' some hurtin' bombs!"

Aesthetically, this might be the richest *Rocky* yet, with Stallone and cinematographer Clark Mathis bathing people in *Godfather* pools of overhead light that transform all of Philadelphia into a makeshift fight club, the see-your-breath chill in the air only heightening the impression of a smoky boxing ring during Rocky and Robert's outdoor verbal rope-a-dopes. *Rocky Balboa* additionally had the good fortune to come along in an era that favours verisimilitude; just as Stallone is governed by commercial caprice as an actor—even *Copland* was mainly a concession to the post-Tarantino indie rehabilitation that was the rage back then[3]—so, too, is he a glorified ventriloquist dummy for the default techniques of the day as a director. If you want to know what 1985 looked/felt like, watch *Rocky IV*. The cost of this—a tonal discontinuity and qualitative inconsistency across the *Rocky* pictures—benefits posterity. By fully embracing its own zeitgeist, each and every instalment Stallone has helmed serves as a valuable historical artifact, and this film's sense of neorealism is rejuvenating besides. *Rocky Balboa* is also an interesting lesson in how to retain the potency of an underdog sports-uplift intrigue in a sequel: wait thirty years to make it, thus letting nature itself renew the stakes. Because everybody ages but few experience the pitfalls of fame firsthand, or are forced to shoulder a nation's weight of anti-communist sentiment in the middle of a cold war, this is the most universally appealing *Rocky* movie since the original, as well as the most resonant.[4] (**BC**)

1.  *Consider that Bond's consistently-overdue makeovers tend to be showered with praise while Stallone has continually*

*kept pace with the times* sans fanfare.

2. To the extent that the back-to-basics Rocky V *seemed somehow more alien than any of the others, so removed from the realities of poverty was Stallone at that point. It was still nakedly autobiographical, though, in that any time Rocky returns to ground zero of his celebrity, Stallone is doing the same. (Stallone made* Rocky, *but the opposite holds equally if not more true.) And of course the movie cast Sly's own offspring Sage Stallone as Rocky's disenchanted son, surely saving thousands in family therapy bills.*

3. He's better in Rocky Balboa, *for what it's worth.*

4. Which is not to regard the Rocky *series strictly as metafiction and discount its value as a modern Herculean mythology. Indeed collectively, at the risk of hyperbole, the films constitute an epic poem.*

## RUNNING SCARED
***/****

st. Paul Walker, Cameron Bright, Vera Farmiga, Chazz Palminteri
w./d. Wayne Kramer

I like Wayne Kramer's *Running Scared* because *Running Scared* isn't ashamed of itself. It's not terribly audacious (in direct contradiction to the consensus opinion that the film is "over-the-top," I found it to be sort of tame in its sexuality, violence, and atrocity) and it's not witty or smart or loaded with the archetype that a direct homage to the Brothers Grimm (the picture is set in the fictitious hamlet of "Grimley") would imply. Its prologue's cliffhanger, for instance, is paid off at the end in absolutely the most spineless way possible, betraying the dark fairytale template of which the film is so proud. (Fairytales were never this squeamish about strangers

actually injuring—sometimes killing—children.) Besides, there's nothing terribly subversive about suggesting that the world is a dangerous place for kids. And yet, there is embedded in *Running Scared*'s clueless schizophrenia (it wants to be edgy even as it's spending the majority of its energy on slick editing tricks, comic-book CGI effects, and a restless camera that doesn't hold still long enough for a fly to land on it) a nasty, seductive class of real cinematic infatuation and a knowledge, idiot savant-like or otherwise, of how to implicate a viewer in the things unfolding onscreen. A neat trick. Neater because the protagonist with which we suture, as it were, is played by one Paul Walker: possibly the worst actor the United States has ever produced, no matter what Armond White says.

To be fair, Walker is excellent in *Running Scared* as a one-note, doltish, monosyllabic, Jersey-mob triggerman whose distinctive gun, which he's used to kill some cops, gets stolen by the abused kid, Oleg (Cameron Bright), of his insane, John Wayne-obsessed next-door neighbour (Karel Roden). Of course Joey Gazelle (he runs, scared, get it?) has to retrieve his shiny revolver so as to avoid the wrath of the bulls on one side (Chazz Palminteri) and the guidos (Johnny Messner) on the other, leading to a long, *After Hours* odyssey through the wild night calling. His wife (Vera Farmiga, a kind of sexually-attractive Claire Forlani), meanwhile, does a little mother bear'ing on her own, saving Oleg from a pair of pederasts (the great Bruce Altman and Elizabeth Mitchell) who cast shadows like Max Schreck's Orlok in the film's most impressive set-piece. Of course there's payback for the ghouls (it's a fairytale, after all), but without an equivalent consequence or learning arc for the heroes, all that's left is another cleverly composed *grimoire* about the absolute righteousness of revenge in a post-9/11 America.

*Running Scared* fits comfortably

alongside a film like *Sin City* or *Kiss Kiss, Bang Bang* in that it's told from a prick's point-of-view—that of Paul Walker's Joey, sure, but moreover the camera lens fulfills its phallic destiny, approximating in its interest and aggression the opening of the penis. I don't think it's an exposé on gun violence in America (unlike any of a number of well-meaning, terrible films about the life of guns), I think it's a celebration of gun violence anywhere and, pointedly, how guns are substitute johnsons. It's wondrously, exuberantly stupid in a very particular, very masculine kind of way: *Jackass* as an underworld crime narrative. The film is all violence and testosterone: the only sex is non-consensual; the only shots in a strip club start at the crotch; the only rule of law is Old Testament; and what's celebrated, ultimately, is a child's ability to wield a weapon.

Although *Running Scared* is often described as ugly, I'm more comfortable saying that it's pretty close to the mark in terms of the darkest fantasies indulged by boys: the mastery of women, the mastery of other men, driving cool cars, having a secret identity, and being the hero of your own thousand faces. It's a recipe for exploitation (and *Running Scared* is indeed exploitation), but it's done with post-Tarantino, music-video skill that's totally in love with its own artifice while maintaining a certain respect for action; its interstitials and time-stutters actually aid in clarification instead of contributing to obfuscation. (For an example of how this shit fails, see Tony Scott's *Domino*.) *Running Scared* demonstrates how style is sometimes substance. It's also an example of a film I recommend simply because it tickled my undercarriage. (**WC**)

## RUNNING WITH SCISSORS
**/****

*st.* Annette Bening, Joseph Cross, Brian Cox, Evan Rachel Wood
*sc.* Ryan Murphy, based on the novel by Augusten Burroughs
*dir.* Ryan Murphy

It would be hard to not be a little moved by the traumatic goings-on of *Running with Scissors*. The film is based on Augusten Burroughs' best-selling memoir, and the author has plenty to forget: not merely the failure of his real family, consisting of a distant alcoholic father and a self-righteous failed-poet mother, but also the nightmare of moving out of *that* home and into that of Mommy's quack psychiatrist. Yet as the horrors pile up, one wonders what's being learned in the midst of all this unburdening. I haven't read Burroughs' book, but Ryan Murphy's screen translation fails completely to draw conclusions from the facts— we're simply dropped in the midst of some seriously unhappy people and left to fend for ourselves. Perhaps the memoirist felt the same way, but without any generalizations drawn it seems rather like that money-grubbing head-shrinker, making hay with other people's depression.

Things aren't going well when we first meet Augusten (Jack Kaeding), who as a six-year-old circa 1971 is in thrall to his wildly ambitious and deeply angry mother Deirdre (Annette Bening). Hungry for recognition, Deirdre takes out career frustrations on her souse husband Norman (Alec Baldwin) with a torrent of psychobabble that would drive anyone to drink. By the time Augusten is 15 (and played by Joseph Cross), he's thoroughly fed up—and then his mother falls in with demented therapist Dr. Finch (Brian Cox). In no time flat, she has transferred Augusten to the doctor's junk-strewn mansion, where the patriarch leads Deirdre into drugged stupors and psychotic episodes while manipulating his daughters—dutiful, co-dependent Hope (Gwyneth Paltrow) and bitter, sensible Natalie (Evan Rachel Wood)— into various states of pliability.

Although it would probably take a battery of biographers and caseworkers to untangle this web of cross-purposes and confusions, the movie doesn't even try. As Augusten's painful experiences—such as a fruitless relationship with 35-year-old schizophrenic Neil (Joseph Fiennes) and the doctor's tendency to read premonitions from his morning bowel movements—pile up, they commensurately weigh us down. Inevitably we respond to so much trauma happening to one person, and at some point it gets to you—especially with Deirdre's stream-of-consciousness ramblings, designed as they are to deflect criticism. Murphy's approach, however, suggests that he neither knows nor comprehends this kind of suffering. He's good at art-directing Mommy's living-room poetry readings in hot canary yellow or finding the right Elton John tune to underscore a moment, but he's all about exteriors: he can't draw you a map to what happens inside.

Buried in this story of therapeutic misadventure is a thesis about the abuse of the psychological model—how almost all of the characters locate a convenient out in the highfalutin' language of Freud and his fellow travelers, as well as how the lingo proves to be a great way to get people to do something they shouldn't, or blame others for their own (admittedly neurotic) sins. But *Running with Scissors* never really connects the dots to this or any other thesis. In fact, it does nothing to change the perception that the recent vogue for tell-all autobiographies (which engendered the hoaxes of James Frey and Laura "JT Leroy" Albert) has mainly facilitated the same sort of displacement in which many of the movie's misfits engage. A more astute filmmaker would have tried to sort out when blame is earned and when it's a devious strategy; Murphy doesn't have anything on his mind beyond "telling a story" and goosing you with madness.

One thinks back to Terence Davies' *Distant Voices, Still Lives*—another amorphous film about a miserable childhood presided over by a tyrant—and observes that presentation and insight are not the same thing. Davies gives you a cause-and-effect relationship between abuse and reactive behaviour—he illustrates the processes by which one is victimized, even if he's at a loss for conclusions. Murphy hasn't nearly as much perspective: presented with a slab of suffering, he shapes it into a conventional Hollywood narrative; you're bombarded by so much and learn so little from it. You feel for poor, confused Augusten and his kindred-spirit "sister" Natalie and indeed hope they save themselves from their assorted guardians. Alas, you also get every thought driven from your head, leaving you exactly where you started. **(TMH)**

**RV**
½*/****
*st.* Robin Williams, Jeff Daniels, Cheryl Hines, Kristin Chenowith
*sc.* Geoff Rodkey
*dir.* Barry Sonnenfeld

Shit, feral raccoons, hillbillies, tits, white-boy Ebonics, more shit, and oodles of forced sentimentality to propel the septic stew down our collective throat as we strain towards it, baby bird-like. Or so the theory goes. In the interest of complete disclosure, the reason Barry Sonnenfeld's excrescent *RV* dodged a zero-star rating from me is that I actually laughed at a perversely perfect sewage geyser. It's one thing when you're all about the slapstick gross-out gag; another when, *National Lampoon's Vacation*-style (the film that, structurally, *RV*, *Johnson Family Vacation*, *Are We There Yet?*, and so on most resemble), your trip across the middle of the United States yields insights into the caste and racial strata of our expansive country. Then you have a feckless relic like this that pulls its punches even in regards to the bigotry it directs at rednecks. There's nothing to hold onto in *RV*, and it tries so hard to please that there's not much joy in taking it down. It's like kicking a puppy, with the puppy trying to lick your boot as you do it.

Bob (Robin Williams) works too hard and doesn't spend enough time with his family and yadda yadda yadda and blah blah blah. He rents/buys a giant RV and convinces his princess wife Jamie (Cheryl Hines) and evil, spoiled children (Josh Hutcherson and something called "JoJo") to go on a road trip to reconnect, but lo, it's secretly a working vacation, the revelation of which will cause the freshly-resurrected marriage to strain for a few minutes. Williams is perfect for this recreational vehicle because he's always liked to combine his antiquated, manic shtick (the picture opens with him doing a surprisingly poor Sylvester Stallone impersonation) with weepy-eyed sentimentality. At least Williams gets a lot of opportunity to work on his self-imitation, although, let's face it, even that isn't in the same ballpark as Jim Carrey's nowadays. And if Williams' gagging feels forced and artificial, the audience's gagging seems entirely genuine.

If you go to this gas trap, you have to know exactly what you're about to experience; as with most things in our culture, garbage like *RV* perpetually regenerates because we want it to. People patronize *RV*, probably propel it to the tops of the box office, because they're either not high on discretion or are being dragged there by the same — they're either stupid or weak, resulting, of course, in entertainment that shares those qualities in spades. Bob's family intersects with a family of backwoods residents led by patriarch Travis (Jeff Daniels) and bimbo wife Marie Jo (Kristin Chenowith) — whom Bob, horrifyingly, speculates aloud is a hooker over dinner she's prepared for him and his family — and rounded out with a trio of children Bob's kids make doe eyes at in just one of the subplots *RV* blissfully fumbles. And the punchline is, you guessed it, that the hillbilly clan is Stanford-educated and moral, which suggests not that Bob's family is un-educated and amoral, but that they're smart and good as well, papering over issues of class and decency.

Rather than bemoan how gifted performers like Hines, "Arrested Development" alumnae Will Arnett and Tony Hale, and Daniels are wasted in this pandering, derivative, interminable dreck, it's more instructive to note how Robin Williams is not. *RV* is an episodic death march that hangs long minutes on gags involving a seat-belt that won't extend and Hines singing **Ronny and the Daytonas**' "Little GTO," tone-free, to the consternation of a disinterestedly-mugging Williams. When the kids are irritating (especially the female named JoJo), they're genuinely irritating — which is either great acting or a really bad idea or both; and when the poignant guitar cues up, that weird noise you hear in the theatre is a few dozen fingernails digging into armrests. *RV* is what it is — up to you whether you take that as either an endorsement or the harshest criticism I can level. (**WC**)

## THE SANTA CLAUSE 3: THE ESCAPE CLAUSE

\*/\*\*\*\*

*st.* Tim Allen, Martin Short, Elizabeth Mitchell, Judge Reinhold
*sc.* Ed Decter & John J. Strauss
*dir.* Michael Lembeck

Much like a TV show that's been on the air too long, the *Santa Clause* films have accrued an unwieldy supporting cast (including those old harbingers of cancellation: grandparents and babies) and begun hitting the reset button on characters thought to be at or near the end of their arcs. Here, workaholic Scott Calvin (Tim Allen) is reminded via the frustrations of his second wife that he might not be husband material—which, all things considered, isn't a bad direction for the series to take, if only because we rarely see remarriage grappled with in any context on the silver screen. Still, as the house style has evolved such that it can no longer accommodate even the quasi-realist, *Oh, God! Book II* trappings of the original, we get that reductive trope about a family man who takes pride in his work being a man who's asking for karmic retribution. Never mind that he's fucking Santa Claus and the needs of the many would appear to outweigh the needs of the few in this case. I suppose it's progress or innovation that Mrs. Claus (Elizabeth Mitchell, whose role as one of the child catchers in *Running Scared* retroactively renders her a subversive presence in these films) is expecting and in her third trimester at that, thus upping the asshole quotient when Santa allows his attention to drift towards other impending deliveries for five-nanosecond stretches—but at the risk of applying logic where it isn't wanted, why would Santa impregnate his wife nine months before Christmastime? It's counterintuitive at best. And if it was an accident, surely there's an 'Abortion Clause' he could've invoked. Maybe they're saving that for a future instalment.

So a beleaguered Santa falls victim to the low-rent scheming of nattily-dressed Jack Frost, played with an awesome and perhaps contagious malevolence by Martin Short: in launching an extended riff on *Back to the Future Part II* (minus the postmodern cleverness) by transporting Santa and Frost into a pivotal scene from *The Santa Clause*, the film is casually mindless of the fact that it's depicting the death of Santa Claus over and over again like some mad Zapruder loop.† (It's still not as ghoulish, mind you, as the Kuleshovian cutaways to the late Peter Boyle, who looks as though someone's propping him up, *Weekend at Bernie's*-style, in his role as Father Time.) The megalomaniacal Frost essentially wants to corporatize Christmas ("Frostmas") and exploit the North Pole's potential as a synergistic theme park, and so, as our own Ian Pugh astutely pointed out in his review of the execrable *The Year Without a Santa Claus*, you have the incongruous image of Coca-Cola mascot Santa Claus conspiring to reclaim Christmas from commercialism. The secularization of Christmas is apparently only selectively offensive—like when it interferes with Tim Allen's personal life, or the hetero orientation of the holiday. After all, the whole Frostmas scenario ultimately reveals itself as a pretext for Short to belt out a show tune in drag.

This third entry in the *Santa Clause* franchise boasts the best production design of the lot, but that's an indication not so much of artistic growth (I mean, the reindeer continue to fart up a storm) as of a concentration of labour, since the film itself is more insular than its forebears. (Suffocatingly so.) The antagonist—anthropomorphized this time around—is uncharacteristically entertaining, but that was a given with the casting of the reliably irreverent Short. Santa's workshop has lost its fascist tincture, but that might simply be the absence of David Krumholtz's problematic Bernard the Jewish Elf. In other words, *The Santa Clause 3: The Escape Clause* creates the illusion that it has learned from previous instalments, though it's really just the same old twaddle. Michael Lembeck returns to helm the production like the veteran sitcom hack he is, directing with a style best described as obsequious—note the hilariously *un*-directed extras littering the margins of almost every shot—and rarely seen outside the realm of live television. Any kind of deference to the material is the last thing this movie needs, as the script is so transparently mercenary in its lack of ambition, coherence, and conscientiousness that it seems to have been composed on the teleprompter between takes. Apropos of recent events, you look at a movie like *The Santa Clause 3: The Escape Clause* and wonder how some screenwriters can have the temerity to go on strike. (**BC**)

†*Need I remind, this got a G rating while* Whale Rider *was slapped with a PG-13?*

## SATELLITE
***1/2/****

*st.* Karl Geary, Stephanie Szostak, Larry Fessenden, Neil Jain
*w./d.* Jeff Winner

Infused with a ferocious air of independence both in its genesis and within its plot, hyphenate Jeff Winner's *Satellite* may prove best remembered for providing a winsome stage to gamine Stephanie Szostak. Indescribably adorable with her slightly buck teeth, wide eyes, and a reedy, Rosanna Arquette-like voice inflected with just a touch of Paris, Szostak has the same ethereal quality to her that's made Nicole Kidman the most over-exposed star on the planet. As Ro, a girl swept off her feet by Kevin (Karl Geary) in something like an urban *Badlands* conceit, she quits her job on a whim, shoplifts on a dare, and agrees to spend a couple of seasons unmoored in the pursuit of a life authentic. Her performance is the most magnetic and winning thing about the film as Winner traces a knowing finger along the delicate line between loving to be free and being anxious that you're not working. It's good, but how much better would it have been to just sit back and behold beautiful, breathless, Godard-ian conflict in the midst of non-conflict than reach, in the last reels, for another genre altogether? Still, it's romantic in a way that avoids sappiness. Ambitious, too: a fairy tale about love. Then again, aren't they all? (**WC**)

## SAW III
**1/2/****

*st.* Dina Meyer, Shawnee Smith, Bahar Soomekh, Tobin Bell
*sc.* Leigh Whannell & James Wan
*dir.* Darren Lynn Bousman

SPOILER WARNING IN EFFECT. If nothing else, the *Saw* saga can be said to defy the law of diminishing returns that normally governs sequels. Both the first and second instalments were equally dumb movies, combining an ambition to be more plot-driven than the average slasher opus while not having the intellectual chops to actually pull it off. Borrowing heavily from *Se7en*'s premise of a moralistic serial killer, the films try to pass off a sub-Rod Serling guilt complex as something resembling theme and subtext; the filmmakers think they're doing more than killing folks in baroque ways, and the combination of brutal violence and twinky piety effectively blunts the former and disqualifies the latter. Which is what makes *Saw III* a semi-pleasant surprise: for the most part, it's far less pretentious than its predecessors, leaving us in the dark without much exposition and deferring the cheesy explanations until the predictably disappointing finale.

In this go-round, Jigsaw (Tobin Bell) is still dying of cancer (this must be the most protracted death in film history) and looking for relief; he finds it in the form of doped-up doctor Lynn (Bahar Soomekh), who has naturally squandered her existence and is thus in need of Jigsaw's brand of superego justice. Intercut with her efforts to save the franchise leader is the confinement and "testing" of Jeff (Angus Macfadyen), who has become consumed with the hit-and-run death of his son and must now face various culprits in that tragedy to see whether he can resist letting them die in nasty ways. If Lynn flees the scene or Jigsaw's heart rate flatlines, a collar she's wearing will explode; if Jeff does nothing to help his tormentors, it's also intimated that something bad will happen. Let the games begin...

The new film deviates slightly from the first two by being more medical drama than police procedural. Where *Saw* and *Saw II* depended heavily upon cops doggedly tracking down our man Jigsaw (the better to skewer their overarching sense of morality), this one features the interpersonal *tête-à-tête* between a doctor, his patient, and that patient's obnoxious protégée, Amanda (returning flunky Shawnee Smith). Distinguishing part three as well is its greater focus on women: while the first two *Saws* were unique in horror for their preoccupation with male victims, this one involves not only the protracted freezing death of a naked bystander to the accident and the flaying death of Dina Meyer's cop, but also the taunting Amanda's confrontational alliance with desperate Lynn. Despite the nastiness of the deaths, the film never quite feels misogynistic, balanced as they are by two women who ultimately overshadow pompous Jigsaw.

Of course, *Saw III* is more interesting in the context of its predecessors than it is as a stand-alone feature. Though one is more invested in this particular outing, that's because you're distracted from the exposition—nobody's explaining anything as they go, freeing you to concentrate on the semi-creative deaths and funky sodium-lamp aesthetic that is now *de rigueur* for these things. But there's absolutely no consistency to the film's moral vision: Jigsaw punishes the hit-and-run driver and his accessories just as he punishes their indirect victim, sort of nullifying the message he appears to want to send his damaged and preoccupied test subject. And, naturally, it all coalesces into one of those everything-is-connected endings that marred the first two, which tries to impress you with "ingenuity" that isn't really there. You could do worse than *Saw III* and its time-wasting sadism, yet its feeble attempts at becoming a genuine movie only remind you that it's not. (**TMH**)

## ANIMATED
## A SCANNER DARKLY
**\*\*\*\*/\*\*\*\***

*st.* Keanu Reeves, Robert Downey Jr., Woody Harrelson, Winona Ryder
*sc.* Richard Linklater, based on the novel by Philip K. Dick
*dir.* Richard Linklater

Our reality has almost outstripped Philip K. Dick's paranoid fantasies, and Richard Linklater's grim *A Scanner Darkly* is the slipperiest take yet on the war between perception vs. reality in a year that knows *United 93*. Keanu Reeves, so often woefully miscast, is wonderfully imagined here as a guy in a "scramble suit": his appearance constantly shifting in a kaleidoscope of mismatched parts—the uniform of future-narcs (seven years from now, announce the opening title) sent undercover to ferret out the dopers and dealers of Substance D. It's a hallucinogen that eventually causes a rift in the individual consciousness (the left hemisphere atrophies and the right tries to compensate) and Reeves' Agent Fred is sent to find out where dealer Donna (Winona Ryder) is getting her shit. But the scramble suits seem mainly used to keep the vice squad's identities from one another instead of their quarry, meaning that Fred goes underground as himself, Robert Arctor, in full grunge, inhabiting his once-cozy suburban nook with tweaked conspiracy theorists Ernie (Woody Harrelson) and Barris (Robert Downey Jr.). Meaning, too, that Fred is asked to spy on Arctor, and that Barris, in a pair of hilarious scenes, informs on Arctor *to* Arctor. It's not the labyrinthine audacity of Dick's delusions that so enthralls, but rather the mendacity of them. What's complicated about *A Scanner Darkly* isn't the compression of identity or the various plots to which its characters imagine themselves hero and victim, but the idea that reality conforms itself to belief—that because life has stopped making sense to you, life has stopped making sense, period.

Animated frame-by-frame using the same rotoscoping process Linklater employed in *Waking Life, A Scanner Darkly* resembles nothing so much as a three-dimensional image frozen and sliced into different, shifting planes. Every second is in motion—sort of a wiggle—that causes faces to slide against themselves and gnash while the characters are talking. It's a mesmerizing technique that has the effect of furthering the film's theme of disconnection. Oppositional ideas in conflict with one another is, after all, the foundation upon which *A Scanner Darkly* and its perception-splitting drug is built. A moment where Arctor looks at his lover post-coitus to see her transformed, replicated later as Agent Fred replays the same moment of discovery (sometimes from angles which we know aren't subject to hidden cameras (a.k.a. the scanners of the film's title)), describes the intimacy of his reality's violation. Because we're watching a live-action feature that's

been animated and then watching our protagonist watching a video that he's secretly taken of himself, the seed of a sneaking suspicion begins to creep in that the drug-induced madness of Fred/Arctor that allows him to separate what he knows from what he sees is of the very same madness the film induces in the audience. I know that this is Keanu Reeves and a cast of indie luminaries in a film directed by Richard Linklater—and then I know that it's an animated adaptation of an engagingly impenetrable book by Philip K. Dick. And still I'm at times incapable of distinguishing its contortions from the truths littering my own philosophy. What does it mean to take art to heart?

Illegal, aggressive surveillance threatens to open *A Scanner Darkly* to an interpretation as an attack on our beloved domestic policy of dirty tricks, but look beyond that to a more wide-reaching indictment of the way we accept information and are fed paranoia, encouraged to trust the diseased skylarks of our drugged minds. If we can imagine it for you, it's true (echoes of Dick's short story, "We Can Remember It For You, Wholesale", which became *Total Recall*), thus this mass media televisual dystopia of ours becomes the angry fix for our atrophied left hemispheres. Day-by-day, we're less capable of reason and more accepting of garbage like *Pirates of the Caribbean: Dead Man's Chest* as entertainment; the appetite for something bigger, louder, and more three-dimensional in our experiential tourism has become insatiable. The lingering indications of our addiction to facility is this inability to connect with one another (Donna rejects physical contact: "I have to be careful because I do so much coke"), to engage in the essential human survival pastimes of fucking and communicating danger—until at the end what's left on the table are suspicion, loneliness, and misdirected rage at anything with the temerity to be difficult to understand. *A Scanner*

*Darkly* is, like the best science-fiction, about you plus me and the time ticking away on the remainder. It says something that I found the film to be almost Pollyannaish when all's said and done: Linklater and Dick seem to hope that a spark of awareness awaits us on the other side of our self-induced doping. But maybe I see too many movies. (**WC**)

## SCARY MOVIE 4
**\*\*/\*\*\*\***
*st.* Anna Faris, Regina Hall, Craig Bierko, Bill Pullman
*sc.* Craig Mazin & Jim Abrahams & Pat Proft
*dir.* David Zucker

The problem with *Scary Movie 4* isn't that the jokes are cheap—indeed, we'd be disappointed if they weren't. No, the problem is that the film has no real point-of-view beyond a) black people are funny; b) gay people are funny; c) lascivious black women are *hilarious*; and d) recent horror movies fit together (however uneasily). The torrent of hit-or-miss gags is perhaps par for the course, but these bits aren't held together by some overarching idea or sensibility—there's no *satire* of current horror titles, just a parade titles and the lazy ethnic/sexual/bathroom humour that is this sort of movie's bread and butter. Which probably won't mean squat to the people who've made the series a cash cow, but anyone looking for genuine comedy (as opposed to listless shtick) is advised to look elsewhere.

After a dumb name-dropping opener in which Shaquille O'Neal and Dr. Phil exchange *Saw* pleasantries, we're more or less introduced to innocent Cindy (the redoubtable Anna Faris) as she's moved into the house from *The Grudge*, which just happens to be next door to Tom Cruise—I mean, Tom Ryan (Craig Bierko)—in *War of the Worlds* country. Though Cindy and Tom immediately fall in love, their relationship gets put on hold by the appearance of Japanese ghosts in Cindy's abode and by the arrival of alien tripods in everyone else's. Long story short, everybody winds up on the run, with Cindy and friend Brenda (Regina Hall) seeking answers in *The Village* and the rest running scared—except, of course, for the President (Leslie Neilsen), who just wants to know what happens in the story with the duck.

I can be reasonably tolerant of this sort of thing: I was 13 once, too, thus my mind can grasp the attraction to obvious jokes like the ones featured here. Still, I've long since outgrown the revue-type spoof; mostly, I stared blankly into my monitor as the writers tried desperately to link some rather disparate material while just as desperately avoiding any *take* on the material. Although I was somehow out of town for the first three instalments of the *Scary Movie* franchise, it's not hard to make out the signs of sequel fatigue: nobody's really interested in doing anything creative, instead merely going through the motions so as to justify paychecks and grease the wheels of commerce. And while that can sometimes result in a freewheeling shambles, here it's resulted in a big whimper, if not a big yawn.

I would not insist on the annoyance of the racial and sexual humour (which manages to rope in not just horror films but *Brokeback Mountain* and *Million Dollar Baby*, too) if it weren't so endemic to the film's problem. Scary Movie 4 is so hung up on the innate hilarity of difference that it's clear it hasn't got anything else in its arsenal: the "surefire" gags of black men with gold chains and two dudes sloppily sucking face are there because the writers know they don't have to break a sweat coming up with a punchline. The transgressions against straight white propriety do the work for them—and everybody breaks for lunch. Leaving aside the issue of appropriateness, it shows the tendency of mainstream comedy to lead away from wit, though the film's success likewise shows such witlessness' indestructible appeal. (**WC**)

## SCHOOL FOR SCOUNDRELS
ZERO STARS/****
*st.* Billy Bob Thornton, Jon Heder, Jacinda Barrett, Luis Guzman
*sc.* Todd Phillips & Scot Armstrong
*dir.* Todd Phillips

## THE GUARDIAN
*½/****
*st.* Kevin Costner, Ashton Kutcher, Neal McDonough, Melissa Sagemiller
*sc.* Ron L. Brinkerhoff
*dir.* Andrew Davis

What the woefully, dreadfully, desperately unfunny *School of Scoundrels* has going for it is the casting of fetching Jacinda Barrett as the leading lady; what it squanders is the opportunity to present anything resembling intelligence or wit in favour of achingly uninsightful jabs at the gender rift and the presentation of idiot Jon Heder in exhibit, oh, about 'E' or 'F' by now, of how he has no known function. Billy Bob Thornton continues his blue W.C. Fields bit (next up, *Mr. Woodcock*), here as "Dr. P," the head of the titular finishing school that specializes in molding the losers and milquetoasts of the world into sunglasses-wearing assholes fond of comparing themselves to lions. His prize student is meter maid Roger (Heder), who, because the script demands it, transforms himself from a doofus into a doofus in a suit, finally mustering up the courage to ask out neighbour Amanda (Barrett). Inexplicably, she has all along been pining for this hermetic, feminized, saccharine troll—after all, what beautiful, smart, funny woman doesn't want to be dating someone with the looks of Napoleon Dynamite and the personality of a serial-killing child molester? Sarah Silverman is wasted (though given her track record, it could very well be that there's nothing left to waste) as Amanda's evil roommate, written with snarky commentary you'd think a perfect fit for her.

Alas, nothing jives in *School for Scoundrels*: not the assertion that black men are scary criminals and probably rapists and homosexuals; not the central love story involving the release of restaurant lobsters; and certainly not the denouement in which everything is instantly revealed and just as quickly forgiven. How something so derivative and appallingly written could have made it to fruition is a phenomenon at once wondrous and depressing. The picture is weak in every aspect from timing to performance, humiliating Todd Louiso and Michael Clarke Duncan and then choking on an awkward cameo by Ben Stiller, various balls-to-the-groin gags, and post-script cards for each of the characters that ring with the poetry of closet Dickensons from your local coffee shop's open mike night. I'm still trying to puzzle out why Dr. P has his students dress up as policemen in one trailer-spoiled sequence beyond an excuse for the punchline of one of them unwisely detonating a canister of mace in an elevator. With no character the slightest bit interesting (save the one who wants to choose as her lover either dumb or dumber, thus making her mentally unfit, if not actually a retarded object of pity), none of the situations plausible or funny, none of the sidekicks edifying, and none of the timing graceful, we're left with a colossal life-suck: a vortex, and another early-Fall candidate for worst of the year.

Surprisingly not a candidate for worst of the year is Andrew Davis' Coast Guard recruiting commercial *The Guardian* (which shares its title with a horror movie about a naked druid nanny), a by-the-numbers action picture that alternates action sequences and sage declarations with metronomic dedication. Kevin Costner is legendary "Rescue Swimmer" Ben Randall, who gets off on the wrong foot with hotshot recruit Jake (Ashton Kutcher, and what better casting would it have been to have Randall played by real-life Kutcher-rival Bruce Willis?) in the usual macho formula epic way before learning to trust and admire the young buck as the May/September version of himself. Daring water rescues are filmed with the force of a large budget (sub "fire rescues," "snow," "climbing," and so on for the lineage and future of this kind of flick), and, even better, with the semblance of coherence so sorely lacking in mainstream actioners nowadays. Costner by now seems comfortable settling into the grizzled saddle-bag portion of his career, the aging jock taking on a promising hatchling of *Bull Durham* fame into eternity—and, in truth, why not? Costner is excellent as a jock/ex-jock or cowboy and little else. *The Guardian's* appeal, such as it is, rests on his still-broad shoulders and thinning pate: a comfortable, congenial quality of not expecting much and getting exactly what you'd expect and not one portion larger. It's not good, but at least it doesn't make you want to poke your eyes out. (**WC**)

### THE SCIENCE OF SLEEP
*½/****

*st.* Gael García Bernal, Charlotte Gainsbourg, Alain Chabat, Miou-Miou
*w./d.* Michel Gondry

### JET LI'S FEARLESS
** /****

*st.* Jet Li, Nakamura Shidou, Sun Li, Dong Yong
*sc.* Chris Chow, Christine To
*dir.* Ronny Yu

A cacophony of cascading whimsy, Michel Gondry's exercise in Freudian bric-a-brac *The Science of Sleep* plays like a movie based on a thrift store specializing in Harlequin novels—*French* Harlequin novels. It adheres to the music-video director's maxim of maximum images per second, and it casts Gael García Bernal as Stéphane, a useless lug endlessly working on a calendar of calamitous events and pining after his across-hall neighbour Stéphanie (Charlotte Gainsbourg), with whom he is too smitten to confess that his mother is her landlord. His dreams take the form of a one-man variety show, while Gondry revels in scenes where he inflates his hero's hands and has him ride an animated patchwork horse. But *The Science of Sleep* is more exhausting than illuminating—more a loud masturbation than any kind of intercourse with the audience. The difference between the Gondry of *Eternal Sunshine of the Spotless Mind* and the Gondry of *The Science of Sleep*, it seems obvious to say, is the difference between a film scripted by Charlie Kaufman and one not, though it's more complicated than that in that the Kaufman of *Eternal Sunshine of the Spotless Mind* is an artist who finally struck a balance between affectation and a much finer connective tissue. Gondry is still just engaged in the twist.

It's hard to see Stéphane and Stéphanie as being more substantive than any of the other dishevelled props Gondry tosses around in his *faux*-romantic fugue. Caring about their stultifyingly cute misunderstandings, then, requires something of a pointless and Herculean effort. *The Science of Sleep* is exhausting instead of revelatory, its sentiment grounded by a lethal dosage of quirk that proves that soulless automatons are wondrous only for their elaborate strangeness. If this sounds like the description for a foetal cult film, I'd offer the example of Gondry's feature debut, *Human Nature*: armed, as it happens, with Kaufman's first screenplay, it suffers from the same variety of visual arrogance and has, ultimately, located itself primarily as a curiosity—and an irritating one at that. Gondry is in love with his auteur mantle; I wonder if he's unaware that it's tied so snugly to Kaufman's particular genius.

It's tied almost as inextricably as Jet Li's is to the epic historical martial arts spectacle. Thus it comes with some sadness that Li has declared *Fearless (a.k.a. Jet Li's Fearless)* his final foray into a genre he's done much to define in the modern era—no less because a moment referencing the classic *Once Upon a Time in China* films (and Li's indelible turn as another mythologized folk hero, Wong Fei Hung) whereby Li holds an umbrella during a fight reminds us that although Li's retained most of his physical skills, *Fearless* is a pretty pale imitation of former glories. The tale of Huo Yuan Jia, a legendary martial arts master who defended China's dignity for a brief period of time against the indignities ladled upon it by the whole of the colonial world, *Fearless* is essentially a series of matches against racial bogeymen (American behemoths, British fencing fops) separated by a long, meditative middle section in which Huo recognizes the error of his vengeance-mongering ways and returns to kick ass in the name of Zen. The message is one from Li, who's said he's turning his back on wushu flicks over a repugnance at the revenge element that suffuses the genre with a red light. It's also clearly a message for our time, when so many of the world's ails continue to be carried on the horn of misdirected reprisals and thinly-veiled racial recriminations.

The fight scenes are serviceable, if rendered almost polite by Tony Jaa's new breed of intimately physical violations and further neutered by the plainness of director Ronny Yu's use of CGI and wirework. A scene where a childhood rival should have, by all rights, perished horribly from a head-first plunge off a thirty-foot platform underscores the comic-book aspect of the project, thus allaying *Fearless* more closely to a travesty like *The One* than to something intelligent like the superior Li vehicle *Unleashed*. There's a lot to admire about Li's desire to offer up his own *Unforgiven*, the swan song

to a career spent in bruised flesh and strained joints, yet for as beautiful as it is in its quiet moments (and for as briefly exhilarating as it can be in its occasional martial arts sequences), *Fearless* is ultimately a picture preaching about the cost of violence that shies away from real, visceral consequence. It's a pretty vessel, a smooth surface over a shallow and empty pond. There are bigger truths in this picture, for sure, but its infatuation with the vagaries of its own shell leaves behind something essential and profound in the translation. (**WC**)

## SCOOP
½* /****

*st.* Woody Allen, Hugh Jackman, Scarlett Johansson, Ian McShane
*w./d.* Woody Allen

Woody Allen's stock had been falling when the surprising restraint and structure of the frankly-just-decent *Match Point* temporarily staunched a hemorrhage of appalling failures. Call *Scoop* a return to form, then, with Allen doing Allen again to rapidly-diminishing returns, spicing things up this time around with a teeny dose of post-modern self-deprecation that seems not so much thoughtful as pathetic. The Woodman plays a fast-talking, stammering, Catskills comedian calling himself "The Great Splendini" (for the "square haircuts," he Rickles) who, as Allen is wont to do nowadays, acts as the panderous mentor for a hot young couple. What's most shocking is that a puff of dust and cobwebs don't erupt from his mouth every time it creaks open to deliver another pun about Trollope/trollop and Ruebens/Rueben (the corned beef and sauerkraut variety). Otherwise, it's *The More the Merrier* ad infinitum: the old fart helping a couple of good-looking kids get their groove on—with the twist of a Jack the Ripper subplot woven awkwardly into the narrative. It's far easier to identify the Victorian rake as

Allen himself, what with his vaguely pedophilic sleights-of-hand lurking in every frame. That's not necessarily bad if the film's about a Tom Ripley sociopath (à la *Match Point*), of course, but it's pretty bad when it's a piece of fluff starring his favorite new obsession.

Said obsession: Scarlett Johansson, perhaps the most gifted and voluptuous, old-fashioned siren this side of Monica Bellucci, shoehorned here into the role of mousy journalism student (cum dental hygienist) Sarah Parentsky and forced to jabber Allen's fossilized patter in a way barely resembling classic screwball. Katharine Hepburn and Rosalind Russell are namedropped, which is of course terribly unfortunate because Johansson, in appearance and function, is a lot more like Marilyn Monroe in *Monkey Business* than like Ginger Rogers in same. (If you believe for a second that sultry Johansson is up to the light comedic chops of Diane Keaton or Mia Farrow, you're either not paying attention or don't have a working pair; Allen, take note.) Woody doesn't miss the chance, however, to twice soak Johansson, head-to-toe, doubling his *Match Point* output of drenchings, so maybe there's lascivious method to his madness after all. For a guy who takes pains to mention Freud once or twice per comedy, Allen should think twice about regularly dunking women younger than his daughter/wife in his pictures.

Sarah is in Britain to interview a famous director, whom she promptly shags in the local vernacular while, simultaneously, veteran reporter Joe (the great Ian McShane) kicks the bucket, takes a ride on the Styx express, gets the scoop that aristocrat Peter Lyman (Hugh Jackman) might be strangling prostitutes, and swims back to the mortal plane to tell a journalist. Soon, Sarah and Splendini (a.k.a. Sid) are masquerading as daughter and father to infiltrate Peter's garden parties and gather "clues" with which to validate their supernaturally-acquired information. Don't ask me why. I lost interest a long time ago. Allen can't write jokes anymore and he's never been able to write thrillers, so *Scoop* ranks among this year's most poorly-written, terribly-plotted pictures. The editing is sad but I'm guessing there wasn't a lot to work with: scenes shot at the magic hour aren't imbued with ineffable light but rather murky and shot through with grain. If it doesn't bother you that Allen hasn't taken much care with the technical aspects of the film, it might bother you that the key to the mystery is found not once, but twice (maybe thrice) in exactly the same hidey-hole, thus making the heroes idiot-naïfs and its villain a cast-iron moron. Or, maybe it'll irk you that the only thing Allen and Johansson port from the screwball tradition is desperation, leaving grace, timing, wit, and chemistry behind in a deflated pile.

Though Johansson is flat awful in this picture, I blame the arrogance of Allen's screenplay: she's so conspicuously wrong for this film that the fact of her casting becomes the one consistently diverting thing throughout. Consider that the only audience Allen's writing his alleged comedies for anymore he's already outlived or disenfranchised—any tittering in the audience is more than likely born of pity and incredulity. That Jackman emerges unscathed should cement his position as heir to Cary Grant's romantic comedy crown, because if this giant piece of shit (and Brett Ratner) can't make him look bad, nothing can. (Ditto McShane (doing his best with the indignities of Allen's kitchen sink spirituality), whose legacy is already cemented by his incomparable run in HBO's "Deadwood.") *Scoop* is painful. It's about five steps slow and in the wrong gear besides, every punchline flat, every moment with Allen and Johansson abrasive and embarrassing. But when the film at last mercifully squeezes off its anemic trickle, it at least has the decency not to linger long in the mind. (**WC**)

## THE SECRET LIFE OF WORDS (see: *FREE ZONE*)

## SEE NO EVIL
\*/\*\*\*\*
*st.* Kane, Christina Vidal, Luke Pegler, Samantha Noble
*sc.* Dan Madigan
*dir.* Gregory Dark

SPOILER WARNING IN EFFECT. Gregory Dark started out directing adult films—I've been told that his award-winning *Let Me Tell Ya 'Bout White Chicks* is a classic of the miscegenation genre—and had moved up to music videos when he was offered *See No Evil*, his first feature film (as well as the first film produced under the WWE banner). The idea that Dark sees this movie as his ticket to the big leagues is as good an explanation as any for its smarmy tone. Still embarrassed about making a slasher picture (and, by extension, his stigmatic beginnings), he distances himself from the material by condescending to it: if he's better than B-movie claptrap then that means he's an A-list filmmaker, right? I have no idea where Dark wants to be near the end of his career, but the attitude he brings to *See No Evil* is that of a climber and not of a serious artist who happens to be relegated to the periphery of the mainstream.

The film's general premise unabashedly rips-off *Se7en*, working explicitly from the tired notion that the slashers in slasher movies are punishing their victims for "sinning." The victims are a motley crew of juvenile offenders assigned to clean a ransacked hotel in order to shave a few months off their sentences; all of them wind up having their respective "sins" turned against them. The black kid searching for a safe full of riches is crushed by it shortly after finding it.

The vegetarian who broke into a dog pound and released the animals before they could be gassed is eaten alive by a pack of strays. The hot blonde shoplifter has a cell phone she pilfered pushed down her throat until she chokes. (I admit that this was an effective bit of Guignol—it literally had me dry-heaving.) And so on.

The killer is Jacob Goodnight, a scowling giant who was trained by his fanatical Christian mother to recognize sin and execute those who possess it. We're treated to flashbacks in which she puts porno magazines in pre-teen Jacob's cage (?!) so he can study the faces within: you see, you can tell which people have sin by looking into their eyes. Eyes are the windows to the soul. Jacob cuts them out of his victims and this is supposed to be his trademark, though I was never quite clear as to why he does this and the film, alas, is more interested in simple sadism than in exploring the psychology of its bogeyman. Jacob collects the eyeballs in jars in his room, implying that they're significant as trophies of his kills and that he is blinding his victims mainly to acquire them. I have to wonder why anybody thought this would be the ideal star vehicle for WWE wrestler Kane. We are given few hints as to how the boy in the cage came to look like a professional wrestler, but—I dunno, maybe it's a joke at our expense.

I tend to view the slasher genre as having two distinct modes: anti-teenager (*Friday the 13th*) and pro-teenager (*A Nightmare on Elm Street*). The anti-teenager genre is what we mean when we say that sex is equated with death. This dictum fits John Carpenter's *Halloween* fairly well, but it's overly specific when dealing with the *Friday the 13th* films. In a *Friday the 13th* movie, Jason slays everybody and anybody, more or less. It isn't that they're having sex, it's more that having sex represents the extent of their existence. Their hedonism speaks to a fundamental bankruptcy of spirituality and intellect; they've reached the end of the line, and so it is only natural that they're executed. In the pro-teenager movies, the killer represents not death incarnate, but rather the corruption of the adult world—they're all about kids creating a future that's better than their present. While Jason is never really defeated, Freddy Krueger is for all intents and purposes vanquished every time out and the *Nightmare on Elm Street* films generally conclude on a positive note.

This isn't a hard-lined binary system: some films, like Manny Coto's underrated *Dr. Giggles*, or the *Final Destination* trilogy, manage to have pro- and anti-teenager elements alike. But the general idea is that a slasher movie consists of an attitude towards its potential victims and an antagonistic villain, something *See No Evil* doesn't get. It never develops a perspective towards the victims, and with no perspective towards the victims it cannot have a perspective towards the killer. I'm pretty broad-minded, I guess—I don't believe that movies need to be populated by flesh-and-blood human beings, nor do I believe that movies need to be particularly healthy or ethical. This lack of conflict between the two worlds is fundamentally alienating, though. It doesn't matter if it's the killer or the victim(s), even a slasher movie must give us somebody with whom we can identify.

In the slasher genre, humour is OK as long as it stays on any one side of the fence. In a movie like *Jason X*, the world of the victims is kind of jokey and plastic, but Jason is a sincere creation. The silliness of the victims' environment translates well into a view that their lives are spiritually bankrupt and that Jason is justified in offing them. In *A Nightmare on Elm Street: The Dream Master*, Freddy Krueger spears and eats a screaming teen who's trapped in the form of a pizza topping. In this instance, it's Krueger who is ironically detached, and this attitude helps to accentuate his omnipotence, as well as the idea

that he has defined the way the world will operate until these guys change it. To that piece of sausage on the pizza, this isn't a laughing matter; the sincerity lies with the victims and that is the heart and soul of those films.

Not getting the basics of the genre right, Dark misapplies the humour. It should come organically from within the film, with the killer laughing at the victims or the victims laughing at themselves. In *See No Evil*, the humour comes from without, as Dark calls attention away from the characters and onto himself with cutesy visual gags. During the opening credits, there's a high-angle shot of the protagonist (Steven Vidler) waking up in his bedroom. The ceiling fan is running in the foreground and its blades overlap the credits with every swoop. Neat! He also uses a lot of elaborate, tonally-inappropriate camera movements such as having his actors wear a camera rig with the lens pointed directly at them while they move around. The idea is to convey panic and paranoia, but as soon as you see it you know why it's a technique rarely employed. His use of reverse- and fast-motion is yet another thing you should never see in a horror film—or anything outside of "Dead Like Me", for that matter.

I'm a Kubrick kid, all right? I like long, unbroken shots. This is indicative of a filmmaker not only totally confident and in control of his medium, but also interested in economy and eloquence. With Kubrick, especially, you get the impression that he is using as few shots as possible because he wants to make each one count. And indeed, each shot does. *See No Evil* is hyper-edited in a way that suggests a filmmaker with nothing to say and far too many toys with which to say it. In the supplemental DVD feature "Do You See The Sin?", Dark defends his "style" thusly: "Having been a music-video director for so long, and I still am, my movies are not very slow-moving. They are very contemporary. I understand the MTV audience, which is the audience for horror movies. The movie is fast-paced, fast-cut..." Wow, there is so much wrong with that statement. First of all, it should go without saying that editing your movie to best reach your target market is beneath contempt and turns film, an art form, into a product undifferentiated from toothpaste.

Secondly, he appears to buy into the clichés and generalizations about music-video directors and their audiences. Music-video directors, and their styles of filmmaking, are diverse. Spike Jonze (**Wax**'s "California"), Michel Gondry (**The White Stripes**' "The Denial Twist"), and Jonathan Glazer (Jamiroquoi's "Virtual Insanity") have all made one-shot videos. Of course, it's possible that Dark is stressing a distinctly "music video" style of editing in order to differentiate himself from his past as an adult filmmaker. (He's not coming from porn, you see, he's coming from the music-video world.) Third, assuming that the "MTV audience" is the primary audience for music videos *and* horror films, it does not necessarily follow that horror films should resemble music videos. Horror films tend to be "slow-paced" for good reason: deliberate pacing is often the secret to suspense. *The Shining*, *Alien*, *The Exorcist*—these are classics for a reason, *non*? Dark says he's paying homage to the slasher films of the late-seventies and early-eighties. Has he actually *seen* the slasher films of the late-seventies and early-eighties? *Halloween* and the *Friday the 13th* films are not action-packed by any stretch of the imagination. What a poser!

Dark delivers on the grue but refrains from giving the audience much in terms of T&A, a disingenuous move for an adult filmmaker, to say the least. Like Dark's aesthetic flourishes, however, the gore effects themselves feel self-consciously cute. In addition to sharing the tidy motif of "turning the sin against the sinner," the murders are so violent that their sheer tastelessness becomes its own joke.

When an axe severs an arm, Dark cuts to a close-up of the fingers convulsing from the death twitch. When a character is impaled by a hook and chain, he makes sure that we see it going through the guy's mouth. Jacob eventually plummets to his death—he crashes through an atrium thereby impaling his heart on his own ribcage. Dark rapidly zooms into Jacob's body for a terrible CGI rendering of his heart being punctured. It's smug and stupid to the point where I felt like throwing my shoe at the screen. Then it gets worse. The closing stinger has a dog pissing into Jacob's vacant eye-socket. One of the picture's ominpresent flies ends this scene by flying into the camera. Ugh!

Easily the most intolerable part of it all is Dark's buying into the "sex is death" mythos and then talking down to us about it. Through the film's high-concept premise, the alleged subtext is purged to the surface, ineffectually establishing Dark's artistic cred while feeding the ravaging masses eye-for-an-eye justice and knee-jerk anti-Christian sentiment. He's grossly underestimated the artistic potential for the genre and he has grossly underestimated the audience for slasher films. I'm sorry, but there's more to it than sexual repression and elaborate death scenes. One can only wonder: is there any experience more insufferable than being condescended to by somebody who doesn't even know what he's talking about? (**AJ**)

## THE SENTINEL
½* /****

*st.* Michael Douglas, Kiefer Sutherland, Eva Longoria, Kim Basinger
*sc.* George Nolfi, based on the novel by Gerald Petievich
*dir.* Clark Johnson

Michael Douglas in a suit gets into an affair with the wrong woman and ends up running for his life to save his career.

Again.

He's a Secret Service agent this time, Garrison, who, like Clint Eastwood's fossilized vet in *In the Line of Fire*, is a legend for saving Reagan from being shot twice, I guess. Like that character, too, he finds himself targeted in a plot to kill the President. The proverbial race against the clock is alas muted because our current real-life President is someone most U.S. citizens have probably fantasized about popping themselves (*Shooter* touches on this with a line having to do with loving the *idea* of the presidency, if not the corporeal manifestation); we learn that there's a traitor in the Service, and because Garrison fails a polygraph test (since he's having an affair with First Lady Sarah (Kim Basinger, typecast as mouth-breathing sex victim)), he becomes Suspect Number One in the investigation led by former best friend/protégé Agent Breckinridge (Kiefer Sutherland).

No stone is left unturned in either Breckinridge's "24"-cum-"CSI" machinations or *The Sentinel*'s rote, piston-repetitive script. Breckinridge even gets a rookie agent and mild love interest in vavoom Agent Marin (Eva Longoria), whose primary function is to spout rote feminist ripostes to leering peers and fulfill the passing-the-baton utility in middlebrow thrillers like this. The end is never in question and the chases and gun battles are curiously antiseptic in a manufactured-for-prime-time fashion, and *The Sentinel* makes no compelling statements about anything *en route* to shedding little light on its stock characters and single high concept. The premise that there's never been a traitor in the Treasury Department's storied ranks of selfless über-yojimbo is the most gratifying thing to emerge from the film—or at least it would be had Tom Clancy not abused it almost as poorly a decade ago. If the current *Wild Hogs* proves anything, it proves that aging boomers enjoy watching other aging boomers doing familiar

shit in three-quarter time.

I'll confess that it took me three months or so to finish watching *The Sentinel* and that it doesn't seem to matter where you cue it up from, it always comes out exactly the same: mesmerically-incomprehensible. All the elements are there, from ex-intimate-turned-worst-enemy to inter-generational relationships paralleled to no good effect, to rote action scenes choreographed like Tai Chi routines for the geriatric set—and none of it matters in the slightest, making the picture almost impossible to concentrate on for more than a couple of minutes at a time. *The Sentinel* is the longest conversation with the world's worst conversationalist: rambling, aimless, something that you've already heard a million times before and wasn't that interesting to start with. It's "Matlock" with a better tailor. The solution is solved the instant the real culprit sulks on screen and there's nothing sultry in its bedroom antics and nothing tense in its interpersonal clashes. It appears to recognize its own fatigue with the desperate insertion of meaningless interstitial montages that document a few of the threats the President receives on a daily basis. Among myriad other explanations for its ineffectiveness as a heart-thumper, because the film is about the sentinel and not the prize it's safe to say that we don't care. (Granted, when the Prez actually *is* directly in the line of fire, we still don't care.) *The Sentinel* is that rare film with absolutely no caloric value. Call it cinematic celery: it takes more energy to successfully ingest it than to turn the damned thing off and watch something else. **(WC)**

## SHORTBUS
***/****

*st.* Sook-Yin Lee, Paul Dawson, Lindsay Beamish, Justin Bond
*w./d.* John Cameron Mitchell

I put John Cameron Mitchell's *Shortbus* on my Top Ten for 2006. This was perhaps more for intent than for execution: '06 was a pretty lousy year for cinema, and I was just happy to see something from this continent that wasn't completely asleep at the switch. Still, I think it's too easy to write the movie off (as many commentators have) as pie-in-the-sky warm-fuzzies. What impressed me most about *Shortbus* was that its famous nudity and hardcore sex had not been severed from the rest of human experience. Mitchell may not be an aesthetic master, but he's onto something that few of the would-be indie rebels are: that there is no separating the person from the body, and that sex is as much a social and personal experience as it is a physical one. As the social/personal body is very likely to be a morass of guilt, doubt, confusion, and fatigue, the upbeat ending suggests a covering for a core of despair.

The plot (worked out through improvs with the rather large cast) begins predictably with a round-robin of sexual behaviour. Ex-hustler James (Paul Dawson) tapes himself performing autofellatio, dominatrix Severin (Lindsay Beamish) abuses a taunting john (and "trust fund Muppet") named Jesse (Adam Hardman), and couples counsellor Sofia (Sook-Yin Lee) has a spirited round of lovemaking with her husband Rob (Raphael Barker). The first two instances end in sadness, the third in frustration: Severin clearly hates her job and her customer; James collapses in tears after he comes; and, during a therapy session with James and his boyfriend Jamie (PJ DeBoy), it's revealed that Sofia, who seemed to us sexually content, has never had an orgasm. Extenuating circumstances make sex a trial or a mystery to all of the main characters—something that cannot be reduced or shrugged off.

A palliative must be found to bear the stress, and the characters seek it in Shortbus, a salon/theatre/orgy run by real-life famed New York scenester Justin Bond. It's here where the lost and the abandoned (and the artsy and the hip) of the city find themselves unwinding, interacting, and acting out—though it only serves as a temporary respite. One is always aware of the despair lurking at the edges of the Shortbus, as if everybody knows that the play is merely a detour from the traumatic confusion of their daily routine. From the personal lives to the collective memory of 9/11, they're trying to outrun their troubles: "It's like the 60's," states Bond, "only with less hope." This is what makes the film's attempts at tying loose ends less disappointing than it might be—there is the Vonnegut sense that we're seeing a snapshot of success as opposed to a foregone conclusion.

At any rate, the ending isn't what stays with me. What does is James' declaring that he hustled so he could learn how much he was worth, Sofia coming up with equivocal reasons for why she's sexually blocked, and Severin tearfully declaring that she's fed up with S&M and just wants a nice house and a cat. And miraculously, the way-hip milieu in which we find ourselves isn't an attempt to seem cool: the film is at once very aware of how hipster accoutrements can be a symptom of something else. Pleasure in every form is respected and mistrusted, welcomed for its good warm feelings and censured for the times when it's a half-understood metaphor for something else.

It's an interesting phenomenon: a film entirely devoted to hipster characters that does its damnedest to deprogram the cheap irony that is the hipster's stock in trade. *Shortbus* is non-judgmental where a hip kitty might be rushing to judgment; it's not trying to knock you out with its superiority, offering instead a low-pressure medium for mixed emotions. At the risk of sounding like Armond White, it's the heart-on-its-sleeve opposite number to something like *The Brown Bunny*—which, despite having been made with a thousand times the aesthetic capacity, is so utterly sure of its transgression and narcissistic in its personal focus that I'm driven back into Mitchell's waiting arms. (*The Brown Bunny* has its qualities, but it's a comparatively conventional take on personal anomie and sexual release.) *Shortbus* is far more cogent about not only the reasons people engage in sexual behaviour but also the baggage they drag into it. It's not perfect, but it's kinder and smarter than many films on the subject. (**TMH**)

## SIDEKICK
**\*\*/\*\*\*\***

*st.* David Ingram, Perry Mucci, Mackenzie Lush, Daniel Baldwin
*sc.* Michael Sparaga
*dir.* Blake Van De Graaf

It would be very easy to write off *Sidekick* as another CanCon mediocrity, as an interesting concept and some enthusiastic elbow grease sadly lacking the conceptual force to bring its ideas to life. But the basic template is so common to Canadian films that it bears analysis—and maybe reproach. *Sidekick* offers Canada's traditional cringing at power while refusing to accept its mantle, and in so doing elucidates the Great White North's default position of Power Bad. Not power in the hands of the unworthy, but power in general, meaning that anyone who tries to establish a personal set of ground rules is in danger of being tagged a bully or worse. The thought that power can be used for good—or, for that matter, can be evenly distributed with checks and balances—never crosses anyone's mind: we'd rather accept the burden of victimhood than risk making a disastrous mistake.

The "disastrous mistake" of *Sidekick* is that of nebbishy tech-boy Norman Neale (Perry Mucci), who notices that office jerk Victor Ventura (David Ingram) is mildly telekinetic and thinks he can mold him into a superhero. We know that Norman is deluded because a) he's obsessed with comic books and b) has no life of his own—a sharp contrast to the misogynistic prick Victor, who is of the world and his own selfish interests. The disaster? As Victor becomes more confident and strong in his superpowers, he has no interest in doing good—he'd prefer to take what he can and kill anyone standing in his way. Norman's power-trip-by-proxy backfires spectacularly by turning a sociopath into a living god: suddenly, he has no means of stopping the heartless monster he's unleashed on the world.

It's quite obvious that this is archetypal Canadiana, as Norman's living through Victor is like Canada's cultural dependence on America, while the undesirability of that American cultural model is taken as a given. But what's important is that rejection of America doesn't mean increased power for Canada: America is so completely identified with power that Canada—typically the inverse of its Southern sister—can't even think about having it for itself. It opposes by offering no opposition, protects its identity by leaving it vulnerable, and fights back by surrendering immediately. It doesn't take a genius to tell you that this sort of passive resistance is tactical suicide—just as it doesn't take a genius to tell you that when applied to a narrative, it becomes instant, tortuous frustration.

Writer Michael Sparaga and director Blake Van de Graaf seem like nice guys, though, and their genial nature comes forth in the movie. The filmmakers don't exactly pull their punches in depicting the double-bind, portraying the business elite as a group of unconscionable pricks, and they find a great performer in Mackenzie Lush, who assumes the role of beleaguered secretary (and object of desire) Andrea. But their conviviality masks a larger failure, i.e. the inability to fight back against injustice. In the Canadian way, they've pretty much accepted their lot and refused to ask for more, resulting in a movie in which the assumption of power also means the assumption of evil. If Canada wants a narrative film culture that's worth a damn, it's going to have to take up arms against its identified oppressors and build a future for itself. To do anything else is to accept the status quo it pretends to critique to the point of self-negation. (**TMH**)

## SILENT HILL
***¹/₂/****

*st.* Radha Mitchell, Sean Bean, Laurie Holden, Jodelle Ferland
*sc.* Roger Avary
*dir.* Christophe Gans

Christophe Gans' *Silent Hill* works as a very fine companion piece to Neil Marshall's *The Descent* in that both are gynaecological horror films that trade in feminine currency (childbirth, motherhood, and menstruation) and happen to be scary as hell. More than their female protagonists, the pictures—*Silent Hill* especially—deal fast and loose with surrealism in narrative and set design, substituting the feminine archetype for standard plot development by manufacturing a sense of real melancholy in the communion (and eventual schism) between a mother and child. Not for nothing are the only (human) male characters in the film relegated to stoic inconsequence, spectators before the mystery of the machineries, literal and emotional, of the other gender—and not for nothing again is the feeling that no matter their contribution to the dance, the motions and choreography of life are ultimately alien to them. Though the chief bogey is a masculine figure, decked out with an enormous metal helmet and a giant blade that redefines notions of "priapic" (note a moment when two of our women heroes are left to dodge the knife in a furnace room (!)), the centre of the picture's malignance is a child-stealing, witch-burning Christian priestess (Alice Krige)—single-handedly a harbinger of the slew of anti-Christian pictures in 2007 and positing *Silent Hill* as, in addition to all its other pleasures intellectual and visceral, the crest of the millennial zeitgeist. I love this movie.

Rose and Chris (Radha Mitchell and Sean Bean) lose their child (Jodelle Ferland) first to night terrors, then to an abandoned mining town, buried in ash and prone to Darkness. Chris, refusing to go along with Rose's decision to "treat" their daughter by eschewing patriarchal avenues of therapy in favour of indulging in the child's "visions," is left behind in a wholly reasonable world as the picture proper follows Rose's search for her daughter in a series of mutating, unreasonable sets. As layers of paint peel away and layers of drywall crack to show the skeletal framework beneath, *Silent Hill* betrays its obsession with the horror of aging and its attendant decay. Buddied up with a cop (Laurie Holden), Rose undermines in turn every attempt Chris makes in the parallel world to locate his missing family (the institutions of law, education, religion)—the unravelling of each quest offering a synchronous disintegration of reason and, fascinatingly, beauty. It's not the old saw of our society favouring the young and the nubile, it's an anthropological examination of why *every* society favours the young and the nubile (for its reproductive capacity, naturally), and of how the revulsion we feel towards deformity and age has little to do with amorality and a lot to do with Darwin. Civilization is the lie that binds; Nature is the truth that mortifies. By the time Rose reaches the picture's conclusion in a Cathedral as much of the Devil's part as Milton, she's endured a hallway of faceless Florence Nightingales, the terminal bedside of a demon child, and a doppelgänger mommy (Deborah Kara Unger) likewise looking to appease her unimaginable loss.

*Silent Hill* is visually stunning—its appearance a character in that every frame serves a thematic function for

Rose's descent into this women's hell. Far from distracting, it draws attention to itself because it's important to the film that we understand the nature of her surroundings and its mercurial shifts. Misread repeatedly as arbitrary, I'd offer that the picture's production design is possibly the best of a year that boasts several landmark fantasies in not only its breadth of imagination, but also its ability to guide Rose's transformation from one stage into the next. The creatures are brilliantly disgusting—nearly human but twisted just south of true; Silent Hill is up front about its intolerance for imperfection by suggesting that Hell is populated by the creatively mutilated. The film at its heart is a Clive Barker thesis on the intersection of Heaven and Hell inasmuch as Heaven and Hell are identified with ideas of beauty and ugliness, purity and corruption (note the doubling in the picture, not the least little girl Sharon and her evil, putrid twin), a mother's love and a mother's inability to let go. A primal horror film, Silent Hill is sticky in more ways than its impressive splatter effects. It digs beneath the quick, transgressing in ways wholly unexpected and possessed of an ending that's satisfyingly uncompromised. Its entire third act, in fact, surprises with the quality of sadness it's able to conjure and sustain. What's more melancholic, after all, than a woman forced to come to terms with her own mortality when faced with her daughter's own inauguration into the schizophrenic cult of womanhood? Silent Hill is a film about duality filthy with doubles, sacrifices teeming with hollow victories, and standing against the dismal tide of fear and fear mongers with just the hope of a surcease of sorrow as sword and guiding light. (**WC**)

# 16 BLOCKS
*½/****
st. Bruce Willis, Mos Def, David Morse, Cylk Cozart

sc. Richard Wenk
dir. Richard Donner

There's a lot to like about Richard Donner's ultimately simpering retread of the long-dormant corrupt-cop/asphalt-jungle genre 16 Blocks. Among the highlights is Bruce Willis' drunken, crooked detective Jack, who—sporting a pot belly, a gimpy leg, bad facial hair, flop sweat, and breath you can practically smell through the screen—makes a decision early on to be the hero at odds with ex-partner Frank (David Morse) in transporting his charge Eddie (Mos Def) the titular sixteen city blocks so that Eddie can testify against New York's finest. Standing in their way: an arbitrary time limit and a whole department of collectors for the widows and orphans club, looking to exact a little Giuliani on the suddenly-vigilante pair. Comparisons to Firewall, that other picture buried in the first quarter 2006 starring an over-the-hill tough guy, are inevitable—and revealing, too, in charting the extent to which ego allows Ford and Willis to age as action heroes (Ford: not at all; Willis: a good bit) and, consequently, how successful these films are in crafting their respective scenarios. The standard against which 16 Blocks will be held, however, is one established by the likes of Prince of the City and Serpico (or even a later Sidney Lumet like Q&A)—it's they to which Donner clearly aspires, what with the picture's setting, its admittedly spurious exposé of bad apples on the force, and at least the first hour of Willis' performance, equal parts broken-down gunsel and brown-bagging wino.

The action is sedate, the tension predicated mostly on intercutting Jack and Eddie on the lam with Frank and his henchmen on the scent, and the script pedestrian—but Willis and Mos Def have a real rapport, and their scenes together are unaffected and bright. The best single moment of the film, though, might be Eddie crying alone in the bathroom. If 16 Blocks were only as observant as this for the rest of its running time, had only focused in on the humanity and fear of its unwilling heroes and their *Logan's Run* plight in which all the representatives of order are poisoned by a crooked ideology. But it lowers itself instead, too soon and too often, to long expository exchanges between Jack and Frank, to clumsy visual metaphors (walls, elevators), to two or three too many trick moments where a gunshot shoots a surprise target or baddies knock down the wrong door, and most egregiously, to an ending so Pollyannaish that I expected a chorus of animated daisies to jump out of somebody's ass.

Since *16 Blocks* doesn't know what to do with its high concept, it decides to crack jokes about Barry White while adhering to a mantra of how a leopard can, in fact, change its spots. (How much more interesting would this picture have been if a leopard could not, in fact, change its spots?) It's a film ruined by its complete lack of conviction and follow-through—that chooses to infuse itself with some slack pseudo-mysticism about "signs" seen by wall-of-noise Eddie rather than anchor itself to the bedrock of societal decay and absolute corruption. Here, a well-conceived hostage situation on a crowded city bus becomes representative of the rest of the picture's failings: veteran cop Jack knows how to work the situation to his advantage, veteran prisoner Eddie understands the peril of being re-arrested, and then, suddenly, there's an adorable little girl, a white business man humiliated, and an impossible situation remedied in a semi-literal *deus ex machina* that renders the entire sequence pointless. *16 Blocks* is a missed opportunity. The settings are excellent and the set-ups are pretty good, too, and for long stretches, Willis and Mos Def make you very forgiving about the precariousness of their high-wire act. But then it gets desperate and goes soft. It's all well and good that Eddie wants to be a baker and Jack wants to be a good guy, but when the film actually lets them, it completes this gritty, dark, urban crime drama's evolution into a campfire love-in to which all the middlebrow are invited. It's Donner's resurrection of his *Lethal Weapon* franchise. I guess we should be glad, at least, that it's not his *Timeline*. (WC)

## SLITHER
***1/2/****

*st.* Nathan Fillion, Elizabeth Banks, Michael Rooker, Gregg Henry
*w./d.* James Gunn

Paying tribute to his Lloyd Kaufman roots with a shot in which *The Toxic Avenger* is on TV in the background, James Gunn's *Slither* is more in line with the hipster revisionism of his screenplay for Zack Snyder's *Dawn of the Dead*. Postmodernism its point, then, drying up the musty cellars somewhat of the films it riffs on, *Slither* misses when it does only because it has little resonance beyond the basic Cronenbergian sexual-parasites thing and the shopworn idea that Americans are voracious, disgusting, ignorant swine. (In truth, the one moment that really bugs me is a fairly demented rape sequence (involving more infant-menace than anything in the new *The Hills Have Eyes*) and its played-for-giggles fallout.) In place of useful sociology, it does for redneck archetypes what *Shaun of the Dead* did for workaday slobs, poking fun at the thin line between slack-jawed yokels (initiating deer season with a barn-busting hoedown) and beef-craving, slug-brained zombies (recalling that NASCAR now boasts its own brand of meat). The biggest surprise is that Gunn appears to have seen and liked *Night of the Creeps*, and that, like that film, *Slither* does what it does without sacrificing too much of its good-natured, self-deprecating sense of humour along the way.

Poor Starla (Elizabeth Banks) is married to heavy-breathing good old boy Grant (Michael Rooker) in the kind of small, backwoods community where the sheriff, Bill Pardy (Nathan Fillion), carries a torch for Starla from way back in elementary school. When Grant goes off in the woods with Brenda (Brenda James) following a night of frustrated amour with Starla, he poignantly pokes a space slug with a stick, gets impregnated with a mind-controlling parasite, makes a nest in the basement out of leaves, and buys a lot of steak. It's a long time before somebody notices that something's amiss with Grant, a gag expanded on later when a family of zombies goes after the eldest daughter (Tania Saulnier), walking like tenderloin-looking space slugs might walk if they suddenly sprouted arms and legs—the idea that the bumpkins of Podunk, USA are ridiculous, graceless cattle, moving in time with the herd. But the satire (it feels more like the kind of ribbing that male friends engage in) is without edge, and the cast is uniformly up to the task of presenting the material with the appropriate level of reverence. Except for that extended alien rape sequence, *Slither* just never feels patronizing or mean-spirited. Granted, rape should never be comfortable to watch, but it's so at odds with the tenor of the rest of the film that it's gratuitous.

The rape establishes, however, a certain lawlessness in *Slither* alongside a real interest in grotesque-ifying the American gothic in a new "household" that Grant (starting to look a lot like Belial from Frank Henenlotter's *Basket Case*—indeed, a bar in the film is called "Henenlotter's") sets up in an abandoned barn, bringing home the bacon, as it were, and spreading his seed in one explosive, crimson *guignol* of a sentient-slug ejaculation. The film is disgusting and, in its way, it's sad, too—and it's that element of the pathetic that reminded me the most of the tightrope described by Ron Underwood's cult classic *Tremors*. In both, there's a tenderness attending the treatment of its essential human relationships as they're challenged by these extreme circumstances—and in both, whenever an innocent is killed, there's never the sense of complete anonymity that would make the bloodshed not less funny, but rather damnably inconsequential. There's the girl who tries to save her little sisters in vain, the fate of the rape victim, the missing posters for dogs named "Roscoe" that start cropping up before the other shoe drops in earnest, the way that Starla plays on Grant's essential loneliness, and a final, apocalyptic *tableau* that's surprisingly affecting. By the end (especially once Starla gets a little enthusiastic in her bloodlust), the laughter starts to sound a little like hysteria—and that's a really good thing. It's possible, in fact, that *Slither*'s subtext holds a lot more than it appeared at first glance—that maybe these orally-transmitted zombies are representative of how minds are changed in our shouting culture; of our dangerous condescension to and marginalization of the red states; and of how the pods and the cult of neo-cons aren't shambling anymore. Now they've got teeth—and a real desperate taste for meat. (**WC**)

## SNAKES ON A PLANE
***/****

*st.* Samuel L. Jackson, Julianna Margulies, Nathan Phillips, Rachel Blanchard
*sc.* John Heffernan and Sebastian Gutierrez
*dir.* David R. Ellis

I tend to think that films should be able to work on their own without requiring any prior training or education on behalf of their audience. I'm against film scholarship in general, as film scholars are hardly ever sufficiently expert in anthropology, family dynamics, theology, history, psychology, sociology, biology, and so on to justify their presumed status as the definitive arbiters of culture. Because knowledge can never be definitive, it should be thrown out as a criterion in evaluating art. This isn't like the social sciences or the hard sciences, where the problems are easily identified and thus finite. Every film produces another problem to be solved, and we would need a crack team of philosopher-kings to conclusively decide if a film like *Resident Evil 2* should be preserved for future generations. And certainly, the film scholar must be able to make those kinds of decisions if he is to have any real utility to civilization. Of course, the deciding factor in choosing which films get studied and which ones don't tends to be something as subjective and arbitrary as whether or not the theorists "liked" the film in question, considerably diminishing their status as scientists. Could we even call it a science at that point? Moreover, if it's not a science, then that almost by definition means it isn't reliant on the acquisition of knowledge.

Now, if knowledge should be thrown out as a criterion for evaluating films, does that mean that you don't even need to watch the film to have an opinion on it? As soon as we establish that an absolute threshold of knowledge is necessary in order to have an opinion, we're forced to admit that knowledge is needed in order to possess an opinion. On the one hand, this is all a sneaky syllogistic trap. An opinion does not properly exist unless it is attached to a subject. If you haven't seen the film, you cannot properly claim the film as your subject. Your subject could more accurately be described as the film's trailer, title, cast, director, marketing campaign, and so on. Seeing the film could not be described as accruing knowledge at this point.

On the other hand, whenever we talk about a specific film, we are never talking about the film alone. Every individual motion picture is really its own micro-civilization, with its own laws, customs, values, and beliefs. When evaluating a film, we are really asking ourselves, "Do I want to adopt this culture as my own?" Film criticism, as I believe it ought to be done, is all about identity formation and forming your own distinct associative group. List-making has often been criticized, justifiably in some cases, for closing down all real discussion about the cinema. When done honestly, though, it can hopefully map out a person's DNA, helping them to define their identity by cherry-picking through a bin of collective experiences. I've opted to associate myself with *8½*, *Taxi Driver*, *Gummo*, and *Glen or Glenda*. I have opted not to associate myself as much with *Chinatown*, *McCabe & Mrs. Miller*, *Failure to Launch*, and, of course, *Resident Evil 2*. They're all collective experiences, pretty much all the films we've seen, but I have picked up the first four and failed to pick up the last four and that makes me a unique individual. There are going to be some you pick up and others you won't. There will be times when you'll go with the Accepted Classics, times you'll go with the high-grossing blockbusters, and others when you'll pave your own path.

My point, before I lose it, is that while you can't judge a film until you've seen it, you can judge the surrounding culture emanating from it without ever having to see it. Seeing the film is therefore on the level of accruing knowledge, helping to crystallize and clarify what you likely already knew. Now, about *Snakes on a Plane*: although I appreciate the attempts to do so, I think it may very well be pointless to try to isolate this movie from the hype surrounding its title. The title is the film and the film is the title. The two things are, for all intents and purposes, completely interchangeable. *Snakes on a Plane* is pretty much precisely what you would expect from something called "Snakes on a Plane" and as such I think it's perfectly legitimate to judge the *Snakes on a Plane* culture and decide whether or not you want to be a part of it, based exclusively on those four words. This is a clear example of where the actual film is simply another aspect of its surrounding micro-culture. Asking whether or not *Snakes on a Plane* "works" is almost beside the point. The real question is: Do you want the words "He liked *Snakes on a Plane*" chiselled onto your tombstone?

Speaking for myself, I would rather be on the side of liking *Snakes on a Plane* than not liking it, but with that said I would rather they chisel on my tombstone that I liked *Taxi Driver* or *Gummo*. *Snakes on a Plane*, as a film *and* as a title, is just plain silly, and while I do feel that the cinema should aspire to be more than merely silly, I'm not opposed to celebrating silliness as a virtue in the cinematic arts. Set in Hawaii, with a title sequence scored by Donavon Frankenreiter's sweetly lackadaisical "Lovely Day" that features lots of second-unit footage of bikini-clad babes walking around the beach, *Snakes on a Plane* is utterly harmless and inconsequential. It works on a slower tempo than most modern action/comedies, which have become loud and portentous and seem to be forcing you to have a good time at gunpoint. This has been a complaint about summer action movies for several years, but I don't think it has ever gotten as bad as it is now. Pauline Kael described the first *Star Wars* film as "a box of Cracker Jacks that's all prizes" and "like taking a pack of kids to the circus." You have to wonder how she would have responded to *Charlie's Angels: Full Throttle* or *Van Helsing*. *Snakes on a Plane* is a throwback to a more restrained age. Perhaps 1992, the year that Wesley Snipes' blissfully average "Die Hard on an Airplane" *Passenger 57* was released.

I reject the argument that *Snakes on a Plane* is not a real cult film because it was not discovered by audiences and the buzz on the blogosphere played a key role in the filmmakers re-shooting scenes to garner the film an R rating, meaning they catered to their pre-emptive fanbase. Utter bullshit on both counts. First of all, the audience that revolved around *Snakes on a Plane* did in fact discover the film, albeit only at the title stage. No, that's not how cult films are usually discovered, but discovered it was and that requirement of cult status has been conclusively satisfied. Secondly, the R-rated content amounts to not much more but a little bit of gore, a little bit of tit and the eminently quotable "I've had it with these motherfucking snakes on this motherfucking plane." You can tell that this was filmed as a PG-13 movie. It *feels* like a PG-13 movie: light, fluffy, and unapologetically targeted directly at the junior-high set.

Maybe even younger. My favourite show when I was six was "Commander USA's Groovy Movies". I saw stuff like *Bloodbath at the House of Death*, *God Told Me To* (under the title *Demon*), *Dracula's Dog*, *Q: The Winged Serpent*, *The Brood*, and *Deathquake*, though my favourite was unquestionably *Night of the Creeps*, an homage to *Plan 9 From Outer Space* by the great Fred Dekker of *Monster Squad* fame. When I turned 13, I found "Mystery Science Theater 3000" and, as Tim Burton's biopic was making the rounds at the time, I got turned on to Ed Wood and actually saw the original *Plan 9 From Outer Space*. What worked for me purely on a surface level at age 6 (killer slugs + aliens + zombies + zombie dog = awesome) was recast through a filter of ironic detachment as a MAD MAGAZINE-reading 13-year-old laughing at Wood's stuff. Yes, while watching *Snakes on a Plane*, 13-year-old boys are going to laugh at the snake-in-the-crotch gags and the "motherfucker" line, but the film's silly tone is also going to help soften the blow of the violence for the 6-year-olds, enabling them to experience action violence much the same way us normal viewers do normally without becoming too overwhelmed. Then there's the sex. There is only enough to titillate a 13-year-old, but to the 6-year-old, knowing that this is something they shouldn't be watching, this little bit of sex is enough to provide a thrill of partaking in the forbidden but not so much as to produce any particularly irresolvable feelings of guilt, like a "real" R-rated film would.

I guess it would be fair to say that my positive feelings towards *Snakes on a Plane* are rooted in a very deep nostalgia for the films of my childhood. Before Z-grade monster movies registered as camp, they were particularly tasty and relatively adventurous children's movies. I don't mean this facetiously, but movies like this provided me with my first taste of cinematic greatness. The small doses of violence and especially sex in the B-movie genre provided me with something that children-directed entertainment never could: the idea that there is an entire world of experience beyond my own. I guess having that kind of childhood makes me feel somewhat privileged; those parents who only let their kids watch kids movies seem to me to have irreparably clipped their wings, but it also makes me feel particularly protective of a film like *Snakes on a Plane*. It encapsulates, near-perfectly, something integral to my person that I don't think I ever want to lose. Something I want to pass down through the generations. You know: the Z-grade monster movie. It may be particularly sick to say so, but *Snakes on a Plane* and films like it may be the medium where violence can divorce itself of any moral dimension and purely exist as entertainment. It's a monster movie for kids, and as such has a distinctly innocent connotation.

If they both haven't left theatres by the time you read this, I would strongly suggest all "children of the '80s" go see *Monster House* and this as a double feature. Neither film really captures the actual '80s, only my memory of the films from the decade. A pressboard of stuff like *Poltergeist*, *Halloween*, *The 'Burbs*, and maybe even a little of *The Monster Squad* (or at least *The Goonies*), *Monster House* celebrates suburbia by blackening it as a haven

for monsters, ghosts and serial killers, even explicitly (perhaps *too* explicitly for my tastes)—equating such bogeys with the encroachment of adulthood: a notion perfectly reflective of that of a wide-eyed film-drunk kidlet like myself. *Snakes on a Plane*'s chief influences are considerably more banal. I see it as being more a product of post-post-Vietnam jingoism. The film does not have Sylvester Stallone, Chuck Norris, Arnold Schwarzenegger, or any close substitute (Samuel L. Jackson's cop is simply not the same thing), but it seems to exist in roughly the same universe.

The monsters here, the snakes, don't represent the encroachment of adulthood like in *Monster House*, but rather the encroachment of a foreign element on hallowed American ground. Like the predator in *Predator* (which casually became confused with the guerrillas who were supposed to be the villains), the snakes have a special monochrome vision and, more notably, like the gremlins in *Gremlins* (which represented an Asian element sullied by American jingoism and arrogance), they're sneaky bastards knowing enough to cut off the electric wiring of the airplane controls and pop out unexpectedly to kill their victims. The snakes were put on the plane by an Asian gangster looking to kill off a (white surfer boy) witness, and later we discover that the snakes are not of North American origin, making the production of enough anti-venom near impossible. These exotic snakes are clearly a manifestation of American xenophobia.

There are no significant tensions between black and white in the film. Yes, Jackson takes on the role of protector of the white surfer boy and the "motherfucker" line plays into white-oriented empowerment fantasies of blacks. And no, black and white sexual relations are never consummated and only formed between black men and white women. But all that aside, blacks and whites are seen as part of the same collective American culture, a notion fully attuned to 1980s racial norms. Black is OK and, generally speaking, equally American to White. Asian and Latin American are not. Asia and Latin America represent alien cultures that are trying to sully the purity of Black/White America. Still, I don't see the film as racist toward Asians, or rather, it's not racist in the usual way. In *Snakes on a Plane*, the distinctly phallic, sensual qualities of snakes symbolize a threat of miscegenation that recasts the Asian man as a sexual being in a way that we never really saw in the actual films of the '80s. One of the passengers in the film is an Asian kickboxer immediately recognized by a male flight attendant, who demonstrates "some of his moves" in the process of hitting on him. The kickboxer replies, in straightforward, unaffected English, with little more than a raised eyebrow and a guarded brush-off. Inexplicably and unfortunately, the kickboxer doesn't fight any of the snakes, making us wonder why they even bothered to introduce him while reinforcing the notion that this is an "us" against "them" conflict. And yet it's a nice scene, even somewhat progressive in terms of screen depictions of Asians (if not so much for homosexuals). His culture seems to be preserved from appropriation by hayseed honkies, the flight attendants attempt towards mimicking his fighting style is laughable, while at the same time equating martial arts as a legitimate sport that the attendant appears to celebrate more for the athletic ability required (and the hunky athletic men involved in it) than for any particular exotic quality.

Early on, the film explicitly ties death in with *la petite mort* through killing its victims with these venomous phallic symbols. A couple goes into the airplane's bathroom to have sex and the snakes lunge at them. They pound against the door and scream while an older stewardess smiles and makes some snide, jealous comments about them joining the Mile High Club. The first thing the snakes bite is a breast. Their next victim (male) gets bit in the bare crotch when trying to use the bathroom, further reinforcing the notion of snake as phallus. Finally, when the snakes make their way outside the bathroom, one slithers under the clothes of a napping fat woman, who expresses sensual pleasure at its touch. By appropriating the slasher movie convention of the sex drive being borne of a more primal death drive, the film helps to further neutralize the volatile racist content of its origins. It reminds us that these characters are wholly inviting of this "Asian invasion."

Don't get me wrong, though: I'm likely making a mountain out of a molehill here. Since *Snakes on a Plane* contains a multiracial cast, it can't help but say *something* about race; and since it contains Asians, it can't help but say *something* about screen depictions of Asians. But the film is ultimately not important or heavy enough for any of this to really accrue any real significance. Most of the characters, the principal ones included, are barely developed and at all times are clearly second banana to the very fact that the film has snakes on a plane. One of the funny things that screenwriters John Heffernan and Sebastian Gutierrez have done in developing the script is give some of the one-note characters a second note. For example, the womanizing, self-absorbed rapper also has obsessive-compulsive disorder. The film also anthropomorphizes the snakes with mildly distinguished personalities, again very much like the gremlins in *Gremlins*. No two seem exactly the same and they have a ringleader of sorts, a giant boa constrictor substituting for *Gremlins'* Stripe. This is level-two screenwriting.

Alas, irreverence giveth and it taketh away. Though he may have overstated his case, director Gil Kenan tapped into something pure with *Monster House*, and this could only be credited to a conscious mining of his predecessors and understanding of the material's potential subtext. *Snakes on a Plane* simply doesn't take itself that seriously. It seems to have more or less unconsciously regurgitated '80s action movie elements without preserving their subversive (relative to us liberal-minded filmgoers) punch or re-contextualizing them in any significant way. While *Snakes on a Plane* uses '80s-era xenophobia as a means of giving Asian men back their sexual charge, the film doesn't recast this as either a critique or celebration of American military interventionism. One of the things that is particularly disappointing about *Snakes on a Plane* is that it offers no catharsis or satirical perspective towards the recent airline regulations restricting the carrying of gels or liquids on-board. The film could have poked fun at the Culture of Fear in the United States post-September 11. It seemed to suggest that airline restrictions could plausibly extend beyond fear of everyday objects like water bottles, to absurdly exotic ones like poisonous snakes. Next it seems they'll forbid marshmallows (under the possible pretense that they could pass for plastic explosives) and feral Capuchin monkeys. Alas, there is no indication that the filmmakers have ever heard of September 11th or the terrorist attacks on America in the last five years. It is entirely free of any subtext along those lines.

*Snakes on a Plane* is an apolitical film sprung from intrinsically political material — the very worst case. Political content has a lot of weight (which, when combined with velocity, provides momentum — the ideal of the cinema) but is limited in its specificity. A truly political film can never quite be truly universal; it's stuck in a specific time and place. The political origins of *Snakes on a Plane* keep it from ever attaining that universal quality, yet the lack of consciousness as to these origins bleeds out all their potential power. The results are more or less enjoyable on their own terms, but ultimately rather sterile and inert. One of the things the experience taught me, or at least reinforced for me, is that it's imperative that filmmakers have an idea as to the ramifications of their material. The problem isn't just that *Snakes on a Plane* is lazy, and it's not just that the material lacks universal applicability. More than anything, it's that *Snakes on a Plane* is a purely right-brain exercise. After they had their title, it seems they were afraid to introduce any degree of introspection lest they "mess" it up.

Obviously, I'm a critic and not an anthropologist and I'm evaluating the film based on my own values and standards. But what kind of people would accept *Snakes on a Plane* as their holy text? Likely people satirizing the very idea of a film forming their holy text, I would think. The film is thin and forgettable, and a vote for *Snakes on a Plane* suggests that the cinema can never evolve beyond the thin and forgettable. Ironic detachment aside, the *Snakes on a Plane* cultists reserve a real hate for movies that attempt to do something other than showing snakes on a plane. It's nihilistic and rather reprehensible. In some key ways, however, I find this lack of significance very refreshing. Inspired perhaps by the film version of Tom Clancy's novel The Hunt for Red October, action pictures in the mid-nineties started to come up with more plausible scenarios featuring more plausible heroes and villains. These pictures attempted to provide the same thrills and chills as their goofier predecessors under a guise of pseudo-political middlebrow respectability and a bleakly serious shredded-wheat aesthetic. Watching these movies was sort of like eating broccoli-flavoured ice cream. I particularly loathed *Executive Decision* and *Air Force One*; just typing their titles is enough to get my blood boiling. As that wonderful title clearly indicates, *Snakes on a Plane* puts on no such airs.

Some pre-emptive critics such as Aemilia Scott in her essay "Hissy Fit" for SALON.COM apparently find this transparency alarming, going so far as to quote cultural philosopher Theodor Adorno's observation that "movies and radio need no longer pretend to be art." The complaint makes absolutely no sense to me. Assuming we can agree on some concrete and conclusive definition of what exactly "art" is, and assuming that *Snakes on a Plane* ain't it, doesn't this naked admission of artlessness represent progress? I mean, that's a good thing, isn't it, that "trash" no longer pretends to be "art"? I personally find the *Air Force One* Republicans, meaning those who feel that *Air Force One* best encapsulates their personal identity, far more reprehensible than those who adopt the apolitical nihilism of the *Snakes on a Plane* culture. Seeking sustenance in *Air Force One* has an irresolvable degree of finality to it. With the *Snakes on a Plane* cultists, there is at least the hope that they will one day wake up to strangely vacant lives and turn to something good to fill up the hole. The difference between *Snakes on a Plane* and *Air Force One* is the difference between preferring the coliseum to the cathedral and mistaking the coliseum FOR the cathedral. Relatively speaking, *Snakes on a Plane* haters, you have bigger fish to fry. (**AJ**)

## STRANGER THAN FICTION
**\*\*\*/\*\*\*\***

*st.* Will Ferrell, Maggie Gyllenhaal, Dustin Hoffman, Emma Thompson
*sc.* Zach Helm
*dir.* Marc Forster

Harold Crick (Will Ferrell) is a thinly-sketched IRS agent who obsessively measures out his life in coffee spoons. One day he hears the stentorian, patrician voice of his own personal narrator, reclusive author Kay Eiffel (Emma Thompson), providing him an interiority with Douglas Adams-like serendipitous surreality. Marc Forster's *Stranger Than Fiction* even winks at the Adams connection with a sentient wristwatch and a moment where Crick's apartment gets demolished, Arthur Dent-like, by an uncommunicated work order. It also features sudden, unexpected love at the end of the universe with Crick's opposite, a free spirit baker named Ana (Maggie Gyllenhaal) who falls under the eye of Crick's glum audit and, as literature professor Jules Hilbert (Dustin Hoffman) informs Crick, only hates him until she loves him if Crick's narrator is writing a romantic comedy. The struggle within the film is the same as the struggle without, then, as Crick tries to determine whether or not Eiffel's calm (and, as it happens, excellently-written) exposition will result in his poignant death or—good for him, bad for us—in his resurrection as a bland, non-descript leading man in another piece too frightened to allow itself the most appropriate ending. One way leads to a surprise masterpiece that soars on the chemistry (surprise again) between Ferrell and Gyllenhaal—the other leads to a film that's a lot better than I expected it to be, weighed down by a resolution that it itself comments on as equivocal, cowardly, and disappointing. To crib the analysis of Prof. Hilbert, *Stranger Than Fiction* is just "okay."

*Stranger Than Fiction* paints itself into an obscure corner by being a comedy that will disappoint highbrow and lowbrow audiences equally while its virtues might be lost on the middlebrow, however reluctant may be to dismiss it offhand. As she struggles to determine the method of Crick's demise, Eiffel tells the story of seeing a picture of a woman who's leapt to her death and commenting on the beatific expression on her face while around her is arrayed a halo of her blood and broken limbs. When the movie recreates that image towards the end, it raises all manner of questions about life and the end of it—and, more, about art (and eternity) versus the relative smallness of an individual's day-to-day. (In that respect, it raises the spectre of John Frankenheimer's *The Train*, of all things.) What sacrifice is worth erecting a monument to art and immortality? There's a rhetorical question posed at the end of the film that if Crick goes willingly to his death in order to honour a work of great art, isn't he the kind of guy we should want to keep around? And the difficult answer is that his life has no greater significance if he doesn't—that Christ Himself would have a different profile had God levitated Him off the cross in the nick of time with a series of half-hearted contrivances and hand-wringing justifications.

The question arises as to whether knowing that it doesn't have the muscle to be exceptional excuses *Stranger Than Fiction* from being disappointing and pandering—realizing at the same time that the only reason anyone would bother to ask the question is that the rest of *Stranger Than Fiction* has proven so oddly affecting. Hoffman, grooved into existential detective roles now with this and *I [Heart] Huckabees*, turns in an effortless a pastiche of tenured urban professorship, and Thompson, pale and jittery, is fine as a writer stricken with a decade-long bout of writer's block. Both pull off the trick of conveying subtlety and complexity at the same time, but it's Ferrell and Gyllenhaal who do the Carrey/Winslet tango—their scenes together are alchemical. Forster's penchant for magic realism finds full flower in the *Fight Club*-inspired graphics detailing the course of Crick's obsessive counting (again simultaneously broad, subtle, and complex), while Zach Helm's screenplay is literate up to and including its pale resolution. Just as *Fight Club* never turned a profit, however, the great irony of *Stranger Than Fiction*'s equivocal ending is that it's not likely to be a box-office bonanza in its current form and that, lacking the courage of its convictions, it's also doubtful that the film will acquire a half-life as a flawed yet

respected, oft-revisited cult classic in the mode of *The Truman Show* or, as it happens, *Fight Club*. It's a smart film indicated by a failure of nerve; a backhanded compliment to call it the first real disappointment of the season. (WC)

## STRANGERS WITH CANDY
*½/****

st. Amy Sedaris, Stephen Colbert, Paul Dinello, Ian Holm
sc. Stephen Colbert & Paul Dinello & Amy Sedaris
dir. Paul Dinello

It may be churlish to hold a film to the standards of a TV show I recently panned, but comparing "Strangers with Candy" the series to *Strangers with Candy* the movie reveals a massive gulf between the two in both wit and style. The show at least had a sensibility and an idea of what it was satirizing, and it always delivered the goods; if those goods were not to my liking, it wasn't for lack of trying. But the stillborn film version has neither a sense of craft nor a reason for being: apparently thrown together over a kegger weekend, it's horribly-paced, ugly to look at, and mostly rehashes the broader points of a sitcom that had moved on from its basic premise by the time it reached its final season. *Strangers with Candy* is neither the movie fans were waiting for nor an attractive intro for neophytes, and will most likely be cable filler before it shuffles off into well-deserved obscurity.

Once again we have Jerri Blank (Amy Sedaris), the 47-year-old "boozer, user, and loser" who wishes to redeem herself after a lifetime of prison and prostitution. Returning home to discover her father (Dan Hedaya, no match for the original Guy Blank, Roberto Gari) bedridden and paralyzed from news of her transgressions, she goes back to high school hoping to rouse him from his stupor. Meanwhile, Principal Onyx Blackman (Greg Hollimon) has misallocated funds and needs something to show for it, thus he rests his hopes on the upcoming science fair. Roger Beekman (Matthew Broderick), the ringer brought in to lend the competition "pizzazz," subsequently drives a wedge between science teacher Chuck Noblet (Stephen Colbert) and art teacher/Noblet's furtive gay lover Geoffrey Jellineck (Paul Dinello). For her part, Jerri sees the fair as a chance to prove herself in the eyes of her catatonic father.

So instead of inflating the concept or covering new ground, the regulars return to the scene of the crime and set up camp—to the degree that you're damned whether you know the series or not. Aside from some new faces (many of the show's cast members had grown too old to reprise their teenager roles) and Noblet's vocational shift to teaching science, anyone who's watched "Strangers with Candy" has seen this all before—only with better form and a higher density of laughs. And if you're not familiar with the lay of the program, the movie is too limp and inert to offer much incentive to catch up. It's little more than a glorified trophy for the creators, an attempt to say they managed to get a feature film out of their cult hit rather than do anything substantial once they got the green light.

It's sad, because the brilliance of the performers still manages to poke through the hideous surface and badly-timed jokes. Sedaris simply can't be stopped as the brutal, lascivious Jerri—often she's the only cinematic thing in the frame. Colbert, likewise, is suitably put-upon despite the narrative's truncation of his relationship with Dinello, and Hollimon again shines as the childish megalomaniac Blackman, who was always the best thing about the series, anyway. They deserve better than to struggle through the flat script, especially as they suffer at their own hands. *Strangers with Candy* is a film with no point-of-view beyond the rote recitation of the show's basic

parameters, from people who don't feel the need to stretch when they know that their fanbase will lap up whatever they give them. (**TMH**)

## SUPERMAN RETURNS
****/****

*st.* Brandon Routh, Kate Bosworth, James Marsden, Kevin Spacey
*sc.* Michael Dougherty & Dan Harris
*dir.* Bryan Singer

The saddest, most desperately lonesome and melancholy mainstream film in recent memory, Bryan Singer's *Superman Returns* is about loss and, as a Scrabble board early in the picture denotes, alienation. It's about fathers and sons and, by extension, why so many of our mythologies are about sons divorced from fathers who spend the rest of their lives, nay, the rest of eternity striving for impossible reunions. Prometheus is mentioned by name while Atlas, Christ, and Lucifer are referenced in image, Singer's transition from fallen Titans to fallen Angels an ineffably graceful symbolic examination of where, exactly, comic book martyrs and gods (of which Superman is both) place in the modern spiritual pantheon. Superman is a figure at a juncture in the middle of pagan and Christian just as he's become something like a transitional icon bridging science and religion, classic comics and the modern superhero era, and Americana and the Wasteland. In the film, Superman is a character warring between what he wants and the destiny his father has charted for him—and aren't we all. When a child in *Superman Returns* takes a picture with his cell phone that we recognize as the cover for Superman's debut, 1938's "Action Comics" No. 1, it's at once bemused and in love with Richard Donner's original vision of the hero, but most of all it's eloquent in its assured, maybe even prickly, recognition of where we were and what we've become.

In that loss of innocence, that black stain of experience, Singer tells his story of Superman/Clark Kent (Brandon Routh, doing a mean, if superficial, Christopher Reeve impersonation)—returned to Earth following a five-year absence during which he was searching for his demolished home planet—spending his first dawn back burying a huge chunk of ruin at his parent's Smallville farmhouse and remembering the day he discovered he could fly. It's weird, uncommented-upon, and poetic (you can imagine that the Kents' acreage is littered with their boy's morbid toy collection), and Singer's decision to retain John Williams' stirring theme music and Marlon Brando's recorded, but unused, monologues from the 1978 film further instil the piece with nostalgia while defining "nostalgia" as a phenomenon that's laced with regret.

Evil real estate developer Lex Luthor (Kevin Spacey), last seen trying to make beachfront property in Nevada, then bargaining for emperorship of Australia, resurfaces, too, after half a decade in the slammer that earned him the hard-won philosophy that "No matter what my gifts, they were worthless against a carton of cigarettes and a metal shiv in my pocket." He's nasty where Superman and love interest Lois Lane (Kate Bosworth), who's found a companion (James Marsden) and motherhood in the intervening years, are tortured and conflicted. The movie has been described as a throwback, and in its prioritizing of character development over action set-pieces, it is. But more to the point, *Superman Returns* is about the toll the last quarter-century has taken on the generation that first believed a man could fly. It's no accident that the climax of the picture is a moment where he can't anymore.

Watch for the way that outer space (visited more often here than in the previous films combined) dissolves into the glow stars that still cling to Clark's childhood ceiling; the way that baseball is resuscitated America's central pastime; or the way that Singer cuts every cornball moment with a little humour at the expense of our childish hunger for it (like Lois sliding down a plastic slide, or a little boy's asthmatic wheeze off-camera). We're invited to laugh knowingly at our craving for innocence, which, by the very act of it, reminds us of the emotional Eden we've left behind. Were the film all whiz-bang, I think it would be much easier to dismiss a visceral response to it. Note how *Superman*'s "Can You Read My Mind" romantic number is transformed into a dangerous waltz between a woman contemplating betraying a good, brave man and a jealous ex-boyfriend using everything in his arsenal to lure her. Called a "boy scout" in the earlier films, the Man of Steel is referred to as a "selfish god" in this one by Luthor, and the transformation from saint to sinner is encapsulated just that neatly. But then there's the moment when Superman says, "You say that the world doesn't need a saviour, but when I listen to it, all I hear are people crying out for one," and everything that's simple about this film as allegory falls away.

*Superman Returns* is a grand thing: an emotional and provocative, spiritual and intellectual, pop and arthouse, and above all mature film about *this* character, an alien, out-of-place and utterly alone, who, when he gets sick, can't even receive a visit from his mother. Singer uses Milton's mnemonic play of "sun" and "Son" to wondrous visual use, porting Gyorgi Ligeti's "Lux Aeterna" in one magisterial moment lifted directly from *2001: A Space Odyssey*, suggesting almost subliminally the link between cinematic fathers and godheads and Singer's response to them from atop their shoulders. He's constantly expanding the central theme of paternal/filial relationships to creators and re-creators (modern and post-modern). To say that the film is assured is an understatement—better to say that despite being almost embarrassingly personal, the movie remains a potent entertainment. Its action sequences are exceptionally-paced, easy to follow, move the plot, and develop the characters. Its sets and costumes are impeccable, and if the performances are more iconographic than emotional, that perceived deficiency I choose to regard as a conscious choice on Singer's part to populate his temple with new archetypes. Spacey is fantastic (even if Parker Posey as his moll is no more complicated than Valerie Perrine's identically-functioning Miss Teschmacher from the first two films): he's the foil and, remarkably, he's the character with whom the audience identifies. Singer is a poet of the devil's part, of course, but I think he knows it. That makes *Superman Returns* "Paradise Lost" for Generation X, and damned if it can't almost bear the weight of that comparison on its sober blue shoulders. (**WC**)

DIRECT - TO - VIDEO
## SUPERMAN II (THE RICHARD DONNER CUT)
***/****
*st.* Gene Hackman,Christopher Reeve, Ned Beatty, Jackie Cooper
*sc.* Mario Puzo, David Newman and Leslie Newman
*dir.* Richard Donner

SPOILER WARNING IN EFFECT. A would-be victim of its own *London After Midnight*-esque mystique, "The Richard Donner Cut" of *Superman II* is marginally superior to Richard Lester's mutilation, but mitigating circumstances prevent it from being a totally viable alternative. Reconstructed from suppressed outtakes with due diligence (if a journeyman sensibility) according to pre-Lester drafts of the screenplay, the film follows the same basic storyline, though it's a little more efficiently plotted. (While a few Lester bits remain, there is almost certainly less

Lester-generated footage here than there is Donner-generated footage in the theatrical version.) Gone is the Eiffel Tower set-piece, replaced by a charming sequence better allied — aesthetically speaking — with the previous *Superman* in which Lois tries to call Clark's bluff by jumping out a window of THE DAILY PLANET's headquarters; now the weapon of mass destruction responsible for freeing the three supervillains from the Phantom Zone is an errant missile from the climax of the original, which is clever but probably made more sense before they transposed the dopey turning-back-time conceit from the second film onto the first. (More on that later.)

All of Marlon Brando's footage has been restored (meaning that all of Susannah York's footage has been elided), setting the stage for the paternal/filial *Sturm und Drang* of *Superman Returns*: composited as a floating head in an appropriately Zardozian fashion, Brando as Jor-El admonishes Superman for wanting to live as a mortal ("Will there ever come a time when I've served enough?" Supes asks rhetorically), then literally sacrifices his soul to rehabilitate Kal-El; as prophesied, then, the father becomes the son. Haste—Clark turns in his superhero badge, gets a rude awakening, and dons the tights again—still makes waste of this development, but a new cross-cutting structure that more methodically parallels Superman's sojourn as a human with the trio of Zod, Non, and Ursa seizing control of the planet seems bravely suspicious of status quo domesticity in a Nero-fiddles-while-Rome-burns kind of way. (Is it a coincidence that Donner waited until he was 55 to settle down?) Too, the fact that Lois now sleeps with Superman instead of Clark takes the vaguely puritanical tang out of Superman renouncing his powers.

Unfortunately, the many virtues of this remix are overshadowed by two significant lapses in judgment, one ultimately pardonable, the other guaranteed to leave you livid. Although Lois Lane's unmasking of Clark Kent's true identity in a Niagara Falls hotel room is a disengaging Frankenstein of screen tests for Margot Kidder and Christopher Reeve shot months apart with discontinuous hair and wardrobe, it's at least conceptually preferable to Lester's prosaic 'fireplace' reveal. But what inexorably harms this redux of *Superman II* is the recycling of *Superman*'s infamous *deus ex machina*, which in context gives off the impression that Superman rewinds the present again largely to repair his tarnished image (the citizens of Metropolis misinterpret his decampment to the Fortress of Solitude during the Battle Royale as an act of cowardice) and causes Supes to look that much more uncharacteristically vindictive when he returns to the truck-stop for a rematch with his assailant, since in this scenario the guy never laid a hand on Clark. It also puts Zod and co. back in the Phantom Zone, thus we're left to presume that he traveled back even farther than before. Wouldn't that mean there's now a Superman doppelgänger roaming around, à la *Primer*? Does this undo Jor-El's demise? Shouldn't Superman have used this get-out-of-jail-free card *before* the big showdown if it were so readily at his disposal? Fool me once, fellas, shame on me; fool me twice, shame on you. (**BC**)

**SYMPATHY FOR LADY VENGEANCE (see: *LADY IN THE WATER*)**

# T

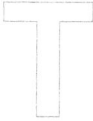

## TALLADEGA NIGHTS: THE BALLAD OF RICKY BOBBY
***½/****

*st.* Will Ferrell, John C. Reilly, Sacha Baron Cohen, Gary Cole
*sc.* Will Ferrell & Adam McKay
*dir.* Adam McKay

I feel about Will Ferrell the way I feel about Jack Black: that they're good second-fiddles on occasion, but put them in a lead role and my eyeballs roll into the back of my head. Imagine my surprise that *Talladega Nights: The Ballad of Ricky Bobby* (hereafter *Talledega Nights*) showcases Ferrell's Faulknerian idiot man-child to great advantage in a vehicle that's sharp, smart, topical, and funny. It's an exuberant satire in every sense of the abused term—a twisting of familiar elements into grotesquerie that brings to light the essential absurdity of the familiar, sketching a portrait of the divide between the blue states and the red states with a feather bludgeon. It's this year's *Harold & Kumar Go To White Castle*, doing for anti-intellectual animals and effete eggheads what that film did for the racism leveled in popular culture at "favoured" minorities. This is the finest document yet of the special brand of idiocy that compels our noble Congress to rename French Fries and French toast in their commissary or, on the opposite end of the spectrum, the air of *noblesse oblige* that taints the highbrow's mincing, *faux*-outraged response. Credit *Talladega Nights* for this: no one's necks have ever been redder than those sported by these self-described retards, and no brainy gay Frenchmen have ever been this gay and French.

Ricky Bobby (Ferrell), shot out of his mother's womb in the backseat of a car, grows up with just a couple of visits from his unrepentant daddy (Gary Cole), from whom he picks up the all-American mantra of "If you ain't first, you're last." With this as his only guiding principle, Ricky takes the wheel of a failing NASCAR team, marries an unbelievably hot pageant princess (Leslie Bibb) whom he screws over a family banquet of KFC and Taco Bell, and sires violent, ill-bred sons named Walker and Texas Ranger. Best friend Cal (John C. Reilly) attempts to bring Ricky out of a coma by telling of the time he posed for PLAYGIRL and "spread his ass and everything," and pit chief Luscious (Michael Clarke Duncan) tries to lever a knife out of Ricky's leg using another knife. Meanwhile, the bad guy, Jean Girard (Sacha Baron Cohen), reads Camus while he's driving and has uncommented-upon dinner parties with Elvis Costello and Mos Def. His "gayness" causes Ricky to faint, but not before picking up the gauntlet and challenging his ideological nemesis to a showdown at the titular Talladega 500. That it all goes down to the tune of Pat Benatar's "We Belong" says it with that hint of a subversive idea that Ricky actually enjoys a character arc in *Talladega Nights*, starting in bestial nationalism, proud imbecility, and base homophobia, and ending in what looks like enlightenment. Forget Oliver Stone's aimless movie-of-the-week *World Trade Center*: this is the picture that offers hope for reconciliation amongst the hawks and doves post-9/11.

There's a moment early on in *Talladega Nights* where a ticket taker at a NASCAR event waxes philosophical; I was shocked to observe I was the only one who chuckled, which made me wonder if it was, in fact, intended as a joke. The lack of response didn't strike me as a failed gag, but as a sobering glimpse at my own bigotry towards race fans. I thought for certain they were hanging this guy out to dry for having emotional intelligence—that a nation populated, at least part, by brutal, ignorant, arrogant thugs would laugh in a certain way here and then later when the Geneva Convention is mocked (like our administration has mocked it) or, moreover, when Ricky declares *Highlander* the "Oscar winner for most awesomest movie ever." But then Cohen's Girard is introduced as a liberal so far to the left that his imposition of lifestyle and privilege become as dire as a fascist fist, clarifying that there's indeed a thin line between assholes who quote William Blake and assholes who quote **Journey**.

As Ricky burns in the crucible of his invisible fire, he invokes every spoke of the modern theological wheel ("Help me baby Jesus, help me Jewish God, help me Allah, help me Tom Cruise"), putting them on an equal plane on the one hand and actually having the wherewithal to talk about them on the other. The picture finds a way to equate other things, too (Don Shula, that Japanese kid who eats a lot of hot dogs, and Rue McClanahan, for instance), that don't often find themselves mentioned in the same breath—it's stream-of-consciousness and non sequitur as Zen koan, almost, buried in *Talladega Nights* amongst uses of the word "chubby" as a noun, Crystal Gayle concert T-shirts, a Member's Only jacket worn without irony, and enough references to erections to fill an architecture textbook. It's the high and the low, then, sure to offend the middle but putting its stake in (pitching its tent?) as the best, most canny illustration of the current culture war. It doesn't take a lot of squinting to recognize the personae of both "Bubba" and "Dubya" mashed into good-ol'-boy Ricky Bobby: stupid and smart; venal and noble; feckless and moral. *Talladega Nights* is a celebration of the dysfunction of being an American—of the possibility of being simultaneously proud and mortified of ourselves, of being "number one" and "last" at the same time, and, at the end of the day, of an ability, almost unique, to nearly live up to our best intentions. **(WC)**

## THE TENANTS
**½/****

*st.* Dylan McDermott, Snoop Dogg, Rose Byrne, Seymour Cassel
*sc.* David Diamond, based on the novel by Bernard Malamud
*dir.* Danny Green

Parts of *The Tenants* are very good indeed. Most of them involve the live-wire presence of Snoop Dogg, who, as an angry black writer named Willie Spearmint, acts as conscience/spur/romantic rival to Jewish novelist Harry Lesser (Dylan McDermott). While Snoop doesn't quite convince as a product of the film's '70s milieu, he's right on the money as a resentful, easily-provoked hard case seeking humiliating assistance from Lesser. Every time he has to flip-flop on some bit of respect or contempt for the cringing whitey, he shoots the movie straight through the ceiling—so much so that *The Tenants* often seems to have more to it than it actually does. As it stands, the film doesn't know what to do with source novelist Bernard Malamud's mash-up between a dithering Jew and a motor-mouthed black with nothing in common except their oblivious monomania for writing.

Lesser is the only tenant left in a tenement slum that landlord Levenspiel (Seymour Cassel) would dearly like to demolish. In fact, the 'lord keeps showing up to alternately heckle and bribe the blocked Lesser, who is dragging his feet on a follow-up to his previous book (an artistic and commercial flop) and won't leave before birthing his literary baby. Squatting in a nearby vacant room, Spearmint arrives on the scene determined to bang out a magnum opus revolving around black oppression. The two open up an uneasy relationship: Spearmint asks for an opinion on his work, flies into a rage when he hears the truth, and then comes back for more, eventually entangling the pair in each other's worlds. This hits a bump once Lesser catches a glimpse of Spearmint's bragged-about white girlfriend Irene (Rose Byrne). It's love at first sight for him, which spells disaster for their respective relationships with Willie.

What keeps the film from greatness is its lack of a thesis. The two writers are complementary—there's an obvious symmetry between them, but it's up in the air as to what that could be. Aside from being painfully serious about their manuscripts, one is eternally passive while the other raises the roof. Just as you think it's illustrating a point, the ground shifts and you can't get a grip—and that's not subtlety, it's just unsureness. If *The Tenants* is about anything, it's about the way that certain artist-types use everything as an excuse to avoid communication, with the pair of them failing to give Irene the attention she needs. But the introduction of the political element demands a little more consideration, and the film doesn't provide much on this front beyond an evocative scramble that pushes your buttons while leaving you wishing for some order.

Still, an evocative scramble is more than most movies provide—there are nuggets of confrontation in *The Tenants* as strong as any I've seen this year. And again, Snoop Dogg deserves much of the credit: his defensive, disappointed anger adds up to one of the most arresting performances I've ever seen. Without him, the film is a literary exercise with a couple of famous people, as McDermott and Byrne—though genuinely fine, both—don't have the fire or edge to sell themselves as anything other than actors playing parts. Snoop makes the movie out of the ordinary by pouring his heart into the material; instead of calling its bluff, he winds up lending it credibility. Had he been matched with a similar personality, this might have had even more power, but as it stands, he forces you to consider the inner life of his character far more than the filmmakers do. (**TMH**)

**THE TEXAS CHAINSAW MASSACRE: THE BEGINNING (see: *AKEELAH AND THE BEE*)**

**THANK YOU FOR SMOKING (see: *INSIDE MAN*)**

PREVIOUSLY UNPUBLISHED
**13 TZAMETI**
**\*\*1/2/\*\*\*\***
*st.* Georges Babluani, Aurélien Recoing, Pascal Bongard, Fred Ulysse
*w./d.* Gela Babluani

The lead-up to and aftermath of *13 Tzameti*'s main event are both pretty underwhelming. In the case of the former, an evocation of Georgian immigrant desolation is upstaged by some clumsy exegesis and sketchy characterizations; in the case of the latter, the tying-up of loose ends proves rather facile and largely unbelievable. But the centre portion—featuring a way-illegal gambling operation in which no-hopers play games of Russian Roulette—is bloody gripping no matter how you slice it. It's for that reason that you sort of forgive the sins of the early portions, which set up the blank-slate protagonist so that we might better project ourselves into his shoes when the guns come out and bodies start dropping. Art it's not, but a nasty good time it most certainly is. Still, the finely-detailed mechanics of the tournament make you wish there were more to this thing, which is on the same facile-topical plane as *American Gangster*—if a damned sight better and more resonant.

The milieu is that of a group of Russian workers labouring on the roof of a neglected house. Said house's owner, Jean-François Godon (Phillippe Passon), is a drug-addicted wreck tended to by a long-suffering wife (Olga Legrand), though the movie is ultimately about Sébastien (George Babluani), the worker who's been watching their behaviour and is up a creek when Jean-François ODs, bringing a halt to construction. Soon Sébastien swipes a letter intended for the master of the house, promising money if he follows instructions—and in so doing winds up, much to his chagrin, as a contestant in the sick tournament described above. Director Gela Babluani then sets out to sketch that tourney in queasy-making detail: you have the rules of the game, the manner in which betting is permitted, the administering of morphine to calm the contestants, the taped-on numbers on the uniform grey T-shirts, and, best of all, the singularly unpleasant master of ceremonies (played with gusto by Pascal Bongard), who shouts out orders and polices the game.

It's an electric, sustained effort, and it's pretty hard not to get sucked in. Alas, the thrills have absolutely nothing to do with narrative: they simply drop an everyman audience surrogate into Hell, and we squirm with masochistic pleasure as he suffers the slings and arrows of rich, sadistic gamblers. Don't get me wrong—that's big fun. But it means that when the film has to do something with narrative interest (such as establish the characters or orchestrate a denouement), it's not so good. *13 Tzameti* actually improves on a second viewing because of this, your knowledge of what's to come impinging on the alternately confused and obvious nature of the set-up. Yet for that first time, you're impatient to get on with it. Although smart in not shooting its wad, the movie doesn't give enough to do while you wait for the central gimmick to arrive, and when it realizes its apparent obligation to give a wrap-up, it's too neat and mechanical to actually convince.

There's also a pervasive sense that *13 Tzameti* is about more than it actually is. The references to working-class desperation and the horrible denials of the competition all raise the stakes for the entertaining nightmare at its core, and there's no sense of flippancy in evoking that desperation. Unfortunately, one doesn't get a sense of what might make such a competition possible, or why people might invest in it. Similarly, the class issues (with the competition clearly designed for people who haven't been able to get ahead) are more alluded to than actually examined. As Sébastien is an intentional blank slate, we can't really gain the proper distance to examine what he feels; the attraction is more sensual, with the grit adding one more level of "authenticity" to the grimy proceedings. And while it expresses a kind of doomed fatalism about people on the bottom of the ladder who try to get ahead, it's nothing that hasn't been expressed far more articulately by hosts of better *films noir*. I liked *13 Tzameti*, but I not only wish it had taken itself further—I also got the impression that the filmmakers might have hoped for the same thing. (**TMH**)

## THIS FILM IS NOT YET RATED (see: *BORAT: CULTURAL LEARNINGS OF AMERICA FOR MAKE BENEFIT GLORIOUS NATION OF KAZAKHSTAN*)

## 3 NEEDLES (see: *THE NATIVITY STORY*)

## TIDELAND (see: *MARIE ANTOINETTE*)

## TRISTAN & ISOLDE
\* /\*\*\*\*
*st.* James Franco, Sophia Myles, Rufus Sewell, David O'Hara
*sc.* Dean Georgaris
*dir.* Kevin Reynolds

After bravely transforming the Robin Hood legend into a case of thirtysomething love jones with *Robin Hood: Prince of Thieves*, Kevin Costner's well-known ex-best friend Kevin

Reynolds turns the *Tristan & Isolde* legend into a WB/TIGER BEAT-friendly, mouth-breathing bodice-ripper indicated by lots of backlighting, orgasmic slow-mo, and dialogue purple enough to blind a Bronte sister. It's shot like a perfume commercial and written like a florid creative-writing exercise, one packed with such AM Gold, Luther Ingram treasures as: "Why does loving you feel so wrong?" Well, it might have something to do with said love being the basis for the Guinevere/Lancelot adultery story in which a woman comes between a king and his most trusted knight, leading to the ideological and literal collapse of a kingdom. Or it might have something to do with the fact that the actors playing the lovers in question never for a moment manage to spark the soggy tinder packed beneath the story. This allows a great deal of time for the sentient beings left in the audience after the ten-minute-mark exodus to suss out why this thing was delayed, then dumped in the middle of the January dead zone. It also, incidentally, caused me to fantasize about somehow harnessing the ability of films like this to make 125 minutes feel like six days for youth-giving effects and racing box scores.

The whole thing is a catafalque for a hideous screenplay and a performance by young stud James Franco that begins with promise but conspicuously peters out as soon as he's asked to do something other than run and swing a sword. He freezes his face and half-fills his eyes as lovelorn fighter Tristan; the very Madame Toussaud effigy of Andy Gibb in a tunic, he lets his leonine mane do the emoting. The story, for the uninitiated, finds ferocious, haunted Pict warrior Tristan seriously wounded in Dark Ages battle and nursed back to health under the tender ministrations of Irish princess Isolde (Sophia Myles). Returned to his king (Lord Marke (Rufus Sewell)) and Cornish cohorts, Tristan proceeds to win Isolde (not knowing it's Isolde, of course) to be his king's queen. Sweaty teen melodrama ensues. A nicely-staged and executed fight to free female captives in a woodland clearing gives way to lots of the same semi-filthy PG-13 arrows-and-furs confrontations so recently bollocks'd-up by the nearly-identically awful Antoine Fuqua demystification (hey, great idea) of *King Arthur*. Though Myles is undeniably beautiful, left to her own devices to fashion Isolde into something other than a silly, inconstant, petulant little kid, she succeeds only in looking like she's going to cry no matter whether she's fucking, fighting, or shopping.

*Tristan & Isolde* is an exhausting film even though nothing much happens in it. A young Tristan is shown to be a pacifist of sorts until goaded into action by a subplot that will have its predictable pay-off in the third act. Meanwhile, nine years pass through the magical graces of a dissolve and a matching shot and suddenly Tristan is a polished swordsman and inspiring leader. Less is offered the heroine: Isolde loses her mother as a child and then, blip, Isolde's a master herbalist jealous of her virginity. You could speculate that the best bits are in those skipped years. You could also say that the picture is economical because it's so meticulous about its set-ups and rim-shots that Victorian robots seem to have graphed the trajectory of the narrative arc—but then there's the problem of its gangrenous bloat in almost every other respect, including a score by Anne Dudley that's comprised of violin notes held into meaningful piano couplets. It sounds like the score for *The Legend of Bagger Vance*, and if you thought that sprightly treacle was bad in a film about a magical black ghost helping a white golfer with his swing, you can only imagine what it's like as the only emotional clues in a Medieval epic romance-cum-Enya video. If you're trapped in a theatre with this adipocere, though, it's fair to wonder how it is that despite much laborious set-up, Isolde still doesn't connect the dots between the pufferfish-poisoned Tristan and her missing betrothed — and once wondered, consider that for all the people to blame for this disaster, maybe we're forgetting to give Reynolds' favourite editor Peter Boyle his fair share. (**WC**)

## TRISTRAM SHANDY: A COCK AND BULL STORY
**\*\*\*/\*\*\*\***

*st.* Steve Coogan, Rob Brydon, Gillian Anderson, Keeley Hawes
*sc.* Martin Hardy, based on the novel The Life and Opinions of Tristram Shandy, Esq. by Laurence Sterne
*dir.* Michael Winterbottom

This whole idea of post-modern meta-movies just doesn't thrill me the way it used to. Nonetheless, Brit maverick Michael Winterbottom's once around on the *Adaptation.* wheel is buoyed by a game cast and an actual purpose: rather than the impossibility of a blocked writer trying to adapt a bad novel, find here a post-modern film about a novel that predicted, in a way, post-modernism itself. Winterbottom addresses the difficulty of translating an 18th century novel concerning the vast chaos of interiority (and writing a novel within a novel); instead of turning it into a film school exercise (like Marc Forster's *Stay*, for instance), he allows it to become a manifestation of that insular chaos. It's the story of a tornado told as a tornado. The eye of the storm is Steve Coogan, who plays an actor named Steve Coogan (who is much like Coogan, but different) cast in the title role of Laurence Stern's The Life and Opinions of Tristram Shandy, Esq., which is directed in the film by an actor (Jeremy Northam) playing a director, with Kelly Macdonald playing his girlfriend. Or is she actually his girlfriend (and is that their kid?), or is the fact of her and their alleged child together merely a pointed echo of the action of the film-within-a-

film of Walter Shandy (also Coogan) on the day of the birth of his son, Tristram? Doesn't matter. What does matter is that the conundrum is right there at the front of your head — and that the doubt is deposited with the sense of embarrassed, absurd propriety that's the hallmark of great British humor. Not so much a mindfuck as a mindlovemaking, *Tristram Shandy: A Cock and Bull Story* is delighted, like the novel, by the incapacity of art to encompass the vast incomprehensibility of life, and so it makes a piece of art that gently reminds us that there's more in heaven and earth than is dreamt of in any philosophy. (**WC**)

## TRUST THE MAN (see: *THE LAST KISS*)

## TSOTSI (see: *CATCH A FIRE*)

# U

## UNACCOMPANIED MINORS

ZERO STARS/****
st. Lewis Black, Wilmer
Valderrama, Tyler James Williams,
Dyllan Christopher
sc. Jacob Meszaros & Mya Stark
dir. Paul Feig

The bare bones of it—misfit kids stranded, The Breakfast Club-like, in a relationship pressure-cooker—seems tailor-made for "Freaks and Geeks" co-creator Paul Feig, but the fact that it plays out in a series of deadening, eternally-unspooling pratfalls and Catskills set-ups and payoffs proves that it's possible for good artists to produce bad art. Feig getting work at all (ditto erstwhile partner-in-crime Judd Apatow, who's sadly already used up a good bit of good will) in Hollywood suggests that the same blindness that finds consistent employment for Michael Bay and Brett Ratner will sometimes smile on good, smart people like Feig. That being said, Unaccompanied Minors is appalling. If it's not offensive in any substantive sense, it's bad by almost every measure of quality. People defending things like this children-running-amuck slapstick piece—which demonstrates precious little in the way of focus or restraint (think Baby's Day Out or any Home Alone sequel, but without the depth)—because their children like it would have their kids taken away from them were they to apply this rationale to food, toys, friends, schools, car seats, and so on. The reason we don't let youngsters vote and sign contracts is that their judgment is for shit, and if we want to keep them from setting themselves on fire we ought to be protecting them from this stuff, too, not indulging their affinity for it.

Lead minor is Spencer (Dyllan Christopher); the girl he's in love with is Grace (Gina Mantegna, daughter of Joe); the black comic relief who dances and sings is Charlie (Tyler James Williams); the proto-lesbian is Donna (Quinn Shephard); and the disgusting fat weirdo is Beef (Brett Kelly). Beef is not to be confused with the similarly vile Chunk from The Goonies or Ham from The Sandlot. Since over-familiarity with the premise and characters is only a small part of the problem, lay the rest of the troubles on the doorstep of gags like a security guard failing to grab a kid, looking at his hands in double-take surprise, and then doing a cartoon catch-up to the accompaniment of calliope music. Most heartbreaking is the presumptuousness of it: the agreement that Spencer is a geek because he apparently works in the A/V room, or that Grace is a shallow bitch-goddess afraid that her secret (she wears glasses!) will be leaked into the smirkosphere. Why, and at what point, did Feig choose to ally himself with the bullies of the world and substitute broad stereotype for insight into character? It always bugs me when shortcuts like these are taken—but it bugs me more when someone like Feig takes them, because doesn't it, in essence, undermine much of what he's stood for up to this point?

Our hero minors take on the evil dean/principal/airport security manager Porter (Lewis Black) when they're stuck at an airport during a blizzard and forced into the gently impotent care of Zach (Wilmer Valderrama). Of course they bristle against the entirely reasonable restrictions placed upon them; of course there's a parallel drama with the hysterical mother (Paget Brewster); and of course there's a metric ton of sub-Abbott & Costello slapstick, forced sentiment, and vaudevillian banter. It's antiquated, creaky, and presented sans timing or anything that could be mistaken for wit. Too easy to say the project is a cash-grab aimed at our youngest demographic (though cash certainly has to have something to do with it)—the real puzzler is how you could manage to reunite three founding members of "The Kids in the Hall" and all you can think to do with them is put them in the background of a couple of shots. *Unaccompanied Minors* is a failure of imagination. Obnoxious and chaotic, demonstrating no unity of vision and no excuse for its own existence, it's neither artistic statement nor triumphant popular entertainment: not personal and not public, either. What it is is a vacuum, sucking up a lot of smart, talented people and leaving no trace of them in its celluloid wake. While I've seen worse films, I haven't seen many this dispiriting. (**WC**)

## UNITED 93
***¹/₂/****

st. Lewis Alsamari, JJ Johnson, Trish Gates, Polly Adams
w./d. Paul Greengrass

I guess when you talk about a movie like Paul Greengrass' *United 93*, you have to talk about the propriety of the project: whether death, fear, and suffering at its most obscene is something we should try to know or gratefully shield ourselves from. Should 9/11 already be an Oprah special and a national holiday? It's an essential question, a defining one—and on either side of the question's divide, you'll find one person who thinks we should see our soldiers' caskets draped in American flags and another who feels that seeing war casualties is somehow bad for morale or, if our fearless leaders are to be believed, somehow unpatriotic. Ignorance is as blissful now as it ever was—it's one aphorism the film honours. Another is that you reap what you sow: the belief that our civil liberties, for which we eagerly fight and die to protect on foreign soil, are the first things we seem to sacrifice in times of peril (including a vocal rabble wondering if we're "ready" for a 9/11 film), is far stickier when the proposition before us

is that Islamic extremists don't like us because of that which defines us as Americans. ("They hate our freedom" is the party line.) So when our government begins to infringe on our personal freedom after a meticulously organized and coordinated terrorist attack took us completely unawares (I still recall with a shudder how then-Secretary of State Condaleeza Rice claimed that no one could have imagined it) more than four years ago, that means—more than over twenty-one hundred military dead (and counting) does—that we've already lost.

*United 93* is a deeply divisive, deeply political picture that, in portraying the "facts" as we either know them or want to know them or want to deny them, paints a portrait of an administration so unprepared for the possibility of a full-scale terrorist attack on American soil that the only person with the authority to set the rules of engagement in that situation for a military response to the immediate threat was unavailable for those precious minutes at the beginning of the crisis, where it could have made a difference. Greengrass is fairly unapologetic as far as Bush Jr.'s conspicuous absence is concerned, and during the height of the crisis as it's portrayed, the frustration of military and civilian leaders waiting for a word from on-high is a key component of the tension. In other aspects, though, there's an equanimity to Greengrass' approach that some will remember from his treatment of another still-fresh historical event, *Bloody Sunday*, a film that recreates the moment the IRA became a viable terrorist organization, just as *United 93* is a film about the moment the United States became an overt stick stirring an already covertly-riled hornet's nest. The two films could be companion pieces in their mutual suggestion that western civilization is sliding backwards—maybe all the way back to the Crusades that Bush Jr. name-dropped so casually, so appallingly, at the beginning of our latest troubles.

Greengrass' film is a clever thing, lingering in its apparent vérité randomness for an extra beat on a sexually suggestive perfume ad in the airport terminal as a terrorist passes by—or on a Westerner's foot resting casually against a stranger's luggage. *United 93* is about a sum of offense; it's about a hijacking of technology by a sophisticated and worthy opponent with a list of grievances; and it's about arrogance, too, the common refrain of air traffic controllers and military watchmen in the film being that it's unthinkable that a hijacking could occur on an American airplane. A foreign passenger presumably more experienced with violations of this sort pleads with his peers to do nothing, demonstrating with subtlety the way that the parameters of the game were suddenly and irrevocably changed by hostiles who had apparently been studying the same rules of engagement. The portrait of their actions is frightening because they don't seem the frothing Hun we'd like to see them as, but rather they appear to be intelligent human beings of the belief that they're doing the right thing in the name of their god and country. They're portrayed as we like to portray ourselves, especially when we're put upon. It's frightening that they can use our technology against us—that they understand that what makes us great is always the same thing that makes us weak. (Greengrass shows how the very qualities that mark the heroes of Flight 93 and those that would cause a country to favour a President fond of championing inarticulate aggression in the name of aggression are one and the same.) Suddenly *United 93* is a sharp, uncomfortable microcosm.

The film's finale, depicting events that will never be known in the detail Greengrass presumes to know them, are the only ones worth a real moral discussion, because it's here that the director dips heavily into conjecture and, in that license, reveals his thesis. At the picture's climax, Greengrass shows passengers and terrorists alike deep in prayer to their respective deities before sending everyone in the whole goddamn mess to their graves in the cool whimper of a cut-to-black. The suggestion is that the only possible resolution in this kind of religious war between fundamentalist extremes is mutually-assured destruction. There are no real heroes or villains in *United 93* (indeed, during the last rush to the cockpit, Greengrass envisions the passengers battering one terrorist's head to a bloody pulp with a fire extinguisher long after he's been neutralized), just victims fed to a complete failure of ideology. In Greengrass' appeal to the bloodlust of his audience, there's a certain contempt for the patness of a bloody Old Testament resolution that's well-placed and, given the hysterical reaction of some members of my screening audience, not at all in vain. It is at its core a cry for reason in the offering of the extreme before an impossible situation escalates into, I guess, what it's escalated into already or, if you take the more cynical view, what it's already been for thousands of years. *United 93* is tightly-constructed—a painstaking progression of circumstances (what some see as a corporate shill of a title, I see almost as an idea of order) and, along with *V for Vendetta*, it's another early-2006 film about terrorism that is complicated, controversial, and, most bracingly, strikes at the heart of how far we've come since 9/11. And how far we haven't. (**WC**)

**UNKNOWN (see: *THE PIANO TUNER OF EARTHQUAKES*)**

D O C U M E N T A R Y
**THE U.S. VS. JOHN LENNON**
**\*\*/\*\*\*\***
*dirs.* David Leaf & John Scheinfeld

Terry Eagleton once remarked that although it was easier to attract the art and English departments to radical politics than it was, say, the folks in chemical engineering, the engineers can at least be counted on to regularly get out of bed. I thought of that double-edged sword while watching John Lennon and Yoko Ono stage their "bed-in for peace" during the hagiography *The U.S. vs. John Lennon*. This is a film that marshals the praise of Bobby Seale, Jerry Rubin, Angela Davis, Tariq Ali, and Ron Kovic—all people not only more worthy of a documentary but also more instrumental in the ferment of '60s/'70s leftism—for the sake of a kind but inarticulate superstar who served as the conduit for their messages. The problem is not so much that the conduit has become the central figure, but that the film takes the position that conduitism is the same as being on the front lines; and while one can commend Lennon for his refusal to fade into the love generation's decline, ending one's political education at his feet is a tad inadvisable.

The piece hinges on the moment where Lennon ceased to be a lovable mop-topped Liverpudlian and became a more committed political voice—a notion given flower by his fateful union with Yoko Ono. Though it downplays Ono's conceptual-art contributions— the press conference conducted in a bag, the aforementioned bed-in, the WAR IS OVER billboards—to their subsequent publicity stunts, it rightly credits Lennon's refusal to be just another loafing rock star, in addition to his willingness to put his money where his mouth was for the cause. Trouble is, that mouth was not especially eloquent—and neither is the movie. Despite that Lennon and Ono are seen in vintage footage extolling each other's "rebellion," their politics are neither systematic nor detail-oriented: more than anything else, they're an outgrowth of youthful revolt. This, of course, is what makes Lennon—as opposed to the people to whom he lent cultural capital—interesting to VH1, under whose imprimatur *The U.S. vs. John Lennon* was produced.

Of course, there would be no film if he hadn't stepped on a few toes. His investigation by the Nixon administration is proof that even toothless dissent scares anyone under the influence of J. Edgar Hoover—and to be sure, the years-long effort to deport Lennon after his arrival in New York is as shameful as anything committed by the FBI during that ignoble period. Still, it's a matter of degrees. Lennon may have been threatened with exile and regularly ridiculed in the press, but he suffered lesser and fewer indignities than half the talking heads in this movie. Yet *The U.S. vs. John Lennon* never wavers in its refusal to contextualize our man's struggle, meaning a whole raft of other considerations get papered over to clear space for hero worship.

True, the filmmakers try to establish the mood in America and provide a reasonable timeline to the events occurring under Nixon's disgraceful tenure. Everything is passed through the filter of Lennon, though, to the extent that he becomes the only serious figure in the film: one isn't aware of the protest culture beyond what he could lend to it, and his radical associates are merely names without referent or ideological definition. I realize this is a music channel's attempt to lionize a big name, and maybe he deserves the attention up to a point. But when photos of the Kent State massacre are wistfully, inexcusably set to "Imagine," it's clear that co-directors David Leaf & John Scheinfeld will do anything to link subject and period. If you come away thinking Lennon was a courageous man, perhaps that's not a bad thing—but if you think you're seeing the model of a dissident, you'd better think twice. (**TMH**)

V

## V FOR VENDETTA
***½/****
st. Natalie Portman, Hugo
Weaving, Stephen Rea, John Hurt
sc. The Wachowski Brothers,
based on the graphic novel by
Alan Moore & David Lloyd
dir. James McTeigue

As documents for the opposition go, *V for Vendetta* may be the ballsiest, angriest picture of the current administration, flashing without apology images of naked prisoners of the state, shackled in black hoods and held in clear acrylic boxes while a febrile talking head and his cloistered intimates (called "fingers") form a closed fist around them. It surmises a future where the government plants stories in centrally-owned media conglomerates, controlling groupthink by providing just one point of view. Woe be unto those with a critical mind because what, after all, is more dangerous to a dictatorial theocracy than a question? But more, the picture is an impassioned plea for alternative lifestyles, exposing the melodrama of *Brokeback Mountain* to be embarrassed, even polite, when the struggle for equal regard is something that should be undertaken with passion and brio— it's life and death, and *V for Vendetta* presents it as such. There are no half measures in a film that takes as its hero an eloquent monologist in a Guy Fawkes mask (Hugo Weaving), his erstwhile, reluctant sidekick a young woman, Evey (Natalie Portman), transformed through the government-sanctioned abduction of her parents and a period of torture and imprisonment into not an avenging angel, but a voice of reason. How fascinating that the reasonable solution in the picture is the destruction of

Britain's Parliament on the Thames.

It gives hope that thoughtful, adult-themed, long-form comics ("graphic novels") can yet be translated to the screen as intelligent, topical, pulp-entertaining films (see also *A History of Violence*), with Alan Moore's The Watchmen awaiting adaptation and Neil Gaiman's near-canonized "The Sandman" in perpetual turnaround. *V for Vendetta* works—like the best literature, the best art—as a mirror to the audience, thus what some individuals might perceive as an attack on their value systems (ones based on mysticism, intolerance, and exclusion, granted) may have others basking in a self-righteousness that, better than George Clooney's aggressively dry but well-intentioned platforms, indicts an apparent attack on common decency. It's a polarizing film, and I confess that I'm too far to one side politically by now to see it in anything other than a ideologically gratifying light, but as a film it's also well-made: slick, exhilarating and outrageous. It reminds a lot more of *Fight Club* than of screenwriters the Wachowski Brothers' own *The Matrix*, and I do wonder if, like *Fight Club*, it won't lose esteem as it drifts away from that extreme topicality. Still, it's useful to remember that today, *V for Vendetta* feels like a slap in the face and a kick in the shorts; damnit if, when the Old Bailey loses its head, I didn't feel a little like whooping with that pleasure of destructive juvenile resistance. Freedom's just another word for nothing left to lose.

Already scourged in some corners as an apologia for terrorism, *V for Vendetta* is instead a cautionary tale about how monolithic governments create revolutionaries from ordinary people when they intimately violate them. The equation couldn't be simpler, nor could the affection V has for Rowland V. Lee's *The Count of Monte Cristo* be a clearer brand that our beloved anarchist is something of a vengeance-driven whack-job. ("I'm sad for Mercedes," says Evey, revealing in that moment to V that she might be the more suitable instrument of rapprochement in his grand schemes. "Dantes loves revenge more than he loves her.") The seeds of the formation of our own country can be traced to being mad as hell and not taking it anymore, our beloved USA transformed in the picture into a barely-glimpsed wasteland embroiled in a civil war after a badly-contained (self-inflicted?) plague decimates its population. The "Ulcerated Sphincter of Asserica" as foaming Rush Limbaugh-esque talking head Prothero (Roger Allam) calls it, receding in the background as the Wachowskis transform Moore's treatise on Thatcher's England into a still-scathing commentary on the toll of totalitarian thought on a public reared on democratic principles. Unlawful wire-tapping made lawful, secret prisons, all-pervasive media saturation, the avian flu, philosophy as science, legislating the bedroom, and the pushing of fear as at once the latest, greatest thrill-drug and the most effective opiate of the people... There is a focus on the suppression of art (and John Hurt as the film's arch villain reminds us that he was Evey prototype Winston Smith in Michael Radford's *Nineteen Eighty-Four*) as the first step towards the death of individual thought—there are, in fact, so many hot-button topics wired into the piece that it's something like a miracle it doesn't collapse in on its own outrage.

But what's wonderful about *V for Vendetta* is that it is, itself, artful. It plays Tchaikovsky next to **Cat Power** next to a wistful WWII croon while Portman provides her first truly great performance as an adult. Somehow, the British accent—a stumbling block for so many actors—has freed her to indulge in her waifishness, spiced with that hint of resolve that made her child-actor turn in *Leon: The Professional* ever so tantalizing a(n unfulfilled) promise. By never allowing its hero a face, and by further obscuring him behind a storm of gilded words, V becomes as slippery a signifier as Thomas Pynchon's <u>Zelig</u>-esque heroine of the same name, reminding of some combination of that literary gadfly and Britain's own King Arthur, thought to return whenever his country needs him most. In a period in our history when the cinema is caught emulating the golden endings of the fifties while constructing the tortured, misanthropic narratives of the seventies, *V for Vendetta* has the big brass ones to make its main characters arrested, criminal (what *is* Evey doing out after curfew?), and invested in the overthrow of the government for, of all things, personal reasons. It's an utterly humanist picture in that sense—and a hopeful one ground in the idea that not every epoch-shattering event growing from one person with one idea has to be the World Trade Center. Sometimes they can be Bastilles. (**WC**)

# W

## WASSUP ROCKERS
**½/****
*st.* Jonathan Velasquez, Francisco Pedrasa, Milton Velasquez, Usvaldo Panameno
*w./d.* Larry Clark

These days, when I think of Larry Clark, I think of Stephen Wiltshire, the outsider artist profiled in Oliver Sacks' An Anthropologist on Mars. Diagnosed with autism early in life, Wiltshire soon after began doing immaculately detailed sketches of animals before moving on to buses and eventually cityscapes. So advanced was Wiltshire's technique at such an early age that Sacks and co. were fascinated to learn that his talent came pre-evolved: as a child, he drew like a grown-up, but he drew like that same grown-up in adulthood. Whatever you think of Clark's directorial debut, *Kids*, there's no denying that he's a natural—a savant, if you will—at harnessing the prickly energy of youth. And yet, although he's since moved on from "animals" (the mindless fuck-bunnies of *Kids* and *Bully*) to "buses" (the emotionally shipwrecked fuck-bunnies of *Teenage Caveman* and *Ken Park*) to "cityscapes" (the El Salvadoran fuck-bunnies of the new film, *Wassup Rockers*), he hasn't—and I don't mean this in the pejorative sense—matured; you can essentially start anywhere in the Clark canon without missing a beat. It's nice to see him grapple with the "other" in *Wassup Rockers*, but all he's really done is turn the tint down on his usual band of utopia-seeking skater punks, and as the picture's relatively tame surface works to offset its intensely nihilistic underbelly (Clark has never had this little regard for human life—and that the victims of the film's Rube Goldberg deathtraps

are by and large pedophiles isn't nearly as self-flagellating as you might presume), the cumulative effect is one of *déjà vu*. Treating the Latino characters' sojourn into Beverly Hills like a social experiment, Clark remains a compelling, primal anthropologist—and the mischief-making in *Wassup Rockers* spreads a surprisingly infectious joy. But there are only so many times you can applaud a one-trick pony. (**BC**)

## WHEN A STRANGER CALLS
ZERO STARS/****
*st.* Camilla Belle, Tommy Flanagan, Tessa Thompson, Brian Geraghty
*sc.* Jake Wade Wall, based on the screenplay by Steve Feke and Fred Walton
*dir.* Simon West

There's nothing patently, obviously offensive about Simon West's abominable remake of the already awful "thriller" *When a Stranger Calls*: it's neither misogynistic nor racist nor really anything more than exactly what you'd expect from a project like this, dumped as it has been in the wasteland of another early-February. It's so studiedly inoffensive, in fact, that you could take an elderly nun to it and there would be nary a flutter in her rigidly tender sensibilities. It tittles no ates, manufactures no suspense, and no one in a packed audience of four-hundred folks at the preview screening rustled an inch when the cat—not once, but twice—provided the false jump before the "real" one, though I confess the reason for that might be that by the time West and company get around to actually having something happen, most anyone with any kind of sense is asleep or halfway home. I've failed to mention that it's acted by heavy-browed lead Camilla Belle (as babysitter Johnson, Jill Johnson) like a toy robot with her key only half-wound. Were she to have run out of juice negotiating a wall and leaned there motionless, I wouldn't have batted an eyelash.

If you want to spend any time analyzing it, the problem with *When a Stranger Calls* is that every single thing it sets up it fails to follow through on. There is literally and metaphorically nothing going on in this film. The narrative (a crank caller menaces an isolated babysitter) is stagnant, the visuals are achingly pedestrian, and the twist (spoiled by the picture's own trailer) is stolen from *Black Christmas*. If it were paint, *When a Stranger Calls* would be pale beige. Whenever a moment is ripe for virginal slasher-film sexual subtext—like when Jill sucks on a cherry popsicle, or when her slutty best friend appears very briefly and threatens to do a few tequila shots—West's matronly chastity causes him to recoil like a finger from the fire. Fireplace poker as surrogate phallus? Nope. Overactive fireplace as devouring vagina? Nope. Maternal instinct awakened subsequent to symbolic deflowering? Fuggedaboudit. Reunification with boyfriend or continued strife with stern father leading to displaced psychosexual vengeance visited upon the mysterious interloper? Nah. And any irony concerning how Jill and co.'s beloved technological crutch, the cell phone, becomes the proverbial rack of choice for some faceless killer (Tommy Flanagan, voiced by Lance Henriksen and given zero backstory or meaning) is ignorantly overlooked in favour of interminable sequences involving West fetishizing the wax-like Belle in medium close-up as she, yes, answers and talks on the telephone. Indeed the killer is only distinguished by the fact that he somehow does his dirty deeds without weapons—which is intriguing in a berserker sort of way, but even that, by the end, is cast aside by the implication that this monster's weapon of choice are his jazz hands. It's scary, sure, but for all the wrong reasons.

Films like this are more sad than anything else. They don't exhibit any malice in their existence, suggesting instead that everyone involved was doing the very best they could and this is what they came up with. Unlike a child's clay ashtray, though, *When a Stranger Calls* invokes a state of permanent retardation in which creative evolution from this point forward is unlikely. What other conclusion can we arrive at when tension is imagined in that old saw of a new car not starting at a moment of crisis? (Where a girl hiding in a koi pond is safe from an attacking bogey who, for whatever reason, isn't allowed to get in the water.) It's an inexplicable PG-13 for the rare reason in modern horror that there's nothing whatsoever in it that would prevent it from being shown on your local PBS station (I've seen rougher stuff on "Bear in the Big Blue House"), and such a stilted, inept mess in every other way that I also can't imagine any television network outside of maybe Lifetime stupid enough to air it. Once the lights came up, not long after one of those fake-out dream sequences (but "faking out" whom?) where the girl imagines that she's hunted still in an ostensible sanctuary, I heard a lot of incredulity and laughter from the exact mainstream audience to which this film hopes to pander. It's good sport to lambaste the popular taste, but you continue to make asinine, incompetent flicks for an imagined demographic of rich morons and the bill inevitably comes due. You can fool some of the people some of the time, but you never fool anyone with loose stool like this. **(WC)**

**WHO KILLED THE ELECTRIC CAR? (see:** *AN INCONVENIENT TRUTH*)

**WHY WE FIGHT (see:** *LOOKING FOR COMEDY IN THE MUSLIM WORLD*)

# THE WICKER MAN
*/****

*st.* Nicolas Cage, Ellen Burstyn, Kate Beahan, Frances Conroy
*sc.* Neil LaBute, based on the screenplay by Anthony Shaffer
*dir.* Neil LaBute

You mark off certain literary flourishes in Neil LaBute's remake of Robin Hardy's classic *The Wicker Man*, and then you can't help but note that beneath the pagan matriarchy that is its villain and the hangdog cop (Nicolas Cage) that is its dullard hero, the film is just the auteur's latest unnecessarily reductive gender deconstruction. It's another major disappointment from the man who put humanity on the spit in *In the Company of Men* and—to a lesser, if no less affecting, degree—*Your Friends and Neighbors*. This redux hates women and, more, it hates femininity—typical LaBute, you could fairly offer, especially after *Possession* and *The Shape of Things*; *The Wicker Man* demonstrates again that LaBute is one of the brightest, most well-read American directors working—and that he's become incapable of focusing his smarts on a target other than the cruel and essentially alien nature of women. Hitchcock's films are arguably as obsessed, but his "wrong men" were hardly free of complicity in the construction of their own downfalls. Fatal to the production, then, is the introduction of an unsullied male hero—a literal martyr this time instead of the figurative types of LaBute's last couple pictures: a man of action (no milquetoast intellectuals here) struggling against a rising tide of castrating, hippie harpies.

Two full moonscapes vs. two orange sunrises (the fullness of the feminine vs. the right reason of the masculine) separate this girl vs. guy bout into neat, equally-spaced rounds. The battle is between chthonic mystery and ratiocination, thus it's a fertility cult that keeps men are on leashes pit against sheriff Edward Malus ("You gonna go for detective?" a co-worker asks Mr. Wonderful), who journeys to lush, remote Summerisle in Puget Sound in search of a missing girl at the beck of his estranged fiancée (winsome, beautiful Kate Beahan). Officer Malus is named after a genus of apple dependant on pollinating insects, making his allergy to honeybees the kind of little joke LaBute enjoys while serving the dual function—after the nod to the original film's virginal protagonist—of introducing Summerisle's thriving apicultural industry. What else would a goddess cult use as their chief source of sustenance and income but a product produced by a queen-led society? (And who else would they victimize but this drone of a man?) Malus' intrusion into the self-described "colony" is met with seriocomic hostility and provincialism; he's doomed to be the only person in any theatre who doesn't realize that his phallo-centric weapons (gun, money, reason) are useless against the wet, enveloping chaos of the islanders.

This would be fine if Malus' idea of order were constantly usurped by the "Key West" of the women—and the original film's establishment of the thorny divide between Christianity and Paganism strikes a resounding chord in that pursuit. But rather than a Wallace Stevens poem, LaBute references William Blake. In a classroom scene that threatens at any moment to become chilling in a way the rest of the film is not, LaBute includes a part of the opening "Argument" from Blake's astonishing "The Marriage of Heaven and Hell":

*Once meek, and in a perilous path,*
*The just man kept his course along*
*The vale of death.*
*Roses are planted where thorns grow.*
*And on the barren heath*
*Sing the honey bees.*

Blake continues with a series of contraries ("Without Contraries is no progression. Attraction and Repulsion,

Reason and Energy, Love and Hate, are necessary to Human existence"), declaring his thesis to be that "Good is the passive that obeys Reason. Evil is the active springing from Energy. Good is Heaven. Evil is Hell." It also happens to be *The Wicker Man*'s thesis, which is all well and good save that Blake's extremes are complicated by his affinity for this "Evil" and, later in the same piece, his disdain for this passive "Good." Heaven for Blake is ironic, making the Heaven of Malus' dedication to reason (and love and attraction, should we follow this argument) the malefactor, and the Hell of Summerisle's mad, procreative Energy the hero.

Yet LaBute takes Blake at face value, turning Malus into the forbidden fruit sampled by the Eves of this Eden and closing on a particularly vile epilogue that believes it's making hay out of a literalization of the concept of the *femme fatale*. *The Wicker Man* is Romanticism without melancholy, handily transforming it into something that feels like a man of straw rather than of wicker, erected to illustrate a point about original sin and the tactics men and women employ to wallow in it. The only irony left in *The Wicker Man* is that LaBute's head, his reason, seems at terminal odds with his carnality—the tantalizing suggestion being that if a successful marriage were ever engineered to join this artist's personal Heaven and Hell, these late cinematic offspring might finally be as vigorous and rich as his firstborn. (**WC**)

**THE WOODS (see: *FEAST*)**

**WORLD TRADE CENTER (see: *LITTLE MISS SUNSHINE*)**

X

## X-MEN: THE LAST STAND
½*/****
st. Hugh Jackman, Halle Berry, Ian
McKellen, Famke Janssen
sc. Simon Kinberg & Zak Penn
dir. Brett Ratner

As an example of what can happen
when a homophobic, misogynistic,
misanthropic moron wildly
overcompensates in a franchise that
had as its primary claim to eternity
that it was sensitive to the plight of
homosexuals, Brett Ratner's painfully
queer *X-Men: The Last Stand* (hereafter
"X3") manages to present its series of
melodramatic vignettes in such a way
as to completely negate any sense of
peril, individuality, or struggle for the
characters. Without a sense of weight,
the references in the piece to genocide
and The Holocaust ("Ink shall never
again touch my skin!" says Ian
McKellen's Magneto) become pure,
laggard exploitation in the service of a
sub-par superhero action film that
shows its true colours time and again
in its hatred of women ("Hell hath no
fury!") and loathing of female
sexuality, as well as in its flat-eyed
regard of children trying to hasp off
their wings while their fathers attempt
to break down the bathroom door. It's
Michael Bay's *Schindler's List*: a
reptilian populist, at ease with the slick
and facile, has been asked to take the
reins of a project that, for whatever its
crimes of pacing and exposition, had in
its Bryan Singer-helmed episodes the
good sense not to kick over ant piles it
wasn't prepared to contain.

The premise this time is that
they've discovered a cure for "mutant-
ism" in the mutant power of a little
boy, Leech (Cameron Bright), meaning
that any close contact with him results
in the negation of mutant powers—
which of course doesn't make any kind
of sense if we're talking about genetic
change, but there you have it. Happily-
imprisoned in Alcatraz (retrofitted
now as a research laboratory (it's a
metaphor, stupid)), Leech sits there
blankly in the style perfected by young
Mr. Bright, waiting for a stupid battle
to take place on his behalf between the
forces of "good" and the forces of
"evil." But these lines drawn in X3 feel
arbitrary, and the scenes of picketers
protesting before "clinics" offering the
cure to unhappy mutants (leading to
the inevitable abortion clinic
explosion), the horrific imagery of a
woman who has had her sexuality
unfettered by a traumatic event going
batshit (Jean Grey/Dark Phoenix
(Famke Janssen))—her entire storyline
reminding of Clive Barker's "Jacqueline
Ess: Her Will and Testament"), and
those loaded *tableaux* of people being
reduced to ash while a troubled
minority exterminates itself all start to
feel dirty, like the world's most
expensive Leni Riefenstahl film.

What should be an excruciating
decision of whether or not to take the
cure for an "unfavourable" mutation—
even the question of how the debate
begins to change once a "cure" is found
over the morality of playing God to fix
one of His works—is ignored in X3 in
favour of rote special-effects sequences
and perfunctory action spasms that
bear no relation to each other. There
are no consequences in this universe.
As with X2 casualty Jean Grey being
resurrected with nary an explanation,
emotional or narrative, when other
main characters die, there's never any
sense of peril or pathos. When Cyclops
(James Marsden) is summarily
dispatched in the early going, for
instance, his absence isn't questioned
for at least an hour, by which time it's
no longer clear if he's actually dead or
was pushed out of the picture by the
sheer volume of characters
introduced—at least in one scene—
through a literal checklist. Dark
intimations that Jean's Id—manifesting
itself as a real strong desire to get

laid—needs to be stringently controlled by Professor Xavier (Patrick Stewart) hint at some real dysfunction in the picture that's neither addressed nor ameliorated by Magneto's late-film semi-intervention. Magneto wants this girl to go wild, and once she does, he's as helpless as the rest of the "brotherhood" before her appetite.

In Ratner's world, tortured men ride motorcycles along winding roads; women (preferably naked) are sexually voracious *fatales* who make decisions based primarily on the likelihood of getting fucked by über-mensch; and androgynous leather freaks typify the difference between dark and light. The final battle—which finds only six "good" X-Men arrayed against an army of "bad" mutants—is cacophonous in no fruitful way, allowing Beast (Kelsey Grammar, probably delighted to get to say "Oh my stars and garters!") to kill a few faceless rabble, while over it all hangs the truisms that Storm (Halle Berry) is completely worthless for someone who can control the weather and that Magneto should just neutralize the metallic Wolverine (Hugh Jackman) and Colossus (Daniel Cudmore), thus reducing his opposition by a third. In the middle of so much ridiculousness (and more: with the seams already bursting, Ratner shoehorns in a romantic ice-skating scene), find young Ellen Page creating, as Kitty Pryde, a character out of whole cloth that feels vulnerable, fully-fleshed, and somehow worth caring about. The great irony of X3 is that even with the inevitable suggestion of another sequel, the promise of a Wolverine spin-off film looming on the near-horizon, and Ratner's continued viability as a big-budget director despite/because of his string, unabated, of sub-par, repugnant, feckless pictures, the star born out of this hateful, clumsy mess is a young woman, Page, who's so obviously too damn good for it. (**WC**)

# REVIEW BREAKDOWN BY STAR RATING & AUTHOR

\*\*\*\*
**CHILDREN OF MEN** (Chaw)
**THE DEATH OF MR. LAZARESCU (Moartea domnului Lazarescu)** (Chaw)
**49 UP** (Pugh)
**THE FOUNTAIN** (Chaw)
**MANUFACTURED LANDSCAPES** (Chaw)
**PAN'S LABYRINTH** (Chaw)
**A SCANNER DARKLY** (Chaw)
**SUPERMAN RETURNS** (Chaw)
**SYMPATHY FOR LADY VENGEANCE** (Chaw)

\*\*\*½
**THE ABANDONED** (Chaw)
**GABRIELLE** (Hoover)
**HOUSE OF SAND (Casa de Areia)** (Chaw)
**IDIOCRACY** (Chaw)
**LETTERS FROM IWO JIMA** (Chaw)
**MONKEY WARFARE** (Hoover)
**MUTUAL APPRECIATION** (Chaw)
**NEIL YOUNG: HEART OF GOLD** (Chaw)
**REQUIEM** (Hoover)
**ROCKY BALBOA** (Chambers)
**SATELLITE** (Chaw)
**SILENT HILL** (Chaw)
**SLITHER** (Chaw)
**TALLADEGA NIGHTS: THE BALLAD OF RICKY BOBBY** (Chaw)
**THE TEXAS CHAINSAW MASSACRE: THE BEGINNING** (Chaw)
**TIDELAND** (Chaw)
**UNITED 93** (Chaw)
**V FOR VENDETTA** (Chaw)
**THE WOODS** (Chaw)

\*\*\*

**APOCALYPTO** (Chaw)
**BORAT: CULTURAL LEARNINGS OF AMERICA FOR MAKE BENEFIT GLORIOUS NATION OF KAZAKHSTAN** (Chaw)
**THE BRIDESMAID (La Demoiselle d'honneur)** (Hoover)
**CASINO ROYALE** (Chaw)
**CURIOUS GEORGE** (Chaw)
**THE DEPARTED** (Chaw)
**THE DESCENT** (Chaw)
**FAVELA RISING** (Chaw)
**FINAL DESTINATION 3** (Chaw)
**GOING TO PIECES: THE RISE AND FALL OF THE SLASHER FILM** (Jackson)
**HALF NELSON** (Chaw)
**HAPPY FEET** (Chaw)
**HOW TO EAT YOUR WATERMELON IN WHITE COMPANY (AND ENJOY IT)** (Chaw)
**IRAQ IN FRAGMENTS** (Hoover)
**JACKASS NUMBER TWO** (Chaw)
**LUCKY NUMBER SLEVIN** (Chaw)
**MIAMI VICE** (Chaw)
**MONSTER HOUSE** (Chaw)
**OFF THE BLACK** (Chaw)
**OLD JOY** (Chaw)
**ON NATIVE SOIL** (Jackson)
**THE PAINTED VEIL** (Chaw)
**THE PRESTIGE** (Chaw)
**THE PROTECTOR** (Chaw)
**THE RITCHIE BOYS** (Hoover)
**RUNNING SCARED** (Chaw)
**SHORTBUS** (Hoover)
**SNAKES ON A PLANE** (Jackson)
**STRANGER THAN FICTION** (Chaw)
**SUPERMAN II (THE RICHARD DONNER CUT)** (Chambers)
**TRISTRAM SHANDY: A COCK AND BULL STORY** (Chaw)

\*\*½

**THE BLACK DAHLIA** (Chaw)
**BRICK** (Chaw)
**THE CHILD (L'Enfant)** (Chaw)
**CONVERSATIONS WITH OTHER WOMEN** (Hoover)
**CRANK** (Chaw)
**DÉJÀ VU** (Chaw)
**DRAWING RESTRAINT 9** (Chaw)
**FACTOTUM** (Chaw)
**FLUSHED AWAY** (Chaw)
**A GUIDE TO RECOGNIZING YOUR SAINTS** (Chaw)
**JESUS CAMP** (Hoover)
**LITTLE MISS SUNSHINE** (Chaw)
**MARIE ANTOINETTE** (Chaw)
**NANNY McPHEE** (Chaw)
**NATHALIE...** (Hoover)
**THE NIGHT OF TRUTH (La Nuit de la vérité)** (Hoover)
**THE OMEN** (Chaw)
**THE PUFFY CHAIR** (Chaw)
**QUINCEAÑERA** (Chaw)
**SAW III** (Hoover)
**THE TENANTS** (Hoover)
**13 TZAMETI** (Hoover)
**WASSUP ROCKERS** (Chambers)

**\*\***
**BAMBI II** (Hoover)
**THE BREAK-UP** (Chaw)
**CANDY** (Chaw)
**CATCH A FIRE** (Chaw)
**CHARLOTTE'S WEB** (Chaw)
**THE DEVIL AND DANIEL JOHNSTON** (Chaw)
**DON'T COME KNOCKING** (Chaw)
**DREAMGIRLS** (Chaw)
**FEAST** (Chaw)
**FREEDOMLAND** (Chaw)
**FRIENDS WITH MONEY** (Chaw)
**THE GOOD SHEPHERD** (Chaw)
**THE GROUND TRUTH** (Jackson)
**HARD CANDY** (Chambers)
**HARSH TIMES** (Chaw)
**HOSTEL** (Chaw)
**JET LI'S FEARLESS** (Chaw)
**LITTLE JERUSALEM (La Petite Jérusalem)** (Hoover)
**LITTLE MAN** (Chaw)
**MAN PUSH CART** (Hoover)
**MATTHEW BARNEY: NO RESTRAINT** (Hoover)
**MONGOLIAN PING PONG** (Chaw)
**NOTES ON A SCANDAL** (Chaw)
**ONLY HUMAN (Seres queridos)** (Chaw)
**OVER THE HEDGE** (Chaw)
**PEACEFUL WARRIOR** (Chaw)
**THE QUEEN** (Chaw)
**RUNNING WITH SCISSORS** (Hoover)
**SCARY MOVIE 4** (Hoover)
**SIDEKICK** (Hoover)
**THE U.S. VS. JOHN LENNON** (Hoover)
**WHY WE FIGHT** (Chaw)
**WORLD TRADE CENTER** (Chaw)

**\*½**
**ACCEPTED** (Chambers)
**THE ANT BULLY** (Hoover)
**ART SCHOOL CONFIDENTIAL** (Chambers)
**BABEL** (Hoover)
**CARS** (Chaw)
**THE DEVIL WEARS PRADA** (Chaw)
**THIS FILM IS NOT YET RATED** (Chaw)
**FIREWALL** (Chaw)
**THE GOOD GERMAN** (Chaw)
**THE GUARDIAN** (Chaw)
**HOOT** (Hoover)
**THE ILLUSIONIST** (Chaw)
**THE KING** (Chambers)
**LITTLE CHILDREN** (Chaw)
**THE PIANO TUNER OF EARTHQUAKES** (Chaw)
**THE SCIENCE OF SLEEP** (Chaw)
**THE SECRET LIFE OF WORDS** (Chaw)
**16 BLOCKS** (Chaw)
**STRANGERS WITH CANDY** (Hoover)

246

\*
**ADAM & STEVE** (Hoover)
**ASK THE DUST** (Chaw)
**BLACK CHRISTMAS** (Hoover)
**BLOOD DIAMOND** (Chaw)
**THE BRIDGE** (Hoover)
**DOWN IN THE VALLEY** (Chaw)
**FAST FOOD NATION** (Chaw)
**FLAGS OF OUR FATHERS** (Chaw)
**FREE ZONE** (Chaw)
**THE HILLS HAVE EYES** (Chaw)
**HOLLYWOODLAND** (Chaw)
**LAST HOLIDAY** (Chaw)
**THE LAST KING OF SCOTLAND** (Chaw)
**LOOKING FOR COMEDY IN THE MUSLIM WORLD** (Chaw)
**LOOKING FOR KITTY** (Jackson)
**MATERIAL GIRLS** (Hoover)
**MISSION: IMPOSSIBLE III** (Chaw)
**THE NATIVITY STORY** (Chaw)
**NIGHT WATCH (Nochnoi Dozor)** (Chaw)
**PIRATES OF THE CARIBBEAN: DEAD MAN'S CHEST** (Chaw)
**THE PROMISE (U.S. version)** (Chaw)
**THE PROPOSITION** (Jackson)
**THE PURSUIT OF HAPPYNESS** (Chaw)
**THE QUIET** (Chaw)
**THE SANTA CLAUSE 3: THE ESCAPE CLAUSE** (Chambers)
**SEE NO EVIL** (Jackson)
**TRISTAN & ISOLDE** (Chaw)
**TSOTSI** (Chaw)
**THE WICKER MAN** (Chaw)

½\*
**AWESOME: I FUCKIN' SHOT THAT!** (Jackson)
**BOBBY** (Chaw)
**THE COVENANT** (Chaw)
**EIGHT BELOW** (Chaw)
**EVERYONE'S HERO** (Chaw)
**FALL TO GRACE** (Chaw)
**FAMILY** (Chaw)
**FUCK** (Hoover)
**GLORY ROAD** (Chaw)
**A GOOD YEAR** (Chaw)
**HOME OF THE BRAVE** (Chaw)
**MAN OF THE YEAR** (Chaw)
**MY SUPER EX-GIRLFRIEND** (Chaw)
**NACHO LIBRE** (Chaw)
**RV** (Chaw)
**SCOOP** (Chaw)
**THE SENTINEL** (Chaw)
**3 NEEDLES** (Chaw)
**TRUST THE MAN** (Chaw)
**UNKNOWN** (Chaw)
**X-MEN: THE LAST STAND** (Chaw)

ZERO
**AKEELAH AND THE BEE** (Chaw)
**ALL THE KING'S MEN** (Chaw)
**THE ARCHITECT** (Chaw)
**BASIC INSTINCT 2** (Chaw)
**BLOODRAYNE** (Chaw)
**CLICK** (Hoover)
**THE DA VINCI CODE** (Chaw)
**DECK THE HALLS** (Chaw)
**ERAGON** (Chaw)
**FAILURE TO LAUNCH** (Chaw)
**FETCHING CODY** (Hoover)
**THE HOLIDAY** (Chaw)
**JUST MY LUCK** (Chambers)
**LADY IN THE WATER** (Chaw)
**THE LAST KISS** (Chaw)
**NIGHT AT THE MUSEUM** (Chaw)
**POSEIDON** (Chaw)
**ROAD HOUSE 2** (Chambers)
**SCHOOL FOR SCOUNDRELS** (Chaw)
**UNACCOMPANIED MINORS** (Chaw)
**WHEN A STRANGER CALLS** (Chaw)

# APPENDIX A

## FILM FREAK CENTRAL'S TOP 10 OF 2006

*I think the start of 2006 held so much promise mainly because it heralded the end of 2005. Not a doomsayer by any stretch, I find myself, at least in my own head, defending the state of film against facile diagnoses. "Books are always better than the movies based on them" and "They don't make good movies anymore" are the common phrases trotted out to simulate critical thought—better yet is the carrying around of the cross of "You just don't like anything." The truth is that books are only superior to the movies made from them about half the time (consider that almost all of Hitchcock's films are based on shitty literature); that good movies are no rarer than usual; and that disliking* Blood Diamond, Dreamgirls, *and* The Holiday *doesn't mean I don't like anything. Still, I admit to taking short rides with those facile phrases over the years, trying them on for size, seeing if and how far they will fly.*

*I don't think it's that I'm getting old in this profession after only five or six years (and isn't there some sadness that the most respected voices in our field have, for the most part, decided that life is too short to bother to criticize a medium that suffers so much insult) inasmuch as we've gotten too good at making movies. A century of cinematic education has made everyone a director—and a critic. Technology has rendered the machineries of fantasy not only portable, but also affordable and readily available. GOOGLE paying 1.5 billion dollars for a service that officially democratizes the filmmaking process and a TIME "Person of the Year" cover sporting a mirror are just more symptoms of the savaging of the privilege of this art. When movie trailers are dissected and reconstructed with withering precision by Internet amateurs equipped with shareware and a broadband connection (and used as a key narrative framework in a major Christmas release,* The Holiday*), Hollywood has something more pressing to fear than the phantom WMD of piracy. The result, perhaps unexpected, isn't a sudden outpouring of sideshow Ed Woods like Uwe Boll, dutifully cranking out films awful enough to actually merit conversation. Instead, we have a glut of workmanlike pictures nigh indistinguishable from one another, rinsed clean of individuality, vision, risk...anything that would identify them as something besides a pure capital investment.*

\*\*\*

*The best of 2006 are a little desperate, a little resigned, a little nihilistic. They're films that by the fact of them refute drippy bits of parasitic sentimentality like* World Trade Center *along with self-important chunks of patronizing, liberal jingoism like* The Last King of Scotland *and Richard Linklater's dreadful, misanthropic, exploitative* Fast Food Nation. *I saw fewer and wrote less this year than last, which was already a low watermark. I missed films like* Idiocracy *because they weren't released in my market and films like* The Death of Mr. Lazarescu *because I was too lazy to seek it out independent of much studio interest in* my *interest. I've become closer to the non-professional this year than I have been at any time since starting out—a significant recoil and possibly a natural evolution that you have to push away, eventually, from too long at even so frugal a repast. I miss the fatigue of overfeeding sometimes, but in the wake of the soul-destroying* The Devil Wears Prada *(likewise* The DaVinci Code, *likewise* X-Men: The Last Stand, *likewise* Glory Road/Invincible/We Are Marshall, *likewise* Mission: Impossible III, *likewise, likewise, likewise), I remember why I don't miss it more.*

**Walter Chaw**
January 2, 2007

# WALTER CHAW'S TOP 10 OF 2006

### 10. *The Descent* (d. Neil Marshall)

I choose to take the domestic and international versions of *The Descent*—released in the U.K. with a different ending (now restored for Region 1 DVD) that has a kind of animal-logical emotional impact veering towards the *Kill Bill* maternal—as Kali-complementary. This is far and away the best horror film of the year, its cave setting utilized with devastating, visceral intelligence and its structure as a series of three births brilliant and pop-prickly. The first of several 2006 pictures that treat physical toil and the toll of violence on the meat of the body politic with intimate, suffocating weight, it's also the first of several that re-introduce humans into the wild only to turn them, unsurprisingly, into something bestial. Impossible in our current context not to view it on at least some level as a commentary about unfriendly incursions in foreign places (it's our *Deliverance*, just as Iraq is staking a claim as our Vietnam), but let's not discount the fact that it's home to one of the most satisfying jump scares in movie history.

### 9. *Tideland* (d. Terry Gilliam)

If the sickening thud of flesh and earth and blood is one theme unifying the best of 2006, another is the firmness of those elements as verities in our fundamental substance. Yet another is family: legacy through procreation and, through that, the potential and grail represented by little girls lost in the wilderness. Terry Gilliam's *Tideland* is very possibly the first honest film of his career: his "cleanest" picture, it's scrubbed of much of the rubbish sale floss that reached its apex (nadir?) in *The Brothers Grimm*, revealing itself to be a Lewis Carroll version of *The Texas Chain Saw Massacre*: no less fantastical, but starring a child looking for a family's approval in an Andrew Wyeth landscape. *Tideland* is unabashedly single-minded in its vision (arrogant, even) and representative of what's missing in our culture of technical perfection at the expense of emotional vacuity. Though it's oft described as discursive, I'm more comfortable calling it difficult; and unlike a lot of puzzles unravelled, its surface grotesquerie houses the disturbance of being human and the perversity of love.

### 8. *Miami Vice (Unrated Director's Edition)* (d. Michael Mann)

With *Miami Vice*, Michael Mann asserts himself as a poet laureate of the post-9/11 Wasteland, now finding its full flower of expression five years hence. A full-grown masculine fantasy of speed, technology, bullets, response-wetness (its villain even lives on a waterfall), and the cool balm of pyrrhic revolt, the picture is digital expressionism—a triumph in form and function. Re-edited for an unrated DVD, it's that version that reaches this list, as Mann trims the already lean vehicle of all its fat, inserts **Nonpoint**'s cover of the series-iconic "In the Air Tonight" into a key sequence, and augments the piece's doomed romanticism. It recasts our idealism as the Byronic hero perched on the ruins of a great civilization: chest full of braggadocio, head full of the lulls between calamities where we try to tend to our gardens.

### 7. *The Departed* (d. Martin Scorsese)

Martin Scorsese's giant fuck-you to mankind, *The Departed*'s extended epilogue of ebullient carnage is a little like the interminable denouement of *The Return of the King* with more brain tissue and arterial splatter. The rest of it is no less discontent with the state of masculine relationships, matching itself with Mad Mel's *Apocalypto* in that sense but more savage in its fashion, as it doesn't have the consolation of birth to soothe its annihilation of father-son bonds. Its parting shot a rat in a city (Boston) described as filthy with the creatures, Scorsese's version of an underwater nativity for all mankind is that there are so freakin' many of us to shoot in the face that we're going to be doing it for a long time. That it boasts as many charms as it does speaks to the seductive quality of misanthropy when clothed in the brimstone of Milton's Satan. It doesn't hurt that Scorsese shoots films that almost literally drip with testosterone.

### 6. *Superman Returns* (d. Bryan Singer)

With Richard Donner's deeply flawed cut of *Superman II* hitting shelves in 2006 as well, there is in that film the literalization of *this* film's themes of the son becoming the father. Poignancy, too, in the fact that Donner's picture is a resurrection in a way while Singer's opens with the revelation that our favourite man-in-tights has started a buried-memorial for his exploded planet. Also discover in Singer's the year's most affecting scene between a parent and child: Superman tells his maybe-son that no matter the incarnation, there is always a father to compare against in a boy's life. This after another virtuoso moment in which Superman floats above the world and informs (boasts to?) his love that the world is crying out for a saviour—and that saviour is him. The burden of the film, though, isn't mankind's on this alien's shoulders, but rather the impossible hopes of a father's and the insurmountable inadequacies of his son.

### 5. *Children of Men* (d. Alfonso Cuarón)

While the bottom of the top 10 is littered with polarized films describing the extraterrestrial landscapes of men versus women, the top (with one notable exception) is populated with pictures that walk a more evenly-weighted line separating the seeker and the sought—the conqueror and the protector. Begin with Alfonso Cuarón's remarkable, lilting *Children of Men*, which appropriates key images from modern art (including the album cover of **Pink Floyd**'s "Animals") in its tale of terrorism and infertility in one of the most poetically-realized futures since Ridley Scott's *Blade Runner* set the benchmark for such things. Clive Owen goes on the lam with the last pregnant woman on a planet that's running down—and discovers in the end the only possible way to honour his own dead son. Littered with canny cameos and scenes of virtuoso, fairytale power, it's parable of the finest sense in that although it's indisputably about 2006, it's also about every period of strife in our past and, one presumes, every stretch of despair to come.

### 4. *United 93* (d. Paul Greengrass)

Subtly politicized and sharp as a tack, Paul Greengrass' updating of his own *Bloody Sunday* does what one thought impossible in treating the subject of 9/11 with a total lack of sentimentality (unlike, it goes without saying, the Oprah-sanctioned *World Trade Center*). It's fair, amazingly so, in presenting both sides of this impenetrable religious sickness, and it does so by humanizing the desire to die, if one must die, for a greater purpose.

### 3. *Letters from Iwo Jima* (d. Clint Eastwood)

Clint Eastwood divorces Paul Haggis, his own personal Chad Lowe, and produces his best picture since *A Perfect World*. *Letters from Iwo Jima* is a doom diary of a proud-standing army on the verge of being decimated by a much smaller ground force because of an almost complete lack of air support, munitions, food, medicine, and hope. Of Chinese heritage, I'm particularly resistant to the idea of humanizing the Japanese during WWII, but between this and the great anime *Grave of the Fireflies*, we have two movies that dramatize the Japanese perspective without glorifying it. Eastwood deals with ideas of a shrinking world in the character of a celebrity Japanese officer who recounts to an American soldier the dinner he once had with Douglas Fairbanks ("Why sure, everyone knows him!") while death and disgrace hover all around them. It's as cruel a dissection of violence's toll on men (and, the film's framing story suggests, the legacy of men) as *Unforgiven*. Another withering excoriation of war in 2006 and the rites that boys endure to satisfy the image that their culture promotes as heroic.

## 2. The Fountain (d. Darren Aronofsky)

Darren Aronofsky's maddening, perfectly imperfect impressionist riff on love and eternity—on the importance of asking the right questions and the privilege of dying for, again, something greater than yourself—grew from his own career-threatening obsession with this story. He suffered massive setbacks and the loss of his A-list star (Brad Pitt, replaced by freshly-minted A-lister Hugh Jackman) in order to realize the story of three time periods and three explorers (or maybe just two) searching for the reason, I guess, why we ever fall in love with people and things that are temporary. The ideas in *The Fountain* are huge and the film is so smart that it doesn't endeavour to answer any of them. It's a lovely picture with a performance by Jackman so committed it approaches maniacal. Devastating from about thirty minutes in, it fits as comfortably into a festival bill with *Eternal Sunshine of the Spotless Mind* as does Steven Soderbergh's *Solaris*. A singular vision that attempts to marry religious imagery with science, *The Fountain* is alive in ways that too few films are anymore.

## 1. Pan's Labyrinth (d. Guillermo del Toro)

Brutal and dulcet, often in the same breath, Guillermo del Toro's extraordinary *Pan's Labyrinth* is about another girl hero in another fairytale wood, tasked with discovering her morality in a morally-bankrupt time and place. Del Toro unearths beauty in his atrocities here, painting his pictures with a sort of indefinable exquisiteness that takes as much care with a boy's face smashed, repeatedly, by a bottle as with the flight of a fairy through a war-clouded sky. Man's desire for progeny and the cruelty of that denial of personal mythology reveals the piece's real concern: that storytelling is the vital thread that gives weight and value to everything in an individual's existence. The characters (arrayed against one another as archetypes of scientist, soldier, mother, child, monster, guide) each understand the importance of their stories—the most jealously guarded commodity in the film is The Word. For del Toro, there is also the eloquence of the immaculately-conceived image; I can't imagine the way that he imagines. *Pan's Labyrinth* is the best film of 2006.

•**Honourable Mentions:** *Apocalypto*; *Stranger Than Fiction*; *Talladega Nights: The Ballad of Ricky Bobby*; *Water*; *A Scanner Darkly*; *Heading South*; *House of Sand*; *Silent Hill*

•**Notably Missed:** *Inland Empire; Omkara; Curse of the Golden Flower; The Death of Mr. Lazarescu*

# BILL CHAMBERS' TOP 10 OF 2006

### 10. *The Death of Mr. Lazarescu (Moartea domnului Lazarescu)* (d. Cristi Puiu)
Form serves function in this overlong, sickly-looking film, a triumph of verisimilitude that makes you fear not the Reaper, but rather sanctimony from within the medical community. Cumulatively devastating; I just wish it hadn't laid on the allusions to <u>The Divine Comedy</u> so thick.

### 9. *Heading South (Vers le sud)* (d. Laurent Cantet)
Unfolding towards the end of "Baby Doc"'s reign of terror, *Heading South* relies a little too much on a working knowledge of Haiti's political history to sort out its narrative ambiguities, but Cantet miraculously manages to exploit Haiti's mystique without falling back on *Serpent and the Rainbow*-isms.

### 8. *Clean* (d. Olivier Assayas)
This is the first time an Assayas film has made me look forward to the next one. It's a return to the humanism of his early pictures, which seemed to bother highbrow filmgoers, maybe because it deromanticizes their ice-queen centrefold Maggie Cheung.

### 7. *Manderlay* (d. Lars von Trier)
Not as good as *Dogville*, though I suspect Nicole Kidman would've helped turn on the afterburners. The relish with which narrator John Hurt says "niggers," it's so wrong, yet unlike the public implosions of Mel Gibson and Michael Richards, *Manderlay* is articulate enough to pre-empt a knee-jerk dismissal.

### 6. *Idiocracy* (d. Mike Judge)
When Luke Wilson's army guinea pig awakens from cryo-sleep 500 years into a future where stupidity reigns, the first person he encounters is literally suckling a nipple attached to his television; *Idiocracy*, however funny (and it's very, very funny), is an angry, terrifying conjecture of a world in which the culture war was definitively lost. It could just as easily have been called *An Inconvenient Truth*.

### 5. *Miami Vice* (d. Michael Mann)
Contrary to Walter, I feel the so-called Director's Edition dumbs down the theatrical version, to say nothing of its careless deletion of the opening smash cut—*the* movie moment of the year, albeit an abstract one.

### 4. *Children of Men* (d. Alfonso Cuarón)
War journalism as a master class in visceral filmmaking.

### 3. *United 93* (d. Paul Greengrass)
### 2. *Pan's Labyrinth* (d. Guillermo del Toro)
### 1. *The Departed* (d. Martin Scorsese)
Narratively and aesthetically, *United 93, Pan's Labyrinth,* and *The Departed* couldn't be more different, but they suggest a trilogy to me, together forming a snapshot of our misanthropic zeitgeist that is as existentially disquieting as it is cinematically galvanizing. (*Children of Men* is actually the most timely

allegory on this list, but unlike my Top 3 films, it finally succumbs to something resembling hope.) All three directors go on a kamikaze mission—both onscreen and off—and they've rarely seemed so alive; if the best movies of 2006 had you feeling like a rubberneck (see also: *Tideland* and *The Death of Mr. Lazarescu*), at least they left you, to paraphrase Scorsese's film, comfortably numb.

●**Honourable Mentions:** *Superman Returns; Neil Young: Heart of Gold; A Scanner Darkly; Dave Chappelle's Block Party*

●**Notably Missed:** *Inland Empire; Old Joy; The Fountain; Letters from Iwo Jima; Marie Antoinette; Brick*

●**Dishonourable Mentions:** *Lady in the Water; Pirates of the Caribbean: Dead Man's Chest; Hard Candy; Looking for Comedy in the Muslim World; The Illusionist*

●**Ridiculous Yet Unshakable:** *The King; Don't Come Knocking; Running Scared; London; Wassup Rockers*

# TRAVIS MACKENZIE HOOVER'S TOP 10 OF 2006

### 10. *Shortbus* (d. John Cameron Mitchell)
Most critics were limited in their praise for this film, and perhaps in a stronger year it might not have made my list. But its bold rewriting of the sexual program—one that included fatigue and burnout—made it one of the few essential American films of the year. Mitchell may only be groping in the dark for his ideas, but at least he's out there looking.

### 9. *Requiem* (d. Hans-Christian Schmid)
The travesty known as *The Exorcism of Emily Rose* gets karmic payback through this sensitive reversal of its more loathsome themes. Without seeming anti-religious, *Requiem* demolishes the pop religiosity that led its based-on-fact heroine to her untimely end.

### 8. *The Proposition* (d. John Hillcoat)
A lovely, blood-and-thunder revisionist western, with all the sadness and torment that implies. Supremely unimpressed with the American rev-west loss of innocence, Hillcoat and screenwriter Nick Cave wind up breathing new life into a lost genre by envisioning an Australia where nobody has innocence to lose.

### 7. *Battle in Heaven (Batalla en el cielo)* (d. Carlos Reygadas)
"We've got one a heavyset chauffeur in love, a rich young client who turns him on, a whorehouse staffed by wealthy teenagers, a botched kidnapping complete with dead baby, a weird climax in a church, fat-people sex, thin-people sex, fat and thin people sex, it's dark, and we're wearing sunglasses." "Hit it."

### 6. *Six Figures* (d. David Christensen)
### 5. *Monkey Warfare* (d. Reginald Harkema)
Readers of THE FILM FREAK CENTRAL BLOG know my frustration with Canadian cinema, so it's my pleasure to announce two films that do my country proud. The first is a delicate, Haneke-esque essay in suburban anomie and uncertain motives, the second a blunt and furious wail for the twilight of the Left and the perversion of its goals. Both are sharp, funny, and more forceful than ten other films I could name.

### 4. *Old Joy* (d. Kelly Reichardt)
Another Left-twilight film sketched in the subtlest possible manner: it's the reunion of two college friends, one of whom has chosen to join the capitalist grind while the other has fallen off the map completely. It's more than that, of course, and Reichardt captures their new ambivalence towards each other with immense respect and sensitivity.

### 3. *The Sun (Solntse)* (d. Aleksandr Sokurov)
This has to be the most entertaining film ever made about Emperor Hirohito, but it somehow never got an American release—thank God for Films We Like north of the border. *The Sun* manages to be funny and sad as the Emperor faces up to his non-godhead status and must end a war for which he was never that enthusiastic; a performance by Issey Ogata crowns an already high achievement.

## 2. *The Death of Mr. Lazarescu (Moartea domnului Lazarescu)* (d. Cristi Puiu)

They say that Romania is the new world-film hotspot, and if Cristi Puiu's Cannes-winner is any evidence then the rumours would appear to be true. This is a trip down the slippery slope from a slight pain to certain doom in the Kafka hell of arrogant doctors and red tape. Though it starts unassumingly, it eventually weighs on you like few movies this year.

## 1. *The Child (L'Enfant)* (ds. Jean-Pierre Dardenne & Luc Dardenne)

The appeal of the Dardenne brothers had eluded me until I saw this devastating essay in irresponsibility and redemption; it was the highlight of last year's TIFF and now it's the highlight of this year's release crop. Jeremie Renier leaves an indelible impression as the feckless hustler who sells his baby only to have to deal with the consequences of getting him back. The incident-packed film doesn't let him down.

•**Honourable Mentions:** *Deliver Us from Evil; The Queen; V for Vendetta*

•**Enjoyed Despite My Better Judgment:** *Crank; Brick; District 13*

•**Overrated:** *Pan's Labyrinth; Babel; Half Nelson; Three Times*

•**Instant Camp Classics:** *Lady in the Water; Little Children; The Nativity Story*

•**2005 Films I Wish I'd Seen In Time For Last Year's Top 10:** *Caché; Keane; The New World*

# APPENDIX B

## TEN YEARS, TEN-LISTS

*To mark the occasion of the mothersite turning ten, all of us at* FILM FREAK CENTRAL—*Walter Chaw, Travis Mackenzie Hoover, Alex Jackson, Ian Pugh, and yours truly—compiled a Top 10 list of our own devising. A new one surfaced every couple of days at the Blog, and they're reproduced here in the order in which they appeared—with mine, the most self-indulgent, coming last.*

*First up: Alex Jackson with a subject close to my own heart. Take it away, Alex!*

**Bill Chambers**
May 25, 2007

# TEN UNDERAPPRECIATED CLASSICS FROM THE 1980s
## by Alex Jackson

*When this project was first announced, my initial idea was to make a list of ten middlebrow films worth going to bat for. But the more I thought about it, the more unoriginal and—in light of Walter's recent two-for-one pan of* American Beauty *and* Forrest Gump*—overly reactionary it sounded. I thought about what I really wanted to say in a Top Ten list and realized that, more than just defending the status quo, I wanted to point people to some buried treasures. The idea of compiling a list of underrated classics was also a little passé—a list of underappreciated classics from the 1980s, however, feels powerfully evocative. For the most part, I stumbled upon these films, guided by a sense of adventure, though a few were referred to me by a particularly strong review. Many were well-received at the time of their release but have since fallen out of fashion, with none retaining a particularly strong reputation. As I see it, this should be one of the focal goals of movie reviewers everywhere: to shine a little bit of light on films that have been ignored or simply forgotten.*

### 10. *Wish You Were Here* (1987, David Leland)
When it was first on Showtime, my dad recorded *Bill and Ted's Excellent Adventure* for me and caught the end credits of this film, which depicted a British street performer dancing on the boardwalk. I watched this for years before my curiosity got the better of me and I did a reverse-lookup of the title on the Internet Movie Database using the name of one of the cast members. The picture is a breezy but bittersweet coming-of-age story about a sassy teenage girl who rebels against her deadening working-class existence with sex and becomes pregnant by the town's middle-aged projectionist—a friend, as it happens, of her judgmental and overbearing father. *Wish You Were Here* is very funny, very peppy, and very brutal in a way that doesn't cancel out the funny or the peppy.

### 9. *Pixote* (1981, Hector Babenco)
It's a little fatty and drags in spots, but who can forget that glue-huffing sequence with little Pixote? Or the last shot at the train tracks? Or the iconic kiss with the prostitute? The fattiness is necessary, in a sense. Given a little room to breathe, sensational material becomes natural, normal, and real. Walter accurately labelled *City of God* "Quentin Tarantino's *Schindler's List*." One need only refer back to *Pixote* for that film's good doppelgänger.

### 8. *Children of the Corn* (1984, Fritz Kiersch)
I've been an advocate for *Children of the Corn* for a while now. To be honest, the script is pretty bad; the dialogue is filled with howlers; there's the it's-just-a-dream-cliché and the woman who gets out of the car when her man told her not to cliché; and everything ends with a big explosion to help out the guys cutting the TV spots. But there's something in the air. Low-budget horror had a different feel in the early-'80s; *Children of the Corn* lacks the slick sheen you encounter even in films like *House of the Dead*. This thing is sparse, quiet, and deadening. And it plays on our fears of the Bible Belt very powerfully, more so than any movie I've yet seen. I find *Children of the Corn* to be much more frightening than Tobe Hooper's *The Texas Chain Saw Massacre* and I think that can be traced back to the

fact that the monsters here are all children. If they're children, what they're doing can't be dismissed as the happenings of one lone band of psychos. It has to run deeper.

### 7. *Life Lessons* (1989, Martin Scorsese)

It's the first segment of the prestigious anthology *New York Stories* and is unfortunately the only thing of real value in that film. *Life Lessons* is as good as anything in the Scorsese canon. I may be revealing my inexperience in saying so, but a sequence where artist Nick Nolte paints on his canvas through a series of rapid dissolves so that it looks like there are several of him working at the same time has to be one of the freshest uses of the cinematic medium I have ever seen. This is a true master at work.

### 6. *Made in Britain* (1982, Alan Clarke)

I know that Alan Clarke has gotten a lot of love around these parts and apparently those serious about film have known about him for years. I heard a little bit about *Made in Britain* from Roger Ebert's near-pan of *American History X* and from interviews with *Gummo* director Harmony Korine, who cites Clarke as a major influence. But to be honest, I wasn't really aware of the guy until **FFC** reviewed a box set of his work. *Made in Britain* is one of the great juvenile delinquent movies. The script (by David Leland, the writer-director of *Wish You Were Here*) is brilliant in making the protagonist (Tim Roth) a neo-Nazi. That single decision renders him more morally ambiguous than the working-class heroes who populate a film like *Brassed Off* and yet more sympathetic than the rebels-without-a-cause who populate our more class-unconscious American films. It's darkly funny, too; I love the moment where the mentally-retarded black kid who gets in trouble because he always follows the crowd participates in a hate crime with Roth.

### 5. *The Mosquito Coast* (1986, Peter Weir)

A very recent discovery for me and I kind of want to get the word out. All the materials seem to be there: a literate script by Paul Schrader; icy, dispassionate direction by Peter Weir; and a flashy but brilliant performance by Harrison Ford. Yet the film never quite caught on like it should've. Believe it or not, the cult that's formed around it on video consists largely of teenage girls lusting after Ford's co-star River Phoenix! *The Mosquito Coast* has two of my favourite ideas for a movie: the intellectual who argues himself outside of the human race, and the teenage boy who gradually realizes that his father, who had been the centre of the universe as he knows it, is batshit insane. The film is about nothing less than a failed god figure, a notion that has the precisely right blend of the romantic and the cynical. Plus, check out the cameo by the great Butterfly McQueen!

### 4. *Nineteen Eighty-Four* (1984, Michael Radford)

It's the rare film adaptation of a classic novel that does the source material justice, and quite surprisingly most who've seen it tend to agree. If only more people *would* see it! The filmmakers appear to have read the book and understood Orwell's thesis that the key to maintaining the totalitarian government is in keeping everybody perpetually miserable. The film is wonderfully grungy and hauntingly ugly—and with the great John Hurt as Winston Smith, it avoids making heroes of the patently anti-heroic. Embarrassingly, the story remains topical today. The idea that we shouldn't criticize our government in a time of war is regularly presented *sans* irony by talk-show pundits who fail to understand that if we don't criticize our government in a time of war, the government can forgo ever being criticized by always being at war!

### 3. *Pennies from Heaven* (1981, Herbert Ross)

Other than maybe home movies shot in Super8, I don't believe there is anything I love more in a movie than lip-synching. I never saw the Dennis Potter miniseries this is based on, but from the sounds of things the miniseries likes its characters whereas the feature film (also scripted by Potter) despises them—it really doesn't paint a very optimistic picture of human nature. *Pennies from Heaven* is sort of an anti-musical, a subversive take on the polluted gender dynamics that populated the Busby Berkeley and Fred and Ginger musicals of the 1930s. When a heart-shaped iris wipe closes out what is unquestionably the rape of Bernadette Peters, the entire genre is violated along with her. This is a work of pure cinema with a heart that is four sizes too small. It uses sarcasm and escapism as a weapon and is nothing short of a masterpiece of audience abuse.

### 2. *Parents* (1989, Bob Balaban)

Like *The Mosquito Coast*, *Parents* is a film about a kid who discovers that his mother and father, the centre of his universe, are nuts. In fact, they're cannibals—but the movie is also about incest, in a disguised form. It sexualizes cannibalism and Mom and Dad want their boy to be a cannibal like them. Moreover, it's about the fear of disappointing your parents. The kid doesn't overtly reject his parents' values; he's just a kid, he doesn't know what's going on. This important fact helps raise the film above the level of an easy attack on 1950s suburbia and into some sort of gonzo, left-of-centre masterpiece.

### 1. *Christiane F.* (1981, Uli Edel)

The titular Christiane F. is a fifteen-year old girl in Berlin who is a huge David Bowie fan, and to fit in with the older and more sophisticated crowd she tries heroin. (Or "H" as they like to refer to it.) The film is perhaps the most brutal Afterschool Special ever made. Once she's addicted, Christiane gives handjobs to older men to support her habit. She and her boyfriend decide they're going to go cold turkey and fight over one last fix to keep themselves going. We see her nude, vomiting, going through withdrawal, and yet, not only does the actress portraying Christiane (Natja Brunckhorst) actually look fifteen, but the film is also told through a teenager's sensibility: it's naïve, romantic, and a little bit stupid. It even ends with Bowie's "Heroes"! The tone clashes with the images that we're seeing and that seems to be precisely the point. *Christiane F.* is so authentic from an emotional standpoint that it's jarring and difficult to take.

*I also recommend:* Paperhouse *(1988, Bernard Rose);* The Monster Squad *(1987, Fred Dekker);* Alice *(1988, Jan Svankmajer);* Friday the 13th: The Final Chapter *(1984, Joseph Zito);* The Race for the Double Helix *(1987, Mick Jackson);* Talk Radio *(1988, Oliver Stone);* Mother's Day *(1980, Charles Kaufman);* Night of the Comet *(1984, Thom Eberhardt);* Personal Services *(1987, Terry Jones); and, with some measure of guilt,* My Demon Lover *(1987, Charlie Loventhal).*

# TEASERS: TEN GREAT OPENING TITLE SEQUENCES
## by Ian Pugh

*It was actually a set of closing credits that gave me the idea for my contribution to FFC's Top Ten List project—the very final sequence of Romero's* Dawn of the Dead, *to be exact. Thinking about how that film's end titles entailed the most eloquent, concise, and chilling example of the film-long equation of zombies with dead-eyed consumerism, the idea of compiling a list of other great thematic "thesis statements" became an attractive one. Ultimately, I decided to head for the opposite end of the chronological spectrum, because while the best opening title sequences establish and epitomize their films' worlds and intentions, they also represent the screenwriters' and filmmakers' eagerness to snatch up the soonest possible opportunity to subdue the viewer with the elusive magic that is cinema. The definition of what constitutes a "title sequence," per se, will be left intentionally vague for the purposes of this list. Many of these selections are pre-credits teasers, while others are the moments that surround the literal credits—basically that grey area between the studio logos and "directed by."*

**10. Magnum Force (1973, Ted Post)**
Sequels don't require the laborious set-ups that original films do—and boy, does the second Dirty Harry film ever know it. As the film begins, we're quite plainly presented with Harry Callahan's familiar .44 Magnum, spread out across a blood-red background. The gun turns towards us and—as Clint Eastwood recites an abridged version of his "do you feel lucky" speech—fires. Call it a simplification of Godard's necessities for filmmaking: all you need is a gun.

**9. Bride of Re-Animator (1989, Brian Yuzna)**
A good chunk of my admiration for Brian Yuzna's scattershot *Re-Animator* sequel lies in its opening stinger, featuring the living, disembodied head of arch-prick Dr. Carl Hill slowly floating towards us as he casts a dire warning directed at his nemesis, Herbert West. The last time we saw the dear departed Dr. Hill, his brains were splattered across the walls of Miskatonic University; he won't be formally revived from the dead in this film for another half-hour. And yet here he is, head awake and fully intact, coming at us with a beautifully melodramatic speech in the Bela Lugosi vein. (After all, beyond the obvious *Frankenstein* connection, *Bride of Re-Animator* is something of an extended tribute to Ed Wood.) Hill has bent the rules of his own metaverse to once again rise from the grave and make life difficult for everyone. It's the ultimate re-animation.

**8. Stop Making Sense (1984, Jonathan Demme)**
"Hi, I got a tape I wanna play." The singularly bizarre sight of the crane-like David Byrne jamming to an acoustic version of "Psycho Killer" on a bare stage makes us wonder what he's hiding up his sleeve.

**7. Dead of Night / Deathdream (1974, Bob Clark)**
*Dead of Night* earned the right to use Hitchcock's familiar "no one will be seated" marketing ploy by turning the jungles of Vietnam into something dark and supernatural even before Andy Brooks (played by a different actor in the pre-credits sequence than in the film proper) is killed in the line of duty and sent back to Mom and Dad as a post-traumatic zombie. So once the film starts

throwing pulsating lights and faraway, ghostly voices at us, it doesn't seem like a leap of logic so much as one step deeper into a void of madness that has already engulfed us. To be honest, the audio alone could almost carry this sequence, as the wails of a dying soldier and the pleas of his doomed friend ("Darren? Darren, Jesus Christ, Darren!") are just as haunting as any other horrors delivered throughout the rest of the piece. With this prologue, Clark implies that his own metaphors may be unnecessary in the harsh face of what was already happening overseas.

### 6. The Untouchables (1987, Brian De Palma)

Pauline Kael famously called *The Untouchables* "an attempt to visualize the public's collective dream of Chicago gangsters." I would call its title sequence an attempt to visualize the public's collective dream of the gangster genre as a series of recognizable abstracts. Start with a sepia background and pillars of shadows that vaguely mimic some aspect of the *noir* aesthetic—maybe the ceiling fan that presides over the archetypal private detective's office, or the Venetian blinds that ominously open and close when he wants a peek at the outside world. They're eventually revealed to be the deep shadows cast by the enormous letters of the title itself, which of course becomes a representation of the purely conceptual heroes from the days of Sam Spade, Mike Hammer, and Robert Stack's Eliot Ness—in our eyes, larger-than-life and, of course, untouchable. Top it off with Ennio Morricone's driving, threatening overture and you're ready for *The Untouchables* despite that there isn't a single fedora or Thompson gun in sight.

### 5. Schizopolis (1996, Steven Soderbergh)

The entirety of *Schizopolis* is something of a gigantic joke on an audience unprepared for the *avant-garde*, and Steven Soderbergh's intro, in which the man himself takes the stage for a brief explanation, serves as a parodic response to folks who demand cohesion and logic from the likes of David Lynch—finally, somebody can tell me what all of this weird shit is about. But all that awaits such expectations are more frustrations: Soderbergh interrupts his stream-of-consciousness speech with random commands to "turn" and retreat to a different camera angle, and concludes that the viewer's lack of understanding in the film's purpose is "your fault, not ours." It's at once a condemnation of the attempt to rationalize a world of subconscious surrealism and an invitation to play by its rules.

### 4. The Spy Who Loved Me (1977, Lewis Gilbert)

I can't list my favourite opening sequences without mentioning at least one James Bond film; out of all of them, I choose Maurice Binder's title sequence from my personal favourite of the series, *The Spy Who Loved Me*. The teaser itself hits all of the familiar marks for a Bond film—and I could probably do without the disco remix—but the surrealistic titles manage to indulge in the typical silliness that comes with the territory (girls on trampolines, fetishized gun barrels) without descending into puerile ridiculousness. Notice how they follow the easygoing flow of Carly Simon's "Nobody Does It Better" while capturing the undercurrent of paranoia in the film's détente subplot: there's actually something self-consciously reckless about how the guns are thrown around here. The vital moment, however, comes when the 007 silhouette knocks over a row of nude women "dressed" as marching toy soldiers.

### 3. Fahrenheit 451 (1966, Francois Truffaut)

The opening "titles" of Truffaut's *Fahrenheit 451* don't feel quite right, as if they were made by someone with only a rudimentary grasp of filmmaking: the credits are read aloud in an indifferent monotone while the camera, armed with obnoxious pastel filters, zooms in abruptly on what appear to be intricate television antennae. It comes from another world, one of illiteracy, artlessness, and suppression—one that's becoming more and more familiar every day.

## 2. Darkman (1990, Sam Raimi)

I absolutely adore the opening minutes of Sam Raimi's *Darkman*—the original, superior version of Raimi's overblown *Spider-Man 3*—because they establish its world of comic book hyper-logic so effortlessly. Raimi kicks things off by filling his frame/panel with a multitude of unique personalities (in the second shot of the film, notice the geek off to the side quickly alternating between popping pills and puffing his cigarette), only to cram more such characters into view a few moments later. Then it proceeds to embroil them all in a manic gang war to determine which band of thugs will serve as the bad guys of this picture. The winners, of course, are the ones whose themes and traits are most consistent with a comic book villain landscape—Robert Durant's penchant to clip the fingers of his adversaries with his cigar cutter; a guy named "Skip" with a machine gun housed in his wooden leg—and those who best prepare the viewer for the fantastic elements that *Darkman* is about to hurl at them.

## 1. A Hard Day's Night (1964, Richard Lester)

**The Beatles** described their experiences with crowds of rabid fans as terrifying— it was apparently the threat of being assaulted with scissors for locks of their hair that finally forced them to stay holed-up in a studio for good. But *A Hard Day's Night* begins with the Fab Four, just two steps ahead of a screaming mob, running for dear life with great big grins on their faces and concocting silly, makeshift plans to escape. It's a spectacular, hyperactive sequence, one that of course sets the stage for the madcap hilarity ahead. But knowing the truth of it, it also says a lot about masking your fear and pain for the benefit of your audience—willingly feeding into a popular perception that there was something fun and cartoony about the disturbing loss of anonymity that attends worldwide fame. I dare say that it transforms **The Beatles'** subsequent horseplay into the work of operatic Pagliaccis. Incidentally, the sequence makes for a fine companion piece to the final, live-action sing-along of *Yellow Submarine*, where the band attempted to exude the same camaraderie when they were actually on the verge of destruction thanks to their clashing egos.

# THE TEN BEST CANADIAN FILMS
## by Travis Mackenzie Hoover

*A collection of genuine gems found among the detritus of my country's cinema. Good luck locating copies of most of these, but if you have the wherewithal, here's a handy guide to Canada's best.*

**10. La Vraie nature de Bernadette (The True Nature of Bernadette)** (1972, Gilles Carle)
Gilles Carle's satirical tragedy involves a free-thinking woman named Bernadette (the implacable Micheline Lanctôt) who flees the city to set up shop in a rural village; all manner of misunderstandings ensue, including the idea of her as a miracle-curing Madonna. Unpretentious yet acid, *La Vraie nature de Bernadette* goes down easy without spoon-feeding you to get there.

**9. Gambling, Gods and LSD** (2002, Peter Mettler)
Training his camera on all things transcendent (from revival meetings to demolition sites to the lights on top of the Luxor pyramid), Peter Mettler shows the profound mystery involved on both the spiritual and the material planes, as well as the plain weirdness involved in being human.

**8. Montreal Main** (1974, Frank Vitale)
This semi-autobiographical work of photographer Frank Vitale places Vitale in an undefined relationship with a 12-year-old boy—and, subsequently, the censure of his circle (to say nothing of the boy's parents). Mournful but somehow not hopeless, the film's melancholy will stay with you for days.

**7. A Married Couple** (1969, Allan King)
Before reality-TV followed people around with cameras 24/7, there was Allan King's cinema-*vérité* masterpiece about Billy and Antoinette Edwards. A wrenching film about two people who talk past each other, with a rewarding moment of clarity close to the end.

**6. Goin' Down the Road** (1970, Donald Shebib)
A man went looking for Canada, and couldn't find it anywhere; the Anglo-hoser *Citizen Kane*: a movie that's satisfying no matter how many times you watch it.

**5. Les Dernières fiançailles** (1973, Jean Pierre Lefebvre)
A brilliantly structural take on the last two days in the disappointing lives of an elderly couple, this is the only film I've been able to track down by the great Jean Pierre Lefebvre, but it seems like it was the one to catch. The camera tracks beautifully as the details come spilling out.

**4. Pour la suite du monde** (1963, Michel Brault, Marcel Carrière, Pierre Perrault)
Another one of the great documentaries: three filmmakers revive the practice of whale fishing in rural *Ile-aux-Courdes* and in the process make a statement on the vanishing traditions of Quebec.

**3. Dead Ringers** (1988, David Cronenberg)
And God said, "Let there be Cronenberg." And when He saw what He had done, He disappeared in a puff of smoke as the master went about his bodily business

in the most profoundly disturbing manner possible. This is Cronenberg's crowning achievement, about two Jeremy Irons who discover that their attempts at bodily control will come to naught.

**2. Yes Sir! Madame...** (1994, Robert Morin)
Technically this is a video, but whatever it is, it's a masterpiece. Robert Morin's bilingual exploration of what it means to live on the knife-edge of two languages and two cultures while living on the margins of society. Blunt, ballsy, and conceptually astounding, this years-in-the-making mini-epic will make your jaw drop.

**1. Les Bons débarras (Good Riddance)** (1980, Francis Mankiewicz)
There has never been a more appalling girl than Michelle, the 13-year-old who demands her mother's undivided attention in the most devious ways. She's the apocalyptic heroine of Francis Mankiewicz's quietly devastating classic: the most powerful film ever produced in Canada, and on the short list of best movies of the '80s. The climax must be seen to be believed.

# TEN FILMS THAT CHANGED THE WAY I LOOK AT FILM
## by Walter Chaw

*In composing a Top Ten list to celebrate the tenth anniversary of an endeavour I've only been a part of for six (six of the most creatively fulsome and rewarding years of my life in this profession, I might add), I ran through a chum-load of possible topics. I thought long and hard about cannibal films—not just natives dancing around a pot in old jungle screamers, but actual on-screen depictions, the hook being that after so many words, I'm probably just cannibalizing myself nowadays. I considered using this as an excuse to write about ten movies I couldn't slot into any particular Top 10 list. At a low moment, I even toyed with doing ten flicks I was wrong about the first time around. But then it occurred to me that the best way to honour a collaboration as important to me as mine has been with Bill (for my writing, for clarifying—to whatever extent that it's clear—my thinking) would be to set down a list of ten films that were, at various points in my life, seminal to the way I think. Ten pictures that are for me like those railroad track junctures leading off into different destinations—not the ten that you necessarily need to see to experience a similar revelation, but the ten that I did. The change in direction hasn't always been easy, some were more like wrecks than like rivulets, but here are ten personal milestones as FFC crosses the threshold of its first decade on the Internet.*

## 10. Trouble Every Day (2001, Claire Denis)

Claire Denis' apocalyptic take on both the banality and reward of companionate love addresses the bestial roots of passion before taking on the terms of endearment we use to leash it. Vincent Gallo is extraordinary as the vacuum at the picture's dark core—and I don't know of a better illustration of what it means to love and fuck and grow old together in the tempest of the temporary. I saw this in a private screening at Boulder's International Film Series; later that week, the only public screening of the film in Colorado saw a few hysterics, including a young woman who locked herself in the bathroom and refused to be coaxed out for hours afterward. For me, the picture is the possibility of cinema as anthropology and as high art—a reminder, at a relatively late date, that there are still things that can get under the skin if the medium is wielded like a scalpel by a surgeon. Odd that a few knock-offs appeared not long after it. Not so odd is the cult that has gathered around it.

## 9. The Killer (1989, John Woo)

John Woo's ballet of bloodlust. The dubbed version with Brother Chow screaming "Dumbo!" as bloody tears stream down his cheeks was met with howls of drunken approval at my first screening of it in CU Boulder's Muenzinger Auditorium. I taught my pals that night how to say "shoot him again" in Mandarin (not knowing at that moment that Woo shot his pictures in Cantonese), and for probably the first time in my life felt a distinct pride in being Chinese in Colorado. Folks only familiar with Woo from his American output are missing the indescribable romantic machismo distilled by the director in his Hong Kong flicks—it doesn't translate. Yellow Power, man, and the wasting of Chow in this summer's *Pirates of the Caribbean* threequel is disappointing for sure. But that he's there at all is a result of this and other collaborations with Woo. I was ecstatic to hear that Chow is back in the fold with Woo's *Chinese* epic *The Battle of Red Cliff*.

**8. Dragonslayer** (1981, Matthew Robbins)
I hid under the seat for most of my first two viewings of Matthew Robbins' *Dragonslayer*—a picture I demanded to see because, unless I'm mistaken, I believed it to be some sort of sequel to *Pete's Dragon*. (A belief that, among other things, confirms that eight-year-olds are almost without exception stupid in the larger sense.) Little did I know that *this* "Disney" picture featured a flash of full-frontal nudity, a beautiful princess consumed by a litter of baby dragons, and the death of one—make that two—kindly father figures. A special-effects dry run for the groundbreaking stop-motion work of *Return of the Jedi*, its beastie Vermithrax Pejorative is pathetic in its majestic, pagan glory. It's helpless in the face of the encroaching Christianity, says one read, but for me at that moment, not-yet-weaned from a steady diet of Disney heroes slaying their shadows in a series of deeply-destructive problem-solving scenarios, it was a shot in the pants of that old-time atheism. I was terrified of the dragon, but I don't recall ever wishing it dead. The marvel of *Dragonslayer* and secret movie-brat Robbins' direction and script is that it proposes a happy ending that's not at all happy. The more I learn about myself through the movies, the better it gets.

**7. Marnie** (1964, Alfred Hitchcock)
I didn't really understand Hitchcock until I saw *The Birds* and then, soon after it, *Marnie*. You get a sense of the formalist (the auto-formalist, maybe) from stuff like *North by Northwest* and *Notorious*, but you don't get a full sense of Hitch's sly, unrepentant wickedness until you view his work through the prism of his Tippi Hedren pictures. I'd go so far as to say that *Marnie* is the Rosetta Stone for *all* of his pictures: you turn to *North by Northwest* for a sense of how Hitchcock's clockwork is wound; but you look at *Marnie* for a little sulphur whiff of the infernal electricity that makes the clockwork turn over. Tippi in this one is raped, and the whole sea reflects her change outside a porthole while Sean Connery—the dim, dashing rake cast perfectly at last—saves an empty glass cage in his room for her, his next and greatest trophy. Just as *The Birds* is Hitch's domestication fantasy for wild Tippi, all of a feminized nature arrayed against her wild individuation, *Marnie* is menstrual fear, sexual paranoia, and the price of carnality against the life of the mind. Though it's as much about artifice and illusion as any of the Master's treatises on the theme, it was my long-in-coming epiphany that the gateway to the secrets of the flesh is through the eyes of the artist.

**6. Grave of the Fireflies** (1988, Isao Takahata)
Isao Takahata's devastating war idyll *Grave of the Fireflies* was the singular event in my turning the corner on a fairly unquestioned bigotry against the Japanese. Raised in a household where a good portion of my mother's side of the family was fed to the Nipponese grinder in Nanking, I was, through glances and smirks and possibly even direct comments, bred to hate the Japanese. Watching this film for the first time my senior year in college, I came to terms at last with a lot of things I just took as plain truth and found myself confronted with the ugliness of my assumptions. The picture is so good on its own that it doesn't need much further endorsement from me: it's not just the best animated film ever made, it's one of the best films ever made in any medium. But for me, the switch that turned over in my heart has rippled into the way I look at everything in my adult life; things are never black-and-white, and the tactics of dehumanization make all manner of atrocity possible. Take the punditry of the modern day and consider something wonderfully acidic Melvin Van Peebles said to me in regards to bigotry in mainstream culture: how it's always possible to isolate our next enemy by identifying the "nigger" in our pictures.

**5. Alphaville** (1965, Jean-Luc Godard)
A houseguest asked once, while searching my library for a film to watch, if Jean-Luc Godard's neo-*noir Alphaville* was a good choice. My wife warned: "It's not conventionally entertaining." Fair enough. Indeed, more than fair—a quick look at most of my collection shows that the DVDs I keep are likewise not conventionally entertaining and, in the case of this selection, almost aggressive in their desire to not be conventionally liked. I saw *Alphaville* for the first time in college and it opened a door for me. It inspired, of all things, research, not into whether such and such a character was really real or this event happened or what have you, but into precepts of critical theory that I'd been using as reference points in the study of British Romanticist and Modernist poetry. The picture connected the dots, so to speak, allowing a dim student to finally understand that all the strategies that have been used for centuries to decode the sublimity of great works could be applied to bear fruit from film. A great picture by one of the great film theorists (talking about *Alphaville* or *Week End* or *Breathless* in terms of signs and signifiers is easy enough: they're textbooks already)—and if the case could be made that movies carry within them the same seeds as music or letters or brush strokes, then movies must also carry within them the possibility to understand the meaning of an individual's life. Of the critical life.

**4. Revenge of the Nerds** (1984, Jeff Kanew)
The first time I saw female full-frontal nudity once I was capable of assimilating what it was; my VHS tape became one of the most prized onanistic totems of my adolescence. *Revenge of the Nerds* has gathered around it a wealth of scholarship since its release because, more so than the oeuvres of Sylvia Krystal or Deborah Foreman, there's something genuinely sticky about the thing. The way that it equalizes gay people, and blacks, and women; the way that Darth Vader is turned into a literal rapist for a generation of boys like me secretly titillated by the fetishistic promise of his cyborg, insect carapace; the way that, the way that... Look, it's a hell of a film, and it holds up now as not a masturbation aid, but a scalpel for the dissection of the way that film is voyeurism incarnate: justification for voyeurism; idealization of voyeurism; and perfection of voyeurism. Too, it's a nutshell of why pornography's genres are such useful tabs for our real peccadilloes. A peek at what we hide between our mattresses reveals the taboos tattooed on our bestial pelts: miscegenation, pedophilia, sodomy, humiliation, promiscuity, water sports—you find these things in *Revenge of the Nerds*, encapsulated in the moment where a weak, physically ineffectual young man takes on the mantel of the Dark Lord of the Sith to rape a grateful Betty.

**3. Apocalypse Now** (1979, Francis Ford Coppola)
A lot of movies made me feel scared; *Apocalypse Now* was the first movie to make me feel *awful*. Was it Coppola himself who said it's not *about* Vietnam, it *is* Vietnam? Call this film the gateway drug for all the films of the 1970s in the United States, our very own *Aguirre: The Wrath of God* about the limits (should we call it "limitlessness"?) of man's ambitions in art and life. It's the siren's call to a period in our cinema (say, 1967-1981) that should be considered, with seriousness, the best of any in any place at any time. Before it, I had equated the decade with bad fashion and Blaxploitation, with Clint Eastwood in monkey movies, with the Burt Reynolds of *Smokey and the Bandit* and not of *Deliverance*; and a uniform grain to the film stock just couldn't hold a candle to the slick comfort of the 1980s blockbusters that were my celluloid teat. I looked at the period with ignorance and disdain—and then I saw this movie, which feels

depraved in a way that few films, especially ones that try to be depraved, do. More than that, the picture sparked in a younger me an interest in T.S. Eliot that eventually led to more general avenues of study while strengthening the bond that film has with an idea of the Sublime in art. If you don't get chills listening to Brando recite lines from "The Hollow Man", you might have a nerve missing.

**2. The Empire Strikes Back** (1980, Irvin Kershner)
I stood in line for two hours to see this film and was rewarded with one of the most miserable moviegoing experiences of my life. What the fuck is this? Luke, behanded; Han in carbonite; Lando not in carbonite; Vader is Luke's mf'ing *dad*; the Republic in tatters; and then it's over?! Since the wait for relief was interminable, my buddies and I declared *The Empire Strikes Back* the worst movie ever, resolutely replaying the action of the picture with our now-priceless action figures, be-handing Darth instead and throwing Boba Fett into dry ice punch bowls, thus proving the maxim that you should never give the public what it thinks it wants. If only Lucas had remembered that before forging ahead—and backwards in his special editions. (Though to be fair, he started destroying his legacy with *Return of the Jedi*.) What *The Empire Strikes Back* did was make me a blockbuster junkie. With *Star Wars* the first movie I ever saw in a theatre, the anticipation I felt for "the next one" was my first taste of delirious anticipation. (Those long summers of youth, you know, they go too fast, but time is elastic in a way that it doesn't seem to be anymore.) When I think about *The Dark Knight*, I get that same tingle—I get it for the new Coen Brothers flick, too, especially because it's an adaptation of a Cormac McCarthy novel. In every way, this first sequel is The First Sequel: the reason I *love* movies—and, hindsight and age being what they are, it remains the only artistically viable film in the *Star Wars* saga.

**1. The Conversation** (1974, Francis Ford Coppola)
I've constructed a sort of personal mythology around this picture—I'm asked about it often in my public-speaking ("What's your favourite movie?") and I think it surprises people that I actually have a favourite movie. The preface is always that *The Conversation* might not be the best film, but it's the single most important film in my decision to try out this movie-critic thing professionally. A product of Walter Murch taking over final cut after Paramount backed a dump-truck full of money up to Coppola's door to make *The Godfather Part II*, it's not finished in the most perfect way imaginable. Still, it cemented in me this lingering belief in authorship in film, and it was the first time, truly, that I began to feel I had ideas about movies that were exciting enough to share. Harry Caul (the name actually an accident—the picture also suggests divinity between the sprockets) is Gene Hackman's quintessential creation: the listener, he is the purity of the actor's craft. The course of the film is a test of fidelity philosophical and technological, while a remarkable cameo by Teri Garr is full of the weight of loneliness that a lot of '70s cinema only hints at. The story is simplicity itself (a dame, a murder, a hero in a trenchcoat), but the execution is as circular and damning as David Shire's piano score. It's the breakthrough in therapy and, six years later, I'm still clicking.

**Also:** *Near Dark; Miracle Mile; Star Wars; Back to the Future; Gandhi; Raiders of the Lost Ark; E.T.; Last Year at Marienbad; Grand Illusion; Peeping Tom; The Life of Colonel Blimp; Hana-Bi; Eternal Sunshine of the Spotless Mind; Once Upon a Time in the West; Die Hard; Predator; Killer of Sheep; The Thin Blue Line; Ferris Bueller's Day Off; The Rescuers*

# TEN WATERSHED MOMENTS IN FFC'S HISTORY
## by Bill Chambers

*You may resent me for not giving you ten more rental ideas, but since I realized that FILM FREAK CENTRAL's tenth anniversary obliged me to recap the site's "origin story," anyway, I just decided to dedicate my list to landmarks in our turbulent history. (Like I warned, "self-indulgent.") Th..Th..That's all, folks!*

**10. 10th Anniversary** (Present)
Woah... Meta.

**9. Press release from New Line** (November, 1998)
I've said many times before, only half-jokingly, that I started FILM FREAK CENTRAL to get free LaserDiscs. Well, that never panned out—and the format was on its last legs by 1997, anyway. Cut to the fall of 1998: out of left field, I receive a press release from New Line Home Video; nothing ventured, nothing gained, I e-mail the address at the bottom asking them to send me review copies of both DVD titles they were promoting therein. The following day, a FedEx truck rolled into my driveway, accompanied—in my head, at least—by the Hallelujah chorus hymn. It was FFC's first fix, the first time the industry acknowledged our existence in any way, shape, or form...and I've probably been chasing that high ever since.

**8. Sued...Sorta** (2001-2003)
They say you haven't made it until somebody wants to sue you. In the interest of self-preservation, I'm truncating the details, but back when FFC was starting to gain some traction on the Internet, a certain web personality I had, contrary to his belief, not heard of before sent me a *j'accuse!* e-mail *vis-à-vis* my alleged trademark-infringing use of the term "film freak." I ignored him at first, but he was persistent, and so I sent him a list of about 30 sites with some variation of "film freak" in their brand (if I was ever going to change the site's name, *that* would be the reason). Well, I guess that pissed him off, because his rent-a-lawyer then couriered me a small forest's worth of paperwork, none of it amounting to anything but evidence that they had toner and they were gonna use it! Suffice it to say, I continued to do nothing, though I took advantage of a free hour of legal counsel from an entertainment attorney, whose advice boiled down to "do nothing." Eventually I got worn down by his passive-aggressive threats of litigation and e-mailed him ("Dear [*name withheld*], I'm not taking the bait. Bill, xo"), at which point I was notified by an Intellectual Property arbitrator that I had something like a weekend to counter his multi-point entitlement claim. This time I did something, but not much; and the committee unanimously decided in our favour. Justice! I still receive the occasional message from his cronies asking why I can't be a "gentleman" and, y'know, undo a decade of hard work by changing FFC's name to appease an ego obviously bruised by every disappointed visitor who goes to his site thinking they're going to ours. Should the day come, I'm partial to Cinema Jolie-Pitt.

**7. Fight with Ebert** (August, 2004)
The most e-mail I ever got in one day (not counting the odd spam flood)

attended Roger Ebert's review of *The Brown Bunny*, wherein he rebutted my Ebert-baiting capsule on the same film. Perhaps more of a private milestone than one for the site, it nevertheless sticks out in my mind as a moment of validation from the establishment—when my own friends and family began to look at FILM FREAK CENTRAL as a legitimate pastime; Ebert did nothing less than make it easier for me to run this operation unabated, at least temporarily. You might be interested to know that I've crossed paths with him many times since (we even powwowed but a few weeks later at a screening of *Saw*), and if there were any hard feelings, I couldn't tell. I missed him greatly at last year's TIFF and wish him nothing but the best as he recovers from his gruelling medical ordeal.

### 6. "Attack of the Drones" (May, 2002)
If you ask me, Walter's written far better reviews than the one he wrote for *Attack of the Clones*, but I doubt he'll ever write another review with the half-life it's had. From being the root cause of our first bandwidth fine to begetting our first special edition of "Reader Mail" to, most notoriously, landing us on Lucasfilm's shitlist so that we were explicitly denied screeners of the *Star Wars* trilogy when it finally hit DVD, it holds a special place in FFC lore. It even, in a roundabout way, led to us interviewing Mark Hamill! For all that, what I like best about it is that it set us apart, at a critical juncture, from the fanboy contingent.

### 5. The Publication of Our Annuals (2005, 2006)
Now's as good a time as any to formally announce that we will not be publishing a 2007 Annual—the first two simply didn't sell enough copies to make it worth our while. But we're not ruling out the possibility of another book of some sort; it's a genuine, selfish thrill for us to see all those bits and bytes quantified like that. And how many film sites can lay claim to two thick volumes of their work? With forewords and blurbs by some of their favourite directors, to boot? The whole experience was intensely gratifying, and it surely revitalized our writing, that intimate awareness of a destination beyond the ether.

### 4. Birth of a Blog (August 23, 2005)
Let me take this opportunity to set the record straight: this blog was Walter Chaw's idea. A lot of the stuff he was itching to write was difficult to contextualize within the traditional parameters of FFC. I was game but leery, seeing as how each of us has a backlog that could stop a river and this would just provide one more distraction. But I'm proud of the community that has sprouted up here and I feel, as I wrote in the introduction to <u>The Film Freak Central 2006 Annual</u>, that it makes great scaffolding for the mothersite. Truthfully, I can't get over how civil the conversation around these parts is on average—the cynic in me is still waiting for the other shoe to drop.

### 3. E-Mail from Walter Murch (January 16, 2000)
I was DVD-shopping in Toronto when I spotted a childhood favourite, *Return to Oz*, sitting on the shelf. "Don't buy it," my friend advised, "it doesn't hold up." But for some reason, even if it wasn't as good as I'd remembered, I knew I would regret not buying it more. A few months after I wrote up the disc, I received an e-mail from *Return to Oz* helmer Walter Murch. He was quite complimentary towards my review, though I suspect he had an ulterior motive to correct a misnomer I perpetrated regarding the film's soundmix. Be that as it may, it took me a day or two to process that the freakin' editor of *Apocalypse Now* had casually struck first contact with me; I replied, paraphrasing Mario Puzo, that if

I'd known he was going to read the review I would've written it better (I'm sure he groaned), then begged him for an interview. I credit the resulting Q&A with forcing me to get serious, truly serious, about FILM FREAK CENTRAL, if only to honour Mr. Murch's generosity and good faith.

## 2. The Hiring of Walter Chaw (April, 2001)
The name Walter has been good to me. You know how they say that some talk shows are host-driven and some are guest-driven? My utopian fantasy for this site was one that was review-driven rather than critic-driven, and when I first started recruiting writers, I wanted to create a cinephiliac supergroup of budding talent. But there's no denying that one voice has risen above the chorus. I can honestly say that while I created this site, with all due credit to esteemed colleagues Travis Mackenzie Hoover, Alex Jackson, and Ian Pugh, Walter *made* it. Dude's a rock star. For what it's worth, when he came aboard, a lot of folks informed me that he sounded the death knell for the site—and I usually responded that it's better to hate someone for the right reasons (Letterman?) than to love them for the wrong ones (Leno?). Unfortunately for Walter, he rarely equivocates in a world that petulantly equates anything but utmost equivocation with "meanness." Politesse has somehow become a greater virtue than honesty, conjuring the image of Rome fiddling while *Nero* burns. It's an honour to provide Walter sanctuary in these cowardly times, to be affiliated in any way with his genius, and to call him a friend. If anything gives me hope for not only the future of not only film criticism, but the battle against anti-intellectualism as well, it's that I detect Walter's influence in a lot of up-and-coming young critics. I'm sure that drives *him* batshit, though.

## 1. The Purchase of the Domain Name FilmFreakCentral.Net (November 19, 1998)
Christ, why didn't I pick *.COM?!*

# APPENDIX C

# HOLDOVERS
*Reviews we neglected to include in the 2006 Annual*

## DEAD & BREAKFAST
**/****
*st.* Ever Carradine, Portia de Rossi, David Carradine, Bianca Lawson
*w./d.* Matthew Leutwyler

Matthew Leutwyler's winking gorefest *Dead & Breakfast* is a spam-in-a-cabin flick that takes its cues from *The Evil Dead* pictures and *Dead Alive* but comes off as a flick wilfully goofy without any commensurate smarts or, really, any truly memorable geek thrills. Lacking much in the way of visual signature, it's a lot of flat jokes layered in among a few uneven gross-out gags. Everyone in the cast is so *Clueless*-ly self-aware that it veers dangerously close to undermining the very undertone of *gravitas* that made the films *Dead & Breakfast* obviously reveres so great. When the movie and its horde of two-stepping hick zombies pause in their siege on our surviving heroes to "Thriller"-dance to Greek chorus Zach Selwyn's hick-a-billy croon, there's just a little too much winking in the air of its one idea stretched until the white shows.

It goes down like this: a group of attractive twentysomethings are stranded in the middle of nowhere, check into a mysterious roadside attraction run by some freak (David Carradine), and before you know it, the whole town erupts with the pitter-patter of the soft-shoe shuffle of the shambling undead. There're moments to love: Jeremy Sisto (essentially the same one-dimensional character he played in the aforementioned *Clueless*) spends the last part of the film as a severed head puppet; a massacre at a hoedown showcases a pretty neat geysering stick-to-the-eye; and a religious fanatic gets the top part of his head blown off. But there's simply not enough energy to the carnage, not enough verve in the jokes, and no centre to the production. In fact, possible heroes keep getting dispatched, and that lack of focus kills any possibility for identification. No Ash emerges from the wreckage—and that's bad news for the picture. *Dead & Breakfast* is a parsing of better splatter flicks; and like a CliffsNote, it's good for cheating but bad for a screenplay. (**Walter Chaw**)

## FEVER PITCH
*½/****
*st.* Drew Barrymore, Jimmy Fallon, James B. Sikking, JoBeth Williams
*sc.* Lowell Ganz & Babaloo Mandel, based on the novel by Nick Hornby
*dirs.* Peter Farrelly & Bobby Farrelly

Ben (Jimmy Fallon), a Red Sox fanatic and middle-school math teacher, falls in love with corporate minx Lindsey (Drew Barrymore), who, as is often the case in Farrelly Brothers films, is perfect. She's beautiful, bug-eyes and all, and when she simpers in her mealy-mouthed way that she loves Ben as much as Ben loves baseball, all the men folk are supposed to melt—but I have serious doubts as to whether Barrymore is romantic lead material. Though she's fine getting hit in the face with a hard foul (her best roles are as the benighted bimbos in Adam

Sandler trainwrecks), much of Barrymore's sultriness has to do with the idea of her as a naughty schoolgirl (*Poison Ivy*), not as a savvy woman of the world. She's no Mary, in other words, and her lack as one-half of *Fever Pitch*'s romantic pairing is distracting—if not actually crippling, since leading man Fallon is himself a stammering vanilla doormat.

So Ben and Lindsey are doing great until baseball season starts and Ben reveals himself to be one of those screaming jackholes on ESPN who quits his job to go to spring training with his team: explanation in a nutshell as to why thirtysomething Ben is single, though no commensurate explanation is offered for why Lindsey is still in the dating pool. (Probably something to do with how she looks, talks, and acts like Drew Barrymore.) The conflict thus established, Ben will have to eventually choose between America's pastime and a starlet past her prime, while both Mars and Venus have three vestigial satellite friends to pad out the running time of this short subject to feature length. It all ends with one of those moments that typically involves horses or karaoke bars, with the celebrated "drastic" rewrite to accommodate the Red Sox finally winning the World Series after decades of futility actually around three minutes of montage epilogue.

There's something about the Farrelly brothers that I like—a lot. It's not the gross-out slapstick, although I think they do that better than most, but rather a level of intelligence and sensitivity that allows them to deliver—under the radar, as it were—strong humanist messages about the objectification of women, the empowerment of people with physical and emotional disabilities, and the importance of establishing in any kind of relationship a measure of compromise and independence. Their comedy works because the Farrellys have not only a keen eye for but also a deep sympathy with human foible; when Jack Black's Hal in *Shallow Hal* scolds his overweight girlfriend's father for denigrating her looks, we get the gag that in Hal's eyes, she's Gwyneth Paltrow, and we likewise understand that many of this fat girl's self-esteem issues probably do have something to do with the amount of support she's getting from the people closest to her. That's a complicated movement in any sort of film—and at least until *Fever Pitch*, every Farrelly movie has had at least one moment in it that's beautifully observed. Adapted from Nick Hornby's soccer-themed novel, *Fever Pitch* isn't terrible, but it's really, really bland.

Besides loving baseball, there's nothing unusual about Ben, and besides loving Ben, there's nothing unusual about Lindsey; the entire film is basically a friction-less exercise in boy gets/loses/gets girl set against Boston's historic championship season. There's no energy to it, no tension, and little chemistry: in fact, by the end of it, it's so unmemorable that it's fair to wonder what's happened to the time. A rival for Lindsey's affections briefly manifests before disappearing without an explanation, and altogether too many extras have eye-blink cameos—just long enough to deliver a wise/snarky bit of advice before vaporizing into the ether. *Fever Pitch* is the kind of film where the main characters have no purpose outside of providing minor challenges for one another, and its hundreds of minor characters are pastiches to give the main characters a rest. Its best moments begin to address how sports can drive people nuts, but even that's ultimately thrown under the wheels of syrup and tripe. ("You love the Red Sox, but has the Red Sox ever loved you back?" Ooooh.) Blame the screenwriting team of Lowell Ganz and Babaloo Mandel, together responsible for some of the most godawful, howlingly boring material to ever glance off the big screen. (Ron Howard and Billy Crystal have them on speed dial.) It takes something special to make the Farrelly Brothers completely ordinary; think of *Fever Pitch* as the phone booth—though the Kryptonite could be any combination of Ganz & Mandel, Fallon, or Barrymore. (**WC**)

# D O C U M E N T A R Y

## THE GRACE LEE PROJECT
**\*\*¹/₂/\*\*\*\***
*dir.* Grace Lee

Documentarian Grace Lee discovers after a white-bread Midwest upbringing (almost identical to mine, it seems) that the greater world outside is rotten with Grace Lees: small, musical, smart, and nice—even when they try to torch their high schools. Lee's exhaustive name-check of all her serendipitous namesakes is as whimsical as it sounds, touching only in an ancillary way on the Asian-American experience insomuch as the feeling of alienation and the crippling effect of "positive" stereotyping runs across the board. Most fulsome is the exploration of Christianity as the foundation for most of the "grace" names, culminating in a particularly devout Grace Lee who all but burns with holy light—an idea, sneaky, that Asians do their homework even when it's something as esoteric as The Bible. There's a running theme in here about shit I could try to formulate into a theory on debasement and irony, but shit is shit. It does get serious with brief forays into a Korean lesbian activist who recants before the film's completion, retracting her permission to be shown (not to mention the bits about two families on the run from an abusive husband), but the attempts at transcendence exist only uneasily with the film's broadly-appealing facility. It's possible that Lee is so good at pleasing (in the Grace Lee mold) that the grit got sanded off the edges. For what it's worth, *The Grace Lee Project* is an easy trip at just over an hour and should prove a popular ticket on the festival circuit. (**WC**)

## KUNG FU HUSTLE
**\*\*\*/\*\*\*\***
*st.* Stephen Chow, Yuen Wah, Yuen Qiu, Lam Tze Chung
*sc.* Stephen Chow, Tsang Kan Cheong, Lola Huo, Chan Man Keung
*dirs.* Stephen Chow

There's a moment near the beginning of Stephen Chow's *Shaolin Soccer* where a reverie about sweet buns turns into a spontaneous, slightly Asian-fied street recreation of the zombie shuffle from Michael Jackson's "Thriller" video. If Chow is going to break through into the American mainstream with more success than fellow Hong Kong émigrés Jackie Chan, Chow Yun Fat, John Woo, Jet Li, Ringo Lam, and Sammo Hung, it'll be because of his savvy and respect for Western pop archetypes. Evidence of this has surfaced with some regularity in all of his pictures to date, no less so in *Kung Fu Hustle*, a delirious-verging-on-surreal send-up of Kung Fu attitudes and traditions mutated with a Tex Avery cartoon. It's the film Joe Dante has been trying to make for the whole of his career: a multi-cultural pop explosion cross-pollinated to produce a fevered hybrid of the post-industrial standard of Asian innovation of Western invention. Chow is Asia's answer to hip-hop: fugitive poetry primed to gratify the Yankee ruling culture while laying out a subtext of Chinese pride that would feel like a threat if it didn't get your hips shaking and your fingers snapping.

Sing, one of Chow's prototypical down-and-outers (Chow's mug recalls Keaton, but his alter ego is pure Chaplin), tries to bully schwag and face by pretending to belong to the infamous Axe Gang. That backfires, of course, not only in the expected way when the actual Axe Gang demands their pound of flesh, but also when his targeted victims in bedraggled Pig Sty Alley turn out to be a collection of retired kung fu masters (played to a large extent by actual retired kung fu masters). Suddenly, Sing finds himself the proverbial Sanjuro in the middle of a gang war mostly of his own bumbling creation.

After a well-publicized (but vehemently denied) falling-out with action choreographer Sammo Hung, Chow hired on master choreographer Yuen Wo Ping, best known in the West as the architect of *The Matrix*'s iconic action sequences, and the result in *Kung Fu Hustle* is a comic *wu xia* epic that feels curiously familiar to Western audiences; the film might be the right one at the right time. Cannily, Chow makes sport of that familiarity, re-imagining moments from *Spider-Man 2* and the *Lord of the Rings* films with a kind of fluid conversance that once connected classic Shaw Brothers and Tsui Hark fare to the Hollywood musical — that once found throughlines bold and brilliant between John Woo and Sam Peckinpah, or Sergio Leone and Akira Kurosawa. In a lot of ways, *Kung Fu Hustle* is China's answer to *Kill Bill*, with Stephen Chow as much the pop-phile dork as Quentin Tarantino. Their films have passion and a meticulous structure, too, that's often mistaken for arbitrary chaos — case in point, a sequence in the ghetto where a landlady (the incomparable Yuen Qiu, returning to the screen after a 28-year absence) punishes her husband (Yuen Wah) by first throwing him out of a window, then dropping a flower pot on his head and turning around to berate a line of parched tenants about their waste. Chaotic on the surface, the sequence in one compact burst of energy references social-minded silent film, cartoons, the Chinese class system, and the sly subtext of individual worth that underpins Chow's work.

Gay stereotypes, rampant misogyny — the dark underbelly of Chinese cinema is addressed herein with screaming queens and castrating mammys before being undermined when they turn out to be the most virtuous, the most ferocious defenders of community and order. *Kung Fu Hustle* comments on its own complexity with a cast of characters that are each more than they would at first appear. It's easy to label the film as another Asian export full of inscrutable philosophies and high-flying, over-stylized CGI effects, but this is a thornier beast, adorned as it is with elements from the West adapted, subtly, to the sensibilities of the East. It's not a perfect film, paced poorly in spots and threatening to become repetitive long before the final curtain drops. But as something that could be remembered as the last film Chow made with complete artistic control in Hong Kong (because it's the first one of his that will appeal to a broad American audience), it's a film to take note of, just as Stephen Chow is someone to watch. (**WC**)